CYPRUS IN TRANSITION
1960-1985

CYPRUS
IN TRANSITION
1960 - 1985

Editor
John T.A. Koumoulides

Contributors
Field Marshal Lord Carver
Nancy Crawshaw
A. J. R. Groom
Sir David Hunt
Ellen B. Laipson
Hon. Sir Peter Ramsbotham
Hon. Paul S. Sarbanes
Hon. C. M. Woodhouse
Roger Zetter

TRIGRAPH — LONDON

First published 1986 by

Trigraph Limited,
West Africa House,
Hanger Lane,
London W5 3QR

British Library Cataloguing in Publication Data

Cyprus in Transition : 1960-1985
  1. Cyprus — Politics and Government
  I. Koumoulides, J.T.A.   II. Carver,
  Michael Carver, *Baron*
  956 . 45'04   DS54 . 9

ISBN 0 947961 03 8

Origination by Lindfield Graphics Lindfield, West Sussex
Printed by Adlard & Son Ltd, Dorking, Surrey
Bound by Skyline Bookbinders, Dorking, Surrey

CONTENTS

CONTRIBUTORS

FIELD MARSHAL LORD CARVER GCB, CBE, DSO, MC, began his military career in 1935 in the Royal Tank Regiment. During the war he served in North Africa and Europe. After the war he held important British and Allied posts. He was Commander of the Joint Truce Force, Cyprus, and Deputy Commander of the United Nations' Force in Cyprus in 1964. From 1971 - 1973 he was Chief of the General Staff. He is the author of numerous books, his latest being *The Seven Ages of the British Army.*

NANCY CRAWSHAW was educated in England and Germany. For many years she reported Greek and Cypriot affairs for the *Manchester Guardian.* She is the author of *the Cyprus Revolt: An Account of the Struggle for Union with Greece.* From 1980 - 83 she was adviser to the House of Commons Select Committee on Foreign Affairs.

JOHN GROOM was educated at the University of London, Lehigh University, USA, and for four years at the *Institut Universitaire des Hautes Études Internationales,* Geneva. He has been Professor of International Relations at the University of Kent, Canterbury, since 1985 and Co-Director, Centre for the Analysis of Conflict. He is Visiting Professor of International Relations at several other Universities. Author and editor of numerous books and articles, his latest being *International Relations: A handbook on Current Theory.*

SIR DAVID HUNT KCMG, OBE, was a Fellow of Magdalen College, Oxford, and an archaeologist before 1939. After war service with the army he entered the Diplomatic Service in 1947; he was

Private Secretary to Attlee and Churchill as Prime Ministers and subsequently High Commissioner in Uganda, Cyprus and Nigeria and Ambassador to Brazil. He is Visiting Professor of International Relations, Unversity of Edinburgh. In addition to other books he has edited and contributed to *Footprints in Cyprus.*

JOHN KOUMOULIDES was educated in the United States at Montclair State College and the University of Maryland and at Fitzwilliam College, Cambridge in England. He is Professor of History at Ball State University in Muncie, Indiana. He has written and edited numerous books on Greece and Cyprus, his latest being *Churches of Aghia in Larissa* (jointly with Mr. Lazaros Deriziotis), which was awarded the 1985 Academy of Athens prize.

ELLEN B. LAIPSON was educated at Cornell University and Johns Hopkins University School of Advanced International Studies. She is a specialist in Middle East and North African Affairs and is a Congressional Research Analyst, Library of Congress, Washington, D.C.

HON. SIR PETER RAMSBOTHAM GCMG, GCVO, was educated at Eton and Magdalen College, Oxford. After war service with the army he entered the Diplomatic Service in 1948. He was British High Commissioner in Cyprus from 1969 - 71 and subsequently Ambassador to Iran, the United States and Governor of Bermuda.

SENATOR PAUL S. SARBANES, Democrat, Maryland, was educated at Princeton University, Balliol College, Oxford (Rhodes Scholar) and Harvard University. He served in the House of Representatives from 1971 until 1976, in which year he was elected to the Senate. Senator Sarbanes is a member of the Foreign Relations Committee and of the Joint Economic Committee.

HON. C.M. WOODHOUSE DSO, OBE, was educated at Winchester and Oxford. During the war he commanded the Allied Military Mission to the Greek resistance movement. He served in the Foreign Office, 1945 - 46 and 1951 - 52 and was Director-General of the Royal Institute of International Affairs from 1955 - 59. He was Conservative MP for Oxford, 1959 - 66 and 1970 - 74 and is now Visiting Professor in the Department of Modern Greek at King's College, London. He has written many books on Greek history, his latest being *The Rise and Fall of the Greek Colonels.*

ROGER ZETTER was educated at Cambridge and Nottingham Universities. He is currently Principal Lecturer in the Oxford Polytechnic in Urban Development and Planning. He is the author of numerous articles on Cyprus.

PREFACE

The problem of Cyprus appears in the press quite often, but I am certain that the greater public knows very little about it and is unable to comprehend its complexities. We may know about the great past of Cyprus, but, alas, at least in the United States of America, very few of us, perhaps, are aware of its tragic present. Most people do not realise that in Cyprus today past and future collide, and that while the past is certain the future, I fear, is quite obscure. In an effort to educate ourselves better about the various facets of the problem of Cyprus and to understand its historical, social, political, diplomatic and strategic dimensions, a series of lectures was planned at Ball State University in Muncie, Indiana. Under the auspices of the University's Greek Studies Programme and the Stephen J., and Beatrice Brademas Lecture Series an international group of distinguished experts on Cyprus was invited to the University. The lectures were delivered during the academic year 1984-1985. The present volume consists of the papers given at Ball State University as well as essays specially written at the invitation of the editor. Taken together they provide an objective and comprehensive look at the problem of Cyprus, mainly from the foreign perspective; the views expressed are in each case those of the individual writer. It is my earnest wish that this volume will be of value to the scholar as well as to the student of the recent history of Cyprus, providing much needed insights into a very complex situation.

I am most grateful both to those who took part in the lecture series and to those who kindly accepted my invitation and contributed essays for this publication. I wish to record my debt of gratitude to the Friends of Greek Studies and the Patrons of the Stephen J., and Beatrice Brademas Scholarship and Lecture Fund of Ball State University, for their dedication to the programme and their generous support of the lecture series. I am grateful to the A.G. Leventis Foundation for generous subventions and to the publishers, Trigraph Limited for including this volume in their list of scholarly publications.

John T.A. Koumoulides

INTRODUCTION

Hon. Paul S. Sarbanes

The history of civilization on Cyprus can be traced back to the neolithic settlement of Khirokitia in the seventh millennium B.C. It has come to us indirectly, through references in the Homeric hymns and through the archaeological discoveries of modern times; the earliest historians remain mute witnesses, for to this day the script in which they wrote remains undeciphered. By contrast, the history of the Republic of Cyprus dates back only to 1960. Although the independent sovereign state was established a mere quarter-century ago, the events of the past twenty-five years, and the situation on Cyprus today, regrettably appear as far removed from general public knowledge and comprehension as the earliest millennium.

There are several factors that anyone seeking to understand modern Cyprus must consider. The first is the strategic location of the island, which has made it for centuries a traditional gateway to East and West, North and South. Cyprus has never had the luxury of the strategic isolation that permits a nation to concentrate undistracted on its own internal development.

The second factor is imperial domination, with Cyprus long held in subservient status by a colonial power. In modern times Cyprus experienced three centuries of imperial Ottoman rule, with a minority Turkish population imposed on an indigenous Greek population. At the Congress of Berlin in 1878 the Ottomans were obliged to cede administrative authority over Cyprus to the British; subsequently, for roughly the last half-century prior to independence, Cyprus was under formal as well as effective British control. The terms of the 1959 Zurich and London agreements which laid down the constitutional framework for the Republic of Cyprus recognized Great Britain, Greece and Turkey as guarantors of the new nation.

The third factor is the brutal invasion of Cyprus in 1974 by

Turkish military forces, and the continuing Turkish occupation of regions in the north which constitute nearly forty percent of the Republic's territory.

The immediate result of the invasion was the violent displacement of some 200,000 Greek Cypriots, who were forced to flee their homes in the north for the south — to live, tragically, as refugees in their own country. Today, twelve years later, the situation on Cyprus remains acute. 1,619 persons missing since the summer of 1974 are still unaccounted for. The Turkish occupation forces are still in control of the territory seized in 1974, although Turkish Cypriots make up less than twenty percent of the population; large numbers of Turkish troops continue to make up the occupying force, and a significant number of settlers from Turkey have been moved into the occupied portion of the Republic. The 200,000 Greek Cypriots are still displaced persons, despite having risen in remarkable fashion to meet the burdens and deprivations which refugee status places upon them.

The political dimension of the 1974 action is as acute as the personal loss. The Turkish military presence has undermined the cohesion of the new Republic and greatly complicated the underlying challenge, formidable enough to begin with, of developing a common citizenship for the Greek and Turkish communities on the island. The continuing stalemate weighs heavily on the delicate balance of Greek-Turkish relations and inevitably creates obstacles to the functioning of the southern flank of the NATO alliance in which Greece and Turkey together play a crucial role. Furthermore, the search for a just and workable solution has been dealt a major blow by the 1983 Turkish-Cypriot unilateral declaration of independence, or UDI, a device with which a Turkish-Cypriot population in the north, supported by Turkey and reinforced by the Turkish military presence, has sought to carve out an independent state in the occupied portion of the Republic.

Such is the situation on Cyprus. The general public tends to assume — erroneously — that because Cyprus is a small country the conflict there is not of great significance and can therefore be permitted to fester, or may even eventually resolve itself. Within the more knowledgeable and limited circle of public officials, scholars, students of public affairs and others already familiar with the Cyprus situation there is keen recognition of the gravity of the situation, and debate about Cyprus's future takes on an urgent and contentious tone.

The purpose of *Cyprus in Transition* is to shed light on the complex history of modern Cyprus, and to create a framework for informed and reasoned discussion. To this end Professor John T.A. Koumoulides has brought together essays by authors with first-hand experience of the many facets of the Cyprus situation, and has himself provided a very helpful historical and bibliographical framework. Professor Koumoulides is eminently suited to the task. Professor of History at Ball State University in Indiana, he is the author of *Cyprus and the War of Greek Independence, 1821-1829* (London, 1974), and *Byzantine and Post-Byzantine Monuments at Aghia in Thessaly, Greece: The Art and Architecture of the Monastery of St. Panteleimon* (London, 1975). He is also the editor of *Greece in Transition: Essays in the History of Modern Greece, 1921-1974* (London, 1977), published in the wake of the return of Greece to democracy in 1974.

The contributors to this volume bring a variety of different perspectives to the issue before them. Sir David Hunt and Sir Peter Ramsbotham, for example, have both served as British High Commissioner on Cyprus. The Hon. C.M. Woodhouse writes on 'The British Point of View' not only as Visiting Professor in the Department of Modern Greek at King's College, London University, but also as one with many years' service in the fields of diplomacy and politics. Among the other contributors are distinguished journalists and scholars, and, in the person of Lord Carver, the former Deputy Commander of the United Nations' Force in Cyprus.

These essays will assuredly be of interest to a wide audience, from long-time observers to those seeking an introduction to contemporary Cyprus. This book thus constitutes an important contribution to the understanding of the current situation, and to the continuing search for a just and workable solution to the crisis which has so disrupted the life of the Republic and its citizens. As a public official who has for more than a decade participated in that search, I welcome the appearance of *Cyprus in Transition*.

Washington, D.C.   Paul S. Sarbanes
                                              United States Senator

CYPRUS:
THE POLITICAL BACKGROUND

Nancy Crawshaw

The Republic of Cyprus was born on 16 August 1960. The reaction of the Greek Cypriots to this historic event was lukewarm. They had reluctantly accepted the Zurich settlement[1] in the belief that any alternative would eventually lead to partition. The Turkish Cypriots would have preferred partition. Nevertheless they looked to the future with cautious optimism.

Independence was achieved by means of three treaties.[2] Britain retained sovereignty over two military bases in an area totalling 99 square miles. Greece and Turkey were entitled to station contingents of their own troops in Cyprus for the purpose of common defence and the training of a Cypriot army. The independence of the Republic, its territorial integrity and the basic articles of its constitution were guaranteed by Greece, Britain and Turkey. The Zurich agreement provided for a presidential regime, with a Greek President and a Turkish Vice-President empowered to exercise the veto either jointly or separately and for a Supreme Constitutional Court. Difficulties over the implementation of the constitution arose from the outset of independence.[3] The first major crisis came in December 1961 when the Turkish Cypriots blocked the budget, the second a year later when President Makarios refused to extend the municipal law providing for separate municipalities. Both communities took action to avoid a breakdown of local government which the Supreme Constitutional Court found illegal in each case.

The constitution was designed to keep the balance between the two communities in the climate of distrust which followed the Greek-Cypriot rising against the British in the 1950s during the struggle for union (enosis) with Greece. The Greek Cypriots became increasingly resentful of the powers given to the Turkish Cypriots who formed only 18 per cent of the population. On 30 November 1963 Archbishop Makarios submitted 13 amendments[4] to the Turkish-Cypriot Vice-President, Dr. Kutchuk for his consideration. These would have abolished the executive veto and the provision for separate Greek and Turkish-Cypriot majorities in the House of Representatives for the enactment of certain laws. Other recommendations would have reduced the participation of the Turkish Cypriots in the public service and the security forces from 30 per cent to 18 per cent. The amendments would have deprived the Turkish Cypriots of vital safeguards to their security and of an effective voice in the affairs of the Republic. In the middle of December they were rejected by the Turkish Government and Dr. Kutchuk.

CIVIL WAR, December 1963 - August 1964

Less than a week after the Turkish Government's rejection of the amendments Greek-Cypriot irregulars, aided by the police, launched a major attack against the Turkish Cypriots in Nicosia after a series of incidents which began on the 21st. Turkish Cypriots were murdered in their homes; 700 were taken as hostages. On Christmas day Turkish war planes flew low over Nicosia; the Turkish army contingent stationed in Cyprus under the Treaty of Alliance moved from its barracks to strategic positions on the Kyrenia road. Fearing a Turkish invasion Makarios reluctantly agreed that a joint truce force, composed of British troops and liaison officers from the Greek and Turkish contingents, should be set up to restore order. By the end of the year British troops had manned the confrontation areas and set up cease-fire lines in Nicosia and Larnaca.

Representatives of the guarantor powers and the Cypriots met in London during January. The conference, which opened in the shadow of the grim disclosure of the massacre of Turkish Cypriots at Aghios Vassilios, ended in deadlock. The Turkish Cypriots insisted that the separation of the two communities was now essential to their safety. The Greek Cypriots wanted the termination of the Zurich agreements and 'unfettered independence' with a unified Cyprus in which the Turkish Cypriots were relegated to minority status. In the meantime the situation was deteriorating in Cyprus. Serious incidents occurred during February in the Paphos district and Limassol. Once the immediate risk of a Turkish invasion was over the position of the British troops became untenable owing to the hostility of the Greek Cypriots.[5] Britain had already informed the American Government that she could no longer carry the burden alone.[6] Proposals for an enlarged peace force to include NATO troops were, however, twice rejected by Makarios. The Archbishop was committed to a policy of non-alignment and under communist pressure to resist any extension of Western influence. On 15 February Britain, supported by Turkey, appealed to the Security Council which on 4 March by a unanimous resolution[7] set up the United Nations Force in Cyprus (UNFICYP). Its functions were to prevent a recurrence of the fighting and to contribute to the restoration of law and order and the return to normality. The fighting nevertheless continued and Turkey threatened to intervene unless it stopped forthwith. UNFICYP finally became operational on 27 March. Britain's importance as a guarantor from now on was substantially reduced, but she provided the largest contingent and most of the logistic support.

The lull which coincided with UNFICYP's arrival was short-lived. In April Makarios abrogated the Treaty of Alliance and accepted the offer of the Greek Prime Minister, George Papandreou, to send large numbers of Greek troops secretly to Cyprus as a precaution against a Turkish invasion.[8] The Turkish Cypriots twice demonstrated against the United Nations in protest against its alleged partiality towards the Greek Cypriots. Intercommunal clashes broke out over struggle to control the Xeros-Kokkina coastal road. At the end of the month, the Minister of the Interior, Polykarpos Georgadjis, led a surprise attack against the Turkish-Cypriot stronghold of St. Hilarion. This onslaught was condemned by U Thant, the UN Secretary-General as 'a planned and organised military effort.'[9] In May the abduction of 32 Turkish Cypriots in the Famagusta area brought Turkey close to invading Cyprus. The incident was a reprisal for the death of two Greek army officers and a Greek-Cypriot policeman who failed to stop when challenged on leaving the Turkish walled city.[10] The possibility of war between two NATO allies and the intervention of the Soviet Union prompted the American President, Lyndon Johnson, to send the Turkish Prime Minister, Ismet Inonu, a blunt warning on 5 June against unilateral intervention and the invasion was cancelled.[11]

The Americans had become increasingly dissatisfied with the Archbishop's collaboration with the Soviet bloc and with President Nasser. These misgivings inspired the proposals for a political settlement drawn up by the former Secretary of State, Dean Acheson. During July and August representatives of Greece and Turkey met in Geneva under the chairmanship of the UN mediator, Mr Sakari Tuomioja, to discuss Acheson's suggestions. These gave the Greek Cypriots the option of independence or *enosis* subject to the establishment of a Turkish military base and two autonomous Turkish-Cypriot cantons, compensation for Turkish Cypriots wishing to leave the island and the cession of the Greek island, Kastellorizo, to Turkey.[12] The plan, which would have brought Cyprus under the NATO umbrella, was rejected by Makarios. A revised version offering the Turks a leased instead of a sovereign military base was unacceptable to them.

In the meantime General Grivas who had returned to Cyprus in June launched a heavy attack on his own initiative against the Turkish-Cypriot villages in the Tylliria area.[13] Its objective was the neutralisation of the Kokkina enclave — the main reception centre for arms and men from Turkey. Several villages quickly succumbed but Kokkina was saved by the intervention of the Turkish airforce which bombarded the National Guard positions with high explosive and napalm. Makarios threatened to order attacks on every Turkish-Cypriot village in the island unless the bombing stopped within hours.[14] A cease-fire called for by the Security Council on 9 August[15] was observed by both sides.

By mid-1964 the Zurich settlement was dead for all practical purposes. The Treaty of Guarantee had proved useless. The Turkish Cypriots maintained that the Makarios Government by its unilateral violation of the treaties had ceased to exist as a legal government and refused to accept its authority. The Cyprus Government no longer felt bound by the Zurich agreements and outlawed the Turkish Cypriots as 'rebels'.[16] Illegal forces circulating in the Republic included the National Guard, with Greek officers and NCO's, private armies and, in the Turkish areas, the TMT. The process of territorial separation had already started after the 1963 fighting with the flight of 25,000 Turkish Cypriots to safer areas.[17]

THE ENCLAVES 1963 - 1967

The years 1963 - 1967 were a period of military expansion by both sides. Greek army officers and NCOs continued to arrive in large numbers. The Makarios Government sought to assert its control over the whole of the Republic. The Turkish Cypriots consolidated the defences of their enclaves under the guidance of Turkish army officers. Hopelessly outnumbered, without Turkey's intervention they could have been overrun at any time. The main sources of tension were the movement of Greek-Cypriot police patrols through mixed villages and the construction of coastal defences. The latter tended to stretch far inland and encroach upon the positions of the Turks who retaliated with new fortifications. Nevertheless after the Kokkina crisis incidents were mostly sporadic and on a smaller scale. A serious gun battle, however, took place in the Famagusta area in November 1966.[18]

The search for a political solution was resumed by Dr. Galo Plaza after the death of Sakari Tuomioja. His report published in March 1965 precluded *enosis* and partition and referred to the possibility of demilitarisation. The Turkish Government rejected Galo Plaza as mediator on the grounds that he had exceeded his terms of reference. The Turkish Cypriots, angered by the suggestion that their interests could be safeguarded by a minority rights charter under a UN commissioner's supervision, also found his proposals unacceptable.[19]

In July the Turkish-Cypriot deputies, who had absented themselves from the Parliament after the 1963 fighting, mainly for reasons of safety, applied to return. But the Government's terms would have nullified their rights under the Zurich settlement.[20] A further blow to intercommunal co-operation came a year later when the Turkish-Cypriot judges after an incident with the Greek-Cypriot police withdrew from the courts permanently.[21]

On 21 April 1967 the Athens Government was overthrown in the *coup d'état* which brought the Colonels Papadopoulos, Makarezos and Pattakos to power. The rise of the junta was to have far-reaching repercussions on developments in Cyprus, but at first little was changed. The summit talks with Turkey planned by a previous government went ahead in September on the Evros frontier. The Greek military leaders however had underrated Turkish objections to *enosis*. The conference failed, bringing to an end the Greco-Turkish dialogue which had lasted fourteen months.[22]

The Kokkina battle ended for the time being Greek-Cypriot hopes of a military victory. They next sought to subjugate the Turkish Cypriots by blockading the enclaves. Kokkina was under siege for nearly four years. The Turkish-Cypriot quarter of Nicosia was cut off by the authorities for two days on one occasion and

5

for two weeks on another. A ban was enforced on strategic materials which included essential commodities used in daily life.[23] Turkish Cypriots moving from one enclave to another were subjected to harassment and humiliating searches by the Cyprus Police.

Early in September Makarios announced a programme of 'normalisation'. This included the restoration of freedom of movement initially in the Paphos and Limassol areas. The Archbishop's move was distrusted by the Turks, as a ruse designed to drive a wedge between the outlying Turkish-Cypriot communities and the Nicosia enclave. Tension rose in October with the arrest of Rauf Denktash in the Karpas. He had returned secretly having been banned from the island by Makarios since 1964. After a visit from Glafcos Clerides he was allowed to return to Turkey. The crisis was thus averted only to be followed by another of greater magnitude.

On 15 November a large force of Greek and National Guard troops, led by Grivas, attacked the Aghios Theodoros/Kophinou enclave. Twenty-seven Turkish Cypriots were killed; many houses were destroyed. The incident, triggered by a dispute about police patrols, brought Greece and Turkey to the brink of war.[24] Heavy storms delayed the Turkish intervention. In the meantime President Johnson's special envoy, Cyrus Vance, had set out on a new peace mission, earlier diplomatic efforts having failed. Turkey's terms for calling off the invasion were the immediate departure of Grivas, the disbandment of the National Guard, the withdrawal of all Greek and Turkish troops in excess of the legal contingents, and compensation for the Turkish-Cypriot victims of the attack. By the end of January 1968 an estimated 10,000 Greek troops had left the island.[25] But the National Guard was not disbanded, nor was compensation ever paid.

The ordeals of the Turkish Cypriots in the enclaves between 1963 and 1967 reached a climax with the Kophinou crisis and were decisive in strengthening their resolve to press for a settlement based on the separation of the two communities. On 29 December their leaders announced the formation of the Provisional Turkish-Cypriot Administration (PTCA) which, they said, was to remain in force until all the provisions of the 1960 constitution were implemented.[26] The Greek Cypriots saw the move as yet another step towards partition and were not convinced by Turkish assurances to the contrary.

6

POLITICAL DEVELOPMENTS AFTER KOPHINOU
December 1967-July 1974

The Kophinou disaster had highlighted the folly of working for *enosis* in the face of Turkey's objections. On 12 January Makarios stated that the failure of the Greco-Turkish dialogue and the departure of the Greek army now made it necessary to seek a solution 'within the limits of what is feasible which does not always coincide with what is desirable.'[27] His re-election as President with 95 percent of the vote on 25 February and the humiliating defeat of the *enosis* candidate, Dr. Evdokas, indicated popular support for the Archbishop's change of direction. On 7 March Makarios lifted the last restrictions on the Turkish Cypriots. The pacification programme was slow to get off the ground, but in June a more hopeful phase opened in Beirut with the start of direct talks between Clerides and Denktash. The latter had been allowed to return to Cyprus as the appointed Turkish-Cypriot representative. At the end of the year the UN Secretary-General reported 'at last the emphasis seems to be shifting from military confrontation to negotiation.'[28]

The talks, which lasted six years, concentrated on the constitutional structure. A wide measure of self-government for the Turkish Cypriots within a unified Cyprus was considered. Differences were narrowed but the crucial issue for the Turkish Cypriots was the degree of state control to be exercised over the autonomous areas. Progress was affected by mounting violence inside the Greek-Cypriot community and renewed agitation for *enosis* by the extremists. Pro-*enosis* speeches by Makarios, intended to placate his rivals, were taken at face value by the Turks.[29]

The small group of EOKA extremists who supported Grivas and *enosis* at any price could not have begun to mount a coup against the Government. Their activities were restricted to intimidation and sporadic violence. The main danger to the survival of Makarios and the policy of independence came from the Greek army officers brought by him to Cyprus for the express purpose of defence against a Turkish invasion. By the spring of 1967 the National Guard had become closely associated with the Greek Army. Its barracks habitually displayed the emblems and Hellenic slogans of Greece.[30] *Enosis* propaganda was rife. Early in 1969 a new threat to stability came with the rise of the National Front, an illegal armed organisation headed by a former EOKA leader and based in Limassol. The capture of Limassol Central Police Station by one of its branches exceeded in scope and military skill anything ever attempted by EOKA against the British.

The National Front, however, disclaimed responsibility for the attempted assassination of Makarios on 8 March 1970 when the helicopter taking him to Makheras Monastery was shot down after take-off by gunmen firing from the roof of the Pancyprian Gymnasium. A week later Polykarpos Georgadjis, the former Minister of the Interior who was dismissed on the Greek junta's orders, was found murdered near Kythrea in mysterious circumstances. Before and after the helicopter incident the local and international communists had widely publicised rumours of a western plot in which a Greek-sponsored coup was about to end the indeendence of Cyprus as a step towards the establishment of a NATO base.[31] On 19 March the Turkish Foreign Minister was quoted as saying 'any attempt to carry out a coup in Cyprus and declare *enosis* would be opposed by Turkey with all her forces and strength.'[32]

On 27 May Makarios referred to the lawlessness which had brought Cyprus to the brink of the precipice.[33] Contrary to expectations parliamentary elections, the first since independence, went ahead on 5 July without incident. The results confirmed wide public support for the policy of independence and the continuation of the intercommunal talks. The strongest backing for Makarios came from Clerides's pro-western Unified Party and the communist AKEL, which substantially increased its strength.[34] The *enosis* candidate was not elected.

The autumn saw the renewal of intercommunal clashes after a long spell of peace. The main focus of trouble was, however, in the months to come centred on the Greek-Cypriot community. In January 1972 the Athenian newspaper *Estia* reported that the Government had imported a large consignment of arms and ammunition from Czechoslovakia.[35] The news alarmed the Greek and Turkish Governments. The junta was afraid that the weapons would get into the hands of the Greek-Cypriot leftists. The Turkish Cypriots feared, as usual, that whatever their immediate purpose the weapons could eventually be used against them. The crisis was not resolved until Makarios finally agreed to the storage of the arms inside UNFICYP's fortified perimeter.[36]

Throughout the winter and spring Makarios was faced with mounting opposition. Grivas who had returned to Cyprus in

September 1971 and formed EOKA-B, was openly campaigning for *enosis* in defiance of government policy. The junta's interference in the affairs of Cyprus was increasing. In February the Greek Ambassador, in a stiff note to Makarios, called for the formation of a government of national unity stressing that Athens not Nicosia was the 'national centre of Hellenism.' The demand was in due course partly met by the 'resignation' of the Foreign Minister, Spyros Kyprianou, and the reshuffle of the Council of Ministers to include politicians who were less openly hostile to the Greek junta. In March the three Cyprus bishops, Kition, Paphos and Kyrenia, accused Makarios of abandoning *enosis* and demanded his resignation as President, claiming that his political role conflicted with his ecclesiastical responsibilities. On 8 February 1973 Makarios was re-elected President unopposed for a third term. The following July the bishops, who had recently stepped up the pressure for his resignation, were themselves unfrocked by decision of the Synod of Eastern Orthodox Churches which Makarios had convoked. In November the Papadopoulos regime was overthrown by a counter-coup engineered by Brigadier Ioannides, commander of the military police.

On 27 January 1974 Grivas died in Limassol. Violence nevertheless continued and on 25 April EOKA-B was proscribed, but to no effect. On 2 July Makarios wrote to President Ghizikis accusing the junta of plotting his assassination and the Greek officers of encouraging EOKA-B in its criminal activities. Even the 'evil spirit which possessed the three unfrocked bishops emanated from Athens' he wrote.[37]

THE GREEK COUP AND THE TURKISH INVASION

On 15 July the National Guard led by Greek officers overthrew the Makarios Government and installed the former EOKA gunman Nikos Sampson, as President. Makarios, at first reported dead, escaped from the burning Presidential Palace to Paphos. From there he was taken by RAF helicopter to Akrotiri base and later flown to London. In New York on the 19th he urged the Security Council to call upon the Greek junta to withdraw the Greek officers and end its invasion of Cyprus.[38] In the meantime Bulent Ecevit, the Turkish Prime Minister, had arrived in London to seek Britain's co-operation for joint action with Turkey under the

Treaty of Guarantee. The British Government, however, was unwilling to commit troops except in the framework of an extended UN operation. On 18 July Ecevit sent the Greek Government an ultimatum calling for the resignation of Sampson and the withdrawal of the 650 Greek officers serving with the National Guard. It was disregarded by the junta. On 20 July Turkey invoked article IV of the Treaty of Guarantee[39] and landed troops by sea and air in northern Cyprus. The same day the Security Council called for an immediate cease-fire, for the withdrawal of foreign military personnel other than the legal contingents and for negotiations between the guarantors for the restoration of peace and constitutional government.[40]

The Greek troops and the National Guard put up a stiff resistance and the Turkish army did not occupy Kyrenia until the 22nd. On the 23rd it failed after heavy fighting to capture Nicosia airport which by agreement with the combatants was put under UNFICYP's control. On the 23rd the junta ordered a cease-fire; Sampson resigned and Clerides became acting President. The next day Karamanlis after eleven years in voluntary exile arrived in Athens to form a civilian government at President Ghizikis's request. Meanwhile British forces and the Royal Navy had started evacuating thousands of visitors trapped in the north.

The Foreign Ministers of Britain, Greece and Turkey met in Geneva at the end of July. On the 30th they signed the Geneva Declaration.[41] This noted the existence of separate Greek-Cypriot and Turkish-Cypriot autonomous administrations, and contained the undertaking that all Greek and Greek-Cypriot forces would immediately withdraw from the Turkish-Cypriot enclaves, that the occupied areas would not be extended and that prisoners should be released. The first two conditions were not honoured. The second Geneva conference which opened on 10 August, was joined by the Cypriot leaders for constitutional discussions. The Greeks wanted a unitary state, the Turks a separatist solution. The Turks submitted two plans; both involved territorial separation and would have brought more than 30 per cent of the island under Turkish control.[42] The talks broke down in the small hours of the 14th. Shortly afterwards Turkey resumed the war. On the 16th she declared a cease-fire. Cyprus was now partitioned by the Attila line which ran from Xeros to Famagusta bringing nearly 40 per cent of the Republic under Turkish control. Two thousand Greek Cypriots were missing. Turkish-Cypriot casualties totalled

932 dead and missing; massacres had occurred in several outlying villages.

Public anger turned against the Americans in general, and Dr. Kissinger in particular. On 19 August the new ambassador, Rodger Davis and his secretary were killed by an unknown assassin firing from a building site during a mob attack against the American embassy. The Turkish invasion had drastic consequences for the NATO alliance. Congress imposed a ban on American military aid to Turkey. The Greek Government, as a sop to an outraged public opinion, withdrew from military participation in the alliance.

On 7 December Makarios returned as President to an island which faced economic and social chaos. Population density in the south had doubled with the influx of 180,000 Greek-Cypriot refugees who had fled as the Turkish army advanced. The Turks controlled most of the grain-producing area of the Mesaoria, 82 percent of the citrus production and the leading holiday resorts of Kyrenia and Famagusta. 83 percent of the Paphos forest had been destroyed by Turkish incendiary bombs.

By the end of the year thousands of Turkish Cypriots had made their way to the north, often at great risk.[43] In January 1975 the British Government allowed 9,390 Turkish-Cypriot refugees, who had been camping in the Episkopi base, to be evacuated to Turkey from Akrotiri airfield for resettlement in north Cyprus. The action, taken for humanitarian and security reasons,[44] precipitated anti-British riots in Greece and Cyprus. The arrival of mainland immigrants from Turkey upset the demographic balance still further.

AFTER 1974: THE SEARCH FOR A POLITICAL SOLUTION

Clerides and Denktash quickly resumed contact to deal with urgent humanitarian problems, and by January they were again discussing the political question. The coup, however, had destroyed any chance of a multi-regional settlement on the lines of the previous talks. The Turkish Cypriots were now insistent on a bizonal federal state with the separation of the communities. On 13 February they established the Turkish Federated State of Cyprus which, it was explained, would eventually form the Turkish-Cypriot wing of a federal republic. The move was condemned by the Security

11

Council as tending to compromise the negotiations for a solution.[45]

Three rounds of talks were held in Vienna under the chairmanship of the UN Secretary-General, Kurt Waldheim, during the summer. They were unproductive apart from an agreement reached by Clerides and Denktash for the transfer to the Turkish area, with UNFICYP's help, of Turkish Cypriots wishing to leave the south, and of Greek Cypriots in the north to the south.[46] By the end of the year 8,033 Turkish Cypriots had moved under the arrangement.[47] On 10 September in New York Dr. Waldheim adjourned the talks for want of concrete proposals. Negotiations were resumed in February 1976 on the basis of the Brussels Declaration signed by Greece and Turkey but again ended in deadlock.

The year 1977 began with two encouraging developments. President Carter launched a new American initiative. Rauf Denktash suggested a meeting with Makarios. On 12 February the two leaders agreed on guidelines for future negotiations. They decided that Cyprus should become an independent, non-aligned bi-communal federal republic; that the territorial question should be considered in the light of economic viability or landownership; that certain practical difficulties which might arise for the Turkish Cypriots should be taken into account when discussing freedom of movement and the right of settlement.[48]

When new talks took place between 31 March and 7 April the Greek Cypriots proposed that 20 percent of the island should be retained by the Turkish Cypriots in a federal republic.[49] The Turkish Cypriots brought up the idea of 'federation by evolution'. Waldheim suspended the summit meeting pending progress at local levels. Talks continued in Nicosia but the atmosphere was contentious, with the Turkish Cypriots indicating that unless the economic embargo ended they might withdraw. A new crisis broke out when Denktash retaliated by threatening to re-settle the empty suburb of Varosha. The death of Makarios on 3 August was a major set-back to progress. Spyros Kyprianou automatically became acting President and was returned unopposed in February 1978.

In April Waldheim received the Turkish-Cypriot proposals,[50] one year after the Vienna deadlock. The Turkish plan provided for dual control at every level of federal government and amounted to a loose confederation which left the door open at some unspecified, distant date for the creation of a full federal republic. The principle of equality was made necessary, the authors stressed, by the fact that the Cyprus federation would be composed of only two states. Described by Waldheim as 'concrete and substantial' in their presentation[51] the proposals were dismissed by President Kyprianou as unacceptable even as a basis for discussion.

During the summer Congress lifted the embargo on arms sales to Turkey. In November the 'American Plan', drafted with the help of the British and Canadian Governments, was submitted to the Cypriot leaders. This provided for a bi-zonal federation and a bicameral legislature with equal representation of the communities in the Upper House, and on the basis of the population ratio in the Lower. As a western proposition it was automatically discredited by the communists. The Government's reaction was also unfavourable.[52] Nevertheless it became the prototype for subsequent formulas.

On 19 May 1979 Kyprianou and Denktash signed a ten-point agreement[53] reaffirming the 1977 guidelines. They also agreed to give priority to the resettlement of Varosha and to avoid any action prejudicial to the intercommunal negotiations (point 6). The talks began on 15 June but broke down after a week. Differences arose over the economic boycott and the Greek-Cypriot tactics of internationalisation which the Turkish Cypriots claimed violated point 6.

The spectacular economic recovery made by the Greek-Cypriots was in sharp contrast to the lack of political progress. Within a few years the vast majority of the refugees had employment — often in new enterprises; exports had doubled in value the pre-invasion figures; by 1981 tourist hotel capacity for the south alone was greater than it had been for the whole island before 1974. In the north the Turkish Cypriots at first lacked the expertise and the manpower to develop the resources left behind by the Greek Cypriots. The Greek-Cypriot boycott and the international stance on recognition[54] deprived the Turkish Cypriots of normal communications and trading outlets. They remained dependent on a large annual subsidy from Turkey, with economic growth and living standards lagging far behind those of the south.

After 14 months the talks were resumed on 9 August 1980 under the new UN Special Representative, Hugo Gobbi. Both communities held parliamentary elections during the first six months of 1981; the Turkish Cypriots also re-elected their President, Rauf Denktash. In the Greek-Cypriot parliamentary elections of 24 May the Communists (AKEL) polled the most votes, but no party gained an overall majority. Sixty percent of the electorate divided its votes almost equally between Glafcos Clerides's pro-western Democratic Rally and AKEL — each gaining 12 seats out of the total of 35. Pre-occupation with domestic politics inevitably slowed down the talks. But in August the Turkish Cypriots submitted a draft constitution with a map indicating minor territorial changes. The Greek Cypriots produced counter-proposals.[55] In November fresh efforts were made to spur the parties on to meaningful negotiations with the Waldheim 'evaluation'.[56] This combined the various earlier proposals into a single working document; as such it was accepted by both sides. In 1982 meetings were speeded up but at the end of the year the gulf between the two communities was as wide as ever on the crucial issues of territory and constitution. In February 1983 Spyros Kyprianou was re-elected President with AKEL's support for a further five-year term. The time seemed ripe for a new initiative — the burden fell to the UN Secretary-General, Javier Perez de Cuellar, a former special representative in Cyprus.

INTERNATIONALIZATION

Perez de Cuellar's task was complicated by the sharp deterioration in Greco-Turkish relations since Andreas Papandreou's PASOK came to power in Greece in October 1981. Publicly sceptical about the value of the intercommunal talks, Papandreou advocated the mobilization of world opinion against Turkey with the object of securing the Turkish army's withdrawal from Cyprus prior to negotiations. After his historic visit to Cyprus in February 1982 the tactics of internationalization gathered momentum.

The Greek Cypriots insist that point 6 does not apply to the international struggle. Acrimonious debate in New York has tended to undermine the search for a settlement through quiet diplomacy. And the Cyprus Government was persuaded to drop its annual appeal during the first two years of the Gobbi talks. In 1983, however, it decided to raise the question again. On 13 May the General Assembly adopted Resolution 37/253 by 105 votes to four against with twenty abstentions. The text renewed the perennial demand for the withdrawal of all the occupation forces and the voluntary return of the refugees in safety to their villages. Paragraph 2 called upon all states to help the Republic to exercise 'its right to full and effective control over the entire territory of Cyprus....' The text was also potentially explosive in that it set terms for the resumption of the intercommunal talks which lay outside the framework agreed by the Cypriot leaders. Two thirds of the nations voting for the resolution were members either of the Soviet bloc or of the non-aligned movement, whose contact group had sponsored the draft. The effect of the debate on the Turks was catalytic, and the intercommunal talks were suspended. The dust had to settle before the Perez de Cuellar initiative could get off the ground, and his 'soundings' were not sent to the Cypriot leaders until 8 August. By that time the Turkish Cypriots had already taken the first step in preparation for independence in their legislative assembly which adopted a motion affirming their right to self-determination by 33 votes to 6.

Perez de Cuellar suggested that the talks should concentrate on the crucial issues of territory and the federal constitution; that the first should be negotiated on the basis of the Turkish Cypriots retaining a maximum of 30 per cent and a minimum of 23 per cent of the island. The Foreign Minister, Nikos Rolandis, the Communist Party AKEL and the main opposition party, Clerides's Democratic Rally, favoured immediate and unconditional acceptance of the Secretary-General's plan. Prolonged hesitation by President Kyprianou, caused Mr. Rolandis's resignation.[57] A revised version to meet the wishes of the Cyprus Government was rejected by Rauf Denktash.

THE TURKISH-CYPRIOT DECLARATION
OF INDEPENDENCE

On 15 November 1983 the Turkish Cypriots established the Turkish Republic of Northern Cyprus. The proclamation offered peace and friendship to the Greek Cypriots, it left the door wide open to the formation of a federation with them and for the continuation of the Perez de Cuellar negotiations. For the Turkish Cypriots the event marked the climax of twenty years of intercommunal strife.

By their choice of date the Turkish Cypriots hoped to avoid compromising the Turkish Government. The interim period before the newly-elected civilian government took over from the military regime provided an opportunity which might not recur for years.

15

Turkey had consistently supported the intercommunal talks; the formal secession of the north was likely to have unfavourable repercussions on her relations with the West and on the supply of American arms and aid. Turkey, however, immediately recognised the new state. International reaction was that of almost universal condemnation. Britain requested an urgent meeting of the Security Council and submitted a draft resolution which deplored the Turkish-Cypriot move, demanded the withdrawal of the declaration, and called upon members not to recognise any state of Cyprus other than the Republic of Cyprus. The resolution was adopted by 13 votes. Pakistan voted against the motion; Jordan abstained.[58]

On 2 January 1984 Rauf Denktash announced a series of goodwill measures including plans for the return of Varosha to the Greek Cypriots and the re-opening of Nicosia airport under UNFICYP's administration. President Kyprianou dismissed the offer as propaganda and insisted that the latest Security Council resolution must be implemented in full. The Turkish Cypriots were adamant that the withdrawal of the independence declaration would take place only if and when a federal solution was reached. Nevertheless they agreed to postpone plans for the consolidation of independence.

In the autumn Perez de Cuellar resumed his initiative with a series of 'proximity' talks held separately with Kyprianou and Denktash. In November as the result of American pressure on the Turkish Government the Turkish Cypriots made important concessions. A settlement of the constitutional and territorial issues seemed within reach. The Turkish Cypriots had agreed to reduce the area under their control to about 29 per cent of the island and to waive their claim to a rotating presidency. The Greek Cypriots had accepted the principle of the equal representation of the two communities in the upper house of a bi-cameral legislature. Summit talks opened in New York on 17 January 1985. Denktash accepted the Perez de Cuellar documents unconditionally. Kyprianou wanted further discussions. The consequent collapse of the summit marked yet one more setback in the unending search for a political settlement.

NOTES

1 *Conference on Cyprus,* HMSO, Cmnd. 680, 1959, pp. 5 - 9.

2 *Cyprus,* HMSO, Cmnd. 1093, 1960.

3 Kyriakides, Stanley, *Cyprus: Constitutionalism and Crisis Government* (University of Pennsylvania Press, 1968), pp. 72-103.

4 Ertekun, Necati M, *The Cyprus Dispute* (Rustem & Bro., Nicosia, 1981, revised edition, 1984), p. 182.

5 Kitson, Frank, *Bunch of Five* (Faber & Faber, London, 1977), p. 233, 237. Patrick, Richard, *Political Geography and the Cyprus Conflict* (University of Waterloo, Ontario, 1976), p. 55.

6 Ball, George, *The Past has Another Pattern* (Norton & Co, London, 1982) p. 340.

7 Higgins, Rosalyn, *United Nations Peacekeeping Documents and Commentary: Europe 1946 - 1979* (OUP/RIIA, Oxford, 1981), pp. 96 - 7.

8 Papandreou, Andreas, *Greek Democracy at Gunpoint* (Pelican, London, 1973), p. 134.

9 UN doc. S/5671.

10 Patrick, op. cit., p. 66.

11 Salih, Ibrahim, *Cyprus: The Impact of Diverse Nationalism on a State* (University of Alabama Press, USA, 1978), pp. 144-52.

12 ib., pp. 47 - 8.

13 Karayiannis, General G., *Ethnikos Kyrix*, Athens, 19, 22, 23 June, 1965.

14 UN doc. S/5950, para. 83.

15 Security Council Res. 193 (9 Aug. 1964). Higgins, op. cit., p. 98.

16 UN doc. S/6228, paras. 53 - 7.

17 UN doc. S/6102, para 45. Patrick, op. cit., pp. 76 - 9.

18 UN docs. S/6228, paras 71 - 6 and S/6881, Adds. 1 & 2. Patrick, op. cit., p. 132.

19 Plaza, Galo, *Report of the United Nations Mediator to the Secretary-General,* 26 March 1965, S/6253, S/6267, S/6267/Add. I and S/6279.

20 Higgins, op. cit., pp. 328 - 31.

21 UN doc. S/7350, paras. 152 - 4.

22 Polyviou, Polyvios G., *Cyprus Conflict and Negotiation 1960 - 1980* (Duckworth, London, 1980), p. 45.

23 Ertekun, op. cit., pp. 14, 189 - 90.

24 UN doc. S/8248 & Add. 5. Harbottle, Michael, *The Impartial Soldier* (OUP/RIIA, Oxford, 1970), pp. 145 - 60.

25 Higgins, op. cit., pp. 139, 259, 356.

26 Patrick, op. cit., pp. 169 - 71.

27 *Cyprus Mail*, 1 January 1968.

28 UN doc. S/8914, para. 87.

29 Polyviou, op. cit., *Cyprus in Search of a Constitution: Constitutional Negotiations and Proposals* (Nicosia, 1976), pp. 68 - 101.

30 UN doc. S/7969, para. 29.

31 *Digest of the Cyprus Press* (BIS, Nicosia, 27 March 1970).

32 *Cyprus Mail*, 20 March 1970.

33 ib., 28 May 1970.

34 Distribution of Seats: Unified Party (Clerides) 15; AKEL (Papaioannou) 9; Progressive Front (Ioannides) 7; Democratic Centre Union (Lyssarides) 2; Independents 2; National Democratic Party (Evdokas) nil.

35 *Estia*, 31 January 1972.

36. Higgins, op. cit., pp. 233, 364.

37 *Sunday Times*, 21 July 1974.

38 Ertekun, op. cit., pp. 240 - 49.

39 Higgins, op. cit, p. 270. Ehrlich, Thomas, *Cyprus 1958 - 1967*, (OUP, 1974, pp. 79 - 81. Nedjatigil, Zaim M, *The Cyprus Conflict: A Lawyer's View* (Nicosia, 1982), pp. 74, 75 - 7, 81 - 2, 86 - 8. Polyviou, *Cyprus Conflict*, op. cit., pp. 15 - 16, 32, 157, 161, 167, 178, 186, 188 - 9.

40 Security Council Res. 353, 20 July 1974.

41 Ertekun, op. cit., pp. 248 - 9.

42 Polyviou, op. cit., *Cyprus in Search ...*, pp. 319 - 80.

43 UN doc. S/11568, para. 48. Oberling, Pierre, *The Road to Bellapais: The Turkish Cypriot Exodus to Northern Cyprus* (Colombia University Press, New York, 1982).

44 *Report of the Select Committe on Cyprus.* HMSO, 8 April 1976.

45 Higgins, op. cit., pp. 115 - 16. Security Council Res. 367, 12 March 1975.

46 Higgins, op. cit., pp. 384 - 6. Note: By 1984 fewer than 900 Greek Cypriots remained in the North.

47 UN doc. S/11900, para. 49.

48 *Cyprus Intercommunal Talks* (Public Information Office, Nicosia, July 1981), p. 27.

49 ib., pp. 29 - 30.

50 Ertekun, op. cit., pp. 321 - 44.

51 UN doc. S/12723, para. 52.

52 *Cyprus Intercommunal Talks,* op. cit., pp. 40 - 45, 87 - 90.

53 ib., pp. 46 - 47.

54 White, Gillian M, *The Turkish Federated State of Cyprus: A Lawyer's View,* 'The World Today', (RIIA), April, 1981. Nedjatigil, op. cit., *Our Republic in Perspective* (Nicosia, 1985), pp. 22, 58, 109 - 21, 133 - 4.

55 *The Cyprus Conflict: A Lawyer's View,* op. cit., pp. 165 - 79.

56 Borowiec, Andrew, *The Mediterranean Feud* (Praeger, New York, 1983), pp. 159 - 64.

57 Rolandis, Nikos, article in *Kathimerini* Athens, 6/7 November 1983.

58 Security Council Res. 541 (1983).

PEACEKEEPING IN CYPRUS

Field Marshal Lord Carver

My direct involvement with Cyprus covered two short periods. The first was from February until July 1964, when I was, for a few weeks, Commander of the British (theoretically the Anglo-Greek-Turkish) Truce Force, and thereafter Deputy Commander and Chief of Staff of the United Nations Force. The second was ten years later, when I was Chief of the British Defence Staff — the equivalent of Chairman of the Joint Chiefs in the USA — at the time of the Turkish invasion in July 1974. I will confine what I have to say to those periods.

Knowledge of the island's historical background is essential if one is to appreciate the motives and behaviour, not only of the Cypriots themselves, but also of the mainland Greeks and Turks; but I will assume that this audience is familiar with it up to 1960, when Cyprus became an independent republic within the British Commonwealth.

That independence was limited, quite apart from the establishment of the British Sovereign Base Areas and the retention of a number of military installations outside those areas. The United Kingdom, Greece and Turkey were nominated as guarantor powers both of the security and independence of the Republic and of its constitution. The Republic was forbidden to attach itself to any other state, and any form of partition was excluded, thus stultifying the respective objectives of both sides. Executive power was in the hands of the President, Makarios, and Vice-President, Kutchuk, each of whom had the right of veto, and a Council of Ministers of seven Greek and three Turkish-Cypriot ministers. This ratio of 70/30 was adopted for all fields of government, and was greatly in favour of the Turks, who constituted eighteen percent of the population. There was also to be a Cyprus Army of 2,000 men in the ratio of 60/40, but it never got off the ground.

There is no doubt that the Turks managed to obtain representation in government service, particularly in the police, out of proportion both to their share of the population and, even more, to their standards of education and ability, because they had been more pro-government in British times and particularly during the EOKA emergency. This merely reinforced the objections of the Greeks, who said that the Turks, apart from the justice of their case, were not capable of filling all these posts with men of equal standards to those whom the Greeks could produce, which was true. More important than this, however, was the fact that, at every level of government, the Turks could practically veto any form of activity. Any measure which did not directly benefit the Turkish Cypriots was therefore liable to obstruction, and the attempt to administer the two communities as two separate entities was hopelessly impractical.

But this was not a problem which was susceptible to a rational solution in purely demographic terms. The Turkish Cypriots knew perfectly well that, if they were exposed on even terms to the full blast of competition from the Greek Cypriots, they would go under, as they had elsewhere in the Mediterranean, notably in Crete. They therefore fought against it as long as they could. The dialogue, moreover, was not just between the Greek and Turkish Cypriots. If it had been, it would have been much easier to solve. Mainland Greece and Turkey were directly involved, and there were influential and powerful bodies in both countries which were determined to achieve, on the one hand *enosis,* and on the other partition.

Faced with this situation, Makarios proposed, early in 1963, thirteen amendments to the constitution. On the face of it, they were reasonable and sensible, and they would have made government of the island efficient and logical; but they would have knocked away all the built-in privileges and safeguards of the Turkish community. Makarios believed, with some justification, that these amendments would be viewed sympathetically by the British Government.

There is no doubt that, from then on, both sides began to prepare to use armed force to support their respective stands. At any rate the extremists did, and the responsible leaders knew perfectly well what was happening, even if they did not actually approve — although they probably did. Who leads whom, in these situations, is almost impossible to determine.

Having got nowhere by argument and discussion, Makarios announced, in November 1963, that he was going ahead unilaterally in January 1964 with certain of these measures, notably the abolition of separate Greek and Turkish local government authorities for the same areas.

It is impossible to be certain where exactly to lay the blame for the initial outbreak of fighting in Nicosia on 21 December 1963. There are undoubtedly indications that the Greeks did not plan to bring matters to a head until June 1964, and there are strong suspitions that the Turks knew this and decided to force the issue in January, before the Greeks were ready. There are other signs that extremists on the Greek side, like Nikos Sampson, provoked incidents which hastened the whole process on, either because they realized what the Turks intended, or because they were impatient of the apparently deliberate policy of Makarios.

Whatever may be the real truth, certain facts stand out: that both sides had armed bodies of men ready to go into action immediately: that the Turks had a plan, which they executed, to leave all government service, and to try and set up a parallel administration of their own, at the same time abandoning a number of mixed and isolated villages and concentrating their population in areas where they were less vulnerable: and that the Greeks had plans, which they executed with brutality and callous disregard of human life, to drive Turks out of certain areas, particularly in the northern suburbs of Nicosia, where their presence was either an embarrassment or a real threat to Greeks.

All these things happened in the last fortnight of 1963. The fighting which resulted, in Nicosia and Larnaca, was a threat to the security of British service and civilian families living there. Its continuance and possible spread to other parts of the island would have threatened the security and viability of British installations throughout the island, as well as that of the 15,000 dependents of the British armed forces, who lived outside the base areas, mostly among the Greeks. Not only would this have threatened British interests within Cyprus, but Turkey might have felt impelled to step in to protect her compatriots. This would have led to the risk of war between Greece and Turkey, the disruption of NATO and even wider dangers, possibly involving the intervention of the Soviet Union. Within the island itself, it was also necessary to prevent a direct clash between the contingents of the Greek and

Turkish armies, stationed at Nicosia under the terms of the 1960 Treaty.

In order to avert these dangers, the British Government pressed both sides to accept the intervention of the small British force stationed in the base areas in order to separate the two sides and restore peace, while the politicians sorted things out. This move was supported by the two other guarantor powers, Greece and Turkey, whose contingents were nominally placed under the command of Major-General Young, Commander of the British army units in the base areas. His combined force was known as the 'Joint Truce Force', and was reinforced with an infantry brigade from England.

At this time, it appeared that the political leaders of both sides were genuinely shocked at what had happened and were anxious to restore peaceful conditions; but neither were prepared to compromise on their political aims, and both were egged on by their more extreme factions, either to take advantage of the situation or at least not to yield an inch to their opponents.

In this atmosphere, Duncan Sandys, the British Secretary of State for Commonwealth Relations, visited Cyprus in the first week of January 1964 and hammered out a series of temporary agreements, under which it was hoped that life could return to normal, while political discussions were transferred to London; but the London conference resulted in deadlock. By this time, the British Government was anxious to spread the load. Not only just the military burden of peacekeeping, as the demand for more and more troops grew, but also the political responsibility and the odium attached to it. Makarios was keen, as he always had been, to transfer the problem to the United Nations, which he believed would favour him. The Turks, for the same reason, were opposed to it. For a time a scheme was mooted for an international force, drawn from NATO countries, for which the British Chiefs of Staff would act as agents; but Makarios realized that Turkey's strategic position would always carry weight with NATO, and he refused to agree to it.

While all this was being discussed, the need for more troops was urgent, and I was sent out with the headquarters of the 3rd Division, which I was commanding at the time, and another brigade. I took over command from General Young, who returned to his job of commanding the troops inside the base areas. I was immediately faced with dealing with the attacks carried out by

Greek-Cypriot fighters on the Turkish areas of Limassol and Polis. In both cases assurances were received from the Minister of Defence and Interior, Polykarpos Georgadjis, that nothing serious would happen, and the excuse given that the local fighters were out of control. All attempts to get the attacks stopped were frustrated, until the Turks had been practically defeated and driven into a very constricted area. The Turks demanded restoration of the *status quo* or total evacuation to the north. The Greeks demanded the surrender of all arms by the Turks as a condition of a return to normal. The Turks refused. As a final compromise, the Turks kept, but did not carry or display their weapons; the Greeks, police and so-called freedom fighters, remained in sandbagged strongholds round the area, threatening the Turks, who continued to live in an atmosphere of siege and subjection, unless they were prepared to submit wholly to the Government in every field of activity, which their policy dictated that they should not accept. This pattern was to be followed on many subsequent occasions all over the island.

By this time, it had been decided to refer the dispute to the United Nations, and I hoped for a period of calm, while deliberations took place in New York; but I was disappointed, as both sides tried to improve their positions, and agitation against the British peacekeeping force was fomented by Nikos Sampson and the hardline Greek Cypriots. A serious situation arose at Ktima-Paphos, in the south-west of the island, on the very day, March 4th, that the Security Council passed the resolution recommending the establishment of a United Nations Force in Cyprus for three months; and also the appointment of a mediator 'for the purpose of promoting a peaceful solution and an agreed settlement of the problems confronting Cyprus, in accordance with the Charter of the United Nations.' The wording of the resolution was of considerable importance. The first paragraph called on all member states to refrain from action or threat of action to worsen the situation in the sovereign Republic of Cyprus or to endanger international peace. This was, of course, principally aimed at Turkey, but could be interpreted to prevent anyone else from interfering, even the British from their sovereign base areas. The second paragraph asked the Government of Cyprus 'which has the responsibility for the maintenance and restoration of law and order' to take additional measures to stop violence and bloodshed in Cyprus. The fourth paragraph authorized the Secretary-General to establish the force and defined its mission as 'in the interests of pre-serving international peace and security, to use its best efforts to prevent a recurrence of fighting, and, as necessary, to contribute to the maintenance and restoration of law and order and a return to normal conditions.'

It will be noted that the resolution placed the basic responsibi-lity for the restoration of peace in the island on the Government of Cyprus; and that the UN Force was given, as its first task, the prevention of a recurrence of fighting; and, secondly, 'as neces-sary' to contribute to what was basically the task of the Cyprus Government. At the same time the UN recognized as the Govern-ment the machine headed by Makarios, which was without its Turkish element, and therefore not subject to the latter's veto. As long as this condition obtained, the Turks could (and, of course, did) complain that it was not the constitutional government, and did not therefore have the authority it claimed, and was given by the UN resolution. But every attempt to persuade the Turks to try and rejoin the Government met with blank refusal, as it was to do ever after. Makarios was, as a result, able to state pretty truth-fully that, in the deliberate absence of the Turks, his purely Greek-Cypriot administration had to carry on the government of the island without the Turks and be recognized as the sole valid autho-rity.

Trouble started almost as soon as the resolution was passed. The Greeks saw it as supporting their view that restoration of normal conditions meant re-establishment of the authority of the Government over all the areas in which its writ no longer ran i.e. the Turkish-inhabited places. In addition, they were most anxious that, when the mediator got to work, he should not start from the basis of *de facto* partition created by the Turks, which the Greeks saw as the principal abnormality of the situation. Their chief com-plaint about the peacekeeping force, whether British or UN, was that its operation tended to equate the Turkish Cypriots with themselves and their claims with their own. To regard the two as of equal weight seemed to them grossly unjust and undemocratic.

The conversion of the peacekeeping force from a purely British one into a UN Force was a slow process. Initially the British troops under my command put on blue berets as soon as the first troops of another nation, the Canadians, arrived. The Turkish and Greek army battalions on the island ceased, even nominally, to be under my command. The only order I had given them, which was the only one there was any hope of their obeying, was to stay where they were and do nothing. The two Greek battalions were in their camps on the southern outskirts of Nicosia, while the Turkish battalion, whose camp had been next to the Greek, had deployed into the Turkish area on the north-west of Nicosia, covering the road to Kyrenia. The Indian General Gyani, who was already in the island as a UN observer, was appointed to command the Force, with myself as his deputy and Chief of Staff. He promptly went back to India for a fortnight's leave, while a Brazilian General from the UN Force in the Gaza strip came over to act nominally as commander until Gyani returned. He sensibly did not attempt to do anything but practise his hobby of photography, while I got on with the job, receiving my political advice from Pier Spinelli, the shrewd representative of the Secretary-General in Geneva.

It is important to remember that the UN Force was not concerned in finding a solution. Not only was this the invidious task of the mediator, but we had no idea what the final solution recommended was likely to be. At the same time it was important to do nothing which might prejudice it. In a national situation, the forces are generally supporting and working towards a political solution, the outline of which is generally at least forecast, even if it may change. In that case, one can direct the activities of the force, or at least attempt to do so, so that they work towards that solution.

But, in this case, no such long-term and general aim existed. One was supposed to be preserving the situation in the most favourable temperature for peaceful solution. However, preservation of an existing situation generally favours one side or the other; and indefinite successful preservation of the *status quo*, by preventing real pressures from acting, can actually work against finding a solution. In Cyprus preservation of the existing situation favoured the Turks in one respect, in that it preserved the *de facto* segregation arising out of the December fighting and made it appear that they could not live together with the Greeks. But it probably benefited the Greeks most, as it left them in sole charge of the Government and all its machinery, as well as control of almost all of the island. But both wanted change: the Turkish Cypriots, in theory, a return to the situation before December 1963, in practice, under the influence of Ankara, partition; the Greek Cypriots a move forward to a unitary state with a government with full powers over the whole Republic.

When Gyani returned from leave on 23 March, he addressed himself to the problem of 'restoring normal conditions' and in particular to the establishment of freedom of movement throughout the island. He was disappointed to find that the transformation of the peacekeeping force into a United Nations one had had little effect on the situation, and he was inclined initially to put it down to anti-British feeling, although he was strongly pro-British himself. But he gradually came to recognize that neither side in the dispute had any real respect for the authority of the United Nations, except insofar as they could exploit it for their own purposes. The Greeks interpreted freedom of movement to mean that the Turks should cease to defend their areas, and admit the Greek-Cypriot police into them, abandoning their reliance on the Turkish-Cypriot members of the Cyprus Police Force who had taken refuge in the Turkish areas and formed a force which took its orders from Kutchuk; and that all Greek Cypriots should be free to enter and pass through Turkish-Cypriot areas. The Turks interpreted it to mean that they should be free to travel anywhere throughout the island without interference from the Greek-Cypriot police, who suspected them, not without reason, of trying to transfer Turkish fighters and their weapons from one area to another. Although the Turkish enclaves of the main towns remained fortresses into which the police could not penetrate, movement was relatively free throughout the island both for the Greek-Cypriot police and for the Turkish Cypriots whom the police, or the Greek-Cypriot fighters, did not suspect as being Turkish-Cypriot fighters or carriers of their weapons and ammunition. Although some incidents continued to occur on the borders of the urban enclaves, the presence of the UN Force there managed to control them and generally prevent them from escalating. It was the question of movement which caused most incidents and problems for the Force. In some cases Turks from villages on or near the main roads interfered, or threatened to, with traffic, particularly any that they thought might be a threat to them. This provoked threats from the police or the fighters to attack the village and remove weapons from the Turks. In other cases, the police would stop all Turkish vehicles to search them for weapons and ammunition. Many of the Turks, particularly in the north-west of the island, relied on exporting fruit and vegetables for the early market in Britain. The police searches appeared to be deliberately designed to prevent them from delivering their goods in time to catch the aircraft or ship due to export them. There was little the UN Force could do to alleviate these sources of dispute, short of attempts to persuade both sides not to provoke the other and to act with humanity and understanding.

A particularly serious incident occurred in April which led to a threat of intervention from the Turkish mainland. For a long time Turkish fighters had occupied the castle of St. Hilarion which overlooked the pass through the Pentadaktylos hills between Kyrenia and Nicosia. A large body of Greek fighters managed to approach it without the knowledge of the UN Force and to deliver an attack, which was eventually brought to an end by the Canadian contingent, leaving the Turks still in possession of the castle. Soon after this there was a serious incident at Famagusta, when three mainland Greek army officers and the son of the chief of police, a friend of Nikos Sampson, all in plain clothes, drove into the Turkish quarter in the old town. They were shot at as they left, all being killed except for one officer, who was severely wounded. In revenge, the Greeks abducted and murdered twelve Turkish Cypriots returning from work in the British base at Dhekelia.

The inability of the UN Force to prevent these incidents incurred severe criticism from many quarters and high-lighted two of the handicaps under which the Force laboured: its lack of information, or what the military call intelligence, and the general limitations on what it could do. A UN Force is not allowed to have an intelligence organization. Any attempt to find out what the fighters of both sides were up to, whether overt or covert, was regarded by them as spying, and produced strong, sometimes violent reactions and protests, the Greeks taking the line that all we were meant to do was to monitor specific agreements and get the Turks to comply with them, while the latter regarded our task as being to protect them against Greek-Cypriot attacks and force them also to implement agreements. I was fortunate in that, through British channels, I had fairly good information about the contacts of both sides with Ankara, Athens and their representatives elsewhere outside the island, but scanty and unreliable information about what was intended within the fighting organizations within the island.

As to what we could actually do, we were constantly under pressure from the UN Secretariat in New York, and also from other quarters, including London and the British press, to place our troops between the two sides and use force to stop them fighting. Although this had been accepted from the start on the Green Line in Nicosia, in spite of the fact that it rested on no legal basis, I was opposed to applying it generally, unless there was no other method of keeping the peace. It antagonized both sides, and, in the eyes of the Greeks, it was justifiably seen as merely providing a reinforcement for the Turks. A better method was for the peacekeeping force to keep in the closest touch possible with the influential people, including the leaders of the fighters of both sides, in order to detect when tension was imminent, to prevent clashes and quickly damp them down when they did occur. But in the last resort, it was the political influence that the United Nations could bring to bear which determined what we could achieve, not the amount of force we could use, which, in the last resort, was very much less than either side could deploy, especially if Turkey chose to intervene from the mainland.

Minimum force therefore had to be the order of the day. Even if any other policy had been desirable, there were facts of the situation which made it impractical. The Force, whether British or UN, was at all times greatly outnumbered by the armed Greek Cypriots, regular or irregular. Dispersed, both generally and locally, as we had to be to do our job of having a presence wherever the two sides faced each other, we were at all times very vulnerable to them. Deliberately to have engaged in active operations against them was therefore as much out of the question militarily as it was politically. One of the difficulties in dealing with this question of the use of force was that it is comparatively easy to convince people that you are doing the right thing if you are preventing somebody from carrying out a deliberate attack. It is not at all as obvious that somebody is using force if he is standing still, holding a loaded weapon and merely threatening to fire at somebody if he comes that way. In other words, he is in an attitude of defence. The latter is just as much using force as the former, although he does not fire his weapon until he is actually attacked. A post established to prevent people coming past it is definitely a use of force. The Greek Cypriots were inclined to be the attackers and the Turkish Cypriots the defenders, not always of areas which could reasonably be said to belong to them. If the UN Force were to prevent the Greeks from attacking, as it frequently tried to do, it should, argued the Greeks with some logic, be equally prepared to use force to prevent the Turks from defending. If the Force acted only against the attackers, but never against the defenders, it merely became a reinforcement to the latter. This was true, and was the main local Greek criticism of the Force, both when British and when UN.

The incidents at St. Hilarion and Famagusta reflected a serious development of that period: the increasing professionalism of the illegal organizations of fighters on both sides. The Greek and Turkish army contingents in the island began to train and get involved in the control of the fighters, and reinforcements for both sides arrived from the mainland. The Turks came by boat by night to the Turkish villages on the coast between Lefka and Polis, while Greek reinforcements, many of them serving members of the Greek army, came by ship to Limassol in the guise of 'returning students'. As the Greek-Cypriot fighters began to be organized increasingly as an army, trained and, in some cases, commanded by Greek army offficers, Makarios and Georgadjis explained to Gyani that this was in response to his demands that the fighters should be brought under stricter control. So often, when fighting had broken out after assurances had been given by them that it would not, the excuse had been that local fighters had taken matters into their own hands. A sinister development in this regard was the return of Grivas in the latter half of June. A week before his presence was revealed, Georgadjis had asked me to spend a Sunday with him, driving up to have lunch at the top of Mount Troodos. The object of the trip was to warn me that Grivas was coming and to explain that it was with the approval of Makarios, in response to Gyani's requests for stricter control. Georgadjis asked me to persuade the British not to object. In the light of subsequent events and of Georgadjis's ultimate fate, I have doubts about whether the Archbishop had approved. I had doubts then, but passed his request both to the UN and the British authorities, neither of whom did raise any objections. This development meant that there were now three rival parties, seeking different solutions: the Turks, who wanted to concentrate their population in the north and bring about partition, whatever the majority of the Turkish Cypriots themselves may have wanted: Makarios, and his moderate supporters like Glafcos Clerides, who wanted an independent unitary state, in which the Turkish and Greek Cypriots were treated alike, and Grivas, almost certainly supported by Georgadjis and most of the Greek army officers, who still sought *enosis.*

When I left on 17 July, after General Thimayya had taken over command from Gyani, I summed up the situation in my report in these words:

'Leaving Cyprus when the peacekeeping force, in its various guises, had been in operation for about seven months, for five of which I had either been in command or deputy commander, one could not but feel that little had been achieved. In all that time no progress whatever had been made towards a political solution. In fact the reverse was the case. Both sides had hardened in their attitudes, the Greek Cypriots in their firm determination to control their own affairs, the Turks in their demand for a separatist solution which would divide them from the Greek Cypriots even more definitely than under the Zurich constitution.'

The only variant of the Greek demand was between the proponents of *enosis,* recently strengthened by the arrival of Grivas and of reinforcements from mainland Greece, and those of self-determination, whose voice had grown louder over the last seven months as the influence of the anti-western elements exploited the Greek-Cypriot frustration, whether in the direction of communism or of the anti-British element in neighbouring Arab countries.

On the Turkish side it was difficult to determine the real feelings of the Turkish Cypriots themselves. Policy was clearly dictated from Ankara, and any deviation from it was liable to lead to condign punishment by the TMT, the Turkish fighters organization. There was considerable evidence to show, as the Greek Cypriots claimed, that a considerable number, if not the great majority, of Turkish Cypriots would have welcomed submission to the Greek-Cypriot demands in order to bring to an end the siege conditions in which they lived. The great difficulty in finding any opening for a move to normality was the failure of the Turks to make any proposals which were conceivably practical in administrative, economic or political terms. After seven months it was clear that neither side had any real desire or intention to return to the constitutional position as it had been before the December fighting.

The operation of the peacekeeping force, in the absence of any advance on the political front, had therefore served to make a solution more, rather than less, difficult, in that it prevented the real sources of power from acting on the situation. Any pressure, military, economic, political or diplomatic, exerted by either side, impelled the Force, in the interests of keeping the peace and maintaining a stable situation, to resist it. As on most occasions such pressure came from the Greek-Cypriot side, the Force inevitably found itself ranged on the Turkish side of the balance, in spite of the fact that all recognized that the solution must favour the Greek rather than the Turkish point of view. The soldier in the field found himself permanently on the horns of this dilemma, subjected directly to the human passions involved: from one side threats and insults, from the other, pathetic appeals to his sympathy, which was at the same time exploited without compunction. In the end he learned to distrust both communities.

If the Force appeared to have achieved little in the direction of helping towards a return to normal conditions or to the creation of a favourable climate in which a political solution could be found, it had at least served the other purpose for which it had been brought into being. Although there had been fighting between the two communities from time to time, it had never been of the indiscriminate type of the December outbreak, and casualties had in fact been remarkably small. A most important factor was that, in spite of all apparent failures and frustrations, the presence and operation of the Force had, at any rate up to the time of writing (i.e. July 1964), prevented events in the island from leading to overt armed intervention from outside, with the attendant risk of war between two fellow members of NATO, and the possibility of escalation and of far more serious disasters, even possibly World War III. The possibility of such escalation hung over every daily struggle with the intractable problems of the island, presented to one by the apparently irresponsible leaders of both communities, who only too often appeared, or chose to appear, powerless to control their own armed men and extreme factions.

One lesson at least was clear: that it was a fallacy to imagine that operations of a peacekeeping force of this nature could be divorced in any way from political affairs, either of the island itself or of the world outside. Any act or any word of every member of the Force at any time could have some political significance, certainly within the island, and often outside also. Even such apparently harmless acts as conducting an invalid or wounded man to hospital, giving him medical care, or carrying letters for those who could not go to the post office, had widespread political repercussions. It was essential therefore that the command of the Force should be intimately linked to its political direction, and this was not always easy to arrange. The ideal was to concentrate the two functions in one man, but General Gyani certainly found the strain of this too much for him.

If, in that report, I had suggested that the Force would still be there in twenty years' time and that no political solution would be in sight, I would have been regarded as a Cassandra, but I would have been a true prophet.

*   *   *

Let me now advance, not twenty, but ten years to July 1974. Britain has been much criticized for taking no military action to oppose the Turkish invasion then. I will briefly recount how I saw the affair as the British Chief of the Defence Staff. In spite of the implication in Christopher Hitchens's book, *Cyprus,* that the British Government knew in advance that a coup against Makarios, instigated by the Greek Government of Colonels, was imminent, no such evidence was available to the British Ministry of Defence or to Air Marshal Aiken, the commander of the British Forces in the base areas. I very much doubt if it was available either to the Foreign Office. Of course we knew that the Greek Colonels were plotting against Makarios; that had been obvious at least since the attempt on Makarios' life in 1970, for which Georghadjis paid with his life, almost certainly at the hands of the Colonels, to attempt to conceal the part they had played in it. But the coup on the morning of 15 July 1974 took us all by surprise. At first, all we knew was that the Presidential Palace had been attacked and that Makarios had disappeared, believed to have escaped. It was not until the late afternoon that it had been fairly reliably established that Makarios had managed to reach Paphos, where he had taken refuge with the Bishop. He must have made his way there through the mountains. The Bishop appealed to the United Nations Force to assume responsibility for his protection. Air Marshal Aiken was now very concerned about the safety of all the families of British servicemen who lived in the outskirts of Limassol, which was a hotbed of former Grivas supporters. The road from Limassol to Paphos went through the base area of Episkopi, and, if British troops or base area police attempted to prevent EOKA-B fighters or Cypriot National Guard from getting to Paphos, all those families would be at risk.

On the morning of 16 July Makarios moved into the protection of the UN Force in Paphos, which was provided by the British contingent. Soon after mid-day, the Bishop of Paphos's palace was under fire from a Cypriot National Guard patrol boat, and a force of the Guard from Nicosia was approaching the town. Makarios, fearing that the small UN Force at Paphos would not be able to protect him, asked the British High Commissioner in Nicosia by telephone to arrange for him to be rescued by the British and taken to the safety of the Episkopi-Akrotiri base. This was passed immediately to the Foreign Secretary, Callaghan, in London and Aiken warned to be prepared to implement a contingency plan which had been in existence since the previous attempt on Makarios' life.

Three-quarters of an hour after he had received the warning, at 3:45 p.m. by Cyprus time, Aiken telephoned me to say that, unless a helicopter was sent immediately to pick up the Archbishop, it might be too late. He did not want to keep him in the base for fear of the reaction of the National Guard, and he proposed to transfer him immediately to an aircraft which would fly to Malta. If the British Government disapproved of this, the aircraft could always return. I was unable to get any ruling from the Foreign Office, as ministers were busy discussing all the implications and were not over-keen on receiving Makarios in London. I therefore gave Aiken the authority he wanted, informing ministers in London that I had done so. For once Mintoff in Malta helped the British Government by persuading Makarios to stay there for a few days.

During that time it became clear that the executors of the coup were the mainland Greek army officers serving in the Cypriot National Guard, acting on the orders of the junta in Athens, notably Brigadier Ioannides. Their choice of Nikos Sampson as puppet head of the Greek-Cypriot Government discredited them with all but their most fanatical supporters. Turkey called on Britain, as a co-guarantor of the 1960 constitution, to restore the 'independence and integrity' of Cyprus, even though this would have meant the return of Makarios, regarded as Turkey's arch-enemy. She made it clear that she expected us to allow her to bring additional troops into the island through our bases and to cooperate with her; failing that, she would act alone.

This put the British Government on the spot. If we acted in cooperation with Turkey, and even more so if we let them make use of the bases, the whole Greek-Cypriot population would turn against us. This would not only prejudice the existence of the bases themselves, but would immediately put at risk the safety of all the service dependents and British citizens living in the island outside them. If however the Turks intervened alone and we did nothing to prevent them, we ran the risk of being equally unpopular with both elements of the population, with risks as great as those involved in active cooperation with the Turks.

By 19 July the threat of a Turkish invasion was appearing imminent, as all the Turkish troops, aircraft and ships on their southern coast had been brought to a high state of readiness. It was impossible to judge whether they had taken the decision to invade or were merely bringing pressure on us to intervene as the only means of preventing them from doing so. On several occasions in the previous ten years they had come as close as this to invasion, and on more than one occasion had actually set sail, only to return under cover of darkness. When, therefore, in the early afternoon of 19 July our air reconnaissance detected two separate groups of ships sailing south from Mersin, it could not definitely be forecast as an invasion. The number and size of ships did not seem sufficent to land more than a brigade, probably at Kyrenia, and an even smaller group — only two ships — heading for Famagusta appeared to be able to do no more than seize the port with the help of the Turks in the old city. In fact they did land about a brigade at Kyrenia at dawn on the 20th; the other group was intended to intercept any reinforcement from Greece by sea. The lack of coordination between the Turkish navy and their air force led to one of them being sunk by the Turkish air force, the crew being rescued by us.

We reinforced our bases with a Marine commando, which fortunately happened to be nearby in a commando carrier. Within the next two days, the Turkish forces had reached Nicosia, but, by the time that a precarious cease-fire had been established on 21 July, they had only secured a fifteen-mile wide corridor between the city and Kyrenia. They had bombed Nicosia airfield and the Greek part of Famagusta, known as Varosha. The Greeks, overflying our Episkopi base, landed about 200 soldiers at Nicosia airfield on the night of 22 July, which provoked further Turkish bombing of the airfield, making life very uncomfortable for the headquarters of the UN Force, which was there. On the next day, in the face of warnings from the Turks and our embassy in Ankara, we carried out a successful naval evacuation of 1,500 civilians of twenty-three different nationalities from the area around Kyrenia. While it was in progress, rumours of an imminent Turkish attack on Nicosia airfield reached us, and tension rose to a high level. The Turks said that the UN had abandoned the airfield and that they now controlled it. General Prem Chand, the Indian commander of the UN Force, reacted to this by announcing that the UN had taken over the airport temporarily and that it had come under UN protection. Ankara kept on claiming that they controlled it, while their ambassador in Nicosia, who knew this was not true, said that they would shortly do so. Callaghan warned the Turkish Government of the very serious consequences of this, and tried to get Kissinger to add his pressure; but it was clear that in no circumstances would the Americans consider taking military action or threatening it. Callaghan was anxious to stiffen the threat against the Turks and persuaded the UN Secretariat to agree to the request that Prem Chand had made, for us to reinforce him from the base areas and provide air support. None of the latter was stationed in the island, but we flew out eight Phantoms within 24 hours and they were ready for action on the 25th, two squadrons of armoured cars and two companies of infantry having been sent up to join Prem Chand.

Fortunately they were not required to go into action as political events in Greece changed the situation. Karamanlis replacing the Colonels in Athens and Clerides Sampson in Nicosia. Callaghan now pinned his hopes on diplomatic pressure to get Turkey to withdraw her troops. But while he chaired a conference in Geneva, the Turks, under cover of a cease-fire in Cyprus, gradually increased their forces there. On 12 August they tabled a proposal, demanding as a Turkish-Cypriot zone the area which they later occupied, and threatened to walk out of the conference by midnight, if it were not agreed, and to take military action next morning to secure their demand. Callaghan was anxious for us to take some action to deter them, but there was little effective action that we could take which held out reasonable prospects of success, certainly not as long as the Americans were not prepared to cooperate in putting pressure on Turkey. While discussion was going on at UN Headquarters at New York about what support we might give the UN Force, the Turks struck at dawn on the 14th, carrying out air attacks on Nicosia, but not making any attempt to attack the airfield. Our ability to take stronger military action was limited. Most of our forces on the island were not combat troops. The number of the latter was limited to those needed to provide local security to the two base areas. We should have needed much stronger forces, if we were to face the possibility of hostilities between us and the Turkish armed forces. If we had decided that we should try and force the Turks out of the island, it would have taken us a significant time to build up the force necessary, and the Turks could always pre-empt this. Quite apart from all the wider political and military implications, it really was not an option open to us.

THREE GREEK ISLANDS AND THE DEVELOPMENT OF INTERNATIONAL LAW

Sir David Hunt

The essence of international relations in the modern world is the elaboration and application of the rule of law. This is in fact the principle on which civilised and democratically governed states conduct their relations; it is highly desirable that those less well governed countries which think it cleverer to pursue wholly individual purposes, and that such a pursuit is made easier in a system of international anarchy, should be brought to see the error of their ways. I apologise if these remarks appear trite. My principal intention, as will shortly become clear, is to speak about Cyprus. Because I have been a professional diplomat I cannot approach such a subject except on the basis of international law. I am the more constrained to that approach because I entered diplomacy after a spell of seven and a half years in the army of which those between 1940 and 1945 were on active service overseas. To have seen at close quarters the breakdown of order in the world gives one a strong feeling in favour of binding rules of international conduct.

In any case there is no doubt that to treat the question of Cyprus as a leading case in international law is correct, both morally and practically. I have therefore divided my treatment of my theme into three, unequal, parts each concerned with a different phase in the evolution of international law. I begin with Crete.

Crete, like Cyprus, lies to the south of the other Greek lands; the thirty-fifth parallel of latitude runs through both. Greek-speaking peoples, closely related, arrived in both in the late second millennium B.C. and have been the dominant element ever since in their racial, linguistic and cultural composition. In the second millennium A.D. both passed from Venetian to Ottoman rule, which lasted until the late nineteenth century. Thereafter their destinies diverged. Both became, for a time, independent. The Cretans, after fourteen years, achieved their long-desired aim of reunion with their fellow Greeks. The Cypriots, fourteen years after their independence, were once more invaded by their former conquerors.

Cretan independence was won under the old system of international law. When in 1897 the violence of Turkish oppression culminated in atrocities which shocked the conscience of Europe six powers intervened. A multi-national force was landed. Two governments, Germany and Austria-Hungary, withdrew after a year but the remaining four, Britain, France, Italy and Russia, took control of Crete, forced the Ottoman troops and administration to quit the island and declared it autonomous. This violent interference with the internal affairs of a state with which all the powers involved remained technically at peace was not authorised by any international body. It was organised in their respective capitals through the normal diplomatic channels. Details were arranged on the spot by the commanders of the national contingents.

The Cretans had no objections. They welcomed, as a first stage, their new state, new flag, new Prince and new postage stamps. (In theory they remained part of the Sultan's dominions, like Bosnia-Hercegovina under the Austrians and Cyprus under the British.) Their real desire was for union with Greece, for *enosis.* This was ruled out by the Powers, as it was, later, for Cyprus; but in 1912, when the coalition of Balkan states went to war to liberate the Christian nations of the peninsula, the prohibition was lifted. From that date Crete has been accepted as a part of Greece without question.

It is obvious how similar up to a point has been the course followed by the liberation struggle in Crete and Cyprus. Both have known insurrection, an international peacekeeping force and independence, followed, in one case only, by reunion with the motherland. The name 'the great Greek island', which had been affectionately applied to Crete before 1912, was thereafter transferred to Cyprus. It may seem strange that so equitable a result could be obtained at a time when the principles of international law were only weakly observed and denied in the modern age, when those principles are supposedly defended by a system endowed with world-wide authority.

The doctrine that the rule of law should be supreme in international as in internal affairs was indeed a long time in developing. Greek concepts going back to Plato were refined by Roman and medieval thinkers until they reached their finest expression in the seventeenth and eighteenth centuries with the works of Grotius and Vattel. Unhappily the actual conduct of international relations was more influenced by the practice of the Renaissance period in which inter-state relations first took the shape that they have since retained. The new nation-states of Europe considered themselves free to pursue their interests by any means they chose. Machiavelli provided what passed for a philosophical basis. The nineteenth-century idealists went further. Hegel deified the State. If the individual was a mere contingent epiphenomenon in contrast to the State, the sole absolute, how could there be any external constraints? Between states there should only be arrangements of convenience, such as the Universal Postal Union, or purely temporary treaties.

It is difficult to realise today the extent to which this enormously popular doctrine dominated political thinking in the late nineteenth century. It was less predominant in Britain than elsewhere because Humian empiricism and democratic scepticism tempered the absolutism of Hegel and Marx; though even so there were many philosophers, particularly at Oxford, who were entranced by the rigour of its logical presentation. Practice was much milder. Although the intellectuals argued that states could and even must do what they pleased, diplomats and statesmen knew that in a given situation they were bound to pay attention to other factors. Individual states had differing, even conflicting, ambitions but the directors of their policy felt a certain affinity based partly on social class and partly on shared experience. There was no great ideological divide. Except in matters where the most paramount national interests were involved it was more comfortable to act in concert with the rest of Europe. There was an *esprit de corps*. In fact a great many important though not crucial matters were settled speedily, efficiently and even justly. The affairs of Crete afford a good example. Indeed the treatment of Balkan matters by the Concert of Europe, up to 1914, was reasonably good when taken as a whole. But that date reminds us that in the background were absolutism and anarchy, ready to destroy the old system and out of its destruction to produce a new concept and practice of international law.

War, says Thucydides, is a harsh schoolmaster. The lessons of the First World War were the basis of the formulation of the Covenant of the League of Nations. It was a new word in diplomacy, adopted to please President Wilson, who was proud of his Ulster-Scottish Presbyterian stock. Under its terms the members of the League renounced both war and secret treaties since the latter were believed, perhaps erroneously, to have contributed in the past to the outbreak of wars. At least it was a fruitful step for the future to provide that only such treaties had validity as were registered with an international body and published. Another valuable step was the institution of an International Court of Justice. For the importance of the League of Nations was that it marked a decisive stage in the evolution of international law. Older conceptions became obsolete.

Let me quote the opinion of Lauterpacht,[1] the great British jurist, 'the substance of its law differs so radically from other international conventions in its scope and significance as a purposeful instrument in the process of the political integration of mankind as to deserve the designation of a "higher law".' That was written in 1936; the concept of a 'higher law' is one that has much occupied jurists since then, particularly with reference to treaties. Lauterpacht's colleague McNair[2] described the Covenant (and the Kellogg pact of 1928, renouncing war, which was widely signed) as having created 'a kind of public law transcending in kind and not merely in degree the ordinary agreements between states.' These dicta are of great relevance today with reference to the Charter of the United Nations.

I need not go into details of how the League of Nations disappointed the aspirations of those who created it. The fact that the United States decided not to take up its position as a founder-member meant that it lacked the necessary degree of universality. It was a pity also that the first large-scale conflict between members of the League, that between China and Japan, was so far removed geographically from the main interests of the bulk of its members. I think, though, that the worst blow to the ideals of the League came earlier. It was the failure to deal effectively with the invasion of another Greek island, Corfu.

Like Crete and Cyprus Corfu had been a Venetian possession. Unlike them it never fell into Turkish hands. Like Cyprus it had also been ruled by Britain, mainly, as in the case of Cyprus, for anti-Russian purposes. After about fifty years the island, with the rest of the Ionian Islands, was ceded to Greece; the Crimean War seemed to have diminished the Russian threat and there were other, largely sentimental, reasons in favour of the cession. It is nowadays usually taken as natural; but the voluntary, unconstrained, uncompensated surrender of territory by a great power was so rare in the nineteenth century that I cannot think of another comparable case.

In August 1923 the Italian dictator Mussolini was anxious for a spectacular success in the foreign sphere. He was fomenting subversion in Malta and recruiting a band of terrorists to operate in Corsica but decided that to attack Greece would produce a quicker and safer return than to take on either Britain or France or both.[3] Having manufactured a pretext — and possibly, to that end, engineered the assassination of an Italian general in Albania — he sent an expedition to Corfu, which he had discovered to be undefended. The Italian navy shelled the citadel, killing sixteen children, Armenian refugees, and the island was occupied. Greece appealed to the League. The French Government of Raymond Poincaré, which was working strongly in support of the Italian case, opposed any League intervention even after the British representative at Geneva had reminded them publicly in the Assembly of their obligations under the Treaty of Versailles. After two weeks, however, Lord Curzon, the British Foreign Secretary, was worn down by French pressure and agreed to a compromise whereby the matter was remitted to an Ambassadors' Conference. This old-fashioned expedient — not that I should wish to say a word against ambassadors — was successful in securing an Italian withdrawal, though on terms patently unjust to the Greeks. But the authority of the League had been flouted and many observers, including Harold Nicolson, the British historian of diplomacy, reckoned it a defeat from which its prestige never recovered.[4] There is a lesson to be drawn from this for those who have placed their hopes on the United Nations.

With your indulgence I shall permit myself a brief digression at this point, to weave Winston Churchill into my theme of the three Greek islands. Reading through his published letters recently I came across one to his wife of 3 September 1923[5] in which he suddenly exclaims 'What a swine this Mussolini is! I am all for the League of Nations ... it is life or death for it now.' This reminded me that he had not been in agreement with Lord Salisbury's policy on Crete, which he thought too pro-Turkish. Writing to his mother from India on 25 February 1897[6] he expressed horror 'that British warships should lead the way in protecting the blood-bespattered Turkish soldiers from the struggles of their victims.' As for Cyprus, no-one acquainted with its history can forget that when he went there as junior minister in the Colonial Office in October 1907 he declared in reply to a memorandum presented to him there that it was 'only natural that the Cypriot people who are of Greek descent should regard their incorporation in what may be called their mother-country as an ideal to be earnestly, devoutly and fervently cherished. Such a feeling is an example of the patriotic devotion which so nobly characterises the Greek nation.'[7]

There is room for argument, as is often the case with public statements by young and ambitious politicians, whether his words should be so punctuated as to indicate that these natural sentiments were shared by the Cypriot people as a whole or only by the eighty percent who were of Greek descent. I should incline to give the philhellene Churchill the benefit of the doubt. He saw the force of the desire for *enosis.* He was a member of the government which offered to cede Cyprus to Greece in 1915, if the Greek Government would honour its treaty obligations to Serbia. The Greek Prime Minister, Venizelos, a signatory of the treaty of alliance, was anxious to do so in any case, even before the great inducement was offered. Unfortunately King Constantine, strongly influenced by his Prussian-educated Chief of Staff John Metaxas, believed that Germany was about to win the war. He had family reasons also for favouring the German side. Under this belief, and this influence, he dismissed Venizelos, a highly un-constitutional act. The offer was withdrawn. The great schism in Greek politics began and has continued. For Cyprus this was one of the missed opportunities of which the twentieth century has provided many other examples.

How the British Government became able in 1915 to propose the union of Cyprus with Greece derives from the reversal of alliances produced by the First World War. The motive for the acquisition of the island was the pursuit of the long-established nineteenth-century policy of keeping Russian power out of Anatolia and Mesopotamia — 'the old Crimean policy' as Disraeli called it. By the Cyprus Convention of 1878 Britain undertook to defend the Sultan's Asiatic possessions, but not his European ones, against Russian attack. The Sultan promised reforms of administration, a promise that he failed to keep. The connection was underlined by the agreement to return the island if Russia restored the fortresses of Kars and Ardahan and the port of Batoum which at the Congress of Berlin had been ceded to the Tsar. (Lenin restored the two fortressses in 1921, but not Batoum.) In itself Cyprus was not regarded as a valuable acquisition. After no more than four years it even lost any pretension to strategic value when Mr. Gladstone's Government, which had deplored Disraeli's acquisition of Cyprus, found itself in possession of Egypt, with much better bases at Alexandria and Port Said. The First World War marked the reversal of 'the old Crimean policy' with Britain allied to Russia and at war with Turkey. It was not until after the Second World War, with another reversal of sentiment, that Cyprus's value as a base for strengthening a front against Russia came once more into prominence and influenced British opinion in favour of retaining it for this purpose.

The present international status of Cyprus derives its origin from the conflict waged against the colonial authorities between 1955 and 1959 by EOKA, the National Organisation of Cypriot Fighters, under the command of Lt. Col. (later Lt. Gen.) George Grivas. It does not represent a success for that conflict, which aimed at *enosis*. For although the anti-colonial struggle may have been the efficient cause, the formal cause of the creation of the Republic of Cyprus is an agreement between the governments of Greece and Turkey. It was hammered out in the Hotel Dolder in Zurich between the two Foreign Ministers. Then it was brought to London for consideration by the British Government, which was willing, indeed eager, to accept any formula agreeable to Athens and Ankara, and by the Greek-Cypriot delegation headed by Archbishop Makarios, which was not. For, to borrow the title of a book by Stephen Xydis, Cyprus was a most reluctant republic.

The Zurich and London agreements were embodied in three treaties signed in Nicosia in August 1960 by Britain, Cyprus, Greece and Turkey. (Britain was not a party to the Treaty of Alliance, signed by the other three.) They gave legal force to the basis of the Greek-Turkish agreement which was the renunciation of *enosis* on the one hand and of partition on the other. Greece, Turkey and Britain recognised and guaranteed not only the 'independence, territorial integrity and security of the Republic of Cyprus' but also 'the state of affairs established by the Basic Articles of the Constitution.' I shall spare you the details of those articles; it will be enough to say that they provided for most elaborate safeguards for the Turkish-Cypriot minority, which was placed in a position to obstruct almost all the functions of government.

Many Greek-Cypriot jurists have denied the validity of all the treaties on the grounds that they were intimidated into signing them by the threat from Turkey of military pressure and from Greece of disinteresting itself. This is the doctrine of 'unequal treaties' of which much has been made by China, for example. It is not yet accepted generally as a ruling concept in international law but at least it provides an explanation for the desire of the Greek-Cypriot majority to modify a constitution which had been imposed on them by *force majeure.*

In 1963 Archbishop Makarios, as President, put to the Turkish Vice-President of the Republic thirteen proposals for amendment of the constitution. When the Turkish Cypriots rejected them — or rather when the Turkish Government, without waiting to hear their views, issued a violently-worded rejection from Ankara — fighting began between clandestine Greek-Cypriot and Turkish-Cypriot armed organisations. To separate the contending factions the United Nations organised a force of almost 7,000 men composed of contingents from the armies of six member states, with smaller contributions of auxiliary services from some others, the whole commanded by an Indian general. This force, known as UNFICYP or United Nations Force in Cyprus, is still there after twenty-one years.

That international force presents at first sight some similar features to the one which was sent to Crete in 1897. But in the intervening sixty-eight years the whole world had changed. A new concept of international law had been evolved. It is accepted by all the nations of the world, which have entrusted to the United Nations Organisation and more particularly to its executive organ, the Security Council, the responsibility for enforcing the rule of law and of creating new precedents if necessary when peace is endangered.

The provision of peacekeeping forces is one of those precedents and it raises very interesting points in law. It is worth following, in brief outline, the steps by which UNFICYP came into existence. On 27 December 1963 the Security Council became seized of a complaint brought before it by Greece accusing Turkey of 'aggression' and 'intervention' against Cyprus by 'the threat and use of force against its territorial and political independence.' Greece was acting under article 35 of the Charter which provides that any member may bring any dispute or any situation likely to endanger peace to the attention of the Security Council. No resolution was adopted on the Greek complaint. In February 1964, after the situation in Cyprus had got worse, the Council met to consider a United Kingdom referral and adopted on 4 March the resolution which is the mandate for UNFICYP. In this resolution the Council merely 'noted' that the situation in Cyprus was likely to threaten international peace and security unless measures were promptly taken to maintain peace in the island and seek out a durable solution. This did not amount to a 'determination' of a threat to peace under Article 39, which is the opening article in Chapter VII, the chapter dealing with enforcement measures. Instead it called for the consent of the Government of the Republic of Cyprus to the dispatch of a peacekeeping force. In so doing it recognised the status of that government as the sovereign authority of a member state.

The action in Cyprus followed the precedent of the operation in the Congo inasmuch as it deployed the authority given to the Secretary-General by the Security Council when exercising its functions as conferred upon it by Article 24 of the Charter. Provision for the Secretary-General to perform such functions on behalf of the Council, and other organs, is made in Article 98. The legal possibilities of combining these two articles have been described as 'inexhaustible' and as giving the Secretary-General 'open-ended authority.'[8] He was empowered to take all the necessary steps to obtain the contingents which should compose the force and to transport it to the scene of its duties. In the regulations issued for its guidance UNFICYP is described as 'a subsidiary organ' of the United Nations. Provision is made for such subsidiary organs in Articles 22 and 29, referring to the General Assembly and the Security Council respectively. The latter article falls under the part of Chapter V styled 'Procedure' and, as such, is not subject to the special voting arrangements in which the so-called 'veto' can be used; but it is open to argument whether that point could be sustained against serious opposition since in actual UN practice disputes as to whether or not a matter is procedural have been treated as substantive.

There was one great difference between UNFICYP and the troops who enforced peace in Crete in 1898. The latter were prepared to impose their will by force of arms, including naval bombardments, to the indignation of the young Winston Churchill and others, and they disarmed any irregular forces they found in the island. The soldiers of the United Nations were forbidden to use their weapons except in self-defence. The order was strictly interpreted. I do in fact remember two occasions from my period as High Commissioner when serious fighting between a large U.N. detachment and forces commanded by Grivas was only just averted. Generally, though, the Force relied on the bad effect which would be produced if they were seriously thwarted in their duties. They were an example of what the authority of the United Nations can effect in controlling situations where only their presence can keep domestic factions from coming to blows. Their record is better, I should judge, than in the other parts of the Middle East where similar forces have been deployed. What they were not intended to be capable of was to counter external aggression.

For of course the dominant factor which has reduced Cyprus to its present deplorable condition, and has brought in question the whole modern concept of the rule of law in international affairs, is the Turkish invasion of 1974. The occasion seized on by the Turkish Government to execute an operation which it had long planned did not arise from any action by the Cyprus Government. That government was rather the victim of the irresponsible actions of another state, of the dictatorship then ruling in Athens. Finding themselves threatened by rising opposition at home the military junta decided on a course which has appealed to other arbitrary rulers in similar circumstances, to bring off a spectacular success in external policy. Their coup of 15 July aimed at the assassination of President Makarios and, to judge by the persons whom they used as instruments, to bring about the union of Cyprus with Greece. Both aspirations failed. Makarios survived, against all the odds, and the Turkish invasion followed five days later. The occupying forces seized, and continue to hold, forty percent of the island. The Greek-Cypriot population there, to the number of 200,000, was driven from its homes. There was heavy loss of life both in the course of the military operations and in attacks on civilians. Property was destroyed and looted and cultural monuments and antiquities suffered the same fate.

It is not relevant to my purpose today to go into details about the sufferings of the people of Cyprus or to describe how the consequences of the junta's action led to its fall and the restoration of democracy in Greece. My theme is rather the application of the principles of international law. It so happens that the Cyprus problem in this climactic phase illustrates the leading aspects both of the earlier and the current concepts of international law. They will arise in consecutive historical order if I begin by considering first the arguments used by the Turkish Government to justify their actions.

The Turkish case is based on a treaty, and invites consideration under that aspect which held sway up to the First World War, during which period many jurists held that the essence of international law was the Law of Treaties. The vital clause in the Treaty of Guarantee is the fourth and last:

> 'In the event of a breach of the provisions of the present Treaty Greece, Turkey and the United Kingdom undertake to consult together with respect to the representations or measures necessary to ensure observance of these provisions. Insofar as common or concerted action may not be possible each of the three guaranteeing powers reserves the right to take action with the sole aim of re-establishing the state of affairs created by the present treaty.'

The second sentence was included at the instance of the Turkish negotiators.

The special class of treaties known as treaties of guarantee is a small one. The reason for this is obvious: that states are not so foolish as to enter into them except in cases of dire necessity. Many countries went to some lengths to avoid them, as carrying the danger of restricting their freedom of action in unforeseeable future circumstances; this was particularly the case with Britain because of the doctrine of parliamentary supremacy. Normally such treaties are designed to strengthen the hands of weak countries that occupy an important strategic position when the strong countries that offer the guarantee do not wish to see that position come into the possession of any of their number. They derive in fact from a decision to prefer self-denial to self-assertion when the circumstances are such that the latter would be dangerous. The best-known examples are the treaties that guaranteed the neutrality and independence of Belgium and Luxemburg, because it was the violation of these, more especially the former, that brought Britain

48

to declare war on Germany in 1914. In such special studies of treaties of guarantee as have been devoted to them by historians and jurists it has been a cardinal principle generally accepted that their terms should be given a strict interpretation. The parties are obliged only to such action as would be consonant with the most literal meaning that the words in the treaty will bear.

Applying these principles to the particular case with which I am concerned it will be observed that the only obligation which the 1960 Treaty of Guarantee imposes on the guarantors is to consult together. When the Turkish Government invoked the treaty in July 1974 the three guaranteeing states honoured their signatures. Consultations at a high level took place in Geneva. In strict law, therefore, there are no grounds on which anyone could reproach, say the Government of Greece, for not carrying out its obligations. Greece was not under any duty, for instance, to resist the Turkish invasion by armed force. Similarly, turning to the wording of the second sentence of the article, there is nothing to justify the Turkish Government's action. Indeed the words to which they appeal for justification tell effectively against them because they specify that any action taken should be 'with the sole aim of re-establishing the state of affairs created by the present treaty.' Neither at the time nor subsequently have the Turkish Government pursued that aim. They have on the contrary presented as their intention one of the two courses formally excluded by the treaty, namely the partition of the island. That was the policy they put into effect in 1974 and in 1983 they brought it to completion, by recognising a Turkish Republic of North Cyprus which purports to be an independent sovereign state.

A more fundamental objection, more consonant with the modern conception of international law, is that the Treaty of Guarantee was void *ab initio*. This argument was first raised in the United Nations in February 1964 – ten years before the invasion – by the Cyprus delegation. It rests on the principle that the obligations which nations accept on acceding to the United Nations are superior to all other obligations. The Charter has been defined by the International Law Commission of the United Nations as having the character of 'a peremptory norm of general international law from which no derogation is permitted.' I do not think any country has attempted to deny this principle though some may have disregarded it in practice or sought to obscure their breaches of it by sophisticated arguments. A moment's thought would be sufficient to show its necessity. The nations of the world, having agreed to set up a system for regulating international relations that is based on obligations mutually exchanged, could not with any consistency allow a few of their number to pledge themselves to action contrary to the whole purpose of the system.

I turn then to the Charter to see how it bears on the current situation of Cyprus and on the right claimed by one party to the treaty of 1960 to pursue its aims by the use of force, a means which is not so much as alluded to in that document. Article 2 is generally taken to be the most important. It sets out the principles on which the organisation, and its members, are to act. The first is that of the sovereign equality of members. The intention of this was explained by the sub-committee which drafted the article and included among its definitions of sovereign equality: 'that the personality of the state is respected as well as its territorial integrity and political independence.' It is plain that for one member to invade the territory of another member and to place a large part of that territory under military occupation must be a violation of the article. Article 2 (4) maintains this view with explicit words: 'All members shall refrain in their international relations from the threat or use of force against the territorial integrity or political independence of any state, or in any other manner inconsistent with the purposes of the United Nations.'

I said that this article was the most important in the whole Charter and it is therefore natural that special provisions should be made to provide against any pretext for its violation. The problem of possible conflict between it and any other international obligations is dealt with explicitly in articles 52 and 53. The effect of these is to recognise the validity of what are termed 'regional agreements.' Whether the Treaty of Guarantee of Nicosia, 1960, falls into that category is a matter of dispute but I shall assume here that it does, since that is the more favourable assumption for those who defend the treaty's validity; however that may be article 53 states plainly 'no enforcement action shall be taken under regional arrangements or by regional agencies without the authorisation of the Security Council.' And to avoid all doubt article 103 declares 'in the event of a conflict between the obligations of the members of the United Nations under the present Charter and their obligations under any other international agreement their obligations under the present Charter shall prevail.'

There is therefore no escape from the conclusion that article

4 of the Treaty of Guarantee did not authorise the use of force unless with the authority of the Security Council. Any attempted interpretation contrary to that principle means that the treaty was void *ab initio* as inconsistent with the Charter. The consequence is that there was no such treaty and neither rights nor obligations can be claimed under it.

It is not sufficient, however, to show that the action of the Turkish Government was contrary to international law without showing what steps should be taken to right the wrong done. The words of the Charter are clear. There is provision for restoring an unjust situation. All nations, including the aggressor in this case, have solemnly and voluntarily subscribed to it. They know what they have to do. They have declared, in article 24, 'in order to ensure prompt and effective action by the United Nations its members confer on the Security Council primary responsibility for the maintenance of international peace and security and agree that in carrying out its duties under this responsibility the Security Council acts on their behalf.'

The Security Council has not avoided its responsibilities in the case of Cyprus. It has acted on behalf of the members of the organisation — all of them, including Turkey — by a series of resolutions which, having been carried by the prescribed majority, are mandatory. I shall not go into the details because everything that matters can be summarised under two heads: after calling on all states to respect the sovereignty, independence and territorial integrity of Cyprus the Council demands an immediate end to foreign intervention and the withdrawal of 'foreign military personnel.' This second demand, for the withdrawal of Turkish troops, is vital. In the negotiations in January 1985 the Cyprus Government rightly insisted on it. A state cannot exercise its sovereignty, and its territorial integrity is violated, when part of its territory is under foreign military occupation.

The demand for the withdrawal of foreign troops is one well within the competence of the Security Council. There are precedents. In the case of Azerbaijan the Soviet Union complied, after some delay, with the Council's orders and withdrew its troops from Iranian territory. In the cases of North Korea and Argentina the aggressors refused to comply and military action under the authority of the Charter had to be taken to enforce the demands of the Council. The possible need for enforcement action was always contemplated by the founders of the United Nations at San

Francisco in 1945, inspired by memories of the failure of the League of Nations and by experience of five years during which the voice of law had been silenced by the clash of arms. They provided their new instrument for peace with a formidable armoury of sanctions, economic and military, to be used against states which violated its principles. They were consonant then with the mood of the peoples of the belligerent nations. I believe that the mood of today also accepts the necessity of sanctions.

I believe in fact that there is greater popular support than some governments realise for the ideals of world order and the rule of law. The authority of the Security Council is not a mere catch-phrase; it is something to which people cling and not only with assent but with affection, mixed with hopes for a better world. They are right also to think that their idealism, as some would call it, is the highest form of pragmatism. If the world is to survive in this dangerous twentieth century it makes more sense to take bold initiatives to support the rule of law, even to run risks for it, than to chase after a consensus that will express the lowest common measure of non-disagreement.

I have traced the development of international law over nearly a century with particular reference to its application to three Greek problems, as is appropriate for a lecture which is dedicated to the memories both of Sir Norman Angell and of Stephen Brademas. If I have fulfilled the task I set myself you cannot fail to be struck by the contrast between the fates of Crete and Cyprus. Those fates were decided — so far as that of Cyprus is yet decided — under widely differing systems of international law. Is there a connection between that and the fact that one achieved unity with its fellow Greeks and the other did not, in spite of their great similarity in character? There is certainly one important difference: Crete is nearer to Greece than to Turkey but Cyprus is only forty miles from Turkey and so more exposed to invasion. That geographical accident should not, on any equitable view, have weighed against the wishes of the people concerned. Self-determination has been exalted by our age to almost paramountcy as a principle; it was regarded much more coolly in the nineteenth century, yet it must be said that the old Concert of Europe could on occasion act more effectively and more fairly. While it held together, its concern for an orderly disposal of the dissolving Ottoman Empire brought about tolerable national boundaries for the successor states. In the second half of the twentieth century the world has provided itself with a more rational system for governing international relations and takes a strong line on principles; but when conflicts of ideologies or national strategic interests intervene the results are not markedly better. Undoubtedly the main reason why the Cyprus problem has not found a just solution is that certain countries, among them the United States, have decided that it is in their national interest not to antagonise Turkey. It would not be fitting for a guest to say more on that theme but it would be well to remember that there are other national interests beyond what are seen as immediate strategic ones. For a peace-loving country which has no expansionist desires there can be no greater national interest than the support of the system which has preserved world peace and stability for these last forty years. It is highly practical to subordinate immediate requirements to the need to strengthen and maintain that paramount interest. If the rule of law is seen to break down in the Eastern Mediterranean, then the dangers in other parts of the world are greatly increased.

NOTES

1   British Yearbook of International Law, 1936, pp. 54 - 65, f.n.1.

2   BYIL 1930, p. 112.

3   Mack Smith, Denis, *Mussolini* (Weidenfeld & Nicolson, London, 1981), p. 72.

4   Nicolson, Harold, *Curzon, the Last Phase* (Constable, London, 1937), pp. 368 - 71.

5   Gilbert, Martin, *Winston Spenser Churchill*, Companion vol. V, Part 1, (Heinemann, London, 1979), p. 60.

6   ib., Companion vol. I, Part 2, p. 734.

7   Quoted by Hunt, David, *Footprints in Cyprus* (Trigraph, London, 1982), p. 252.

8   Draper, G.I.A.D., 'The United Nations Force in Cyprus', in *Revue de Droit Penal Militaire et de Droit de Guerre*, VI - i, (Brussels, 1967).

CYPRUS:
A QUARTER CENTURY
OF US DIPLOMACY

Ellen B. Laipson

OVERVIEW

A careful account of twenty-five years of US policy toward
Cyprus needs to take into consideration multiple and sometimes
competing perspectives. For American diplomats directly involved
in the numerous crises over the decades, Cyprus represents both
successes and failures. The United States can claim credit for averting armed clashes, and has generally managed a cordial relationship
with the island nation, but is also considered complicit in Cyprus's
most tumultuous crisis — the summer of 1974 — and the resultant
division of the island that has plagued its history for the past
decade. To many observers, Cyprus is a small country, marginal in
the great power balance, and the policy of one President or another to Cyprus would provoke little controversy. Yet for others,
US policy to Cyprus epitomizes the failure of the West's super-
power to take into account moral and legal factors when formulating its strategic goals and policies.

The story of US policy to Cyprus is interesting for a number
of reasons. Americans who have served there or been involved in
US policy become attached — to its culture, to its climate, and
to the challenge posed by the seemingly chronic crisis of its
twentieth-century being. By and large, it has been a hospitable
place for Americans, and often, in the past decade, a welcome
refuge from the war-ravaged lands to the east. Yet at times it
has not been friendly. Cypriots murdered the American Ambassador in 1974, and attacks against various US facilities on the
island have forced evacuations and raised security concerns.

The evolution of US policy to Cyprus over a quarter of a
century by and large reflects the major trends and patterns in post-

war US foreign policy with all its seeming contradictions: how to define the Soviet threat, measure Soviet intentions, balance regional and global priorities, accommodate strategic considerations with moral values, and protect US interests from nearby sources of instability.

A dramatic asymmetry plagues the US-Cyprus relationship. The differences in size,[1] resources, and perceptions of their respective world role have made it difficult at times to keep the bilateral relations on an even keel. The Cypriots of course resent the size and power of the United States, and sometimes have unrealistic expectations about the degree of attention they merit from busy policy-makers. At the same time, Americans can often be impatient, misunderstanding why the Cypriots can't be more accountable for their fate, more decisive in vital matters. US officials have also occasionally failed to appreciate Cypriots' sense of vulnerability.

This asymmetry problem is true of US relations with many small states, yet one should not view US-Cyprus relations as typical of that pattern. A number of factors make US-Cyprus relations unique. Cyprus is not a Third World country. Its economy is highly developed along capitalist lines, its population highly educated and mobile. In addition, it is rare that US relations with a country are so totally dominated by consideration of the state's very identity. The bilateral US-Cyprus agenda rarely escapes the all-consuming problem of the island's political identity. This lends a special sensitivity to the relationship. Americans, especially in the past decade, have tended to think of Cyprus as a problem, more than as a country with which to conduct normal state to state business.

While newly emerging nations of the post-war period generally have thought of the United States as instinctively anti-colonial, US relations with those nations can sometimes be strained by US ties to their former colonial powers. In the case of Cyprus, this is triple jeopardy. US ties with Britain, Greece, and Turkey are often seen to play a more important part in American decisions relating to Cyprus than Cyprus itself. Cyprus's network of relations with the three states that were guarantors of its independence (and, in the view of many observers, restrictors of its sovereignty) complicates US policy. US relations with Greece and Turkey can be, at best, a window through which Cyprus is viewed, or, at worst, a screen that blocks US ability to view

Cyprus clearly.

In the recent decade, US policy to Cyprus has been characterized by an unusually high degree of domestic interest and involvement. While Americans of Greek heritage have long been concerned about US foreign policy in the Eastern Mediterranean, it was the Cyprus crisis of 1974 that galvanized their concern and encouraged them to organize a highly effective lobbying effort in Congress, which was willing to confront the Administration over its handling of that crisis for a variety of reasons. This domestic involvement and chronic friction between Congress and the executive has been a more sustained and salient element in the management of US relations with Turkey, Greece and Cyprus than with most other areas of the world.

Managing the relationship has also been complicated by the way in which decisions are made in Washington. There is a difference between the decision-making process during crisis times and in relatively peaceful times that is particularly acute in the case of small countries. Cyprus, in the crises of 1964, 1967, 1974 and 1983, has held the attention of Presidents and Secretaries of State, who tend to place the problems of Cyprus in a large, general context. Yet the relationship during non-crisis times is managed by lower-level diplomats more accustomed to viewing Cyprus on its own terms, in its particular context.

There are many strains in US policy to Cyprus that reflect the multiple and sometimes conflicting parts of the American character and its expression in public policy. There are aspects of US policy that sometimes seem naive to the weary peoples of the Eastern Mediterranean, and too full of idealism — of Americans' belief that different peoples and cultures can coexist, and that problems can be solved by good faith and compromise. Other features can be estranging in the opposite direction: US policies are often defined in terms of global and strategic interests with little sensitivity toward the people and lands that are used to obtain these goals.

This paper explores these different themes and the changes in American policy in its different phases. It focuses primarily on the important policy changes mandated by crises on the island. It looks at how US policy reflects changing perceptions of the settlement process and the UN role, and of the salience of the East-West and Greece-Turkey dimensions of the issue over the years.

SCARCELY PRESENT AT THE CREATION:
US POLICY 1955-1963

The United States was not active in the events that led to the creation of an independent state of Cyprus in 1960. While already deeply engaged in Greece and Turkey under the terms of the Truman Doctrine, the United States initially considered the post-colonial struggle for a new status for Cyprus to be a British problem.

According to some accounts, efforts by Greek Americans to move US policy-makers to endorse *enosis* (union with Greece) for Cyprus began soon after World War II. Greeks and Cypriots saw the United States as a logical source of funds and political support.[2] Yet despite several resolutions of support from the US Congress, *enosis* was never adopted formally as a US position. The United States voted against a Greek proposal in 1954 to put the Cyprus question on the UN agenda. The following year, with the outbreak of violence on the island, the US Ambassador to the UN, Henry Cabot Lodge, explained that the United States was even less inclined to find the United Nations an appropriate forum for conflict resolution. The US preference was for a more discreet forum, involving primarily Britain, Greece and Turkey.

By 1956, the United States began to gradually disassociate from total support for the British. US officials condemned the deportation of Archbishop Makarios, and urged the British Government to resume contacts with the Cypriot parties. The US Ambassador to Greece praised the statesmanship of the Greeks and complimented them on the progress toward achieving self-government for Cyprus. Some have interpreted this more as a US effort to bolster Karamanlis than an international rebuff to the British position.[3] When the United States abstained in 1957 on the annual Greek resolution in the UN calling for an exercise of self-determination for Cyprus, the shift from a pattern of negative votes was considered by some to be a further nod to the Greek position. Violent anti-US and anti-British protesters in Athens did not appreciate the subtle distinction.

As terrorist incidents on the island continued in 1958 and 1959, the United States took a passive stance, and tried to avoid alienating either Turkey or Greece. The primary US interest was in limiting the issue's damage to NATO, and averting escalating the tension between Greece and Turkey.[4] In 1958, the United States agreed to attend a NATO parley on Cyprus, which did not take place due to Greek objections. The subject of Cyprus was raised, however, at the NATO Ministerial Council in December. There was no direct role for the United States in the subsequent London and Zurich talks which produced the agreements leading to Cypriot independence. But US praise for the achievement of the agreements revealed the American attitude: State Department Deputy Undersecretary Murphy spoke of the happy solution and the statesmanlike action of our allies, and said 'all Americans wish success to the people of Cyprus in their effort to create a new state based on the cooperation of different ethnic communities and born out of the understanding and mutual friendship of Greece, Turkey and the United Kingdom.'[5] American policy-makers may have expected a prompt implementation of these accords, yet another eighteen months of political jockeying occurred before independence was declared. The United States recognized the new republic on August 16, 1960, and President Eisenhower appointed Fraser Wilkins, formerly the Consul-General in Nicosia, the first American Ambassador to the Republic of Cyprus.

One account describes the main goals of American policy in the early days of optimism after independence as: establishment of political stability in Cyprus as a bulwark against communism; development of a strong economy, democratic institutions, and a pro-western orientation; unrestricted US use of the communications facilities on the island; and maintenance of the British Sovereign Base Areas for access by friendly western nations.[6] In support of this policy, the United States offered $20 million in aid in the first three years of Cypriot independence. The United States also supported cultural and educational programs that strengthened conservative political groups, to balance the growing popularity of leftist organizations on the island, which concerned US officials.

The early optimism was soon replaced by a more sober view that the power-sharing arrangements reluctantly accepted by the parties in 1959 did not guarantee peace and stability for the island. While never faced with an acute crisis on the island, President Kennedy sensed the prospects for trouble, and in 1961 called for a more active American role in Cyprus to avert instability in the Eastern Mediterranean.[7] Two years later an era of greater American involvement would begin. When fierce fighting between the two communities broke out in December 1963, one month after Makarios formally submitted his proposal for constitutional revisions, limiting Turkish-Cypriot rights, the United States offered to join British efforts to end the fighting and monitor the cease-fire President Lyndon Johnson's Christmas 1963 letter to Cyprus called for an end to the fraternal strife.

ACTIVIST PHASE OF AMERICAN POLICY: 1964-1978

1. 1964-1967

In 1964, the United States was remarkably active on Cyprus, and was involved in unilateral, multilateral and NATO efforts to stabilize the situation on the island. US policy included responding to developments on the island, often in coordination with the British; it also involved generating new initiatives and establishing a more independent and assertive stance on the Cyprus problem. This new posture created a new problem: most of the actors in the Cyprus question became wary of American motives and have remained suspicious and uneasy ever since about what they began to view as the secret agenda of US policy.

To quell the violence that broke out in late 1963, leaving over three hundred dead, the United Nations created an emergency observer force under an Indian commander. At the same time, the British worked furiously to create a more permanent force under NATO auspices, and approached the United States, France, Italy and West Germany. Only the United States responded positively, although it named two conditions: that the Government of Cyprus would approve of the force, and that the three guarantor powers would suspend their right to intervene on the island for three months. These conditions may have been intentionally designed to doom the proposal to failure:[8] Makarios' opposition to NATO sponsorship was well-known, and the Turks were loath to give up their right to intervene as outlined in the 1959 London-Zurich agreements. Yet by demonstrating its willingness to provide troops, the United States was in a stronger position to claim a direct interest in the outcome of the dispute.

The United States and Great Britain formally offered a NATO force of 10,000 troops on January 31. Local reactions were strong: the US Embassy was bombed on February 4, leading to the evacuation of American dependents. US Agency for International Development (AID) and Information Agency (USIA) missions were temporarily halted, US officials citing a lack of confidence

59

in the Cypriot police. The anti-American reaction seemed to correspond with President Makarios' view that a NATO-sponsored force would constitute a threat to Cypriot sovereignty and would jeopardize its non-aligned status.

Subsequent to the rejection of the US-UK troop offer, efforts focused on the creation of an alternative peacekeeping force. George Ball was authorized by President Johnson to conduct the necessary negotiations. In the weeks that followed, several alternatives to a UN-supervised force were suggested. But in March, the UN Force in Cyprus (UNFICYP) was created, with the United States pledging financial support and help with the air-lift of the 1,150 Canadian, 700 Finnish, 700 Swedish and 500 Irish troops who would supplement the 3,500 British troops already engaged in peacekeeping on the island.

The status of the 1959 treaties and the responsibilities of the guarantor powers were retained, although the Greek Cypriots argued that the creation of UNFICYP constituted an abrogation (welcome, in their view) of those commitments. In April President Makarios announced his Government's abrogation of the Treaty of Alliance, although the other parties considered his move illegal and continue to this day to consider the treaty in effect.

The decidedly western tint of UNFICYP alarmed the Soviets, who warned the Cypriots against permitting western intervention in their affairs through the creation of the force. Soviet Premier Khrushchev pledged his support to the Cypriot President, praising Makarios' efforts to restore peace, efforts that he construed to be sabotaged by the meddling NATO countries. The strong Soviet identification with the Government of Cyprus prompted an American riposte: President Johnson assured the Soviets that American policy was formulated through cooperation with the Cypriot officials, and was aimed at restoring a peaceful situation on the island.

This exchange in early 1964 is one of the few times that the Cyprus question provoked direct Soviet-American consultation: the East-West dimension of the Cyprus issue was muted in the waning years of the Cold War. According to one interpretation, it was precisely because of the lowering of East-West tensions in the 1960s that Greece and Turkey came to turn so much attention to their 'national question', permitting the Cyprus issue to resurface in such a provocative way.[9]

Yet the East-West theme, in a relatively non-urgent fashion, continued to shape American attitudes toward Cyprus and the new UNFICYP. For American observers at the time, and in the years that immediately followed, UNFICYP as a peacekeeping force was a satisfactory substitute for a direct NATO presence on the island, particularly since the participating countries did not include any eastern bloc nations. Its other mandated role, that of peacemaker, continued to trouble American officials, who wished to avoid providing an *entrée* for the Soviet Union or for the more strident of the non-aligned countries by opening the process up to the UN Security Council or General Assembly. That prospect motivated American officials to continue to back alternative peace mediation efforts, while supporting the UN peacekeeping role, which was fundamentally compatible with American interests in restoring calm and stability to the island.[10]

The shooting ceased in May, but trouble on Cyprus continued to brew beneath the surface. Greek and Turkish troops in excess of those permitted under the 1959 agreements began arriving on the island during the summer, in numbers variously reported as 10 to 15,000. Turkish Cypriots, who looked to UNFICYP 'for security and justice,'[11] were still subjected to attacks and intimidation by the extremist Greek-Cypriot forces, who failed to distinguish between Turkish soldiers, Turkish-Cypriot guerillas, and Turkish-Cypriot civilians.[12]

Turkey responded to the continuing tension by moving naval forces closer to Cyprus, and by demonstrating its air power. While one account concludes that the Turkish Armed Forces were simply not adequately trained or equipped for a landing on Cyprus,[13] high ranking officials in Washington decided to respond to the ominous signals coming from Turkey with what has become a watershed in US-Turkish relations.

President Johnson wrote to Turkish Prime Minister Inonu on June 4, warning that the allies would not feel obligated to defend Turkey should its intervention onto Cyprus result in a Soviet attack. For Turks, the unusual bluntness of the letter, which George Ball called the most brutal diplomatic note he had ever seen, raised serious anxieties about NATO protection in the event of Soviet hostilities, and soured what had been the generally trusting and warm relationship with the United States evolving since the early 1950s.

Yet Washington officials believed the letter had its desired effect, since no Turkish military action was taken. American officials continued to watch developments on the island, including the return of the *enosis* advocate General Grivas, who was appointed head of the Cypriot National Guard and all security forces, and President Johnson invited the Greek and Turkish premiers to Washington later in June. Both parties demonstrated their distance from the American position: the Turkish leader expressed dissatisfaction with the studied American impartiality, and the Greek leader publicly stated his preference for a UN mediation role over any American efforts.

Accounts of the Johnson presidency note, somewhat paradoxically, that Johnson became quite personally involved in the 1964 events on Cyprus, yet at the same time delegated considerable responsibility and authority to his envoys, George Ball, Dean Acheson, and later Cyrus Vance. Particularly ironic, in the light of events a decade later, was the commentary that Johnson operated on Cyprus with a free hand domestically, in contrast to his policies toward Panama or the Dominican Republic, because the Cyprus issue 'never deeply engaged the interest of Congress.'[14]

President Johnson, in a speech to the American Bar Association in August, 1964, lauded US conflict resolution efforts in Cyprus and Vietnam, citing both as examples of US problem-solving through peaceful and orderly processes. In the speech, the President also revealed that his primary interest in Cyprus was its relevance to stability in Greece and Turkey, 'two of our best friends.'[15] US efforts in Cyprus were 'our duty to the alliance.' No mention was made of the Government of Cyprus, the character of its relationship with the United States, or US concern with its survival and sovereignty.

As the Johnson meetings in June with the two Prime Ministers produced no tangible results, George Ball was able to convince the United Nations to attempt a new negotiating effort, since the military build-up on the island boded ill for stable conditions. The meetings began in Geneva on July 4. No Cypriot officials participated.

The United States, though not a formal participant, sent Dean Acheson as an interested observer. This understated title belies the fact that he presented a provocative new American initiative aimed at solving the Cyprus problem by disbanding the independent republic and achieving both partial *enosis* (union) with Greece and *taksim* (partition) to protect Turkish interests. The Acheson plan, while never published officially, has been outlined in numerous sources as entailing:

- the union of the island with Greece;
- the establishment of a sovereign Turkish base on the northern part of the esland;
- creation of at least two Turkish-Cypriot cantons, one in Nicosia, exercising local autonomy;
- compensation to Turkish Cypriots choosing to leave the island; and
- cession of the small Greek island of Kastellorizo to Turkey.

Within the region, the plan had considerable appeal to Greece and Turkey, whose national interests and strategic concerns were at least partly addressed. Both countries initially responded favorably to the plan, and both tried to bargain for better terms. Turkey reportedly requested an increase in the size of the sovereign base, to 20% of the island, and Greece asked Acheson to grant the Turks only leasing rights for their base, not permanent rights. As might have been expected, President Makarios rejected the plan, which was woefully unattuned to emerging Cypriot aspirations and to an understanding of the cultural and political distance that had developed between the two Cypriot communities and their respective motherlands.

US officials recalling that period say the Acheson plan's import has been exaggerated; it was a trial balloon, a suggestion, not a formula to which American diplomats and strategists were firmly tied. For some of its advocates, the plan was worth considering because it addressed general NATO needs (by integrating the island into the alliance and removing it from possible interference by Soviet or pro-Soviet forces) as well as regional interests (by presumably removing Cyprus as a contentious issue in Greco-Turkish relations). While few at the time believed the Soviets intended to take strong measures on Cyprus, the Acheson plan's double *enosis* or *enosis/taksim* solution could be viewed as a far-sighted preventive policy.

Some in the US policy debate have assessed the Acheson plan as more stridently anti-Soviet and anti-Cypriot. They suggest that the prevailing view among some of the Johnson administration, with its much-touted analogy between Cyprus and Cuba, Makarios and Castro, was that an independent Cyprus was unreliable and likely to play directly into Soviet schemes. The activism of President Makarios in the non-aligned movement, the steady strength of the pro-Moscow AKEL Communist Party on the island, Makarios' friendly ties with neighboring Egyptian President Nasser, and signs of increasing Soviet confidence about their ability to play a role on Cyprus, including their new naval presence in the Mediterranean, combined to move some US officials to advocate a radical change in the situation.

Today, the legacy of the Acheson plan is felt among elements of the Cypriot elite who cite it as a symbol of the strategic mind-set that has frequently dominated American thinking on Cyprus, one which places NATO interests above those of Cypriot sovereignty and the survival of a weak independent state. Some Cypriots believe that there are those in the US defense establishment who still favor an Acheson-like solution to the Cyprus problem, and this perception has had its effect on subsequent US settlement efforts.

The Acheson plan was still-born, and the island remained in a volatile condition. A second American warning to the Turks not to intervene was delivered in August, after the Turks began air-strikes on the northern part of the island in response to Greek-Cypriot attacks against Turkish-Cypriot villages. US objections to Turkey's muscle-flexing provoked anti-American demonstrations in Ankara and Izmir, and in subsequent months the United States tried to heal the wounds with Turkey by public statements renewing the US commitment to the NATO umbrella, and by a delivery of C-130 transport planes.[16] The Turkish strikes had had one salutory effect on the island: they apparently sufficiently inhibited hostile actions by the Greek irregulars to bring the island some needed rest. An uneasy calm prevailed on the island until 1967.

For the next two years, the settlement process limped along: UN mediator Galo Plaza's efforts were thwarted by negative Turkish responses to his report of March 1965, which called upon the Greek Cypriots to abandon *enosis* and the Turks to abandon *taksim*. The United States shared the Turks' view that the Galo Plaza report would not move the process along, and when he resigned in late 1965, no successor was named. At the same time, secret talks between Greece and Turkey were apparently focusing on variations of the Acheson formula, making more understandable a US reluctance to see the UN process consolidate or reinforce the pro-independence factions on the island.

A precarious balance on the island was maintained, with the help of the UNFICYP forces and repeated behind-the-scenes American efforts to keep tempers from flaring. The generally tolerable *status quo* made the settlement momentum difficult to maintain. The effectiveness of UNFICYP, according to one former US diplomat, was in reducing tension. But in so doing, it made finding a more permanent solution less urgent. 'We have peace but no progress,' he said.[17]

When the Greek military seized power in Athens in April 1967, new tensions were felt on the island. US policy was focused on the dilemma posed by the fall of the democratic regime, although first the Johnson and later the Nixon administrations found rationales for unusually close cooperation with the junta in Athens. This added a new layer of intrigue and suspicion for those already wary of American objectives and attitudes towards Cyprus, and increased the interest of congressional observers of US policy in the area.

In November 1967, new intercommunal fighting broke out, caused in part from mounting stresses within the Greek Cypriot community between factions that supported President Makarios and those who followed General Grivas. When the Greek-Cypriot National Guard under Grivas surrounded two Turkish-Cypriot villages, killing 26 villagers, Turkey threatened to intervene, and massed troops on its Thracian border with Greece, in addition to readying amphibious units for transport to Cyprus.

The United States responded to what had quickly escalated to intra-NATO brinkmanship by sending a new presidential envoy, Cyrus Vance. His shuttle diplomacy brought him first to Ankara. Ten days later the crisis was defused when Greece agreed to withdraw the 10,000 troops it had put on the island in 1964, and Turkey agreed to draw down its invasion force. The Vance mission, widely praised at the time, essentially employed the same techniques and viewed the problem in the same way as in the 1964 crisis. While successful in the short run, there was considerable evidence to suggest that Turkish patience with the situation on the island was wearing thin, and that the Turkish military could not be talked out of taking definitive action repeatedly. The Vance mission constituted the third and last time the United States was able to convince the Turks that intervening on the island was not in their interest. It also sowed the seeds for future troubles, according to one interpretation, by weakening the defense capabilities of the Republic of Cyprus with no clear concessions or pledges on Turkey's part, thereby making the decision to intervene, seven years hence, relatively easier for Turkish decision-makers.[18]

The Turkish Cypriots consolidated their separate status on the island with the establishment of the Turkish Cypriot Provisional Administration. Neither the Government of Cyprus nor the United States recognized the new political arrangement as legal, although American diplomats were required to devise flexible protocol responses so that their contacts with the Turkish-Cypriot leader Dr. Kutchuk and his deputy Rauf Denktash could be maintained.

2. THE LULL 1968-1973

No acute dilemma arose for the United States over the next six years. Perhaps because of the 1967 crisis resolution, there was virtually no intercommunal fighting: General Grivas left the island and the Turkish Cypriots consolidated their position in enclaves, further diminishing contact between the two communities. Separate elections were held in February 1968, returning President Makarios and Turkish-Cypriot leader Kutchuk (Vice-President under the 1960 constitution) to office. A quiet intercommunal process was initiated in 1968, which mirrored, to a certain degree, a Greco-Turkish dialogue initiated by junta leader Papadopoulos.[19] The existence of bilateral, discreet talks between the two NATO partners and the close working relationship between Washington and Athens combined to convince American decision-makers that the Cyprus question was a manageable problem. While neither of these sets of talks led to significant breakthroughs, the semblance of a negotiating process was sufficient to draw the attention of US policy-makers to other, more pressing matters, including the upheavals in the Arab-Israeli zone which resulted from the 1967 war. In addition, letting Greece and Turkey try and solve the problem (presumably along pro-NATO lines) was also compatible with the Nixon Doctrine promulgated in 1972, calling for greater regional responsibility and reduced American involvement in small-scale conflicts.

Cyprus became a less acute US policy concern for global as well as regional reasons in these years. As the Nixon administration pursued detente, its perceptions of the Soviet threat and Soviet intentions were altered. The Johnson premise that the Soviets would intervene in Cyprus should instability occur was replaced with a more sanguine view that Soviet and American governments might have convergent interests in a stable Cyprus, and that the Communist Party on the island, AKEL, was not an effective instrument of subversion for Soviet aims.

The management of US-Cyprus relations in this period occurred within the Near East Bureau of the State Department, and its view of Cyprus and its Government generally prevailed in official thinking. The image of President Makarios as the Castro of the Mediterranean was replaced, at least temporarily, with the notion that Makarios was a popularly supported leader whose involvement in the non-aligned movement need not be inimical to American interests, and that Cyprus under President Makarios was tolerable and deserved more unequivocal support as a friend of the United States. At the same time, however, tension was building between Makarios and the junta in Greece, and General Grivas returned secretly to the island to reinvigorate the pro-*enosis* forces, who viewed the overthrow of Makarios as crucial to their cause. As a result of these developments, a competing viewpoint in US Government circles emerged that Greece should be allowed to handle the Makarios problem.[20]

A shipment of Czech arms to the Government of Cyprus in early 1972 infuriated the Greek Government, the Grivas forces, and the Turkish Government, and Makarios was pressured to turn the arms, intended for his personal guards, over to UNFICYP. The Government in Athens decided to take advantage of the situation and demanded that Makarios reform his Government and remove ministers who were critical of the junta in Athens. Both Greek and American officials were surprised at the extent of popular support for Makarios — all political factions rallied to the President and supported his resisting the blatant pressure from Athens.

The widespread backing of Makarios' resistance to the Greek ultimatum seemingly strengthened the position of officials in Washington who opposed US acquiescence in Greek domination of Cyprus. Yet some argue that the United States could have more actively intervened in this period to assist the Cypriot Government in its struggle against the Grivas forces, who worked with Greece to undermine the independence of the island's Government.[21]

But in its greater concern about growing instability in the governing circles in Greece, US policy neglected the repercussions on the island, for which it would pay dearly two years later.

3. 1974 CRISIS

The crises of the summer of 1974, deriving from the Greek-engineered coup attempt against President Makarios, formed a dramatic turning point in US policy towards Cyprus and fundamentally altered US-Cypriot, as well as US-Turkish and US-Greek, relations for much of the decade to follow. The events of 1974 also dramatically changed the way in which the Cyprus question is viewed in the United States. Cyprus is often cited as a major failure in the foreign policy of the Kissinger era — Kissinger himself reportedly considers the crisis his greatest failure. There is no question that American influence, prestige and credibility were damaged seriously in Cyprus, as well as in Turkey and Greece, as a result of some of the policy choices made in 1974.

In the spring of 1974, rumors and reports of the wobbly Greek junta's plans to remove Makarios from power were frequent. Signals that President Makarios was a likely victim of a coup attempt were available to US officials and working level officers attempted to generate a policy response that might prevent the deed. Their efforts bore no fruit at higher levels of the policy process, who considered the alarm-ringing the work of 'cry-babies' or 'boys crying wolf.'[22]

Some US officials familiar with developments on the island consider Makarios' open defiance of the ultimatums from Athens the real *coup de grace,* and they believe Makarios himself could have averted the coup by trying to appease the regime in Athens. Yet Makarios apparently believed the United States had the power to rescue him, as he believed had happened in 1972.[23] There were, however, real limits to US ability to reshape decisions made by an insecure Greek leadership, although the US Ambassador to Greece was instructed in June to try to convince the Greek Government not to carry out the coup.[24] Additional messages were conveyed to various levels of the Greek Government July 2 - 9.

The coup was executed on July 15. Greek-Cypriot National Guardsmen seized the Presidential Palace, and President Makarios only narrowly escaped, making his way one the following day to

London via Malta. Through an unexpected series of developments, including the death of General Grivas a few months earlier, the putschists had difficulty finding an appropriate successor to the President, and settled on the unsavory character, Nikos Sampson, a former EOKA activist who was anathema to the Turks and Turkish Cypriots.

In Washington, a Special Action Task Force was created to monitor the crisis and coordinate American responses. One complicating factor in managing the crisis was the spring 1974 adminstrative decision to transfer the office covering Turkey, Greece and Cyprus from the Near East to the Western Europe bureau at the State Department. This meant that higher level officials, at the Deputy Assistant Secretary level and above, were making key decisions although they may not have been well schooled in the complex history of Cyprus.

US official statements failed to strongly condemn the coup. Instead, non-commital statements that the political situation was unclear characterized the American response. Suspicions about possible American support for the coup were reinforced when the US Ambassador to Cyprus, Rodger Davies, met with the Foreign Minister of the Sampson regime on July 18, reportedly the only foreign emissary to grant him such recognition.[25] On subsequent days, officials continued to equivocate on whether the United States still considered Makarios the legitimate President of the Republic, and whether the junta in Greece was responsible for the coup.

The Secretary of State sent his deputy, Joseph Sisco, to London to meet with the parties to try and avert the worst scenario from an American point of view — hostilities between Greece and Turkey. Kissinger and other officials were generally optimistic about the prospects for averting a serious crisis: past incidents had been defused, and the United States had access to all the parties. Yet Turkish leaders, under Prime Minister Ecevit, a socialist whose attitude toward the United States could be considered ambivalent, had already determined that the time for intervention had arrived. In London, they argued for joint British-Turkish action as consistent with their obligations as guarantor powers.

On July 20, Turkish troops began landing on the island, and Greece declared a general mobilization of its armed forces. Within two days, the United States had arranged a cease-fire, and Nikos Sampson was replaced by Glafcos Clerides, the moderate Speaker of the Parliament. Clerides, well-liked by the Americans, was subsequently viewed by American officials in Nicosia as a satisfactory alternative to Makarios, whose political fortunes they thought and/or hoped were finished.

At Geneva, a declaration promising peace talks was signed by Greece, Turkey and Britain on July 30. The United States was optimistic that this would bring stability to the island, although US attention was drawn more to the ramifications of the coup in domestic politics in Greece and the subsequent transfer of power to a civilian government. Although Geneva talks resumed on August 8, sporadic fighting on Cyprus was hardening attitudes on all sides. By August 14, the talks had collapsed, Greece announced its withdrawal from the military command of NATO, and Turkey began a second offensive on the island, expanding the area under its control to 37%.

It was the second Turkish military move that galvanized public opinion in the United States and provoked extreme anti-American reactions in Greece and Cyprus, where the conviction was strong that the United States could have prevented the Turkish action. On August 19, Greek-Cypriot Guardsmen fired shots into the US Embassy from a bluff to the east, and killed Ambassador Davies, who was crouching in the corridor with other Embassy staff members. Of the many issues that clouded US-Cypriot relations in the following months, the failure of the Cypriots to satisfactorily investigate the murder and of the United States to demand such satisfaction was troubling for some of the US diplomats involved.

On Capitol Hill, it was the second invasion that provoked questions about the Turkish use of US-supplied weapons. The Defense Department said on August 18 that it would look into possible arms agreement violations, and on August 20, the Legal Advisor of the State Department was asked to prepare a memorandum for the Secretary on Turkey's action. From a small group of Congressmen initially concerned primarily about the fall of the junta in Greece, the congressional role expanded. Resolutions calling for a withdrawal of the Turkish troops were introduced, and congressional demands for information and policy responses from the executive increased dramatically.

This issue appealed to a surprisingly wide range of members of Congress. In addition to Members interested in foreign affairs and the Eastern Mediterranean in particular, the activists on the Cyprus issue included members whose attitudes were shaped by the crisis in presidential leadership and by the enhanced congressional role in foreign policy as a result of the war in Vietnam. Cyprus touched a nerve for members who were concerned about congressional authority, the executive branch's seeming lack of respect for the rule of law, and the arrogance of Henry Kissinger.

Throughout the fall of 1974, the congressional forces concerned about Cyprus and Turkish use of American weapons were frustrated by what they considered executive branch obfuscation.[26] After heated debates and negotiations within and between the branches, Congress voted to suspend military assistance to Turkey in December, although they granted the President until February 5, 1975, to permit negotiations to continue. Editorial opinion in US newspapers favored President Ford over Congress on the embargo question.[27] Yet despite efforts by President Ford and other Administration officials to convince Congress that the embargo's imposition would damage rather than improve the prospects for settlement on Cyprus, the embargo went into effect in early 1975.

There are multiple assessments of how US policy went awry in 1974. The policy process is faulted for poor management and for inadequate or inaccurate intelligence. According to some, the US mismanaged its response to the information it had of plans to overthrow Makarios, and could have more effectively staved off Greek action. Others argue that the information was not adequate, or was not effectively transmitted within the labyrinth of the US Government. The chain of command between a concerned Cyprus desk officer and the higher levels of the diplomatic decision-making process became a subject of inquiry by a congressional committee in October 1975.[28]

Once the coup took place, critics charge, the United States was slow to respond, did not react decisively enough, and failed to predict and prevent the Turkish intervention. Others suspect a secret agenda: the United States knew about the coup and chose not to act, because it saw its strategic interests served by a change of government on the island. An entirely different line of criticism focuses on the Department of State's handling of congressional inquiries and concerns. The blocking of legal opinions about Turkey's possible violation of its agreements with the United States to the Congress was disturbing, as were numerous other examples of the Secretary's highly personalized approach to US policy on Cyprus in fall, 1974.

This litany of grievances in Washington was matched in fervor by the parties in the Eastern Mediterranean, none of which felt that US policy was sufficiently attentive to its position. To the dismay of American officials, the new democratic government in Greece saw fit to pull out of the military command of NATO. Turkish officials warned repeatedly that the imposition of the embargo would cause them to reassess their role in NATO and their bilateral defense arrangements with the United States, although their decisions about closing US installations were not made until summer 1975. Anti-Americanism on Cyprus was rampant, and US diplomats serving there describe a state of siege atmosphere. US efforts to cooperate with UN programs, including the transfer of Turkish Cypriots from enclaves in the south to the Turkish-controlled zone in the north, were broadly condemned as American plots, and provoked violent incidents at the Embassy and Consulate.

4. 1975-1978 EMBARGO YEARS

One task for US diplomats in the following years was to restore a semblance of good-will in the region towards the United States. In addition, the newly politicized Greek-American community became a new factor in formulating a domestic consensus on US policy, and that community and congressional activists on the Cyprus issue continued to engage executive branch officials in a debate over which US policies would best promote the achievement of a peaceful and just solution to the problem. During this debate, the Greece-Turkey dimension of the problem received high attention, and US officials not familiar with the Eastern Mediterranean and its legacy of problems became involved in the embargo issue, which came to be defined more as a NATO crisis than a Cyprus crisis.

On the island, population resettlement was the priority, and US involvement in the relief and resettlement efforts was for the most part not a contentious issue in the formulation of US policy. The two communities conducted formal talks in early 1975, focused on the immediate population and humanitarian issues, not on a larger political settlement. Relief efforts managed by the UN High Commissioner on Refugees received broad support from the international community, although the US contribution was the largest. There were virtually no armed clashes, and the industrious Cypriots moved quickly to improve living conditions for the island's newly displaced citizens, so Cyprus was removed from the headlines as one of the world's trouble spots.

In Washington, the Ford Administration began to restore a climate of trust with Congress, and strenuous efforts were exerted to convince members to suspend the embargo against Turkey. The Senate voted as early as May 1975 to lift the embargo, but the House of Representatives was firm in its resistance. The Administration, whose arguments about the weak state of the western alliance were given added potency by instability in Spain and Portugal, stressed US security concerns as the tantamount consideration for members of Congress. In one of the more interesting hearings of the period, diplomatic luminaries from past Cyprus crises, George Ball and Cyrus Vance, testified in favour of retaining the linkage between Turkey's security assistance program and demonstrated progress on Cyprus, although they both supported a partial lifting of the embargo.[29] Congress eventually approved such a partial lifting and $125 million in military aid was granted to Turkey for fiscal year 1976. Some embargo advocates concluded that the effectiveness of the tool was gravely compromised.

Members of Congress whose main concern was the situation on the island — including the housing, missing persons, and enclaved Cypriots issues — complained that US policy had not been sufficiently forthright in identifying Turkish-Cypriot and Turkish intransigence as the key obstacles to progress. They called for more explicit US pressure on Turkey. In addition, those concerned with the refugee and humanitarian aid aspects of US policy were critical of the Ford Administration's tendency to treat US contributions to the UNHCR's programs as a form of bilateral assistance and of subjecting projects to review and approval by American experts. They were also discontented with the practice set in 1974 to distribute American aid on an 80/20 basis to the Greek and Turkish communities respectively. They argued that Turkish financial support to the Turkish-controlled area should be taken into account in allocating the funds on a need basis.[30]

During the 1976 presidential campaign, Democratic candidate Jimmy Carter pledged to seek an objective policy on Cyprus and end unwanted American intrusions on Cyprus. This was interpreted as a commitment to distance US policy from support for Turkish positions, and to depend more on efforts under UN auspices. His position was warmly welcomed by Greek Americans as well as Greeks and Greek Cypriots. Yet newly appointed Secretary of State Vance concluded that resolving the Cyprus problem was a direct American concern. A study mission was sent in early 1977, prompted in part by congressional prodding to make Cyprus a priority issue. In fact, the new administration shelved temporarily a pending base agreement with Turkey and focused instead on Cyprus.

Important talks between President Makarios and Turkish-Cypriot leader Denktash enhanced the prospects for demonstrable success on Cyprus. Held under UN auspices, their summit led to agreement on a set of general principles between the two communities. The United States wanted to encourage the process, and presidential envoy Clark Clifford went to the region. He convinced the two sides to make even more concrete proposals, including the first offer of territorial compromise by the Greek Cypriots, providing for a Turkish-Cypriot administered zone of 20%. According to some accounts, this move by President Makarios was a great gamble for him, and one he regretted until his death a few months later.

US officials were disappointed when this process faltered in June 1977. Six months later, the Turkish Government announced its willingness to submit new territorial and constitutional proposals, which facilitated the Carter Administration's surprise April 1978 decision to work to lift the embargo. The battle between the branches over the embargo was one of Carter's foreign policy challenges of the year, and the administration was aided by occasional conciliatory gestures from the Turkish side, including the July 1978 Turkish-Cypriot offer to permit resettlement by Greek Cypriots of the coastal town of Varosha.

The legislation to lift the embargo passed both chambers in September 1978, after a compromise was formulated which remains in the Foreign Assistance Act. The section entitled US Policy Regarding the Eastern Mediterranean (620C) contains repeated references to US support for a just and lasting Cyprus settlement, one that ensures a free and independent government on Cyprus and the protection of the human rights of all the people of Cyprus. It also requires the President to report to Congress every sixty days on progress made on a negotiated solution of the Cyprus problem.

In some ways, the most significant section of the 1978 compromise is found in subsection (b) (4): 'Security assistance for Greece and Turkey ... shall be designed to ensure that the present balance of military strength among countries of the region, including between Greece and Turkey, is preserved.' From this language evolved the unusual practice of allocating military aid to Greece and Turkey on a 7:10 basis. While never legislated, the ratio has served as a vehicle for congressional critics of the stalemate on Cyprus, because it has theoretically punished Turkey for its military control of northern Cyprus and forced the administration to link the Greco-Turkish balance with the seemingly more expendable Cyprus dispute.

Yet the utility and effectiveness of the ratio for Cyprus can be questioned. Both the Carter and Reagan administrations have opposed the informal ratio practice and have viewed it as an irritant and an undesirable precedent. Military aid levels to both Greece and Turkey have steadily climbed, absent a Cyprus settlement. Congress, in the annual wrangling over the ratio, reminds the administration of congressional dissatisfaction with US policy impotence, but the ratio has also permitted Congress to avoid getting involved directly in the details of the technical issues blocking a settlement on the island, and places the Greece-Turkey aspect of the Cyprus question in the forefront.

The last US-sponsored initiative in Cyprus resolution efforts was the Nimetz plan offered in November 1978. Technically co-sponsored by Canada and Britain, the plan summarized the progress that had been achieved during the 1977 Denktash-Makarios summit and the Clifford mission. It called for a bizonal, federal solution, the formula that has been used in all subsequent negotiations. The Nimetz proposal, acknowledged by US officials who had tried to keep it secret, can be seen as a logical endpoint of the Carter Administration's commitment to both Congress and the parties in the eastern Mediterranean. It was a sign that the decision to lift the embargo entailed an obligation to reinvigorate the settlement processl

The Nimetz plan was coolly received by both parties, some of whom considered the confederal formula to be a form of partition, and as such, a pro-Turkish position. It was formally rejected by the Greek Cypriots. The intentionally low-key American attitude toward the exercise seemed to reflect US resignation to the fact that an American label to a peace plan was a sure way to fail. The bruises of 1974 were still too fresh to permit an assertive American posture, and the new and fragile domestic consensus on US policy might not survive such a bold stance. Yet the plan's main components were used by the UN Secretary-General and were reflected in the 10-point agreement reached by President Kyprianou and Mr. Denktash in May 1979.

LOWERED PROFILE ON CYPRUS 1979-1985

The United States has lowered its profile on the Cyprus issue since 1978. Some view this as only a tactical shift, reflecting the judgment that the parties prefer a more discreet American role. The United States, according to this view, remains the key external factor, though it has more effectively used the UN as its formal intermediary. Yet others argue that the shift is strategic: the United States can live with the *status quo* on the island and has leaned from past experiences that it may not be worth the political costs to expend considerable resources on the problem, until the parties themselves are ready to negotiate. Therefore, while the United States wants to maintain cordial relations with the countries of the Eastern Mediterranean, it is content to see the UN Secretary-General play the lead role on Cyprus talks, and has effectively lowered the prominence of the Cyprus issue on its bilateral agendas with Greece and Turkey. The strategic view is also premised on a lowered salience of the East-West dimension: Cyprus remained in this period an unlikely arena for US-Soviet rivalry.

Consistent with the widely held view that private talks are more productive than public debates, the United States has opposed the use of the UN General Assembly as a key forum for airing the differences of the parties on Cyprus. This has placed the United States at odds with the Government of Cyprus, which considers its support from the international community its greatest asset, and the Government of Greece under Prime Minister Papandreou, who has seen 'internationalization' of the issue as the alternative to the current impasse.

Yet there has been no total convergence of American and Turkish views either. The United States has never supported the

Turkish-Cypriot claim for equal power and representation in a future federal system, and has repeatedly, though not forcefully enough in the view of many, impressed upon the Turks that their military occupation of 37% of the island is an untenable diplomatic position.

Cyprus has also continued to be an annual irritant in the congressional-executive consultations over the foreign assistance program, although from the lifting of the embargo to the November 1983 declaration of statehood by the Turkish Cypriots, it was a manageable problem for the Administration. In 1984, with the help of reinvigorated Greek-American organizations and the Government of Cyprus, Congress succeeded in making the inter-branch interaction more acutely uncomfortable for the administration, and in requiring more active official involvement in resolution efforts.

Cyprus was not one of the foreign policy issues that was debated in the 1980 presidential race. But the security orientation of President Reagan's foreign policy logically led to a policy of strong support for Turkey, particularly in the light of the Iran and Afghanistan troubles that were cited as evidence of Carter administration weakness.

The Reagan administration's optimism about its ability to solve problems, including Cyprus, led to the June 1981 appointment of Reginald Bartholomew as Special Cyprus Coordinator. Congressional critics had urged the creation of such an office, to demonstrate higher level concern about Cyprus, although administration sources say that congressional interest was not a key factor in Secretary of State Haig's decision to create the post. This symbolic gesture was coupled with a dramatic increase in administration requests for military aid to Turkey, alerting some interested members of Congress to a possible loss of US leverage over the parties to the Cyprus conflict.

By 1983, congressional impatience with the moribund Cyprus talks and concern with the growing US strategic alliance with Turkey led to a new legislative initiative designed to freeze levels of military aid to Greece and Turkey until troop reductions on the island were made. The provision was narrowly defeated after eleventh-hour administration interventions.

Administration and congressional leaders were of the same mind when the Turkish Cypriots declared their statehood on November 15, 1983. Condemnations of the act as counterproductive to settlement efforts were heard on both ends of Pennsylvania Avenue. The Greek and Cypriot Governments praised the united American response, and the Turks expressed a kind of sad understanding. These reactions and subsequent requests by the parties for a more direct US mediation role were in striking contrast to attitudes of the mid to late 1970s.

The administration was not pleased by the multiple efforts exerted by Congress in 1984 to make the Turks accountable for the statehood move by Mr. Denktash. While the specific circumstances were new, the arguments were well-worn and familiar: the administration challenged the view of the congressional activists that such public pressure on Turkey could lead to positive results, and that Turkey was so clearly the Turkish-Cypriots' master. Instead, they argued for discreet diplomacy and for a separation of the Cyprus issue from security cooperation with Turkey.

Of the numerous legislative proposals debated in 1984 (cutting aid to Turkey by various amounts, linking a portion of Turkey's aid to transfer of Varosha to interim UN control) it is worth noting that none linked aid directly to a troop reduction on Cyprus. Congressional activists may have quietly conceded that the security issue is the card the Turkish side has to play, and it must be dealt with in a comprehensive approach. The Varosha proposal, for example, was seen by its supporters as a more positive approach than past efforts because it seized upon a Turkish-Cypriot idea and merely provided encouragement, not coercion, to carry it out.

By the same token, the administration may have tacitly bowed to the congressional perspective when it urged the Turks to take advantage of the opening provided by the UN 'proximity talks' that took place in New York in late 1984. According to many accounts, American messages to Turkey were a contributing if not determining factor in Mr. Denktash's surprise concession in mid-December to accept a territorial settlement granting the Turkish side under 30% of the island.

US diplomats have been able to play an active role, albeit behind the scenes, in the UN-sponsored settlement efforts underway since late 1984. One explanation may be a mellowing of Cypriot attitudes towards the United States, and a greater appreciation of the constructive role which American diplomats can play, albeit discreetly, in support of UN talks. In addition, in those optimistic periods when experts on both sides start to focus on operational details, the US experience as a federal system comes to the fore, and that special US expertise has proven of great interest to Cypriot leaders contemplating a future as a unitary federal state.

The reelection of President Reagan in 1984 promised continuity in official attitudes toward Cyprus, and increased attention or new priorities at the high levels are unlikely for the foreseeable future. Special Cyprus Coordinator Richard Haas, who along with former Congressman, now State Department Counselor Edward Derwinski, brokered the Cyprus issue on Capitol Hill, left at the beginning of 1985. His departure coincided with the change in the Department's top Europe slot, and none of the new team of Assistant Secretary Rozanne Ridgway has inherited his special coordinator title. In Washington, the annual debate between Congress and the executive over aid levels to Turkey and the continuation of the $15 million annual aid program to Cyprus, despite executive views that the program is unnecessary, continues in its predictable pattern. Only important changes in the status of intercommunal talks or conditions on the island would be likely to alter the debate.

There is no magic formula to guarantee good relations between Cyprus and the United States. The American system's tendency to focus only on current crises, not long-term issues, the political and cultural antagonism between the two communities and the higher profile of the two NATO interested parties will continue to be factors that affect US policy responses, to the recurrent dismay of some Cypriots. Cypriots may continue to have unrealistic expectations about the degree of interest and attention they will get from US policy-makers. But prospects for greater mutual understanding have increased in recent years. A realistic prospect of restoring the stability of Cyprus through a new federal system of government would be welcomed and actively supported by involved US political leaders and policy-makers. American generosity in the island's economic development after a settlement, as already promised in the Administration's 1984 peace and reconstruction fund proposal, is a certainty. Absent a total breakdown in the negotiating process, there is ample reason to believe that the course of the second quarter-century of US-Cyprus relations will be smoother sailing than the first.

NOTES

1   Cyprus is about the size of the state of Connecticut. Its population of 650,000 ranks it between Syracuse, New York, and Akron, Ohio, the 59th and 60th largest U.S. metropolitan areas, according to the 1980 census.

2   Crawshaw, Nancy, *The Cyprus Revolt: An Account of the Struggle for Union with Greece* (George Allen and Unwin, London, 1978), p. 59.

3   ib., p. 173.

4   Couloumbis, Theodore, *The United States, Greece and Turkey: the Troubled Triangle* (Praeger, New York, 1983), p. 28.

5   Address by Deputy Under Secretary Murphy, as printed in the Department of State Bulletin, May 4, 1958, p. 628.

6   Adams, T.W., 'The American Concern in Cyprus', *The Annals of the American Academy of Political and Social Science,* vol. 401 (May 1972), p. 98.

7   Schlesinger, Arthur M., Jr., *A Thousand Days: John F. Kennedy in the White House* (Fawcett Premier, New York, 1965), p. 394.

8   Geyelin, Philip, *Lyndon B. Johnson and the World* (Praeger, New York, 1966), p. 115.

9   Couloumbis, op. cit., p. 41.

10 See, for example, Adams, op. cit., p. 99 and Adams, T.W. and Cott-ressi, Alvin J., 'American Foreign Policy and the U.N. Peacekeeping Force in Cyprus', *Orbis,* vol. XII, No. 2 (Summer 1968), p. 503.

11 Denktash, Rauf, *The Cyprus Triangle* (Rustem and Bros and George Allen and Unwin, London, 1982), p. 30.

12 Hitchens, Christopher, *Cyprus* (Quartet Books, London, 1984), p. 55.

13 Harris, George, *Troubled Alliance: Turkish-American Relations in Historical Perspective 1945 - 1971* (American Enterprise Institute, Washington, D.C., 1972), p. 107.

14 Geyelin, op. cit., p. 116.

15 Department of State Bulletin, August 31, 1964, pp. 298-301.

16 Harris, op. cit., pp. 120-21.

17 Dobell, W.M., 'Division over Cyprus', *International Journal,* vol. XXII, No 2 (Spring 1967), p. 290.

18 Van Coufoudakis, 'U.S. Foreign Policy and the Cyprus Question: An Interpretation', *Millennium,* vol. 5, No. 3 (1977), p. 255.

19 Evriviades, Marios, 'The Problem of Cyprus', *Current History* (January 1976), p. 20.

20 Coufoudakis, op. cit., p. 259.

21 ib., p. 260.

22 Couloumbis, op. cit., p. 86.

23 Coufoudakis, op. cit., p. 261.

24 The chronology of events and U.S. responses in 1974 is taken largely from 'Aspects of U.S. Foreign Policy and the 1974 Cyprus Crisis: The Relationship between Intelligence and Policy Initiatives' by Richard Preece, Report of the Congressional Research Service, November 1975, 39 pp., and a chronology of events 1974 - 1976 by Richard Preece which appears as Appendix 1 to U.S. Senate Judiciary Committee. 'Crisis on Cyprus 1976: Crucial Year for Peace'. Staff Report, 94th Congress, 2nd session, January 19, 1976.

25 Couloumbis, op. cit., p. 89.

26 For more detailed treatment of the interaction between the Congress and the Executive, see 'Congressional-Executive Relations and the Turkish Arms Embargo', a committee print of the U.S. House Foreign Affairs Committee. Published in June 1981, this was vol. 3 in the Congress and Foreign Policy Series.

27 Foster, H. Schuyler, *Activism Replaces Isolationism: U.S. Public Attitudes 1940 - 1975* (Foxhall Press, Washington D.C., 1983), pp. 363-4.

28 U.S. House Select Committee on Intelligence. 'U.S. Intelligence Agencies and Activities: The Performance of the Intelligence Community'. Hearings, Part 2, 94th Congress, 1st session, September - October 1975 (U.S. Govt. Print. Off., Washington, D.C.), pp. 683-792.

29 U.S. House Committee on International Relations. 'Suspension of Prohibition Against Military Assistance to Turkey'. Hearings 94th Congress, 1st session, July 10, 1975, 158pp. (U.S. Govt. Print. Off., Washington, D.C.)

30 U.S. Senate Judiciary Committee, op. cit., p. 21 - 22.

CYPRUS:
THE BRITISH POINT OF VIEW

Hon. C. M. Woodhouse

The primary interest of British governments in Cyprus, like that of earlier foreign powers in occupation of the island, has always been strategic. That was the logic of the description of Cyprus as a *'place d'armes'* when it was first occupied in 1878. The same logic was made explicit in 1954 by the statement of a Colonial Office minister in the House of Commons that 'nothing less than continued sovereignty over the island could enable the United Kingdom to carry out its strategic obligations in Europe, the Mediterranean, and the Middle East'.[1]

There has often seemed, however, to be a discrepancy between the declared purpose and the real character of this strategic interest. The original purposes defined in the Anglo-Turkish Convention of 1878 were two: to enable Britain to support the Sultan in resisting pressure from Russia on the northern provinces of Turkey, and to help to ensure that the Sultan carried out internal reforms, especially for the protection of Christian communities such as those in the Lebanon.[2] Only the first of these purposes was strategic, and it never became operative. Nor was any other strategic use made of the island for well over half a century. Not surprisingly, it was suspected that the British, like other occupying powers over many centuries, had installed themselves in the island chiefly to make sure that nobody else did so. The strategic interest was seen to be essentially negative.

It was not long before disappointment set in over Britain's new acquisition. The Admiralty had pointed out from the first that Cyprus had little value as a naval station because of the inadequacy of its harbours. As for the non-strategic purposes of the occupation, there was no sign of internal reforms in the Ottoman Empire, nor did the British Government make a serious attempt to promote them — for example, by persisting with its declared intention to appoint military consuls to report on them throughout Anatolia. The only significant development was an increased interest on the part of British capitalists in the construction of railways in Anatolia and Mesopotamia. As early as 1881 the British Ambassador at Constantinople recommended that Cyprus should be relinquished. But since that would mean the island's restoration to an unreformed Ottoman Empire, which was still nominally the sovereign power, nothing was done.

What is surprising is that no mention was made of a more important and obvious strategic interest in the island. In 1875, three years before the Cyprus Convention, the British Government had acquired the Khedive of Egypt's shares in the Suez Canal Company. The security of the canal — at first as a stage in the route to India, and later to safeguard the supply of oil from the Middle East — then became a major consideration. If Cyprus had a strategic utility at all, it was in connection with the Suez Canal. But the British occupation of Egypt in 1882 side-tracked this consideration for over 70 years, until the occupation was ended by the Anglo-Egyptian Treaty of 1954. Consequently it was not until 1956 that for the first and only time the island was required to play an active part in operations related to the security of the canal; and on that occasion the operations were disastrously unsuccessful, at least in a political if not in a military sense.

It might reasonably be argued, therefore, that those who opposed the continued occupation of Cyprus were justified. During most of the three-quarters of a century which followed its acquisition, Cyprus was a forgotten island. It played a minor role in Colonial Office reports, and was seldom mentioned in Parliament. The occupation was publicly justified, when necessary, by claims to have instituted social and economic improvements, and by statements that the people of the island were prosperous and contented. Not only were they said to be better off than they had been under Turkish rule, but also better off than they would be under Greek rule.

Nevertheless a number of public figures — including Gladstone, Lloyd George and Churchill — spoke sympathetically about the possibility of ceding the island to Greece. But with two exceptions, both short-lived, they took no initiative in that direction when they were in office. The first exception, which was not publicly known until half a century later, was the series of informal discussions held by Lloyd George and Churchill with Venizelos in the winter of 1912-13.[3] Their theme was that Cyprus might be ceded to Greece in exchange for naval facilities at Argostoli in Cephallonia. The proposal was overtaken by the turmoil of events, and was never submitted to the British Cabinet. But it provided at least a preliminary sketch of what might have been a solution to the Cyprus problem a generation later.

The second exception came at a critical moment in the first world war. When Bulgaria attacked Serbia in 1915 the British Foreign Secretary offered to cede Cyprus to Greece if Greece would carry out its obligations under the Treaty of Bucharest (1913) by declaring war on Bulgaria, and thereby joining the Entente. The Greek Government declined the offer, under pressure from King Constantine, and it was never renewed. What is remarkable about it is that Britain sought no permanent *quid pro quo* in the form of strategic facilities elsewhere in Greece. This was tantamount to an admission that Cyprus had little if any strategic value in itself. Certainly no significant use was made of the island during the First World War.

The same was true in the Second World War. For a brief period in 1941, after the Germans had overrun the Greek mainland, it was feared that their next target for an airborne operation might be Cyprus. But when the target turned out to be Crete instead, which was captured at almost prohibitive cost, the momentary anxiety faded. The Germans did indeed try (without success) to gain control of Syria and Iraq, but in doing so they bypassed Cyprus entirely. Once more the island ceased to play any role in the strategy of either side.

The two world wars nevertheless had by-products in Anglo-Greek relations over Cyprus. The official annexation of the island by Britain in 1914, and the recognition of that annexation by Turkey in the Treaty of Lausanne (1923), stimulated the belief among the Greeks that *enosis* would not be long delayed. (A little-noticed fact about the Treaty of Lausanne was that in the relevant clause only Turkey recognised the British Annexation; Greece was not mentioned.) When the Greeks found their hopes disappointed, they resorted to non-cooperation in Cyprus, and eventually to violence in 1931. But colonial officials continued to believe that the discontent was artifically inspired, and that they need do no more to suppress it than to lock up or deport a few bishops.They followed the same policy with even less success in the 1950s. As with the Jews in Palestine, they failed to see that a basically European population could not be dealt with simply as 'natives'.

*　*　*

This examination of earlier history, lying strictly outside the chronological scope of the present volume, has been necessary in order to establish the point that Britain's interest in Cyprus, which was essentially strategic, grew with the passage of years rather than diminished. It is probably more important in the post-colonial era than it ever was under colonial rule. This does not, however, invalidate the argument that Britain could have had all the strategic facilities which she now has in Cyprus, and more besides, even if the island had been ceded to Greece at the opportune moment in 1945.

Why was that opportunity missed? It must be remembered that when the issue was raised, in the summer of 1945, a new Labour Government had only just taken office. (By a striking coincidence, the Cyprus crisis in 1974 also occurred just after a Labour Government had taken office.) A new government is naturally hesitant to take drastic and irreversible decisions within its first few weeks. In 1945, moreover, it was beset with conflicting advice from three distinct centres of power: the Colonial Office, the Foreign Office, and the Chiefs of Staff (who were later to be merged in the Ministry of Defence).

The Colonial Office put up automatic objections to the relinquishment of any part of the Empire. When the process began with the grant of independence to India and Pakistan, colonial officials did not yet regard it as the writing on the wall, since India had not been a colony and was in any case administered by a separate department of state. But they were determined to halt the process, at whatever point seemed practical, before it became a landslide. In the case of Cyprus, they did not trust the Greeks to treat the Turkish minority with the same consideration as they had shown themselves. When independence finally became the favoured solution, the only ground on which it was tolerable was that it dissatisfied all parties equally.

The Foreign Office, which was the second power centre, was more realistic. It had to conduct diplomacy with Greece and Turkey, and to meet international criticism. Its officials knew that

85

Cyprus could not be indefinitely contained within the concept of 'domestic jurisdiction'. In both world wars, Foreign Office minutes indicated that there was no insuperable objection to the cession of Cyprus to Greece. Turkish objections, if they arose, were not to be taken seriously: in the first world war, because Turkey was on the enemy side; in the second, because the Turks had neither the legal right, nor the moral standing, nor probably even the inclination to object. In 1945 a number of Labour ministers, as well as senior officials, positively favoured the concession of *enosis.*

But there was also the third power centre: the Chiefs of Staff, and later the Ministry of Defence. The new Labour government quickly discovered that when two of the power centres agreed with each other, it was difficult if not impossible for the third to outmanoeuvre them in Cabinet. Over Cyprus, the Chiefs of Staff sided with the Colonial Office, and that was decisive. It was decisive not only on the immediate issue, but also for the long-term future. In 1945 the cession could have been carried out painlessly, and even with public approval; but never thereafter.

During the following decade all parties took up non-negotiable and irreconcilable positions, which became enshrined in sacrosanct slogans. The Greeks claimed *enosis* as a national cause; the Turks demanded either partition or (contrary to the Treaty of Lausanne) retrocession of the island. The Colonial Office claimed that Cyprus never had been Greek; the Foreign Office encouraged the Turks to be obdurate; and the Chiefs of Staff insisted that they must have not 'a base on Cyprus' but 'Cyprus as a base'. It was therefore to no avail that the Greek Government had offered, in return for *enosis,* to provide Britain with strategic facilities not only on Cyprus but in other parts of Greece as well.

Why was the Greek offer not accepted? It had affinities with the plan discussed by Venizelos, Lloyd George and Churchill in 1912 - 13. It would have given the Chiefs of Staff at least as much as they asked for, perhaps more; and certainly more than they have had since 1960. It would also have ensured that Cyprus became part of the North Atlantic alliance when Greece joined NATO in 1951. Since Turkey was also about to join NATO, the Turks would have gained in compensation a military presence in Cyprus, just as the Greeks gained a presence at Izmir (Smyrna). This was the last opportunity of a settlement in friendly instead of hostile circumstances.

It was rejected from force of habit. The habit, which has persisted and hardened ever since, rested at first on three interrelated assumptions. The first was that Britain, after the Second World War, still remained and would continue to remain the predominant power in the Eastern Mediterranean and Middle East. The second was that the Soviet Union was a potential threat to that predominance, which must be countered at all costs. The third was that one of the ways — perhaps the likeliest — in which that Soviet threat might be realised was through the establishment of communist control in mainland Greece. Therefore Cyprus could not be ceded to what was later described by a Secretary of State for the Colonies as a 'friendly but unstable country'.

The passage of time has reduced the first of these assumptions to nothing more than a ghostly survival, but the ghost has not finally been laid. The second and third assumptions still persist, though in modified form due to changing circumstances. But the force of habit dies hard. Whatever the changes of circumstance, the actual arguments are much the same. Greece is still regarded as a 'friendly but unstable country', and the Soviet Union is still the potential enemy. Although the arguments need to be re-stated and re-examined, the conclusion is the same: the less change, the better. The *status quo* must, so far as possible, be preserved, although it is totally different from the *status quo* which had to be preserved a generation ago.

The first assumption is the most completely invalidated of the three. Whereas in 1945 Britain controlled the eastern Mediterranean and Middle East from Cyrenaica to Iraq, excluding only Turkey, by 1957 the whole area had been lost to British influence except only Cyprus; and even Cyprus was then engaged in an armed conflict which portended the end of British rule. Paradoxically, however, in 1957 a new situation had just been created, in which Cyprus was used for the first time in its original role as a *place d'armes*. In the closing months of 1956 the Anglo-French attack on Egypt, aimed at overthrowing President Nasser and restoring control of the Suez Canal, had been partly based on Cyprus. The Chiefs of Staff therefore had a new argument for maintaining Cyprus as a military base.

Its usefulness as a base in 1956 had been limited. It could not accommodate major units of the Mediterranean fleet. But the landing facilities were essential to the RAF, and also to the French Air Force. The island had accommodated GHQ in the Middle

East since its evacuation from the Suez Canal Zone in 1954. As a centre of communications and intelligence, Cyprus was becoming more valuable. The facilities available there had not been developed, but they could be. Even the concurrent struggle against EOKA under Colonel Grivas did not make it impossible to use the island as a base. All these considerations were reinforced by the appointment of a prominent soldier, Field-Marshal Harding, as Governor.

The conception of Cyprus as a strategic base therefore took on a new lease of life in 1957. A surprising feature of Harding's appointment was that he offered Archbishop Makarios much the most favourable plan for the future of Cyprus ever put before him, which could hardly fail to lead to *enosis*. Unfortunately Makarios rejected it, partly because it implied a strategic role for the island in the interim period. No doubt he misread the significance of the appointment of a senior soldier to the governorship. The result was that attitudes hardened on all sides. The Chiefs of Staff adhered to their conception of 'Cyprus as a base'. Although they were compelled only three years later to accept the reduced conception of 'a base on Cyprus' instead, the belief in a strategic role for the island still persisted; and it still persists today.

One reason why it still persists can be seen in the parallel survival of the second assumption on which British policy rested after the Second World War. The assumption that the Soviet Union constitutes a threat to the Eastern Mediterranean and Middle East has taken on a new form. It is now seen as a threat to allied interests, not merely to British interests; and it has been reinforced by the emergence of a Soviet fleet in the Mediterranean. It is therefore still arguable that a *place d'armes* is valuable, especially as so many others — Palestine, Egypt, Libya, Malta — have been lost. Cyprus is still unserviceable as a naval base, but in the age of aircraft-carriers that is less important. It is more valuable than ever as a base for aircraft, communications and electronic intelligence.

The third assumption made in 1945, that Greece was in danger of succumbing to communist control, and must not therefore be allowed to drag down Cyprus with her, might be thought to have lapsed after 1949, when the Greek Government, with American help, defeated the communist-led rebellion. But the bogey of 'instability' remains. The only direction in which Greece has seriously deviated from democracy since 1949 led to the right-wing military dictatorship from 1967 to 1974. That was unwisely regarded by the leading powers in NATO — the USA, Britain, and even Turkey — as a reinforcement of the western alliance. It proved to be a disastrous mistake, leading to the catastrophe of July 1974 in Cyprus. But even after the fall of the military dictatorship and the restoration of democracy in Athens under Karamanlis, the fear of Greek 'instability' remained. Karamanlis, himself, after all, had often spoken of the instability of his compatriots' political habits. If a right-wing dictatorship could come to power unconstitutionally, what assurance was there that a left-wing coup would not succeed?

A left-wing coup would be different, because it was unlikely to have the support of the Greek Army. But since the Greek Communist Party (KKE) was restored to legality by Karamanlis in 1974, it had become increasingly strong and obtrusive. It appeared to have an undue influence on the Socialist Government of PASOK, which came to power under Andreas Papandreou in 1981. Papandreou himself showed tendencies which alarmed the western allies. He argued that he was merely restoring Greek policy to a position of balance between the western world and the Soviet block. But in contrast with his predecessors' firm commitment to the West, this new position was interpreted as anti-western and pro-Soviet.

The anxiety caused by Papandreou's stance naturally caused a reaction which affected both the Mediterranean generally and Cyprus in particular. The reaction could not be the same as in the 1940s because the conditions were totally changed. The status of Cyprus was different: after being established as an independent republic in 1960, the island had suffered a *de facto* partition as a result of the Turkish invasion of 1974. Also, it was no longer Britain alone which reacted: the Americans were now just as much involved in Mediterranean policy, not least in Greece. Britain's stake had been reduced in 1960 from 'Cyprus as a base' to 'bases in Cyprus'. The trend of policy in mainland Greece made it highly unlikely that Britain would contemplate giving up those bases in the foreseeable future.

British commitments in the Mediterranean had been reduced commensurately with the reduction of the British stake in Cyprus, but they were still important. They were now all of an international or allied rather than a national character, being undertaken on behalf of NATO. Some of the commitments were only occasional, such as support for the international interventions in the Lebanon; others were more permanent, such as support for allied surveillance of Soviet military activities by aircraft, radar or other electronic installations. For all such activities, the British sovereign bases in Cyprus were useful.

It can be argued that these facilities would equally have been available if Cyprus had been ceded to Greece forty years ago. But arguments about 'what might have been' are necessarily speculative. In this case the speculation can also be reversed, by reference to the fortunes of the US bases on the Greek mainland. After the crisis of 1974, when the western allies did nothing to avert the Turkish invasion of Cyprus, Karamanlis withdrew the Greek forces from NATO command and placed restrictions on the US defence facilities. When Papandreou became Prime Minister in 1981, he insisted on re-negotiating the terms for the use of the US facilities, and refused to renew them for longer than five years. It would be illogical to extrapolate from these events to speculate on what would have happened to the British bases in Cyprus if the island had been under Greek sovereignty, because in that case the particular crisis of 1974 could not have occurred in the way it did. But some other crisis could well have taken its place: and the inference that Greece might prove an unreliable ally, especially under a left-wing government, would have remained.

* * *

To question the reliability of the Greeks as allies naturally provokes the legitimate question: have the British themselves proved reliable? Manifestly the answer is negative. This answer would come as a surprise to the broad mass of public opinion in Britain, but that is only because public opinion has given little attention to Cyprus. Only a small minority even of well-informed people was aware in 1974 that Britain had obligations under the Treaty of Guarantee (together with Greece and Turkey) to safeguard 'the independence, territorial integrity and security of the Republic of Cyprus.' There was therefore no public reaction comparable to that which was to be experienced eight years later over the Falkland Islands, except in one limited but highly significant respect. It was accepted in both cases that Britain had an obligation to rescue British subjects in danger; but in the case of Cyprus, it was not thought that Britain had any further obligation to restore the

90

status quo under the Treaty of Guarantee.

Ironically, the contrast between Cyprus in 1974 and the Falkland Islands in 1982 is made sharper by the fact Britain had much more physical power to intervene in the former case than in the latter. There were British troops and combat aircraft stationed on the island when the Turkish invasion took place, and HMS *Hermes,* which eight years later was to travel 8,000 miles to recover the Falkland Islands, was only a few hundred miles from Cyprus. Naturally the prospect of an armed conflict between British and Turkish forces was extremely unwelcome. But the possibility of averting conflict altogether by a pre-emptive show of force was readily available. What else, in the circumstances, was the Treaty for?

What the British Government in fact did was bound to seem evasive to the Greeks, although it could be represented as fulfilling the bare letter of the Treaty. The Foreign Secretary of the day (James Callaghan, who was later Prime Minister), when asked in 1976 before a Select Committee of the House of Commons whether we had a right to intervene, replied:

> 'I dare say legally we had. In political, practical terms we had none because the constitution had not been working since the early 1960s.'[5]

This was hardly a convincing apology for the failures of the previous decade.

It was more or less true that the constitution had not been working. But the constitution was one of the things which Britain (with Greece and Turkey) had undertaken to safeguard under Article II of the Treaty of Guarantee, together with the independence, territorial integrity and security of the island. All of them had come under threat during the years 1963 - 74. Only once did the British intervene effectively, when at the end of 1963 troops from the sovereign bases helped to restore peace after President Makarios' attempt to enforce constitutional changes had led to inter-communal conflict which almost provoked a Turkish invasion. Apart from that one occasion, the initiative was left, if any was taken at all, to the United Nations or the United States. But British responsibility remained, under the letter of the Treaty, although Britain did nothing to honour it.

Callaghan, who had been Opposition spokesman on colonial affairs when the Treaty was negotiated, was certainly aware of its contents. In particular, he must have given his attention to Article IV when the crisis occurred in July 1974. That article contained two separate provisions in case of a breakdown of the settlement established by the three powers in 1959-60. The first provision was that the signatories would consult together 'with respect to the representations or measures necessary to ensure observance' of the Treaty. The second provision was that if consultation failed to produce agreement between the three powers, then each of them reserved 'the right to take action with the sole aim of re-establishing the state of affairs created by the present Treaty.' An advisory opinion was given to the Secretary-General of the United Nations by his legal advisers when the Treaty was signed to the effect that action by armed force under this article would be contrary to the UN Charter.

When the Greek Military Government launched its attack on Makarios and its attempt to subvert the independence of Cyprus, Callaghan correctly called a three-power conference at Geneva. But no agreement resulted. The Turks then took unilateral action by force; but their invasion did not result in the re-establishment of the state of affairs created by the treaty. The British Government did nothing more to uphold the treaty. It sent HMS *Hermes* to rescue British nationals from the path of the Turkish invasion; it authorised the RAF to facilitate Makarios' escape; and later it allowed Turkish-Cypriot refugees in southern Cyprus to be re-patriated through mainland Turkey. But that was all.

Many excuses were given for this inactivity. One was naturally the risk of war with Turkey. Another was that the Greeks had only themselves to blame (meaning the Military Government, which had in fact destroyed itself). A third was that the Treaty permitted but did not oblige signatories to take unilateral action; it therefore also permitted Britain to take no action at all. The Greeks might well ask why, in that case, it was called a Treaty of Guarantee?

It seems clear not only that the Labour Government behaved in a pusillanimous and evasive fashion in 1974, but also that neither Labour nor Conservative governments, nor their civil and military services, had ever given serious consideration to the obligations which they were undertaking from the first. The guarantee was given to Cyprus in 1960 in much the same way that similar guarantees were given to several east European states in 1939, on the assumption that the mere existence of the guarantee would deter aggression and ensure that the guarantee never had to be honoured. Successive British governments failed again to foresee that by mid-1974 they would be dealing with Greek and Turkish Governments which had no scruples about disregarding treaties.

It is fair to say that a Conservative Government would have been no more likely than the Labour Government of 1974 to react boldly to the crisis. It was a Conservative government which had signed the Treaty in the first place without considering the implications. Neither government was under pressure from public opinion to find a satisfactory solution to the problem of Cyprus. On the contrary, public opinion only became interested in Cyprus at times of crisis, when British interests, lives or property were at risk; and provided that these were safeguarded, public opinion asked for nothing more.

On the whole, with the exception of liberal intellectuals, the British tended to be more sympathetic to the Turks than to the Greeks. In the context of Cyprus, this was partly because the Turks were a minority, and partly because it always appeared to be the Greeks who started the trouble which affected British interests, lives and property — for example, in 1931, 1955-59, and 1974. It was symptomatic of the attitude described that even during the First World War, British soldiers judged that 'Johnny Turk was a gentleman'; and that in 1955 a leading article in the London *Times* could surprisingly describe Turkey as 'our ally in two world wars.'

A decade after the crisis of 1974, most sectors of British public opinion were content to live with the *de facto* partition of Cyprus into a Turkish north and a Greek south. Ordinary people had no interest in the island as a problem, only as an agreeable holiday resort. The Chiefs of Staff still had their bases intact. Governments, both Conservative and Labour, saw infinite difficulties in trying to bring about any substantial change in the new *status quo*. They would naturally support UN resolutions and encourage inter-communal discussions; they would oppose provocative gestures, such as the proclamation in 1983 of a supposedly independent 'Turkish Republic of Northern Cyprus'; but they would not risk destabilising the precarious balance which grew out of the crisis of 1974.

Officially, the British Government continues to favour the re-establishment of the Republic of Cyprus, with a new constitution recognising the demographic and other significant changes which have taken place since 1974. But a more convincing guarantee of independence, territorial integrity and security would be needed. The United Nations would not be a satisfactory guarantor; NATO might be, though it was NATO, in the Greek view, which failed so abysmally to respond to the 1974 crisis. Privately, the British Government would probably be prepared to acquiesce in the annexation of the two parts of Cyprus to their respective Greek and Turkish mainlands: in other words, what used to be called 'double *enosis*' or *de jure* partition. But the obstacles to any such settlement are formidable, and perhaps insuperable.

The temptation to leave things as they are and hope for the best is strong. But although the present state of affairs is quiet, it is not stable. British governments and officials have less justification than anyone for regarding it with complacency, since no one bears greater responsibility for bringing it about.

NOTES

1   H.C. Deb. *Hansard,* 5., vol. 531, 28 July 1954, col. 511.

2   *Annual Register,* 1878, Part II, pp. 251 - 2.

3   Michael Llewellyn Smith, *Ionian Vision* (London, 1973).

4   C.M. Woodhouse, *Karamanlis: the Restorer of Greek Democracy,* (London, 1982), pp. v, 24, 116 and *passim.*

5   *Cyprus* HMSO, Cmnd. 1093, 1960, App. B., pp. 86 - 7.

IMPRESSIONS OF ARCHBISHOP MAKARIOS 1969-1971

Hon. Sir Peter Ramsbotham

During my mission in Cyprus I saw a great deal of Archbishop Makarios who was then at the height of his popularity. My impressions of the Archbishop date from this period, although we met once again briefly in Washington in 1974 shortly after I had taken up my post as Ambassador to the United States. He had come to seek American support in the aftermath of the Turkish invasion of Cyprus and the usurpation of his position as President by a notorious, former EOKA gunman. The Archbishop had asked to see me privately and, though I do not recall the details of our conversation, I was again impressed by his poise, dignity and inherent courtesy which he never seemed to lose, whatever predicament he was in.

This natural dignity was one of his major assets. On the great feast days of the Greek Orthodox Church in Cyprus his stately hieratic figure, in imperial purple and bearing a sceptre, dominated the scene for all the world like one of the last surviving priest-kings. The imperial purple and the sceptre were two of the three privileges granted to the Archbishops of Cyprus by the East Roman Emperor Zeno in A.D. 488. The other archiepiscopal privilege was to sign their names in red ink — which Makarios never failed to do.

He exuded dignity and cheerful confidence. His sense of humour, often impish, was used effectively to disarm. His favourite technique at interviews was to listen with the utmost courtesy and to appear to indicate assent, but without commitment. Usually his interlocutor was naive enough to depart believing that he had carried his point, or at least that the Archbishop had heard him out in good faith and with good will.

Resilient by nature, the Archbishop seldom allowed reversals of fortune to rattle him. At moments of crisis or physical danger he showed cool nerves that even the most phlegmatic would envy. He believed that he was protected by Providence and this feeling was strengthened by what he surely considered to be his miraculous escape from assassination in 1970.

I well remember this dramatic event. It was early in the morning when I woke up to the crackle of machine-gun fire. The High Commissioner's Residence at that time was not far from the Archiepiscopal Palace, where Makarios had taken off from the courtyard in his small helicopter to attend a ceremony at a monastery in the south of the island. The would-be assassins had stationed themselves on the flat roof of a nearby house and opened fire at almost point-blank range as the helicopter flew by, riddling the pilot with bullets in the lower part of his body, but not so much as grazing the Archbishop, although he was sitting on the side nearest to the gunmen. Somehow the pilot managed to land the helicopter in the street. Makarios commandeered a passing car and rushed him to hospital. The unknown gunmen escaped, but it was generally assumed that they had been hired by some military element in Greece.

The Archbishop's habits were formed in his early youth as a shepherd boy in a small village near Paphos, when he would sometimes spend months in the mountains with his father in a tiny hut beside the sheep-fold; and later as a novice in the great medieval monastery of Kykko, where he received his early education.

The best account of Makarios' personal way of life can be found in a book[1] written in 1957 by Captain Le Geyt, a retired Indian Army officer, and his wife, who were given the task of looking after the Archbishop and his three co-prisoners during their nine months exile in the Seychelles. Mrs. Geyt, who gave Makarios his daily English lessons, came to know him as a man as few have done before or since; it was perhaps the only time and place when he came near to revealing himself.

He would rise at 6 a.m., take a walk before breakfast and then study in the grounds of the villa, reading his bible and meditating until 10:30, when he went to his room to write or study until lunch-time. After a short siesta he would have his English lesson and then go for a long walk, usually into the mountains, returning to the villa for supper; after which he would converse with his Cypriot colleagues on the verandah and retire at 10 p.m. She describes him in those days as a deeply religious man, keenly interested in comparative theology and church history and practice, with an open mind to new ideas. He was, she wrote, an outstanding student, quickly absorbing the intricacies of English conversation which he practised by recounting to her his personal experiences of his boyhood, his school days at Kykko and student days in America. He enjoyed climbing the mountains in the Seychelles and took physical risks in order to reach the summits: on one occasion, to mark his achievement, he carved his initials on a tree at the top.

The Archbishop's habits had not changed when I knew him twelve years after his exile. His way of life then was austere and self-disciplined. He rose early and devoted himself to prayer and study before spending the morning at the Archiepiscopal Palace, where he attended to religious matters in his capacity as Archbishop. Later he repaired to the President's Palace to conduct government business.

The Archbishop ate sparingly and took care to preserve his lithe figure with a regular regime of physical jerks in the early morning. His physique was superb and he was proud of it. I remember one occasion when he invited me to join him at his country retreat — the former 'lodge' of the British Governor, high up in the Troodos mountains and looking down across the vineyards and fields to Paphos and the sea beyond. He seldom got away alone to the mountains which he loved, and that day he was in high spirits. We walked along the spur above the valley where he had grown up as a shepherd boy and where to this day the young men take part in an annual race up the mountain to test their stamina. The Archbishop stopped to display his physical prowess, stretching his arms downwards with knees straight and with the palms of his hands flat on the ground. Then he stood back with a smile and invited me to follow suit. I felt all the weight of the British Empire on my shoulders as I bent downwards, managing just to touch the ground with my finger tips and quivering at the knees. Satisfied with his triumph, we spent a pleasant afternoon together.

The Archbishop's ascendancy over all his associates in Cyprus was unquestioned. He also thought he was cleverer than any political leader in Greece at that time, and this was probably true. But he was patient with lesser mortals — listening sympathetically to the pleas of villagers and humble people who daily came to seek his advice and help. Surprisingly for one so astute and shrewd, he sometimes took a child-like pleasure in flattering courtesies. I recall an occasion when I had to go to see him about some awkward matter on which we could not agree. I brought with me a coloured photograph of the recent Commonwealth Prime Ministers' Conference, showing Makarios seated by the side of the Queen, by virtue of his seniority as a Head of State. He was delighted and quickly conceded the point in dispute. There were other indications too that he valued the Commonwealth as a unique, non-aligned institution which helped to promote understanding between many different nations and to provide Cyprus and himself with a wider international platform.

The Archbishop was conservative by temperament and imbued with the prejudices of his island and his church. He was quick in understanding, but had a cautious mind and a preference for temporizing and moving forward only by consensus. Such limitations in a political leader had all too often caused him to delay a decision until his hand had been forced, or to offer too little, too late. Like most of his countrymen he was an able tactician but not a far-sighted strategist, preferring to work with time, not against it.

He seemed to have no intimate friends nor even persons whom he felt he could trust implicitly. I think he was conscious of the danger of being misled by favourites and sycophants who brought him news of the outside world and tried to impose their views on him. He used to hold a morning levee, attended by junior hangers-on. There was also a daily stream of Cypriot visitors who diversified his sources of information about what was going on in the island. His fund of information was, indeed, remarkable. The 'bush telegraph' was well developed in Cyprus and Makarios made good use of it.

Like most Greek Cypriots, and in keeping with his peasant origins, he paid close attention to commerce. His particular interest was in property and tourist development and he personally managed the considerable investments of the church. If one wanted to start a conversation on matters outside government business a good topic was always about some property in which he was interested; a hotel in Larnaca, I remember, was of special interest to him. There was no evidence, however, that either he or his relations profited from these business transactions, though he was criticised for mingling church and state affairs.

The Archbishop was a man of genuine personal kindness, commanding affection as well as admiration amongst those who were close to him and whose judgment was, I think, good. But he was capable of being, at the same time, both generous and vindictive. For all his innate caution he could display a streak of recklessness when he would stop at nothing to achieve his ends.

His name is indelibly associated with EOKA whose violence he never condemned nor publicly condoned. The extent of his implication with EOKA was never proven, but there is good evidence that he gave his approval to their murderous tactics against the British in 1955 - 58 and later, in 1963, against the Turkish Cypriots. He never disclaimed responsibility for the many acts of political thuggery at the time of independence and the early years of the Republic. But I doubt whether he ever directly ordered an act of violence. It was not in his nature to give direct orders. He preferred the oblique hint, leaving himself free to withdraw from a position which had become untenable or to disown those who had acted according to his intentions.

Violence was historically part of the stock-in-trade of a Levantine prelate. During the 19th century Orthodox bishops were often the national leaders in wars of resistance. As Ethnarch Makarios would regard it as his traditional role to lead his people in resistance to the 'conquering' power. And yet, however understandable in the light of history, the fact remains that under Makarios' leadership Cyprus reaped what was sown in the EOKA period and the same deadly fruit nearly killed him in 1970 and again in 1974.

The Archbishop believed that his first responsibility was to his church, to which he devoted a surprisingly large amount of his time. On many issues he was opposed by the regional bishops in Cyprus, but he kept his grip on church affairs. This church background coloured his approach to politics, people and the social problems in Cyprus. He treated his government and people like a monastic community. Himself accustomed to obedience, he ruled directly through chosen and manageable instruments. He selected as the ministers in his government those who had no political following of their own and who could, therefore, be changed or dropped with the minimum of fuss. He did not understand, indeed he had no experience of, the art of delegation nor the merits of coordination. All matters, weighty or trivial, appeared on the weekly agenda for his Council of Ministers, over whom he presided like a bishop in the chapter house of his cathedral. Any form of political schism was anathema to him as a good churchman.

Though he was constantly criticised by the right wing for pro-

moting the growth of communist influence in Cyprus, the Archbishop continued to regard communists as errant members of his
flock and did not hesitate to rely on their support. Those members
of the illegal right-wing movement, the National Front, many of
them ex-EOKA fighters who had 'repented', were treated by him
as prodigal sons. Such an attitude and disposition on the part of the
Archbishop fed the impression of his indecisiveness and dis-
heartened some who would have been his natural supporters.

This apparent indecisiveness stemmed from his conviction that
he had, at all costs, to keep his options open in order to maintain a
political equilibrium. Centuries of experience under foreign occupation had taught the Greek Cypriots how to profit from their
own weaknesses. Makarios, like a smaller version of General de
Gaulle, perfected the art of international ju-jitsu; playing one interest off against another, never allowing himself to become beholden to a stronger power (not even to the United Nations),
while enhancing his own importance by deliberately making a
nuisance of himself, though taking care not to provoke a hostile
reaction. This balancing tactic is well described in Stanley Mayes's
book written in 1960, shortly after the EOKA period.[2] 'In dealing
with his opponents, whether inside or outside the island, Makarios
uses an effective double bluff. He presents the people of Cyprus
as being solidly behind him, at the same time showing that he
cannot move forward because of the pressure against him. This
keeps him in equilibrium and pushes him a little higher, forcing
his opponents to make concessions.'

It was, I think, this innate desire to keep his options open as
long as possible which governed his attitude towards *enosis*. As
the Ethnarch of Cyprus he considered himself above party and to
have been elected as the national, as well as the spiritual, leader of
his people. But when he spoke of the people of Cyprus he really
meant the Greek-Cypriot people. He believed that there was no
one else in Cyprus who could shoulder the responsibility. In this
he was probably right. Every archbishop in Cyprus for the past
200 years had also been a political leader by virtue of his office;
and until 1959 Makarios' record as a supporter of *enosis* was entirely consistent with the tradition of the Ethnarchy. But on the
19th February 1959 he compromised over *enosis* in signing the
London Agreements, the settlement whereby Cyprus became an
independent republic. Right up to the last moment he had preva-
ricated and it was only under considerable pressure from the

Greek Government that he had finally agreed.

That was a traumatic experience for Makarios and it left an indelible mark on him. He did not wish to go down in history as the Ethnarch who finally ended the dream of *enosis*. Nor was he prepared to accept any compromise with the immediate objective of a Cyprus dominated and run by the Greek Cypriots. He was therefore content that Cyprus should continue as an independent state as long as he was President, though his secret wish may well have been to bequeath Cyprus to Greece on his political death-bed.

As Ethnarch Makarios was haunted by the fear of partition ('double *enosis*' as it came to be called), with the Turkish Cypriots attaching themselves to their Fatherland in Turkey to match the Greek Cypriots uniting with the Greek Motherland. And this led him to oppose any move which might tend to confirm the loss of Cyprus to a greater Greece or demolish the territorial heritage.

The Archbishop's whole outlook and style was at variance with those of the junta which governed Greece at that time, not least in his alliance with the communists in Cyprus, his use of left-wing advisers and his close personal relationship with King Constantine. It is possible that his ambitions extended beyond the narrow limits of Cyprus and that he hoped to play a positive role in Greece at some future time of upheaval and political change. He once told me that he would willingly act as a mediator if the terms were favourable for a restoration of the King; 'I am a Hellenic monarchist' he said.

The Greek Cypriots had long felt that they belonged to a greater Greece — the common language, the Orthodox Church, the Hellenic and Byzantine heritage, the shared experience under the Ottomans. They identified themselves with the nation state of Greece, while insisting on being wholly independent of the Government in Athens. And for most moderate Greek Cypriots that was the extent of their interest in *enosis*: they did not really want a political union, still less an economic one. Conscious of their fast-rising standards of living they considered that they were doing well enough on their own. And so they were caught in a contradiction. Their emotions and traditions were at variance with the reality of Cyprus's recent birth as an independent republic — a country artificially created almost overnight in 1960. They never really wanted independence in that form. Foreigners who encouraged and advocated a greater sense of national identity in

Cyprus were sometimes accused of being hostile to *enosis,* even in its cultural and linguistic guise.

It would, therefore, have been unrealistic to expect the Archbishop openly to renounce *enosis* for ever in the name of an independent Republic of Cyprus. Even if he had wished to, he would not have dared; it was, literally, more than his life was worth.

Makarios had little conception of the office of President, as opposed to that of Ethnarch. The susceptibilities of the Turkish Cypriots were constantly being offended to a degree which indicated either deliberate provocation or poor judgment of the Turkish character. So it was not surprising that they came to regard him as the central figure in their demonology. Like many of the older Greek generation he underestimated the potential of the Turkish-Cypriot community, which was no longer lethargic, poverty-stricken and insignificant. Even moderate Greek Cypriots, who remembered how in the early 50s the Turkish Cypriots were their poor cousins, tolerated and patronised, came to resent the sight of these same people behind their barricades with their own cinemas, cars and new buildings.

They seemed to go out of their way to make it harder for the Turkish-Cypriot community to cooperate as the junior partner in the economic and administrative life of the country. They treated them as an impoverished minority who might be permitted a share in the island's growing prosperity, provided that they knew and kept their place.

If the Archbishop had handled the Turkish Cypriots with as much shrewdness and statesmanship as he displayed when he attended the meetings at the United Nations in New York, he might have come nearer to his objective of a Cyprus fully controlled, in fact if not in appearance, by the Greek Cypriots. By his short-sighted policies towards the Turkish Cypriots he realised his own worst fears — the *de facto* partition of Cyprus. For their part the Turkish Cypriots did little to lessen the fears and suspicions of their Greek compatriots that they were secretly working for partition and the creation of a Turkish state within Cyprus. Indeed, they seemed intent on fostering such fears by ostentatiously giving military training to their young people. It was these inherent attitudes which made the prospects of an inter-communal settlement so remote.

During my time in Cyprus there were many instances which, but for the presence of the United Nations forces, could have led to more widespread violence: the attempted assassination of the Archbishop; the murder of a former minister with the suspected involvement of Greek mainland officers; plots and counter-plots and a bomb exploding outside the British High Commissioner's office; and always the danger of intercommunal hostilities as the two sides eyed each other distrustfully across the 'green line'.

By 1970 it was clear that 'creeping separatism' as I called it then (whereby the economic and administrative separation of the two communities was becoming more deeply entrenched) was a greater danger to Cyprus than the bogies of *enosis* or partition. But I had no success in persuading the Archbishop that the more he and his ministers encouraged the *enosis* drum to be beaten, the more they were also encouraging the Turkish Cypriots to protect themselves by developing their own institutions and moving towards that state of quasi-partition which it was his avowed purpose to prevent (and which is sadly so far advanced today).

The Greek Cypriots themselves, cheerful, intelligent, helpful people, proud of their island and their name, had little faith in their country's future. Few believed that, left to themselves, Greek and Turk could work out a solution to their own problems. Sooner or later there would, they thought, be another initiative to impose a settlement.

Had the British had a better understanding of the Archbishop's complex personality and ambitions we might, I suppose, have found some *modus vivendi* for an inter-communal settlement. But I doubt it. The conflict had at that time become too intransigent. The Archbishop himelf seemed to have calculated that time was on his side and that, provided there was no crisis nor excessive pressure on him from Athens, the existing situation was acceptable. In due time, he thought, the Turkish Cypriots would be absorbed without violence as a privileged minority within a Greek Cyprus.

When I left Cyprus in 1971 the Archbishop was a vigorous man of 57, capable of continuing his dominant rule of the island for at least another 10 years. But nothing grew in his shade. Vanity, as much as political instinct, made him reluctant to talk about grooming a successor. The uneasy political stalemate which prevailed at that time suited him well enough. A political settlement would have presented him with unwelcome problems: control of the Communist Party would have been more difficult; any non-*enosis* solution would have alienated the Orthodox

Church; and his own unique position as leader of the Greek Cypriots in the 'national struggle' would probably not have survived unchanged. Yet, paradoxically, he was also the one important element of stability in that volatile island, in so far as the *status quo* could be regarded as stable when the prospects of a settlement seemed so remote.

Certainly during the 30 years of his Ethnarchy no settlement would have been possible without his acquiescence. He kept the island in a precarious balance between the rival powers of Greece and Turkey, both of whom were shaping to their own national interests the sad division of Greek and Turk in Cyprus. It was not in his temperament to reach for any clear solution to Cyprus's problems — call it equivocal, sly, temporizing to preserve his own position, or call it a brilliant and shrewd balancing act, a recognition of the volatile elements which had to be controlled.

Makarios was a brilliant opportunist, single-mindedly devoted to the Greek-Cypriot cause and fully conscious of his historical role as both national and spiritual leader of the Greek-Cypriot people by whom he had been elected. He was a genuine Cypriot patriot as patriotism is understood in Cyprus. He was determined, despite many calculated hints to the contrary, never to allow an effective union of Cyprus with Greece. But he was equally attached to his ideal of a greater Hellenic sphere of influence with himself as its Patriarch. A most remarkable man, who incited devotion in some and hatred in others; half devout priest and half shrewd politician. Whatever criticisms — and there are many — can be levelled against him on other scores, his commanding presence and his genius for political and physical survival helped to preserve an uneasy peace in the Eastern Mediterranean for a long span of years.

His was an enlightened despotism admirably suited to the criteria of the 18th century, but not calculated to prepare Cyprus, after his departure, for a future as an independent and self-contained republic. Yet he gave the island an international status and it will be many years before Cyprus will again find a leader of his stature.

I do not pretend to have understood fully his complex character. He was neither hero nor villain. He was a mixture of strengths and weaknesses. I found him a fascinating person and enjoyed my dealings with him. Cyprus was not big enough for him; on a larger stage his remarkable abilities would have had more scope.

NOTES

1 Le Geyt, Captain P.S., *Makarios in Exile* (Nicosia, 1961).

2 Stanley Mayes, *Cyprus and Makarios* (New York, 1960), p. 238.

REHOUSING THE GREEK-CYPRIOT REFUGEES FROM 1974

Dependency, Assimilation, Politicisation

Roger Zetter

1. INTRODUCTION

It is now some twelve years since the traumatic months in middle and late 1974, when over one-third of the island's population was forcibly separated by the Turkish invasion to form two completely segregated ethnic communities.[1]

The refugee tragedy has been masked by the fragile yet rapidly expanding economy. A remarkably efficacious programme of employment creation and rehousing has formed the cornerstone of government policy to reactivate the economy and integrate the refugees. The refugees, however, left behind their land and property as they fled the occupying forces. Of inestimable cultural value, these are the roots of generations which still form vivid memories.[2] Thus despite the evident achievements of the initiatives, the refugees are still a critical force in the present and future political framework of the island, whether it remains divided or becomes reunited. The refugees are both a resource in, and a symbol of, the unresolved political situation.

In this paper I examine some of the significant political dimensions that the refugees have come to represent. Especially in the context of the rehousing programmes, I shall focus on the reactions of the refugees; on the paradox of assimilation and dependency; and on how these characteristics have given the label refugee a highly politicised texture in the island.

For two reasons the analysis is only concerned with Greek Cypriots. First, by any international standards, the volume of refugees proportional to the total ethnic population was enormous (some 40%). This has made the problems of absorption, rehousing and perhaps eventual resettlement correspondingly complex. By contrast, the 40,000 or so Turkish-Cypriot refugees did not face such problems of shelter provision. The second reason takes us to the heart of the political context of the refugee issue, because both ethnic communities have sought a totally different cultural reconstruction of political realities since 1974.[3] The Turkish Cypriots through a variety of cultural symbols (renaming settlements, comprehensive dehellenisation of the north, erecting monuments to the 1974 'liberation') are seeking to convey the message of permanent separation and independence. Many thousands of Turkish-Cypriot refugees exist. To admit this however is of course to deny the very message that the reconstructed reality is intended to convey.

For Greek Cypriots a contrasting ideology exists. Partition of the island and occupation of the north is conveyed as impermanent. In this reconstruction of reality, the resettlement of the 200,000 refugees becomes a powerful, indeed a pre-eminent, factor which is endorsed in a number of formal and informal arenas. To this end, the very label of refugee is one of the greatest symbols of that reality — providing crucial political leverage both nationally and internationally against accepting the present division as permanent. And it is important to note that in the intercommunal negotiations since 1974, the concept of refugees has only been promoted by the Greek Cypriots, never the Turkish Cypriots.

Thus, the burden of a large dependent group and the high political profile that the refugees have come to represent, have an important bearing on the Cyprus situation. In this paper I consider this importance in four interrelated sections. A brief *résumé* of the policies and programmes is followed by a second section which examines some of the experiences and attitudes of the refugees.

Significant contradictions between the intention and outcome of the policies are evident and the third section argues that one explanation of these contradictions is that the refugees have been incorporated through the housing policies and the processes and procedures. In the light of this interpretation the fourth section reformulates the current situation of the refugees showing how politicisation and dependency, integration side by side with the will to return, are now dominant aspects in their lives.

2. REHOUSING AND REACTIVATION

Following the 1974 invasion some 49,000 dwellings and associated farmland, villages and towns were lost as the Greek-Cypriot population fled to the south. The immediate response was to provide temporary accommodation. When it became clear that the scale and duration of housing need were going to require far greater provision, the government's housing policy moved rapidly from tents and prefabricated shelter to an ambitious policy for the construction of permanent dwellings.

The rehousing programme has consisted of three main components.[4]

First, there are comprehensively planned estates on the periphery of the three main towns in the south of the island. Rather like British new town neighbourhoods, these have an average size of about 400 units; the largest is 1,000. About 12,000 units have been built and those eligible for these houses are the poorer and larger refugee families. Second there are self-build schemes where refugees, with government grants and loans, build their own homes to prescribed plans on serviced government land. Again these are located, by and large, on the urban periphery but in some village locations.

Popular because this method mirrors pre-1974 housing processes, nonetheless, like the estate houses, the regularity of form and layout provides a dramatic contrast to the pre-existing morphology of towns and villages. About 10,500 units have been built in this fashion. In the larger self-build and government estates, schools, shopping centres and other community facilities have been built. Third, similar assistance is available for those fortunate refugees who owned or who have been able to buy their own plots of land freehold. A range of other initiatives exists: 7,000 families have occupancy licenses in property vacated by Turkish-Cypriot refugees and an assisted purchase scheme for flats has recently been successfully introduced. In all, about 40,000 families (including second generation) have so far (1985) been rehoused in a remarkably short space of time. Importantly, all the estate housing is rent-free and self-build loans are at concessionary rates; equally important, the refugees have no property title.

The programme had cost some C£116 million by 1982, accounting for about 55% of Special Relief Fund expenditure for refugees and some 35% of all expenditure (including Ordinary and Development budgets) on refugee needs.[5] On completion of the programme an estimated C£220 million will have been disbursed on housing. The mobilisation of a successful housing programme has been part of a wider set of policy initiatives, set out in a sequence of Emergency Action Plans from 1975 through to 1986, to rebuild the shattered economy.[6] Agriculture, tourism and the construction industry have been effectively re-established and now exceed pre-1974 levels of output and production (in only 60% of the island) and manufacturing industry, notwithstanding the small domestic market, has expanded substantially.

Of particular significance to this study are the reduction in unemployment, the resuscitation of the construction industry as a leading sector of the economy and the expansion of the urban-based manufacturing sector. As we shall see, in these facets of economic change the refugee population has been a significant resource.

3. REFUGEE REACTIONS

How have the refugees themselves adapted in the intervening decade? What has been the impact of the Government's dramatically successful policies on their lives.

The housing estates are developing their own identity despite the rigid layout and design. Houses are being extended and small backyard industries and businesses are developing. Adobe ovens and richly-planted gardens, old traditions, are the symbolic hallmarks of new roots being established. Self-build estates are hives of activity; there is considerable personal investment and an air of permanency. A form of adjustment is taking place. The refugees have also been rapidly assimilated into the urban economy in the factory estates springing up near the housing areas. The Government and the refugees may be the paradoxical victims of their own success. For these emerging characteristics appear to demonstrate a growing suggestion of permanency.

Yet this conclusion is by no means unambiguous. There have

been difficulties in tranferring from rural to urban life-styles: refugees comment on the monotony and regularity of wage employment and estate life, compared to farming activity and the familiar bustle of village life — the environment from where a majority of refugees came. All the refugees are preoccupied with the difficulty of building up, what they call, 'trust' in their fellow refugees in the housing estates. This is because the criteria used to prioritise housing needs have been large family size and low income, rather than regrouping villages. Appropriate though these criteria may be, they have cut across the timeless and seamless web of community identity and the inherited social conventions of each village. The rural districts each had their own unique traditions and intuitively understood norms; these have now been lost.

The diaspora of summer 1974 rendered the alternative, of regrouping villages in the south, immensely difficult to achieve. As it is, tens of villages are represented on each estate — a randomness which simultaneously heightens refugee resistance to assimilation and intensifies the desire to recreate the familiarity of past structures. They are 'strange people in a strange situation' as one refugee described her estate.

Many other social changes are evident. The extended family facilitated by the provision of a dowry house is now difficult to maintain. Some refugees sagely accept that perhaps this modernisation is a change for the better; but more likely it is a rationalisation that they no longer have the land to build on or sell to raise the necessary capital to perpetuate the tradition. And the government houses provide insufficient accommodation anyway. Realising this problem, the Government is now building small old people's dwellings on estates; but these are too few as yet. The loss of large village weddings is much regretted because of lack of space in the houses and lack of finance. Parents suggest that control over children is more difficult since the broader controls of village life, where everyone knew everyone else's children, no longer exist in the estates. Many married women now have to take paid employment in factories to help the family budget. This is a radical change from pre-1974 days of strong domestic orientation and work on the farm. The women in particular regret the increasing monetisation of their lives. Food has now to be bought rather than exchanged with neighbours in an informally accounted way.

As with many refugee groups the 'myth of the return' is an

ever present feeling for the Greek Cypriots.[7] It is exceptionally strong amongst the women. Children are inculcated into the life and history of their villages in the north even though they may have been born after 1974. Photos of houses and family life before 1974 are prominent in most homes. The coffee shops and stores are named after towns in the occupied areas. Exhibitions and revival of interest in cultural traditions and ethnic identity (costumes, dancing, vernacular achitecture) are also evident. Another phenomenon is that many refugees have deliberately settled in estates from where they can see their villages in the occupied north, vividly to keep alive the memory of the past.

4. INSTITUTIONAL PROCESSES

By no means are these reactions unique to Cyprus. Such social, cultural and psychological fragmentation is a widely documented response by refugees in many parts of the world.[8] Whilst these discontinuities in Cyprus cannot all be attributable just to the housing and reactivation policies, the widespread impact and the very success of these policies means that they have come to figure very highly in the lives of most refugees. How then might we account for these contradictory experiences in a more systematic fashion? And how might such a patterning help to explain the politicization of the refugees as perhaps the most significant interest group in future developments on the island?

By definition, the Cypriot refugees, like all refugees, have accepted major changes in their lives. These changes were then accompanied by new needs, opportunities and aspirations — expressed as resource requirements for housing and jobs. At one level, therefore, rehousing and reactivation stood by themselves as both necessary and humanitarian. Important though this is, there is another level of analysis which suggests a different interpretation of these policies and their impact. A client group existed with specific needs. Accordingly, institutions had to be organised and procedures developed to define what precisely these needs were, how they should actually be provided, how plans might be implemented and then how the products (houses, serviced plots,) should be distributed in an equitable way. In short, in post-1974 Cyprus, behind the superficially clear objectives, we may see needs and policy responses becoming institutionalised. Thus, as the refugees became absorbed by institutions and procedures designed to house them, their needs and values became filtered by administrative rules and were structured more and more in a form that the Government felt able to handle. Intentions and outcomes thus began to diverge as refugees realised that what was provided was not necessarily according with their own preferences; especially, that what was being provided might be creating consequential and perhaps unwanted effects on their lives and long-term aspirations — socially and politically.

This tension or discrepancy between intentions and unforeseen outcomes, is a fundamental theme in analysis of public policy and administrative action.[9] Moving from this theoretical setting to an examination of what the outcomes in Cyprus have come to mean, three facets of the programme demonstrate how this tension has emerged and how the refugees have become incorporated, not necessarily unwillingly, as a political resource.

LOCATION AND DESIGN: After 1974 large-scale estates appeared on the island for the first time. This presented a radical contrast to the piecemeal, plot by plot, incremental and culturally determined processes before the invasion. Physical shelter was an overriding priority after the disaster — the more subtle long term implications were of lesser immediacy. What now, in retrospect, seem functional designs, uniform in style and layout, acknowledging little of the preceding cultural or vernacular characteristics, were perhaps an inevitable institutionalisation of needs — rendering the problems technically manageable within the humanitarian obligation to rehouse.

It is perhaps still too soon to detect the full conditioning effects of the radically different housing styles; but some of the changes in social norms and cultural values which are emerging have been documented in the preceding section. Alienation exists, doubtless accentuated by the growing feeling of the permanency of the island's division which now pervades the Greek-Cypriot community.

Clearly the government housing, although of a very high standard, is proving inflexible to physical change (with small plots, terracing and integrated layouts) and thus, as we have seen, inflexible in meeting social norms. Housing is for nuclear families, thus refugees find it hard to maintain the obligations of the extended family and dowry provision. Co-occupation of dwellings

112

between two sometimes three generations of a family exists. These problems may increase as time goes on. There may be similar tensions between refugees and housing agencies with respect to the 'non-conforming' uses — backyard industries, grocery shops — so much part of the village and town life before 1974 but resisted, not always effectively, by the housing management policies.

By contrast, the self-build schemes offer much greater similarity with the pre-existing processes in Cyprus; this makes it all the more surprising that this type of provision has not assumed a larger share of government initiatives. A partial explanation is that in the early years after the invasion the refugees did not have the resources to build for themselves; additionally their refugee status was only temporary — why build a house if one was soon going to return to the north?

The government housing has high 'political visibility' and will be an important resource if some kind of repatriation takes place. But self-build housing by refugees gives another message: the houses are of extremely high standard — far higher than the government loans and grants require — suggesting considerable personal investment; might this also suggest a belief that settlement in the south is now permanent?

The differing attitudes of Government and refugees to these two housing modes indicate, therefore, important differences in the perception of control and autonomy that institution and beneficiaries might have.

There are consequences from the locational choices as well — effectively to urbanise a predominantly rural population (60% of the refugees). Major changes in rural land tenure were not contemplated: and from the government's perspective, the implementation of the programme in urban locations could capitalise on existing land holdings, infrastructure and service provision. In addition the object of providing good housing and community facilities — as material and social welfare compensation for what had been lost — was more economically satisfied in urban areas. But it should not be forgotten that these locations provide a convenient labour force for an economy restructured around a manufacturing not an agricultural base.

The estates have not yet linked effectively into the urban fabric. Many estates are not contiguous with existing urban areas, necessitating long journeys to work and making communication and integration difficult.

Thus, semi-isolated and with a readily recognisable physical form, they have generated a distinctive identity for the label refugee and may have accentuated the development of a 'refugee consciousness'.

The refugees do not complain that they did not participate in the shaping of the policy. Whilst grateful for the housing, yet they feel stigmatised to an extent despite the ethnic and religious identity with their hosts — they are all Greek Cypriots. Prejudice, if it exists at all, is more subtle than is usually found in such situations. Some feel that non-refugees now begrudge them the housing programme despite their losses. In part the obviously recognisable housing estates may have encouraged this enmity. Moreover, the earlier estates generally accommodate larger, poorer families accentuating a socio-economic differentiation. It may be that smaller estates located closer to existing facilities would have fostered more effective social and physical integration. As it is, the pattern of housing which has emerged fundamentally changes rather than replicates the pre-1974 format. This heightens dependency and differentiation and institutionalises further changes in, for example, the decline of the extended family.

ACCESS AND ALLOCATION: So far it might be assumed that the label 'refugee' is clear cut. By many criteria the situation is consistent with what the label implies. Cypriots have been forcibly removed from land and livelihood. Substantial UNHCR assistance (as proxy for US aid) gives added legitimacy. Nonetheless, the beneficiaries are not technically refugees; they are in their country of origin and not deprived of their 'national' status. In a narrower interpretation, the designation is thus misapplied. An important consequence of this distinction (if it means anything to the refugees in practice) is that the label must presume some, and pre-empt other, methods by which a political settlement might be structured. This in turn conditions perceptions of the housing programme objectives.

Moreover, not all refugees are equally eligible for housing. Different rules, some categorical some discretionary, exist to ensure priorities and equality of access to the programme and then the allocation of resources from it. Applications have to be prioritised, queues ordered and matched to the building programmes. Income levels have to be determined against thresholds of eligibility and family size determined, so that poorer larger families may be allocated houses early on. First and second generation refugee status also conditions different levels of eligibility in different districts, as does family size. The importance of these entry points to the housing programme — organisational connections, procedures, encounters between beneficiary and distributional agencies — are examined in some detail elsewhere.[10]

Being labelled a refugee has come to mean a number of different things over time; it is not quite the same as being eligible for a house, a plot or a housing loan. And of course, the criteria represent the necessities of the programme as well as the client group for whom the programme has been intended. The beneficiaries have become incorporated. What is the evidence and what are the consequences?

Use of income and family size criteria was intended to prioritise those under greatest threat of poverty and assign them estate houses. Defined in this way it was the poor, rural, landless or small farmers, the urban poor suddenly unwaged and large families, who were rehoused first — since their wealth and income, such as they were, were highly location specific in the north. Civil servants, salaried income earners, large land owners or wealthy farmers, although refugees, were all excluded. To this extent the access criteria have been progressive in impact.

There are perplexing outcomes. There is a perception, real or illusory, that the larger older estates are problem or ghetto estates, with uniform age, family and socio-economic structure. Of course, these are the precise images of the definitional criteria but not, obviously not, the intended outcome. Contrasted with the highly heterogeneous residential spatial pattern of socio-economic groupings before 1974, there is now an impression of socio-economic class segregation on the estates which derives more than from just being a refugee. Stereotyping is taking place. These are difficult experiences to which refugees have to adjust — as the reactions noted above indicated.

Conversely, newer estates tend to be smaller and the houses better finished. For the self-builders more generous grants now available allow higher standards to be achieved. The queue can occasionally be beneficial. Refugees in the pending category, smaller families, those better off, those in short, excluded on these criteria but who now have access because the criteria are less stringent — they unintentionally may be 'better' housed in the popular image.

These criteria, defining eligibility, are the corollary of perhaps the most fundamental issue affecting the refugees as they attempt to reconstruct their lives — that is the break-up of the villages in the diaspora. This is the 'strange situation' that the refugee was trying to communicate and the reason why building up trust is so problematic.

The allocation mechanisms for houses, reliant as they have been on bureaucratic definitions of need, have unfortunately endorsed this fragmentation. Understandably, from the government's viewpoint, the criteria are fair, equitable, workable and sound. management in the circumstances. Looked at from a refugee's point of view, in straightforward terms he is a refugee having fled the invasion. Income, first or second generation — these are not predetermined by thoughts of permanency and thus housing programmes, access rules and eligibility. Yet these are the crucial criteria for identifying and defining needs — not the community of the village. More complex though it undeniably would have been, regrouping villages might have fostered more rapid adjustment and re-establishment of past traditions. Simultaneously, the refugees' political profile and dependency may have declined — perversely what neither the Government nor the refugees themselves would have actually wished.

Just as the form and location of the housing has tended to accentuate the differentiation between refugee and non-refugee, the access criteria also have tended to differentiate, but between refugee and refugee. And in just the same way, therefore, we can appreciate the contradictions that arise. A continuing ennui which the criteria underscore, and thus a wish for some other outcome, is one consequence. A superficial policy failure in attempting integration exists in parallel with the desire that it should not be too successful since this would mean losing the label and thus losing pressure for resettlement.

Who is a refugee therefore, especially since housing is the most dramatic identification of the label, assumes meaning which, whilst socially divisive at one level and not necessarily how the group perceives itself, becomes instrumental in achieving some of the group's objectives despite the contradictions which are created.

REFUGEES AS A RESOURCE: Costs of damage, replacement costs, balance of payments deficits: these are the usual factors emphasised in post-disaster studies. But in Cyprus we can conceptualise the economic impact of the disaster of 1974 in a rather different way. The disaster can be seen as a developmental disequilibrium[11] used to accelerate the long-run growth of the economy both spatially and sectorally.

The construction sector has been a leading sector in rebuilding the economy and within this sector the housebuilding industry has been the most significant element in investment and output. In 1973 housing accounted for 41% of Gross Domestic Capital Formation (GDCF) in the Cyprus economy (high by international standards) and for the post-disaster period 1975-81 averaged the same percentage.[12] But what is significant, of course, is that whereas before the invasion the government's contribution to the housing sector was about 0.5% of the GDCF, after 1974 it averaged over 21% for the 1975-81 period and was especially high in the early years after the invasion. It is the government's investment in the refugee housing programme which has comprised the substantial proportion of the housing sector growth. These linkages suggest that the housing programme has been at least a very significant component of the contruction industry's revival, at most a central factor in re-establishing the leading sector role.

In parallel there is the dramatic restructuring that has taken place, with the pre-emptive growth of the manufacturing sector (from 11.7%-16.4% of GDP, 1970-81), almost inversely related to the slow decline of agriculture (from 17.6%-11.4% GDP, 1970-81). These were trends already taking place, but they have been powerfully underwritten by the Emergency Action Plans.

The impact of the government's labour absorption policies is similarly dramatic, reducing unemployment from over 30% after the disaster to 2% by 1978. On the assumption that about 60% of the refugees came from rural areas and on the assumption that non-refugee Greek Cypriots were unlikely to have changed employment after 1974, then it was rural refugee Greek-Cypriot labour (both men and women) which provided the rapid replenishment of a workforce for the government policy of labour intensive industrialisation.

How do these changes help to explain the reactions of the refugees and the outcomes of the policies? In part the pursuit of economic development stands by itself. The Development Plans were designed to achieve for the domestic economy 'the attainment of the highest possible growth rates under conditions of full employment.'[13] A dynamic economy for the Greek Cypriots, as existed before 1974, was important to self-esteem as well as perhaps an important lever in negotiations for a settlement. But a reconstructed economy was also construed, in the Emergency Action Plans, as a primary element in the integration of the refugees. This objective is stated quite unequivocally-

'The whole philosophy for the reactivation of the refugees ... aimed at exerting gradual efforts for the gradual restoration of the previous order through the reintegration of households with productive means and by assisting refugees to activate themselves once again....'[14]

Equally, however, the process can be construed the other way round. Reactivation of the economy was dependent on the refugees as resources in spatial and structural terms and thus the generation of specific programmes in that context. If the disaster has been a successful growth-inducing mechanism for the economy then the main resource in rebuilding the shattered economy has been the refugees — a resource both as producers and consumers: on the supply side providing labour for construction and urban-based manufacturing industry and on the demand side for housing.

It was not simply good quality housing that was being provided for the refugees, but a model of economic development, rapidly incorporating the refugees from an agrarian to an urban economy and into housing which reflects the needs of a mass programme — not responses family by family, house by house. The beneficiaries' perception of the housing programme was not necessarily, therefore, congruent with the government's. Hence the contradictory reactions of the refugees — gratitude yet resistance especially by women; incomes as a means for survival but earned in unfamiliar and disorientating ways. Government policies have inevitably structured responses. In so doing they have directed beneficiaries to certain other, perhaps, unwanted goods — at least unwanted with conditionality that is attached to them: that is, houses which may not have been preferred and a mode of integration which in the refugees' terms may be unsatisfactory. In this way the distinctive location and design of housing, production processes and allocation rules and economic regeneration forge a powerful institutional framework. This is a framework as much identifiable with technocratic assumptions as with the explicit needs of the target group and links again to the thematic concern of this paper — the divergence of outcome from intention; policy objectives compromised by institutional processes.

5. DEPENDENCY, INTEGRATION AND POLITICISATION

Refugees, more than many target groups, suffer from the dilemma of programmes which seek to integrate and include, but perforce create, dependency and differentiation. Accordingly, whilst the intention has been, through the housing and economic programmes, to integrate and reactivate, at the same time the distinctiveness of the Greek-Cypriot refugees has been accentuated.

And so, in Cyprus the refugee label has come to assume an explicitly politicised meaning as the material and economic requirements designed to satisfy short-term needs now look increasingly like long-term solutions; an interpretation which says something about the sense of assimilation yet dependency which the refugees have experienced. We now review some aspects of the political context which the ambiguities have come to represent.

The commitment of both the Government and the refugees is to repatriation. Whilst the form of repatriation is by no means clear, the policies and programmes for the refugees obviously embody certain broad political assumptions about the kind of Cyprus that the Greek Cypriots envisage.[15] The refugees then are a central element in any negotiations; consequently the degree to which they politicise their objectives becomes an important facet in the stance of the Government.

The refugees have effectively and not unreasonably exploited the ambiguities of the programme to maintain and consolidate their political profile. Extension of housing obligations for second (and eventually third?) 'generation' families is one example of this. Longer term, unforeseen and wider provisions will be required beyond original assumptions about physical shelter needs. These are the outcomes of institutionalised provision and the creation of dependency, which in part the refugees want.

For the Government, of course, an urban-based housing stock, as well as being part of an economic strategy and political statement, is also an important resource under its control if resettlement takes place.

Yet the programme was equally and ambiguously designed for quite opposite reasons. Indeed, as we have seen, the objects were reactivation and integration. In this formulation, through housing and economic policies, political unrest and refugee consciousness have been defused. This may partially explain why the refugee issue was handled within the existing ministerial framework, despite the enormous size of the problem, rather than by creating a separate ministry to handle all refugee affairs. Strongly argued as it may be that depoliticisation was not intended, it is becoming an unwanted but inextricable part of the institutionalised response.

The commitment is to repatriation; but paradoxically the very conditions giving rise to that need have also created policies and outcomes which make that object increasingly difficult to achieve. A number of parameters define increasing assimilation. Even pre-supposing a political solution, self evidently from the preceding analysis, the division of the island has been reinforced. Housing, jobs, new social infrastructure and the now substantial disparity between the economies of the prosperous south and poorer north may all tend to consolidate and reinforce the *de facto* division and, paradoxically, to undermine political aspirations.

All the outcomes lead to this paradoxical conclusion; all, that is, with one exception — the refusal to give property title to the rehoused refugees. This maintains the impression of a binding commitment to the refugees that the situation is temporary, they are not integrated and that they will return. Giving title would imply permanency. Again therefore one set of objectives (national) undermines another (social). This is not unacceptable for it em-phasises the no-compromise position of those who will never accept anything less than repatriation. Title would manifestly represent a softening of negotiating positions with the Turkish Cypriots. Clerides's proposal to give title, in the 1983 presidential elections, partly as a disengagement from continuing commit-ments to the refugees by non-refugees, was defeated for what it implied. The 'refugee consciousness' with its refusal of title ensures that special status is not lost. Families say they would refuse the gift of title to their houses even if they were gilded. With so comprehensive a programme this is perhaps the last vestige of a belief that the situation is temporary. Title removes dependency — and this means permanency.

Withdrawal of support merely strengthens the tendency for the refugees to politicise their needs as a special-interest group.

This attitude is similarly encapsulated in second generation provision: decoupling from this aspect of provision would arouse the same anxieties as the suggestion of granting title. Yet, ambiguously, admitting this category was a politically uncomfortable recognition that resettlement was not on the immediate agenda. Dependency means therefore that the providers find themselves having to adopt new responsibilities and commitments to a wider and continuing support, generation by generation.

Any suggestion of withdrawing refugee support, for example, by imposing maintenance charges or low levels of rent or limiting access of subsequent generations, is vigorously opposed. Each year the Pan-Cyprian Refugee Committee obtains from the Government progressive extension for estate housing eligibility and self-build support. Yet in the politicised environment in which the refugees exist this is what one would expect; for it maintains the label of impermanency and dependency. Dependency and assimilation go hand in hand.

When we suggest that the refugees have become politicised our concern is with the way the dependency, which the refugees have now come to experience, might best be deployed vis a vis state interests to achieve as favourable an outcome as possible for their aspirations. There has not emerged a political party, to articulate these interests. This is perhaps not surprising given the large size of the interest group and its needs. Instead the refugees are represented by the Pan-Cyprian Refugee Committee, which is recognised across the spectrum of political parties as an organisation expressing a certain identity but not necessarily a consensus.

The politicisation cannot at present therefore be explicitly classified in terms of specific right or left wing representation or a class interest; but the articulation of such interests may be commencing — a development which the continuing division of the island will enhance. Whether a proletarian political class on the estates has been created and whether this might become a key issue in the relationship between the state, capital and a refugee/left wing class struggle, is an important but still open issue.[16] Broadly speaking, amongst the refugees, AKEL, the Communist Party, commands most support. This is hardly surprising; the left has always attracted about one third of the vote in Cyprus. Since is is the poor, who lost all in 1974, who form the bulk of the refugees in the housing areas, their political loyalty is by and large a continuation of past trends. It is their spatial consolidation which is the new and in this context important change. A consciousness therefore exists and one might expect this consciousness to be mobilised by the left. This could be through the pursuit of active resettlement policies as a way of confronting the vested interests of capital which are currently benefiting so widely from the economic and housing policies of the divided island; paradoxically, again, this is not the case, for the time being at least. This is consistent with AKEL's very conservative pursuit of any changes to the contemporary free market orientation of the island. It is also consistent with the equally low-key approach to a political settlement. Since, however, the continuing policy of support for UN initiatives and intercommunal talks has achieved nothing in the past decade, the pressure is on AKEL, as on the other political parties, to search for a more active position. This is in line with the hardening attitudes of the refugees and Greek-Cypriot opinion as a whole.

The right has already developed new policies for the refugees — the soundly defeated proposals to grant title. Ironic as that might be, this rejection has been clearly explained in this paper. This was a departure of course from the generally more 'dynamic' policy towards a settlement which the right is now pursuing — keen to re-establish itself after the 1974 debacle. But there is ambiguity too in this new policy direction. Despite the nationalistic perspective, the right has benefited so far from the incorporation of the refugees, both economically and in forestalling a political identity. Removing support from the refugees might reduce the financial burden on public revenues, but it might also intensify the development of the identity of a 'class under threat'. Conversely, classified as 'refugees' waiting to return — this has an apolitical and less threatening implication.

Inevitably speculative in nature, these observations are indications of the entangled strands of political interest with which the refugees can now be identified. The state incorporates, in part intentionally, yet wants to disengage. The refugees accept dependency but also want to disengage from unwanted outcomes of the policy. Dependency and independence, assimilation and repatriation occur ambiguously together.

6. CONCLUSIONS

Tragedy and trauma have been the dominating experiences of Greek-Cypriot refugees. This paper has analysed a rather different set of experiences which have been characterised as incorporating the refugees into a set of policies and programmes where contradictory outcomes are an inevitable consequence. This perspective on a public policy is not at all suggesting that the outcomes are deliberately conceived. Manifestly the policies in Cyprus reflect remarkable community solidarity and support and a reconstruction which is almost miraculous. Rather, the outcomes are inevitable, but not deliberate, because they reflect the constraints within which any agency operates: the constraint of trying to meet assumed needs with programmes and procedures which simultaneously inhibit those needs being satisfied.

Accordingly, with its emphasis on material and economic needs, the Government has created a resource — housing — which has come to symbolise assimilation, settlement, non-repatriation. Yet, equally, it is manoeuvered by the refugees as a negotiating resource because of what goes with it — differentiation, dependency, a proxy for repatriation — housing ironically gives the refugees a convoluted, tenuous link with this last possibility.

For the Government of course the idea of integration, an object never in fact clearly defined, was itself perhaps self-defeating. Integration could never have been intended to achieve a level where it would begin to undermine the strength of the original intention — that the programme was a staging post for repatriation.

These are the unresolved dilemmas of the policy and its institutional formulation. They have become a vehicle for incorporating refugees and for their own contradictory and uncertain experiences of dependency or assimilation and how this has emerged as a politicised expression.

It is the personal sense of loss which remains so strong — small parcels of farm land, perhaps no more than one or two acres and a house vividly remembered. It is the alienation from land, so symbolic to Cypriots, which has fragmented the refugees' lives the most and generates intense symptoms of grieving and bereavement.

By many criteria the refugees would seem to be being assimilated; but whatever the material conditions a refugee is always a refugee. And so it is their appeal to the moral argument, that their own land has been illegally occupied, that keeps alive most strongly the refugee consciousness and dependency on the government to provide the means for them to return — even though only fragments of their lives could ever be reassembled.

NOTES

1   Hitchens, C., *Cyprus* (Quartet Press, London, 1984). Hitchens, C., 'detente and Destabilisation', *New Left Review,* No. 94, 1975, pp. 61-73. Polyviou, P.G., *Cyprus Conflict and Negotiation 1960-1980* (Duckworth, London, 1980). Ehrlich, T., 'Cyprus, the Warlike Isle: Origins and Elements of Current Crisis', *Stanford Law Review,* vol. 18, No. 5. Markides, K., *The Rise and Fall of the Cyprus Republic* (Yale U.P., Newhaven, 1977). These provide the best discussion of the events of 1974 and background to this paper.

2   Loizos, P., 'A Struggle for Meaning. Reactions to Disaster Amongst Cypriot Refugees'. *Disasters,* vol. 1, No. 3, 1977, pp. 231-39. Loizos, P., *The Heart Grown Bitter. A Chronicle of Cypriot War Refugees* (C.U.P., Cambridge, 1981).

3   King R., and Ladbury, S., 'The Cultural Reconstruction of Political Reality: Greek and Turkish Cyprus since 1974'. *Anthropological Quarterly,* vol. 55, No. 1, 1982, pp. 1-16.

4   Zetter, R., *Housing Policy and Social Change in Cyprus 1960 - 1980: The Reactions to Political Instability.* Oxford Working Paper No. 56, Department of Town Planning (Oxford Polytechnic, 1981). Zetter, R., 'Housing Policy in Cyprus — A Review', *Habitat International,* vol. 6, No. 4,1982, pp. 471 - 86.

5   Republic of Cyprus, *Cyprus, The Refugee Problem* (Public Office of Information, Appendix 1, Nicosia, 1983).

6   Republic of Cyprus. *Emergency Economic Action Plan.* First 1975/76, Second 1977/78, Third 1979/81, Fourth 1982/86 (Planning Bureau, Planning Commission, Nicosia).

7   Cruise O'Brian, R., *The White Society in Black Africa: The French of Senegal* (Faber, London, 1972). Schaffer, B., *Political Integration,* IDS. DP No. 53 (University of Sussex, 1974).

8   Stein, B.N. and Tomasi, S.M. (eds.) 'Refugees Today', *International Migration Review,* Special Issue, vol. 15, No. 1 (Centre for Migration Studies, New York, 1981), pp. 1 - 141.

9   Schaffer, B.B., *'Official Providers: Access, Equity and Participation.*

Division for the study of Development, (UNESCO, Paris, 1977). Schaffer, B.B. and Huang Wen-Hsien, 'Distribution Theory and Access', *Development and Change,* vol. 6, No. 2, 1975. Schaffer, B.B. and Lamb, G., *Can Equity be Organised?* (Gower/UNESCO, 1981).

10 Zetter, R., 'Refugees — Access and Labelling', *Development and Change,* vol. 15, 1985.

11 Abril-Ojeda, G., *The Role of Disaster Relief in LDCs,* Draft PhD thesis (University of Stockholm, unpublished, 1981).

12 Republic of Cyprus, *Economic Report 1981,* Ministry of Finance, Tables 12 - 23, Nicosia, 1983. Republic of Cyprus, *Cyprus Monograph on the Human Settlements Situation and Related Trends and Policies,* for UNECE, CHBP, (Department of Town Planning and Housing, Nicosia, Cyprus, 1982), pp. 12 - 20.

13 Republic of Cyprus, *Emergency Economic Action Plan* (Second), p. 44.

14 Republic of Cyprus, *Emergency Economic Action Plan* (Second), p. 5.

15 Tornaritis, C., *Cyprus and its Constitutional and Other Legal Problems* (Public Information Office, Nicosia, 1980), 2nd edition.

16 Loizos, P., op. cit. 'A Struggle for Meaning....'

CYPRUS, GREECE AND TURKEY
A Treadmill for Diplomacy

A. J. R. Groom

THE CYPRUS CONFLICT

The Cyprus conflict, like most conflicts, is one that manifests itself at many levels. In some instances the focal point lies in the
intra-community relations as Greek or Turkish Cypriots sort out
their domestic politics and their policies towards 'the other side'
in the context of their internal rivalries. The inter-community
talks, which have continued intermittently over two decades,
reflect both intra-community concerns as well as outside pressures as the parties strive to come to grips with the difficulties of
establishing a new working relationship between the communities
that is satisfactory to both. These talks usually have the active
involvement of the UN in the shape of a mediator and as a
forum. Other fora, each with a different institutional impact on
the respective parties, include the Commonwealth, the Non-
Aligned Movement and the Islamic Conferences. To complicate
matters still further both communities on the island cherish their
relationship with their respective co-ethnic neighbours, Greece and
Turkey, but it is not an easy relationship in either case and squabbles
can ensue. Moreover, Greece and Turkey have had a long period
of animosity even though they share a deep-rooted heritage —
however much they may wish not to acknowledge it. At the international political level there is therefore a triangular relationship
between Greece, Turkey and Cyprus but the interests of other
states are also involved. It is salutary to remember that Britain
acquired Cyprus over a century ago as a *place d'armes* in the context of the Eastern Question. The strategic significance of the
island remains, with the British maintaining sovereign control of

126

two military bases some use of which is also made by US forces. The Eastern Mediterranean, like the Near East generally, is a flash-point in world politics and thus an ever-present concern of the super powers as well as of regional powers.

Given such complexities, which even then only skim the surface, the wonder is that there are ever any grounds for optimism about finding a way out of the Cyprus conflict in the various contexts in which it has to be achieved, and especially the Greco-Turk relationship. Yet there have been several such occasions since 1980 when inter-communal talks were resumed in an atmosphere better than had hitherto existed. At the time the Greek Government was taking a relatively low profile on Cyprus as it was concentrating its efforts on what it saw as its European vocation and the new military government of Turkey was quick to give a green light as far as it was concerned. But the talks eventually lost their momentum and a new chain of events was set in motion which led to the Turkish Republic of Northern Cyprus on November 15th, 1983. When the storm engendered by that event had subsided, the two parties met for 'proximity talks' under the active chairmanship of the UN Secretary-General Mr. Perez de Cuellar — an old Cyprus hand — and with considerable encouragement from Britain, the United States and Turkey. This process culminated in the high-level talks between two community leaders — Mr. Denktash and Mr. Kyprianou, together with the Secretary-General — in January 1985 amid high hopes for a significant breakthrough. This was not to be. A determined effort has been made since to pick up the pieces by inducing the Turkish Cypriots not to take Mr. Kyprianou's 'No' for an answer and to stand by the essence of the offer they made in January 1985 while at the same time reassuring the Greek-Cypriot leader, who had been chastened by his own community, that the considerable movement on the part of the Turkish Cypriots was indeed a gift horse that would bear looking in the mouth.

However, the unfulfilled promises of the last five years suggest that not only must the policies and interests of the parties be examined but also the process whereby they have attempted to settle their differences. Are there any lessons to be learned from this failure of traditional diplomatic methods to achieve a mutually agreed resolution to the conflict? Is there an alternative process, not a competitive framework, for a parallel attempt to move towards a resolution? After all, every conflict ends, even those which are seemingly intractable and interminable, and some-times they end in a resolution satisfactory to all parties in terms of their own interests as they see them, without coercion, and with their eyes fully open — France and Germany are in many ways a case in point.

FROM 1974-1980: COMING TO TERMS WITH REALITY

An important benchmark in the Cyprus conflict occurred in 1974 when, following the *coup d'état* against Archbishop Makarios and the subsequent Turkish military intervention, there was a territorial consolidation of the two communities. Much was changed thereby, but not the definition by the Greek-Cypriot leadership and community of the situation in majority/minority terms. The Cyprus Government maintained its international status and used it to the full to campaign for the withdrawal of mainland Turkish forces. It sought a return to the *status quo* with some guarantees of the minority community's rights and a full restitution of the human rights and material assets of the refugees. The international campaign of the Greek-Cypriot com-munity was pursued with vigour and with success. It was supp-lemented locally by a tight economic blockade of the northern Turkish-held part of the island so that the only effective means of access to the outside world for the Turkish-Cypriot community was through Turkey. The reaction of the Turkish-Cypriot com-munity to this was that which might be expected in such circum-stances. It clung to Turkey whose intervention it believed to be necessary for its physical survival and whose continued military presence seemed to be a guarantee of its future tranquillity and economic well-being. The Cyprus Government and Greek-Cypriot community therefore seemed to enjoy a 'Pyrrhic' victory, since its very success drove the Turkish-Cypriot community closer to Turkey and thus reinforced just the situation which its campaign had been designed to terminate — the presence of Turkish troops on the island. Nevertheless, there was an evident belief on the part of the Cypriot Government and the Greek-Cypriot people that time was on their side. But Turkey and the Turkish Cypriots weathered this diplomatic and economic storm. Moreover, as time passed, *de facto* partition seemed to be the most likely outcome. Transaction patterns had changed due to the movement of population. The Turkish Cypriots had organised an administration and had begun to act internationally and a new generation of Cypriots was coming to maturity that had experienced no contact whatsoever with the other community except through (usually unfavourable) stereotypes.

The stark fact therefore facing both communities was, and remains, that partition is the most likely outcome of the conflict, an outcome which neither community sees as the most desirable one. Cypriots, and especially Greek Cypriots, have tasted the heady delights of independence, but while a *de facto* or truncated state in south Cyprus is viable, it is also vulnerable to many pressures, political and economic, in a volatile part of the world. A united Cyprus would lessen such vulnerability and perhaps be in a position to contribute positively to a diminution of tension in the area as a whole. But time was not working in this direction since the logic of the situation was such that as time passed the Turkish Cypriots would, failing a resolution of the conflict, seek to regularise their situation either by declaring their independence and seeking to accrete international recognition slowly or to move towards full integration with Turkey. They chose the former route, but moved circumspectly and in such a way as never finally to close the door on their preferred solution of a new relationship with the Greek-Cypriot community in a single state. Archbishop Makarios, and after his death his successor Mr. Kyprianou, both seemed implicitly to recognise this: their prime policy was to use such coercive means as they possessed (international opprobrium, an economic blockade of north Cyprus) to nullify the effects of the Turkish military intervention by restoring the essence of the *status quo ante.* However, at the same time, both Greek-Cypriot leaders met with Mr. Denktash, the Turkish-Cypriot leader, and agreed upon two important declarations of principle that even today act as parameters or reference points for inter-community discussions. It was not a case of 'if you can't beat 'em, join 'em' but one of 'beat 'em *and* join 'em'. Coercive diplomacy, even if compelling (and it was not), was, and remains, hardly likely to be a sound basis for the resolution of inter-communal differences and the legitimisation of a new political regime for the island.

By 1980 the Greek-Cypriot community's leaders in both government and opposition seemed to recognise the self-defeating nature of their policy. The Greek-Cypriot definition of the situation appeared to be changing — no longer was the relationship viewed as that of a majority and a minority, but as one in which two communities existed, both of which would have to be satisfied before a viable political entity uniting them could be founded. From the Turkish-Cypriot viewpoint, the new Greek-Cypriot perception recognised reality and fulfilled for them an essential precondition for dialogue. But that dialogue would not be easy since the two communities were asymmetric in many ways. However, there remained, and still remains, a fundamental self-identification of each community as being Cypriots and a recognition of the other community as also being Cypriot in addition to having a Hellenic or a Turkish dimension. This sustained their desire to maintain at least a semblance of unity, or talks about it, in the island. If the Cypriot dimension was essentially functional in character, the national dimension was more sentimental. In a sense, too, there was another change because the Greek-Cypriot community now saw itself to be in a minority status since Cyprus was firmly ensconced, and had been since 1974, in the Turkish geostratigic sphere. This perception is revealed in the fear that many Greek Cypriots have expressed that ultimately, when the time is ripe, Turkey wishes to incorporate the island *in toto* into the mainland Republic. It is not a fear that the Turkish troops will extend the area under their control in the near future, but rather that one day Turkey will use what it considers to be provocative events as a pretext for incorporation in order, they might say, to stabilise a volatile situation. This, after all, was the scenario in 1974. This fear appeared in 1980 to give a new rationale for attempts at *raprochement.*

To the extent that there was a change in Greek-Cypriot perceptions, the Turkish-Cypriot leadership was put in a very unfamiliar situation in the talks which began in 1980. In the past the Greek-Cypriot definition of the situation had, for the most part, been so unacceptable to them, and the policy of diplomatic and economic chastisement had been pursued with such vigour, that the Turkish-Cypriot leadership's prime aim had been to get its presence acknowledged and its views known. The principal exception to this was the set of principles agreed by Archbishop Makarios and Mr. Denktash in February 1977 with their mention of a 'bi-communal federal republic', but despite the subsequent Denktash-Kyprianou meetings little progress was made and Turkish-Cypriot perceptions and outlook remained the same. The

Greek-Cypriot community's leadership was seeking to win, whereas the basic aim of the Turkish Cypriots was not to lose. The situation was thus defined in win or lose terms. However, by 1980 there was a possibility of conceiving a relationship without losers. There was also, for the Turkish-Cypriot leadership, another problem of defining in practical terms what winning actually meant for them in the context of both communities winning. In general terms what sort of relationship would the Turkish-Cypriot leadership deem acceptable, and more specifically, what actual proposals was it prepared to countenance? Did it wish to remain under Turkey's wing as a prelude to eventual absorption? Did it wish to establish a fully-fledged Turkish-Cypriot state on a genuine basis of independence? Did it take the idea of Cyprus as a goal, and if so, how could that goal be defined and a strategy evolved for getting there in concert with the Greek-Cypriot community? For the first time Turkish Cypriots had to think in practical terms about what they would prefer rather·than what they did not want. It also seemed that genuine negotiations were possible and, perhaps, the conflict might be moved towards a resolution without coercion, to the satisfaction of both communities. The way was clear, or might become clear, for both sides to win.

Thus in 1980 there was the prospect of an historic breakthrough on the basis of the acknowledgement of the identity and security concerns of the Turkish-Cypriot community by the Greek Cypriots in return for a Turkish-Cypriot commitment to the idea of Cyprus and an undertaking by the latter to co-operate in a practical manner in a thorough amelioration of the Greek-Cypriot refugee problem. It required the Greek Cypriots to face the fact that they could not win in the sense of restoring the pre-1974 situation, to face that they were most likely to lose everything through partition or even worse and that their best hope for a better future was to accept the reality of near-partition in return for relief of an immediate and pressing human-political-economic problem, that of the refugees, and the prospect of the re-integration of the island in the long run. It was doubtless a bitter pill, nevertheless as Lenin would say, it was a policy of 'one step backwards, two steps forwards', or *reculer pour mieux sauter.*

But the question was, would Turkey agree? Turkey was relevant because any territorial adjustment which might be necessary to ease the refugee problem had implications for the Turkish army in its defence of the Turkish-Cypriot community. The changes that might be required were, from the immediate military point of view, tactical rather than strategic in nature but the changes did imply, in the long run, the withdrawal of the Turkish armed forces. It would require a delicate balance to be found in which the Turkish armed forces would continue for a time to reassure the Turkish-Cypriot community of its security guarantee without thereby enhancing Greek-Cypriot security fears. But once the process of reconciliation was started the difficulty would ease since the Turkish Cypriots would require less reassurance and the Greek Cypriots would therefore have less to fear as Turkish armed forces became irrelevant in terms of the security considerations of both sides. Nevertheless, even in the fearful initial stages there were considerable compensatory advantages in the offing for the Turkish Government. Even if Turkey was never likely to abandon the Turkish-Cypriot community, it would welcome a reduction in the cost of its commitment — economic, military and political. If the Turkish-Cypriot community was satisfied with a new constitution and a set of relationships with the Greek-Cypriot community then it was unlikely that Turkey would demur or object to a territorial adjustment.

At last the two communities seemed to be free to settle their own destiny. But they did not start with *tabula rasa.* They have a conflict of some thirty years' standing marked by uprooting, trauma, intervention, violence, atrocity, destruction and death. After thirty years they needed then, and they need now, help in the form of a supportive framework in which they can themselves build a new relationship — a supportive framework that does not judge them on the merits of their case, nor on their past, nor seek to guide them in one direction or another, but merely to support them in articulating the nature of the problem as they see it and the possibilities for its resolution in a manner which would be mutually acceptable. Each community was aware of the formidable problems that they faced, they were aware equally of the favourable possibilities of 1980. Furthermore, they seemed to be aware that their problem was a shared one (and remains a shared one) and that neither community could win separately — they can only win together.

132

1980-1983: THE LESSONS OF FAILURE

What, then, went wrong? The seemingly promising starts but subsequent setbacks need to be analysed so that past mistakes are not repeated and appropriate lessons are learned. There are many causes of the lack of success, both conceptual and procedural, which in the last five years have fed upon each other. In 1980 and later both communities did not fully realise that time was on neither of their sides which led them to be unwilling to let the serviceable for the present be sufficient for the day. Both felt in the long run that they could in some sense win, perhaps in one fell swoop, rather than starting a process of amelioration towards a situation in which there would be no losers. In particular, the Greek Cypriots maintained their policy of economic and political sanctions despite their evident lack of success and self-defeating nature. Indeed, sanctions rarely work: they seem to be effective only if they are immediate, if they are overwhelming and if they are seemingly implacable — and it is not possible to apply sanctions of this sort in Cyprus. While the many successes and support gained in international fora for the Greek-Cypriot cause raised their morale, nevertheless, they also fortified the determination of the Turkish Cypriots and seems to have had very little instrumental effect. Moreover, the world has become a little bit tired of Cyprus. There is a sentiment growing of 'a plague on both their houses' because no blood is being spilled, and the economic well-being on both sides is considerable in absolute terms even if there are significant relative differences. The world has more pressing problems so that in a sense the Cypriots are on their own.

In the discussions that took place after 1980 too much emphasis was put on the constitution. Constitutions cannot command behaviour, they can only reflect it, otherwise they are empty vessels — propaganda weapons. In general, it is more fruitful to start with behaviour, building local ties of a practical nature, not with great issues of constitutional principle; the discussion of reality is more fructuous than debate over unreal conjectured situations. Moreover, it is salutary to remember that in heterogeneous societies a strong central government would actually intensify the struggle to control it with subsequent disaffection of the losers, as has occurred so tragically in Zimbabwe. It would therefore exacerbate communal conflict rather than mollify it. Cypriots, however, were passionate in debating all aspects of the constitution from the founding myth of the Republic to detailed clauses dealing with eventualities the probable realisation of which was so low as to render them of no consequence. Frequently constitutions require things to be stated in clear terms and 'for ever' — all or nothing or at least an unambiguous compromise — so that bargaining becomes zero sum in nature. This is fatal when the need is for the parties to feel their way, without any great commitment for the long run, so that confidence can be built and there is no fear that a 'concession' now will be rued by generations to come.

Moreover, the constitutional debate led to bargaining. If in a jocular fashion, it could be said that the national sport in the United States is suing people, the national sport in the Near East is haggling. But the future of Cyprus is rather too important for haggling. The best should never in such circumstances be made the enemy of the serviceable, as in fact it was. If one side negotiates to win, and the other one must therefore necessarily lose, then as likely as not both will end up losers, because in this instance the partner does not have to stay in the game. He can leave, as the Turkish Cypriots have done.

Only the parties themselves can bring about agreement and those parties are the two communities, and even they are not monolithic. It is evident that the Turkish Cypriots are heavily dependent on Turkey but they can act independently. We have many examples of the tail wagging the dog in such circumstances, repeatedly so in the case of Israel and the United States. It is also important for each party to remember that the problems of the other party are also its own problems, because if one party cannot resolve its problems then it will remain a problem for the other party. The concerns of all, therefore, must be met if the conflict is to be resolved. It is not a question of simply bargaining to win but one of solving problems, individual problems and mutual problems without which no one can win.[1]

Not all of these comments and strictures apply with equal force to both sides, nor is the list complete. Moreover, it is not a question of sitting in judgment even if account has to be taken of past experience. Perhaps the greatest lesson of 1980 to 1983 was that the process of discussion was such that both sides, at different times, were allowed to slip back into the old familiar ways of confrontation. What was needed was not an arena for debate but a supportive framework to identify and then to solve problems. The inter-communal talks which started in 1980 at the Ledra Palace under the auspices of the United Nations were conducted on a very different basis from this.

1983-1984: ONE FOOT OVER THE RUBICON

When the Ledra Palace talks lost their *élan* the UN Secretary-General endeavoured to give them a new lease of life with an initiative in August 1983. The Secretary-General asked the parties if they would be prepared to negotiate on the basis of three indicators or to suggest other indicators. The first indicator concerned territory and set parameters of between 23% and 30% for the Turkish Cypriots, who make up 18% of the population and presently hold 36.5% of the land. The lower chamber of the legislature, it was suggested, would be elected by proportional representation or split on a 70 to 30 ratio in favour of the Greek Cypriots. Finally, it was proposed that there should be a Greek-Cypriot President and a Turkish-Cypriot Vice-President with a 60 to 40 representation in favour of Greek Cypriots on the federal executive, or a rotation of the two posts with a 70 to 30 ratio on the federal executive in favour of the Greek Cypriots.[2]

These proposals, although made only in the form of tentative soundings, split the Greek-Cypriot community. AKEL (the Communist Party) and Mr. Clerides's Democratic Rally were favourably inclined, the head of the Church in Cyprus, Archbishop Chrysostomos, fulminated against it and Mr. Kyprianou equivocated to such a degree that his Foreign Minister, Mr. Rolandis, who advocated a positive response, resigned. The Turkish Cypriots, who had a reaction ready, felt that with Greek-Cypriot indecision they could hold their hand. In the event another chain of circumstances was in train and Turkish-Cypriot minds were concentrating on that and its implication for them — a declaration of independence.

The Turkish military intervention in Cyprus in 1974 was occasioned by the Greek Colonels' regime in Athens promoting the overthrow of Archbishop Makarios' Government in Nicosia. Makarios survived both personally and politically, but the Colonels' regime was overthrown. Subsequent Greek governments took a low profile on Cyprus until the arrival in power of Mr. Papandreou. Mr. Papandreou's advisers on this issue, of whom several have been of Greek-Cypriot origin, have given an impression of a hankering towards the old policy of *enosis* — albeit an *enosis* by instalments and in disguise.[3] They reflect the strong position of Greeks from the Diaspora in the Greek foreign affairs establishment.

Mr Papandreou decided to play a more active role on the Cyprus issue in part because PASOK has populist roots, and the continuation of Turkish military presence in Cyprus offends Greek national sensibilities, and in part because in other aspects of the Greco-Turkish relationship — such as the Aegean — Greece was in the comfortable position of wishing merely to maintain its position, whereas in Cyprus it wished to change it. When asked to specify the most important element of the Greek-Turkish differences both politicians and officials in Greece usually put Cyprus first before the Aegean. The greater Greek activity was exemplified by a visit to Cyprus by Mr. Papandreou, the first ever by a Greek Prime Minister. To a certain extent Mr. Kyprianou's Government was embarrassed by the greater Greek activity. Both AKEL, the Government's ally, and Mr. Clerides's party were calling for greater and more conciliatory and imaginative efforts to come to terms with the Turkish Cypriots and together they represent a majority of Greek-Cypriot voters. Mr. Kyprianou, however, was being pressured to take a harder line by the Greek Government and, in particular, to internationalise the issue — a move which was anathema to the Turkish Cypriots since in every international forum they have an inferior status and only in the Ledra Palace framework of intercommunal talks do they have equal status — a status which for them is fundamental to their political position. The cross pressures on Mr. Kyprianou were considerable and were reflected in the stormy relationships between the Kyprianou and Papandreou Governments.

Possibly as a result of the urging of the Greek Government, the Cyprus Government decided in 1983 to reactivate the Cyprus question in the UN General Assembly. Moreover, it did so in such a way that the Turkish Cypriots felt made it more difficult for them to participate effectively in the debate. The Turkish Cypriots saw this as a major breach of the understanding, that while the intercommunal talks were continuing, the Cyprus Government would make no use of its favourable position in international fora to seek international support for its cause. However, the Greek Cypriots felt that the Turkish Cypriots were not taking the intercommunal talks seriously and that there had been no significant progress for some time so that they suspected that the

136

Turkish Cypriots were merely dragging their feet in the talks simply to deprive the Greek Cypriots of a valuable asset, namely, their international legitimacy as the Republic of Cyprus.

The Turkish Cypriots, nevertheless, sent a high level delegation to New York where both Cypriot delegations started to meet together informally. This fructuous beginning however came to an abrupt halt because, according to the Turkish Cypriots, after two days contact was broken off by the Greek Cypriots at the instigation of the Greek Government and the public polemics were resumed. But this episode had a considerable impact on the Turkish Cypriots because it was a contributing factor to their belief that agreement was not possible and that they must look to the obvious alternative of independence.

After the Turkish-Cypriot declaration of the Turkish Republic of Northern Cyprus on November 15, 1983 the Greek Cypriots again managed to get a considerable degree of international support. The Security Council deplored, by thirteen to one against (Pakistan) with one abstention (Jordan), 'the declaration of the Turkish Cypriot authorities of the purported secession of part of the Republic of Cyprus' which it considered to be 'legally invalid' and called for its withdrawal.[4] Other organisations followed suit with verbal condemnation but there was little by way of action. Practically all states have a vested interest in condemning secession, which they did on this occasion with ritualistic fervour, but few believed in the efficacy of sanctions against either Turkey or the new state. Such sanctions had been tried in the aftermath of 1974 Turkish military intervention in Cyprus and had proved to be dysfunctional. Yet this failed policy was the very one chosen again by the Cyprus Government.

Mr. Kyprianou made frequent visits to Athens, London, New York and Washington in an effort to get the United States to put very strong pressure on Turkey, and through Turkey on the Turkish Cypriots, to withdraw their declaration. He also refused to talk to the Turkish Cypriots on a direct basis and Greece declined Britain's offer of a meeting of the guarantor powers to discuss developments in the island. Although the Greek Cypriots secured condemnations of the Turkish-Cypriot action, and the subsequent Turkish recognition of it, there was little else. Moreover, it is difficult to see what might have constituted effective sanctions especially when the Turkish-Cypriot declaration was so exquisitely timed — in the dying days of the old Turkish military

137

regime so that the new civilian regime had 'clean hands' on the issue and could claim innocence. But if the USA and the UK could not, or would not, move effectively in the direction desired by the Greek Cypriots and Athens, what alternative did Athens and Nicosia have?

There were strong indications in early 1984 that if the United States could not be persuaded to exert compelling pressure against Turkey then Nicosia and Athens might contemplate engineering a crisis on the island of such a dimension as to 'force' the United States to intervene. This the US would do because of the NATO connection and the risk of war between Greece and Turkey. However, this scenario did not take into account that any US reaction could affect adversely both Greece and Turkey and, indeed, that it might be stronger on Greece than Turkey, given the normal predilection of the United States for Turkey and the particular predilection of President Reagan for democracy with a military tinge over socialism with a nationalist or 'communist' tinge.

Turkey has made it clear that it will not tolerate any threat to the place of Cyprus in its geostrategic sphere of influence. At the moment Turkey has a considerable military force on the island and control of the air. It is determined that it will not allow itself to be 'encircled' by Greece from Thrace to Cyprus. Thus the issue of Greek troops on the island is a touchstone for Turkey. In 1984 Turkey suggested that there might be anything up to 5,000 mainland Greek forces on the island. *The Military Balance 1984 - 85*[5] suggests that 1,750 Greek forces and 17,000 Turkish forces are based on Cyprus with Greek-Cypriot and Turkish-Cypriot forces 10,000 and 4,500 strong respectively. There was discussion between Athens and Nicosia that 'a Greek division' in addition should be sent to Cyprus on the grounds that the Turks are unwilling to withdraw their forces and therefore the Greeks have the right to 'balance' them. Wiser counsels however prevailed over this perilous step for it seems likely that Turkey would react to any such move by neutralising the island. This would not be too difficult militarily as they are already well-placed to seize Larnaca airport and a sea, air and land operation to gain control of the new airport at Paphos would effectively seal off the island without the Turks having to occupy large Greek-Cypriot centres of population. But such a possibility, while perhaps serving as a deterrent to military adventures initiated in Athens or by Greek Cypriots, would bring an adverse international reaction against Turkey and the knowledge of its feasibility gives an edge to Greek-Cypriot fears about their security at the best of times. Fortunately the potential crisis of the 'Greek division' did not materialise.

But what in the meantime of the Turkish Cypriots? If the Greeks and Greek Cypriots had put one foot over the Rubicon with talk of 'a Greek division' and thoughts of escalation as a means of forcing the issue, the Turkish Cypriots had even more dramatically straddled that river with their declaration of independence. This declaration was striking in its timidity — as though they were tip-toeing out of the door leaving it carefully ajar so that they could quickly and easily come back in again. The declaration reads almost like a classic case of *reculer pour mieux sauter* in the direction of a pan-Cypriot polity. The Turkish-Cypriot community had, in the months before independence, clearly signalled its intentions. Mr. Denktash was reported in the *Turkish News* of July 1983 as saying 'I have always maintained that going to Federation with the Greek Cypriots passes through the way of establishing our own State first, because the Greek Cypriots will not accept us as their equals.' Indeed, the constant theme of Turkish-Cypriot apologists was that an independent state was necessary to assert their status as co-founders of a future federal republic and to ensure that the sovereignty of the republic would be derived from the existing two states joining together as equals to form the future federal republic. Thus, for the Turkish Cypriots, independence solved their identity problem and assured a future basis for negotiation. Moreover, they did not consider that they had seceded but had been 'ousted from the 1960 bi-national republic' and had 'had no alternative but to establish their own State ... step by step since 1963.[6]

The diplomatic response of the Greek Cypriots to the Turkish-Cypriot declaration was to amass resolutions in diplomatic fora, to attempt to galvanise the United States into putting pressure on Turkey and to discuss a 'package deal' with the US and the UN Secretary-General among others. Mr. Denktash took a different route. First of all he protected his rear by getting unanimous support in the Turkish-Cypriot Parliament, despite the strength of the opposition parties.

Early in 1984 Mr. Denktash made a number of suggestions for consideration by the Greek Cypriots, both in public and through the good offices of the United Nations. These concerned Varosha, the opening of Nicosia International Airport, the reactivation of the Committee of Missing Persons and a host of other suggestions in a variety of functional domains.[7] Some of these proposals were old hat, and some reflected initial bargaining positions, but there was also much that was new and constructive and, therefore, not *per se* worthy of instant dismissal. At the same time Mr. Denktash blew hot and cold on the international status of the new state. Only one recognition has so far occurred, that of Turkey, although there has been speculation about the intentions of Bangladesh, Malaysia and Pakistan to mention some states. Mr Denktash has not seemed to pursue recognition over-actively nor did he initially take all the domestic provisions that he might have done to bolster up his international legitimacy thus giving the impression that the new statehood was as reluctant an acquisition as it was verbally claimed to be. Mr. Denktash continued to express his willingness to talk to Mr. Kyprianou on a person-to-person basis as community representatives with no recognition implied. For Mr. Kyprianou, however, there could be 'no talks before withdrawal of independence.' It thus appeared that the *impasse* in Cyprus had become a solution. The attempts at movement from 1980 until 1983 had failed and the logic of the situation prevailed as the Turkish Cypriots declared their independence. Dramatic change, or attempts to achieve it, could court disaster whereas everyone could survive without too much discomfort in the situation at the end of 1983 under the prevailing arrangements. Moreover, there were conveniences to be had if a friendly divorce could be arranged which could become the tentative beginnings of a reconciliation. Basically the Turkish Cypriots had 'won', but at a price: they were isolated and beholden to Turkey. However, they were likely, slowly, to accrete international legitimacy in the form of recognition. But there was another way if the Greek Cypriots were prepared not to lose. Their situation in early 1984 put them always at the risk of having to bear the consequences of the broader Greco-Turk antipathies. They risked, therefore, losing as tragically as in 1974 unless they were prepared to acknowledge the *status quo* as a starting point from which to build a reconciliation, which both parties desire and which is so patently in their separate and mutual interests, in the form of the mutual conveniences of cohabitation on the island. Neither party, when it came to it, was prepared to cross the Rubicon and once again the UN Secretary-General sought to bring the parties together.

1984-1985: TO THE 'HIGH-LEVEL' MEETING

The UN Secretary-General has had for many years a 'mission of good offices' conferred upon him regarding Cyprus.[8] In June 1984 Mr. Perez de Cuellar and his colleagues rightly judged the moment propitious to arrange 'proximity talks' with and between the two Cypriot parties (thereby circumventing the Greek-Cypriot refusal to talk directly with Turkish Cypriots). The talks progressed well and at the end of the third round the Secretary-General was able to inform the Security Council on December 12, 1984, that he expected the interlocutors at the 'high-level' meeting arranged for January 17, 1985, would 'conclude an agreement containing the necessary elements for a comprehensive solution to the problem, aimed at establishing a Federal Republic of Cyprus'.[9] UN diplomacy had been strongly backed by the United States and Britain. President Reagan had written to President Evren in November in an effort to convince Turkey and the Turkish Cypriots that they could relax their demands, which they did. An agreement on Cyprus, it was pointed out, would make it easier to overcome the difficulties in the US Congress in regard to policy towards Turkey. Moreover, an agreement would avert the danger for Turkish Cypriots that, as a result of their declaration of independence, they would be denied the benefits of aid from and economic access to the European Communities as Cypriots. With strong Turkish backing Mr. Denktash made such substantial concessions that Mr. Perez de Cuellar felt warranted in being optimistic in his report to the Security Council and that Mr. Papandreou was led to declare on January 2, 1985 that the Turkish Cypriots had 'undoubtedly made significant steps in the direction of a viable and just settlement of the Cyprus problem'.[10] Indeed, Mr. Papandreou appears to have encouraged the Greek Cypriots to be conciliatory. Prior to the final sessions of the proximity talks, after the Turkish-Cypriot side had given their full agreement to the Secretary-General's document Mr. Kyprianou consulted his own and the Greek Government and then gave the green light to the Secretary-General. Mr. Kyprianou is reported to have commented 'everything is fine; our side has obtained the best possible conditions.'[11]

What, after the proximity talks, was the Secretary-General proposing to which he thought the parties had agreed and on which they could set the seal in 'an hour' when the 'high-level' meeting convened in January? It is generally said that the notion of an independent, non-aligned, bi-communal and bi-zonal federal republic was reaffirmed. The powers of the federal government were defined and the Upper House would have equal Greek-Cypriot and Turkish representation while the Lower House and the Executive would have a ratio of seven (Greek-Cypriot) to three (Turkish-Cypriot). The Presidency would not rotate between the two communities as had at one time been proposed, but the Foreign Minister would be a Turkish Cypriot. Constitutional guarantees would be given to both communities and an equal political status in the federal government. Of great significance was the Turkish-Cypriot agreement to a territorial adjustment to 29% (less than the magical 30% and only 1% more than the 28% for which Archbishop Makarios had been willing to settle). It was suggested that the Turkish Cypriots would relinquish control of large areas around Morphou, Varosha and a substantial zone between Famagusta and Nicosia. Moreover, foreign armed forces would be withdrawn from the island and international guarantees made. A transitional government would be established and funds set up to facilitate economic equilibrium between the two parts of the island and the resettlement of displaced persons. Nicosia airport would be re-opened to all and the UN would administer certain territories on an interim basis. The details would be settled in working groups. Nothing like this had been seen before and it justified the Secretary-General's jubilant tone to the Security Council.[12]

When the 'high-level' meeting convened on January 17, 1985 in New York it was, for the Secretary-General and Mr. Denktash, a matter of signing the Secretary-General's document and then getting on with the establishment and business of the working groups. Mr. Denktash accepted the document *in toto* as an 'integrated whole'.[13] Mr. Kyprianou caused a sensation and dismay by disagreeing. As the Secretary-General put it,

'Both sides started from the above-mentioned documentation. The Turkish-Cypriot side stated to the Secretary-General that 'it fully accepts the draft agreement'. The Greek-Cypriot side stated to the Secretary-General that 'in conformity with its clear understanding it accepts the documentation presented by the Secretary-General as a basis for negotiations in accordance with the integrated whole approach aiming at a comprehensive and overall solution to the Cyprus problem, and that it came to the high-level meeting in absolute good faith with the view to having constructive and meaningful negotiations.'

Once again the best hopes and efforts of the international community had not proved sufficient to bring the Cypriots fructuously together. It was therefore, time once again to reflect upon tactics and processes.

TACTICS AND PROCESSES

Over the years the predominant aim has been for a political reconciliation in the form of a general settlement. The tactics have been to elaborate a set of principles on the basis of which a package deal could be based. This approach encourages haggling because the stakes are large, so that each issue has to be fought over in the context of the whole rather than being considered on its merits. Immobility and obduracy frequently result from this: both parties are frightened to make concessions since they may undermine hard won principles or create an unfavourable precedent. This is the antithesis of reconciliation: if haggling means winning, in an albeit limited zero sum context, it does not encourage that element of vision, and a willingness to sacrifice short term point scoring for a longer term mutually beneficial situation, which is characteristic of reconciliation. The approach also encourages pretentious and academic debate over principles — particularly constitutional principles. In short, the approach has been typical of traditional diplomatic negotiation and bargaining techniques which aim at a settlement based on a compromise which reflects the prevailing balance of coercive forces of all kinds, be they military, economic sanctions or whatever. When the balance of forces changes, so will the settlement. Sometimes, however, a settlement grows into a genuine self-sustaining resolution in which behavioural patterns are legitimised and therefore no longer dependent on the balance of forces. The parties are content with their relationships, which they see as beneficial and which have been freely arrived at on a basis of their intrinsic merits and not as a result of a coercive compromise. Such can be the only basis for an end to the conflict in Cyprus, as the coercively imposed settlement of 1960 illustrates. But are there ways of facilitating the moves from settlement to resolution? Can the formal

143

and traditional negotiating track be supplemented by a second facilitating track?

Such facilitating processes have become a commonplace in industrial relations and in community relations. They are also a feature of various forms of social work. Moreover, they have been tried, with varying degrees of success, in international and inter-communal conflicts at a time when the parties are in an actual state of armed hostilities.[14] This approach can no more claim to be a panacea than traditional approaches, but it does constitute a viable and sometimes fructuous alternative, or indeed supplement, to traditional approaches. Unlike the traditional approach it does not start from the parties and their capabilities for coercive diplomacy, but from the problem. It seeks not compromise nor settlement, but resolution. Parties do not negotiate a compromise but rather they explore their relationship in all its aspects, in a supportive framework supplied by a third party. This third party is not there to provide solutions, or to make judgments, but to facilitate processes and provide information of both a factual and a theoretical nature. Such exercises are usually of a low political cost because they are frequently private and engage no one politically since the individuals participating, although authoritative in their ability to express the views of their party, speak only in their own name. Such processes require all the relevant parties to be present — no matter how deviant or murderous they may seem to some — if they are necessary for a consensus to emerge on which a resolution can be based. Moreover, if there is to be such a consensus then the vital interests of all, as individually they see them, must be incorporated. It is indeed a tall order, but not an impossible one.

There is a need for such a second track insofar as Cyprus is concerned. Repeatedly a promising political initiative has run into sands. While, ultimately, a formal set of political arrangements is necessary, the processes by which they are achieved might well involve the use of, and interaction between, both tracks. Groups from all walks of life from both parties can meet with a supportive third party. For example, members of the two new parliaments could meet together in an academic framework. Educationalists might meet to discuss the creation of a regional university of international standing which is sorely lacking both on the island, which has a severe brain drain, and in the region. Experts in other areas, such as health or those concerned with the jointly used infrastructure of electricity, water and sewerage, might also begin to make contact and move towards building up a network of functionally based, mutually acceptable and mutually beneficial ties. Those concerned with the preservation of the heritage of Cyprus might likewise have much to benefit from such an exchange. Such meetings will not always generate sweetness and light, but a supportive third-party presence could have an enhancing function when the potential for progress emerges and a damage-limitation function in less happy cases.

If this multi-track, multi-dimensional approach is tried (and it had a significant role in Franco-German reconciliation in Europe), and proves successful, or at least ameliorative, difficulties do not end there, for the Cyprus conflict is embedded in other conflictual relationships, not least that between Greece and Turkey, to which such processes can also be applied. Moreover, if the Cyprus conflict is to be resolved so, too, must that between Greece and Turkey since they are related in so many ways. A solution in Cyprus would always be vulnerable to sabotage if Greece and Turkey were at odds. It is thus to relations between Greece and Turkey that attention must now be given and especially the evolution of the Aegean question and domestic politics in both countries. Indeed, it goes beyond that to the very sense of their own identity that Greek and Turkish elites and masses have of themselves and their interpretation of the way that they think that others see them.

GREECE, TURKEY AND THE AEGEAN

Apart from Cyprus the biggest bone of contention between Greece and Turkey is the cluster of questions that fall under the rubric of the Aegean.[15] Significantly, the Greeks lead on Cyprus and the Turks on the Aegean since they are both content with the *status quo* on the other question. The issues in the Aegean comprise six elements: territorial waters, air space, the continental shelf, flight information regions (FIR), demilitarisation and the 'Army of the Aegean'. These issues are immensely complex but can be simplified crudely for the sake of exposition. Greece operates a six-mile limit for territorial waters, but insists on the right to extend this to twelve miles — a right hotly disputed by Turkey to the extent that it states it would consider any such Greek extension as a *casus belli.* Insofar as air space is concerned, the Greeks have, since 1931, claimed ten miles of national air space, a claim disputed by Turkey which reserves the right to fly in the space between six and ten miles and on occasion exerts that right with military aircraft. The continental shelf, the Greeks argue, is attached to each island in the Aegean with an attendant economic zone, and they deny any Turkish rights in areas to the west of the Greek islands since this would lead to enclavement with a consequent threat to sovereignty. For the Turks, on the other hand, the Aegean is a special area which, they suggest, should be delimited on an equitable basis. Equity and national security are the grounds upon which Turkey argues that the FIR and military command boundaries should be moved westwards, while Greece supports the *status quo*. The islands concerned with demilitarisation are Lemnos and Samothrace, Lesbos, Chios, Samos and Ikaria, and the Dodecanese, and different arguments apply to each of these three groups. However, the gist is the same with Turkey accusing Greece of violation of legal obligations in not respecting the demilitarisation of the islands and the Greeks either denying the validity of such obligations or the fact of violation.

Of current interest is the question of Lemnos. Lemnos is in a strategic location in the northern Aegean, not just in terms of the Aegean but also for the Mediterranean as a whole, since it commands the seaways into the Dardanelles. The demilitarisation of the island was agreed upon in the Lausanne Convention of 1923 but at some point its militarisation took place — legally according to the Greeks because of the Montreux Convention of 1936, a fact recognised politically, they suggest, by the Turkish Prime Minister of the day in a speech. Turkey does not accept the militarisation, which became significant after the Turkish intervention in Cyprus in 1974, nor agree with the legal interpretation. Mr. Papandreou insists that Greek forces on the island, and the island itself, should be included in NATO exercises thus gaining an implicit alliance acknowledgement of the Greek case. This Turkey cannot countenance and so NATO is unable to hold exercises in the Aegean in order to avoid offending either of its members. The Turks suspect that NATO would prefer Lemnos to be militarised despite the absence of exercises. Such is the stuff of Greco-Turk relations and the impact of Cyprus therein.

A related issue is the Turkish 'Army of the Aegean' formed at the same time as the increased militarisation of the Greek Aegean islands. This army is based in the Izmir area and about the size of which there are considerable differences of opinion. It is a 'chicken and egg' situation in which the Turks point to the need for such a force due to Greek militarisation of the islands and the Greeks talk of the need for militarisation because of the Aegean Army. A recent North Atlantic Assembly report suggests that Greek fears may be the result of a somewhat over-heated imagination. The Army of the Aegean supposedly takes its name from the Aegean provinces of Turkey, not so much from the sea itself with its implications for the Greek sovereignty of the islands. It is situated in the Izmir area because the climate favours its role as a year-round training army. The army contains no combat-ready units nor is Izmir a naval base. The presence of a large number of landing craft there is a canard.[16] The sovereignty of Greece in the Aegean is not challenged by Turkey, although the latter argues that Greek sovereignty is not absolute since it is limited by international agreements, but the essence of the situation is that Greece fears its effective exercise of sovereignty could be circumscribed significantly by Turkish claims for equity, and it feels, therefore, that its interests are best served by their vigorous defence in legal terms rather than by an arrangement of mutual equity which would be dependent on a mutual understanding which the Greek Government does not feel to be likely in the present situation.

In terms of acts Greece has not, for the most part, been provocative and has been content to hold what it has and to justify its position in legal terms. This is understandable since it is basically content with the *status quo,* and although its legal position is not impregnable on all points, it is a good first line of defence for any *status quo* Power. However, sometimes there can be an element of paranoia in some Greek reactions to the Turkish 'threat' in that there are those who see a Turkish master plan for the encirclement of Greece. Turkish tactics are salami tactics, it is alleged: first Alexandretta, then Cyprus and next the Aegean as part of the Turkish security sphere — its 'vital space'.[17] Other less lurid views of officials stress the legal position of Greece and the political attempt by Turkey to change the *status quo* either because of domestic problems in Turkey, the promise of 'black gold' or simply to stake a general claim that might be useful in the future. No Greek analyst seems prepared to admit that Turkey might have a case, or something to fear. This is part of the Greek obsessive antipathy or addiction for Turkey, an obsession that is not reciprocated, although Turkish policy and reactions are not without antipathy. The most liberal view among Greek politicians and officials is that Turkey does respond to a carrot but not to a stick. In this view the Aegean questions can be dealt with bilaterally in such a way that a diplomatic arrangement could be made on some issues, it is possible to live with some issues, and others could be set aside. The feeling in this camp is that the Turks see the islands as Greek but, nevertheless, the Turks feel that they have some rights over them. Thus the question is a psychological one in that the Turks feel uneasy, unnecessarily so it is claimed, that they may be imprisoned in the Aegean or even attacked, and this is translated into a demand for a degree of influence in the area. The need, therefore, is for Greece to provide psychological reassurance to Turkey that it has nothing to fear. This view is, of course, a far cry from that which sees a relentless Turkish pressure for domination. However, for the moment the situation in the Aegean is calm with few 'scares'.

Turkey does not appear to be as mesmerised by Greece as Greece is by Turkey. Indeed, for Turkey economic questions now assume a greater prominence that the relationship with Greece. However, Turkey does view the cluster of issues in the Aegean as serious ones. The belief is that a bi-lateral dialogue is necessary, but the issues are not irreconcilable provided the approach is clear-headed. For the Turkish Government the basic parameter is the Treaty of Lausanne, and it would not wish to change this even though many aspects of the Treaty are not seen to be in Turkey's favour. On the practical issues Turkish arguments are a mixture of legal arguments, political arguments and appeals on a basis of equity. At worst, if Turkey feels that it will be boxed in then there will be war, and the Soviet Union and other Black Sea states share a common interest with Turkey over any Greek extension of territorial waters beyond six miles. At best the Aegean could become an area of fruitful co-operation between Greece and Turkey to their mutual benefit after the manner of France, Germany and the European Coal and Steel Community. The Turks have proposed a similar functional approach but for the moment, at least, the Papandreou Government is standing pat on the issue of sovereignty since it feels that any movement is likely to be to its detriment. For example, Mr. Ozal, the Turkish Prime Minister, has offered several olive branches such as abolishing visas for Greeks visiting Turkey, which resulted in a Greek tourist 'invasion' of Istanbul, and suggested the supply of water and electricity from the mainland to the Greek islands.[18] In March he stated that 'we are ready to participate in [comprehensive] negotiations anywhere, any time, and at any level they [the Greeks] like.[19] The offer was rejected.[20]

The apprehension of both sides is understandable but their largely coolheaded reactions for the present may not always be the case and this cannot ultimately be to the interest of either side. If Turkey has anything less than an insatiable appetite then, if Turkey has fears, Greece will have problems. Likewise if Greece has fears then it will be to Turkey's discomfort. What is needed, once again, as in Cyprus, is a means of exploring the problem in a non-negotiating, non-coercive, problem-solving framework so that there are not winners and losers, but only winners. The potentiality for such an outcome is evident but the process for reaching it has not yet been broached.

THE REMAINING AGENDA ITEMS

Cyprus and the Aegean are central areas of contention between Greece and Turkey, but they do not exhaust the list. There is, in addition, the question of minorities and especially that in Western Thrace. The upheaval caused by the large scale movement of population after the First World War eventually had an overall beneficial effect after much suffering but there still remained some minorities which at the present time number some 5,000 Greek Orthodox in Istanbul, who are not in an ideal situation, and about 130,000 in the Turkish or Moslem minority in Thrace. The Greeks contest the degree to which the latter are necessarily ethnic Turks and the minority also has links with the Turkish minority in Bulgaria who are at present the victims of an attempt at their enforced Bulgarisation. The Greeks did not take retaliatory action against the minority in Thrace when a large number of Greeks were summarily expelled from Istanbul in the 1960s, nor did they retaliate against them in 1974 after the Turkish military intervention in Cyprus. Nevertheless, the minority in Greece, if not intolerably ill-treated, like that in Istanbul, suffers from some organised state discrimination against it and is significantly circumscribed in its activities. The question remains a festering sore, which in a healthy (diplomatic) climate could heal, but if there is a general deterioration in the Greco-Turk body politic, it could equally lead to amputation. For the moment it is not a burning issue.

In the Balkans Greco-Turk relations are happier. It is Greece that has taken the lead and, although Turkey had not responded with any notable enthusiasm, it has not been obstructionist. After the brief flurry of interest aroused by the short-lived Balkan Pact of 1954 a more sustained Balkan policy was followed by post-Colonels governments in Athens. Mr. Karamanlis did not fare particularly well, but he prepared the ground. Mr. Papandreou's policy is to mend fences with Greece's neighbours, especially Bulgaria and Albania, and more generally to dissolve the line of confrontation — NATO-WTO-Non-aligned — in the area and to help establish a Balkan *détente*. This has involved official visits, functional agreements and conferences on topics such as a Balkan nuclear-free zone. The idea of a nuclear-free zone is on the cards, in the Greek view, because nuclear weapons in both Greece and Turkey and elsewhere in the Balkans are obsolescent if not obsolete. The Greek Government has also exhibited concern at the deployment of US Cruise and Pershing missiles in Europe, in practice, if not so much in principle. In taking an initiative on a Balkan nuclear-free zone the Greek Government claims to be aware of the difficulties, but feels that the game is worth the candle.

Turkey has not had such a vigorous Balkans policy but, nevertheless, there have been a number of visits of a political or economic nature and contact generally is increasing. Turkey has responded cautiously but not negatively to Greek initiatives for Balkan co-operation although it does not always demonstrate the same priorities as the Greeks. For example, like some other NATO countries, which generally welcome these cross-alliance ties, Turkey feels that the nuclear-free zone is likely to be a non-starter, therefore should be at the bottom of the agenda and that co-operation should begin with those areas where there might be possibilities of fruitful, frequently functional, activity. But this is a central area of concern for neither Greece nor Turkey: it is likely to be a victim of their antagonisms but flourish in a permissive climate. Balkan co-operation can only be successful and supportive if there is progress elsewhere.

Whereas in the Balkans co-operation is in part a function of Greco-Turk relations, they are much more clearly separate 'decoupled' actors in the Arab world. Both Greece and Turkey have identity problems when dealing with the Arab world to which they both have a ready access in terms of their Levantine or Near Eastern heritage. Despite the splendour of some of this heritage they have turned their backs on it in promoting their European vocation. Mr. Karamanlis, like Ataturk before him, has tried to make his countrymen 'Europeans' — which is something that they have to become since they are not so 'naturally'. In so doing there has been a tendency to deny their very self as Levantines with predictable difficulties in self-identification, loss of heritage and loss of opportunities. Turkey has come to terms with this more readily than Greece but there is little acknowledgement of the positive side of the shared Ottoman heritage with the Arab Near East by either side. An officially rigorously secular Turkey, but one in which Islam plays a great role in the life of the masses, can not flaunt its Islamic character as an attraction to its neighbours for it would be a denial of Ataturk and a green flag to fundamentalists in Turkey itself.

Turkey began to make moves to get itself accepted in the Near and Middle East as an indigenous state in the 1960s. The task has not been easy given the Ataturk heritage and membership of NATO and formerly of CENTO and the like. However, the need for markets, oil supplies and development funds has pushed Turkey in this direction. In particular Syria, Iraq and Libya are important as neighbours and partners and they have been specially cultivated in the 1980s for both political and economic reasons. Libya is a particularly important trading partner and recipient of Turkish guest-workers, while, with Iraq, Turkey has undertaken military operations on Iraqi territory against the Kurds. Iraq is Turkey's largest trading partner and Iran its third ranking trading partner which helps to explain why Turkey has been neutral in the Iran-Iraq war and, indeed, has managed to maintain good relations with both belligerents. These good relations could become a valuable asset in attempting to resolve that costly conflict.

Greece has been somewhat less successful in cultivating its ties with the Arab world. Although Greece has the capacity, like Turkey, to be an invaluable bridge between Europe and the Near and the Middle East, and Mr. Papandreou recognises this, nevertheless the Greeks feel a certain degree of disillusion in their relationship. The economic link with Libya, although substantial, has gone sour, the economic ties with Saudi Arabia have not always fulfilled Greek hopes and the strong support of Mr. Arafat and the PLO has not always paid dividends, whatever its intrinsic merits. The problem for Greece, as for Turkey, is that to be a bridge between the Arabs and Europe requires a self-identity as such, and that it be more than an allusion to geographical propinquity. The real bridge, of which Greece and Turkey historically, culturally and in many other ways form part, is the Levant or Near East. That there is need for such a link is evident as is the capacity of Greece and Turkey to fill it. But they must make it their principal role to which they are whole-heartedly committed and that raises the broad issue of Greek and Turkish self-iden tification.

Both Greece and Turkey have, in the past, exhibited claims, or at least aspirations, to be 'European' and in all probability the notion signifies 'West European'. Yet they share a common heritage — the Ottoman-Levantine heritage of the Near East — which still seems to the casual outsider to impregnate their social, economic and political fibre along with that of other countries in the area including Cyprus, Syria, Jordan, Palestine and Egypt. It is, however, a heritage that neither, for their different reasons, wishes to acknowledge. Therein lies a problem, for neither state is at peace with itself because, to deny a part of one's own past which lives on in the present, is to deny one's own very identity. Yet their Ottoman-Levantine heritage could be the very stuff of the bridging role between Europe and the Arab world which they both aspire to play. Moreover, they could play that role so much more effectively if they did it together to the benefit of all, and not least themselves.

President Karamanlis, when he was Prime Minister, tried to make the Greeks into fully-fledged Europeans and this reflects a Greek lack of self-confidence. Greece had been subject to centuries of humiliation which tends to make Greeks particularly sensitive to any slight. They resent the application of the term 'Byzantine' in a derogatory sense to the diplomacy of Mr. Papandreou, and they attach great significance to any denigrating comment regarding Greece's identity and its sense of historical and linguistic continuity with the ancient Greeks. An issue such as the return of the Elgin marbles is of considerable significance to them. They are stung by the comment that whatever independence they have got came as much from the efforts of others as from themselves.

Mr. Papandreou's diplomacy reflects some of these tendencies. He has given Greeks a sense of pride and of purpose. They have a feeling of independence and his initiatives have struck a deep national chord not necessarily because of their intrinsic merits, which may not always appear to take fully into cognisance their long term implications, but because they are clearly independent Greek initiatives. Popular sovereignty and social liberation depend, for Mr. Papandreou, on national independence. Thus, a distancing from the Super Powers and a movement towards non-alignment in a Mediterranean context corresponds to Greece's search for its identity. It could also serve a useful purpose for others in a Euro-Arab bridging role and wider still.[21] But the high level of animosity towards and obsession with Turkey is a hindrance to this goal. In their heart of hearts Greeks feel superior to Turks and they very much resent the fact that they are, generally speaking, weaker and likely to become more so. Turks, on the other hand, while not so obsessed by a small country do feel that the Greeks want in some sense to diminish them.

In the context of Europe, Turkey was always at a disadvantage when compared with Greece because of Greece's Christianity. Nevertheless, Ataturk and his successors have made it a point of honour to lead Turkey in Europe's direction and, like the Greeks, to renounce their Ottoman and Levantine past. As Mr. Papandreou is questioning this policy so are many young Turks who likewise see themselves on the 'Periphery' of the 'Centre' with more of the problems and interests of the third world than of Europe. Moreover, another group, strongly influenced by the Islamic revival, takes succour from the Iranian revolution and sees Turkey's role more in the Islamic World. Western ties — economically with the EC and militarily with NATO — are thus questioned, or at least thought to be irksome. Modern Turkey's initial foreign policy was, after all, a sturdy independence. There is little wonder then that both Greece and Turkey have been 'touchy' in their relationships with the EC and NATO, where they are treated as junior partners who are a nuisance, particularly when they have the example of non-alignment from Yugoslavia and Sweden and the siren call of their old stamping ground in the Near East and beyond.

One of the great barriers to such an assertion of independence and identity is their animosity. Not only does it cause them to deny their past, and thus to inhibit their future, it also rivets them into NATO as they seek to get the upper hand in their arms race. Furthermore, their rivalry is projected into European organisations such as the EC and the Council of Europe as each seeks to do the other down. Their future well-being as a bridge is thus not credible or possible, and catastrophe is a possible outcome. Reconciliation is, therefore, a prime necessity, and this is recognised by both of them. If France and Germany can achieve it then it is conceivable; but how can it be made practical?

Present methods do not appear to be very promising. Bilateral negotiations of any parties to a serious conflict frequently result in deadlock as each rehearses its version of history with its betrayals, atrocities and the like, and points to the ethical validity, in legal and moral terms of its case when compared with that of its adversary. Offers of reconciliation made by one and spurned by the other are cited and the parties quickly become locked into unbending and hostile stereotypes of the other from which a 'worst case' analysis emerges. Attempts by third parties, such as NATO, to mediate, are resented since they frequently involve a judgment on the merits of the case by the mediator, an attempt to suggest the content of a settlement of the issue based on compromise and in the background, a hint of institutional coercion. Recourse to law or compulsory arbitration is judgmental and takes the outcome out of the hand of the parties as well as often favouring the *status quo*. Conciliation, however, has some positive advantages in that it is not a judgment, it does not involve coercion, the parties can participate fully and the conciliator does not see his role necessarily as that of suggesting outcomes on a basis of compromise. Problem-solving as a technique has grown out of conciliation: the role of the third party is to be supportive of all the parties in the search for a resolution of the conflict in which no one is the loser. It is a technique which encourages the parties to bring all their values into play so that the totality of their values is maximised in terms of minimising opportunity costs in the context of the interests of others. But it is more than just bringing a greater element of rationality into decision-making by eliminating self-defeating strategies, it also seeks to bring out the submerged issues such as, in the Greek and Turkish cases, a feeling of lack of participation and an identity crisis. But at this level of basic values there need be no competition. A sense of identity and participation by one does not necessarily imply a denial of it to another. Moreover, within the context of a mutual satisfaction of these basic needs for all, problems such as the Aegean or Cyprus then assume a different aspect making it easier to find legitimised ways of dealing with the scarce resources and limited roles which do exist. The need is to solve problems rather than to win fights. Problem-solving is not a panacea, but it has had some successes in difficult conflicts. Perhaps it is a way for Greece, Turkey and Cyprus finally to stop the diplomatic treadmill which is wearing them out in endless confrontation.

NOTES

* This essay has benefitted from interviews accorded on a basis of non-attribution by both officials and politicians of the Greek and Turkish-Cypriot communities, Greece, Turkey, the UK and the USA. I would like to record my grateful thanks to those concerned. It also makes use of material published in *Arès 1984-5*, vol. VII in my contribution '*Chypre, la Grèce, la Turquie: Un casse-tête pour la diplomatie*'. For permission to use this and for many insights provided by Professor J.-F. Guilhaudis and his colleagues, I am likewise grateful.

1 The theory and practice of problem-solving as a method of conciliation and facilitation is discussed in J.W. Burton, *Conflict and Communication* (Macmillan, London, 1969). C.R. Mitchell, *Peacemaking and the Consultant's Role* (Gower, Farnborough, 1981) and Michael Banks (ed.), *Conflict in World Society* (Wheatsheaf, Brighton, 1984).

2 See *The Guardian*, 15 October 1983.

3 This impression was gained while interviewing in Athens in 1984 and confirmed at the time by an independent Greek analyst. It may no longer be the case.

4 Security Council Resolution 541 (1983).

5 Published in London by the International Institute for Strategic Studies.

6 Mr. Korhan, Speaker of the Turkish-Cypriot Constituent Assembly, *Turkish News*, March 1984.

7 For details see *Turkish News*, February 1984.

8 Security Council Resolution 367 (1975).

9 Para. 51 of UN Secretary-General's report to the Security Council.

10 Athens News Agency.

11 Letter from former Foreign Minister Rolandis in *Fileleftheros*, Cyprus, 25 January, 1985.

12 *The Times*, 15 December 1984.

13 As stated in a Turkish-Cypriot Official Statement, *International Herald Tribune*, 26 February 1985.

14 See J.W. Burton, *Conflict and Communication*, op. cit. and Michael Banks, op. cit.

15 For an excellent analysis replete with factual detail see Andrew Wilson, 'The Aegean Dispute', *Adelphi Paper 155*, Winter 1979-80 and also Duygu Bazoglu Sezer: 'Turkey's Security Policies', *Adelphi Paper 164*, Spring 1981 and Thanos Veremis: 'Greek Security: Issues and Politics', *Adelphi Paper 179*, Winter 1982.

16 See North Antlantic Assembly. Political Committee. Interim Report of the sub-Committee on the Southern Region. Mr. Ton Frinking, Rapporteur AB 206 PC/SR(84)2, November 1984, pp. 29-30.

17 See, for example, the glossy brochure published in English by the Journalists' Union of the Athens Daily Newspapers — and also a 'carbon-copy' Turkish response!

18 *The Guardian*, 25 July 1984.

19 *International Herald Tribune*, 14 March 1985.

20 *International Herald Tribune*, 16 March 1985.

21 See A.J.R. Groom, 'The New Cold War: A Need for a Concerned but Independent Western Europe?', *Non-Aligned World*, April 1983 and J.W. Burton, A.J.R. Groom, Margot Light, C.R. Mitchell and D.J.D. Sandole, *Britain Between East and West: A Concerned Independence* (Gower Press, Aldershot, 1984).

BIBLIOGRAPHY

This is a short list of selected books on the recent history of Cyprus. Those interested in a more extensive bibliography should consult the useful work compiled by Paschalis M. Kitromilides and Marios L. Evriviades, *Cyprus*, (Oxford, UK and Santa Barbara, USA, Clio Press, 1982), which constitutes volume 28 in the World Bibliographic Series.

ADAMS, Thomas W., *AKEL: The Communist Party of Cyprus* (Stanford, 1971)

ALASTOS, Doros, *Cyprus in History,* (London, 1976)

ATTALIDES, Michael A., *Cyprus: Nationalism and International Politics* (London, 1979)

AVEROF -TOSITSA, Evangelos, *Istoria Hamenon Efkairion: Kypriako 1950-1963* [History of Lost Opportunities: Cyprus 1950-1963], 2 vols., (Athens, 1981)

BITSIOS, Dimitris, *Cyprus: The Vulnerable Republic* (Thessaloniki, 1975)

CLERIDES, Glafcos, *The Demands of the Turkish-Cypriot Community Since 1955* (Nicosia, 1974)

COYLE, Dominick J., *Minorities in Revolt: Political Violence in Ireland, Italy, and Cyprus* (London, 1983)

COUFOUDAKIS, Van., (Editor) *Essays on the Cyprus Conflict* (New York, 1976)

CROISET, François, *Le conflit de Chypre* (Brussels, 1973)

CRAWSHAW, Nancy, *The Cyprus Revolt: An Account of the Struggle for Union with Greece* (London, 1978)

DENKTASH, Rauf R., *The Problem of Cyprus: Constitutional and Political Aspects* (Nicosia, 1974)

DENKTASH, Rauf R., *The Cyprus Triangle* (London, 1982)

EHRLICH, Thomas, *International Crises and the Rule of Law; Cyprus 1958 - 1967* (Oxford, 1974)

FOLEY, Charles, *Legacy of Strife: Cyprus from Rebellion to Civil War* (London, 1964)

FOLEY, Charles, (Editor), *The Memoirs of General Grivas* (London, 1964)

FOLEY, Charles and SCOBIE, W., *The Struggle for Cyprus* (Stanford, 1975)

FOOT, Sir Hugh, *A Start in Freedom* (London, 1964

HARBOTTLE, Brigadier M., *The Impartial Soldier* (Oxford, 1970)

HILL, Sir George, *A History of Cyprus,* 4 vols. (Cambridge, 1940 1952)

HUNT, Sir David, (Editor), *Footprints in Cyprus* (London, 1982)

KOUMOULIDES, John, (Editor), *Greece and Cyprus in History* (Amsterdam, 1985)

KRANIDIOTES, Nikos, *Dhyskola Chronia: Kypros 1950 - 1960* [Difficult Years: Cyprus 1950-1960] (Athens, 1981)

KRANIDIOTES, Nikos, *Anochyrote Politeia: Kypros 1960-1977* [Unfortified Nation: Cyprus 1960 - 1977] , 2 vols. (Athens, 1985)

LOIZOS, Peter, *The Greek Gift: Politics in a Changing Cypriot Village* (London, 1975)

LOIZOS, Peter, *The Heart Grown Bitter: A Chronicle of Cypriot War Refugees* (Cambridge, 1981)

MARKIDES, Kyriacos, *The Rise and Fall of the Cyprus Republic* (New Haven, 1977)

MAYES, Stanley, *Makarios: A Biography* (London, 1981)

MEYER, A.J., *The Economy of Cyprus* (Cambridge, 1962)

OBERLING, Pierre, *The Road to Bellapais* (New York, 1982)

POLYVIOU, Polyvios G., *Cyprus: The Tragedy and the Challenge* (London, 1975)

POLYVIOU, Polyvios G., *Cyprus in Search of a Constitution: Constitutional Negotiations and Proposals 1960 - 1975* (Nicosia 1976)

POLYVIOU, Polyvios G., *Cyprus: Conflict and Negotiations 1960 - 1980* (London, 1980)

PURCELL, H. D., *Cyprus* (London, 1969)

SALIH, Ibrahim H., *Cyprus: The Impact of Diverse Nationalism on a State* (Alabama, 1978)

SARRIS, Neokles, *I Alli Plevra* [The Other Side] , 2 vols. (Athens, 1977)

STEGENGAN, James A., *The United Nations Force in Cyprus* (Ohio, 1968)

STEPHENS, Robert, *Cyprus: A Place of Arms* (London, 1966)

STERN, Laurence, *The Wrong Horse: The Politics of Intervention, and the Failure of American Diplomacy* (New York, 1977)

VANEZIS, P.N., *Makarios: Faith and Power* (London, 1971)

VANEZIS, P.N., *Makarios: Pragmatism v. Idealism* (London, 1985)

XYDIS, Stephen A., *Cyprus: Reluctant Republic* (The Hague, 1973)

CHRONOLOGY OF EVENTS

B.C.

c.
7000   First evidence of habitation: Neolithic city of Khirokitia.

c.
2700   to *c.* 1050 — Bronze Age.

c.
1190   Beginning of immigration from Greece.

c.
1050   to *c.* 545 — Cyprus part of the Persian Empire.

333   Cyprus liberated by Alexander. Ruled by him and his successors until 30 B.C.

A.D.

45   Missionary journey of SS Paul and Barnabas; conversion of Roman governor.

330   Inauguration of Constantinople as capital of the Roman Empire. Visit to Cyprus of Empress Helena.

488   Emperor Zeno declares Church of Cyprus autocephalous.

1185   to 1191 — Byzantine Governor Isaac Ducas Comnenos proclaims island an independent empire.

1191   Capture of Cyprus by Richard I of England.

1192   to 1489 — Cyprus ruled by French Lusignan dynasty.

1374   to 1464 — Genoese capture and administer Famagusta.

1489   Queen Catherine Cornaro, last Lusignan monarch, cedes Cyprus to Venetians.

1571   Cyprus invaded by Turks and annexed to Ottoman Empire; Turkish ethnic element introduced.

1821   Execution of Archbishop and Orthodox hierarchy.

159

1878	Under the Cyprus Convention Britain assumes administration of the island which remains formally part of the Ottoman Empire; Sir Garnet Wolseley first High Commissioner.
1881	First elections under limited rights granted by British; seats in Legislative Council for 9 Greeks and 3 Turks.
1908	Riots in Nicosia over election of Archbishop.
1914	Cyprus annexed by Britain in consequence of outbreak of war with Turkey.
1915	Britain offers Cyprus to Greece on condition Greece honours its treaty obligations towards Serbia.
1923	Under Treaty of Lausanne Turkey renounces claim to Cyprus in favourof Britain.
1925	Cyprus declared a Crown Colony. Greek-Cypriot members of Legislative Council resign.
1931	Pro-*enosis* riots in Nicosia; Government House is burned down; constitution suspended.
1947	Colonial government of Cyprus convenes Consultative Assembly for study of proposals which provide for constitutional changes and constitute in effect some degree of self-government; proposals rejected by Greek Cypriots who demand complete self-government.
1950	Archbishop Makarios II holds plebiscite of Greek Cypriots which shows 96% in favour of *enosis*. Makarios III elected Archbishop.
1954	Further British proposals for a Legislative Council are rejected. Frustration of first appeal to UN by Greece leads to strikes in Cyprus. November — Lt. Col. George Grivas arrives secretly to organise liberation struggle.
1955	1 April — Campaign in favour of *enosis* started by EOKA (National Organisation of Cypriot Fighters) under Grivas, code-name 'Dighenis'. Tripartite conference in London. Anti-Greek riots in Istanbul. Harding proposals for self-government. A state of emergency is declared.

1956	March - Makarios exiled to the Seychelles.
1957	Radcliffe proposals rejected. Turkish Cypriots declare for partition. Makarios released from the Seychelles but banned from Cyprus.
1958	Macmillan plan, a system of condominium of Cyprus by Britain, Greece and Turkey.
1959	February — The Zurich and London agreements were signed by Britain, Greece, Turkey, Archbishop Makarios on behalf of the Greek Cypriots and Dr. Fazil Kutchuk on behalf of the Turkish Cypriots. Under the agreements Cyprus becomes an independent state; Treaty of Alliance; Treaty of Guarantee; Britain retains 99 square miles as sovereign areas; Treaty also provides for a Greek and a Turkish contingent to be stationed in the island. March — Archbishop Makarios returns to Cyprus. December — Archbishop Makarios elected President and Dr. Fazil Kutchuk Vice-President.
1960	July — General elections to House of Representatives. 16 August — Cyprus becomes an independent republic. Cyprus joins the United Nations and the Commonwealth.
1961	Cyprus becomes a member of the Council of Europe.
1963	November — Archbishop Makarios submits proposals for amendment of the constitution. December — Outbreak of intercommunal fighting; 'Green Line' dividing communities in Nicosia is established.
1964	Turkish officials withdraw from administration. Turkey threatens invasion. March — Security Council resolution in support of Cyprus sovereignty denounces threat or use of force. May — conscription is introduced. President Johnson warns Turkish Prime Minister Inonu against invading Cyprus. June — Grivas returns and assumes command of National Guard. August — Fighting in Tylliria area.
1965	March — Galo Plaza, UN Mediator, publishes report and proposals; rejected by Turkish Government and Turkish Cypriots. UN General Assembly adopts resolution reaffirming the absolute sovereignty of the Republic of Cyprus.
1966	February — Joint communiqué signed by the Governments of Greece and Cyprus that any solution exluding *enosis* would be

unacceptable.

1967   April — Military coup in Greece.
November — Fighting between National Guard under Grivas and Turkish Cypriots in Kophinou area leads to Turkish ultimatum; accepted by Greek junta which withdraws troops and Grivas from Cyprus.
December — Turkish Cypriots announce formation of 'Provisional Cyprus-Turkish Administration'.

1970   Attempt on Makarios' life.

1971   Grivas returns secretly to Cyprus.
Start of renewed campaign for *enosis* by EOKA-B.

1973   February — Makarios re-elected President.

1974   January — Death of Grivas.
July — Makarios demands withdrawal of Greek officers.
15 July — Conspiracy against Makarios inspired by Greek junta; Presidential Palace destroyed; Nikos Sampson declared President.
17 July — Turkish Prime Minister Ecevit flies to London for talks.
20 July — Start of Turkish invasion; Turkish troops land on Kyrenian coast and occupy a 15-mile corridor reaching to Nicosia.
22 July — UN Security Council demands 'the cessation of hostilities and the withdrawal of all foreign troops from the territory of the Republic of Cyprus'.
23 July — Democracy is restored in Greece.
24 July — Glafcos Clerides, President of the House of Representatives takes over as Acting President of the Republic of Cyprus.
25 July — Peace talks between Great Britain, Greece and Turkey open in Geneva.
30 July — British, Greek and Turkish Foreign Ministers sign Geneva declaration precluding extension of areas under military control of either side and setting up of buffer zones.
14 August — Deadlock in negotiations; Turkey launches second phase of invasion.
16 August — Turkish forces reach 'Attila Line'; Security Council calls for cease-fire.
22 August — Declaration of autonomous Turkish-Cypriot Administration.
30 August — Greece announces intention to re-negotiate foreign military bases.
1 October — President Makarios in UN Assembly rejects geographical federation.

1975   January — Greek and Turkish Cypriots agree to resume negotiations on the basis of federal government.

February — US imposes arms embargo on Turkey. Turkey withdraws from Cyprus talks.

10 February — 'Turkish Federated State of Cyprus' declared in area occupied by Turkish troops; condemnation by UN Security Council.

28 April — Intercommunal talks start in Vienna under UN Secretary-General; agreement to set up committee on constitutional matters.

May — Karamanlis and Demirel meet in Brussels, declare support for inter-communal talks.

July — Third round of talks in Vienna; Greek-Cypriot negotiator Glafcos Clerides agrees to allow 10,000 Turkish Cypriots in southern Cyprus to move to Turkish-held north. Turkish-Cypriot negotiator Rauf Denktash promises comprehensive proposals for remaining problems before next talks.

September — Fourth round of talks in New York called off due to lack of formal proposals.

1976   February — Fifth round of talks in Vienna; agreement to exchange proposals simultaneously within six weeks.

May — Makarios rejects Turkish-Cypriot plan for bizonal federation.

September — Parliamentary elections.

1977   27 January — First meeting between Makarios and Denktash.

12 February — Second Makarios-Denktash meeting; guidelines for a Cyprus settlement agreed.

31 March — Sixth round of talks in Vienna; Greek Cypriots propose two-region federation leaving 20% under Turkish-Cypriot administration. Turkish-Cypriot proposals appear to provide for confederation.

21 April — Carter Administration seeks partial relaxation of US arms embargo.

20 May — Karamanlis says Greeks will not rejoin Nato until Turkey withdraws from Cyprus.

3 August — Death of Makarios.

Spyros Kyprianou, President of the House of Representatives becomes Acting President of the Republic.

Bishop Chrysostomos of Paphos becomes Archbishop.

August — Denktash threatens to declare independence of Turkish-Cypriot state.

1978   January — Kyprianou is elected unopposed President for a five-year term.

April — Greek Cypriots reject as inadequate recently-submitted Turkish territorial and constitutional proposals for Cyprus settlement.

November — UN General Assembly passes resolution calling for the withdrawal of Turkish forces from Cyprus; insists on implementation of Security Council resolutions.

1979   January — Greek and Turkish Cypriots agree to accept UN formula for a resumption of negotiations.
May — Some Turkish forces withdrawn from Cyprus.
19 May — Kyprianou and Denktash meet in Nicosia in an attempt to resolve differences at a meeting chaired by the UN Secretary-General.

1981   Elections for House of Representatives under new electoral system (reinforced representational).

1982   Greek Prime Minister, Andreas Papandreou, pays official visit to Cyprus.

1983   February — Kyprianou is re-elected President for a second term.
15 November — Unilateral declaration of 'Turkish Republic of Northern Cyprus' in the part of Cyprus under the occupation of Turkish troops; Security Council condemns the declaration and calls on member-countries to respect the independence, sovereignty and territorial integrity of the Republic of Cyprus.

1984   Kyprianou and Denktash submit proposals for a solution to the Cyprus problem.
September — UN Secretary-General convenes 'proximity talks' between Kyprianou and Denktash in New York.

1985   January — 'High-level' meeting between Kyprianou and Denktash under the auspices of the UN Secretary-General proves fruitless; proposals accepted by Denktash, rejected by Kyprianou.

INDEX

China, 41, 45
Chios, 146
Chrysostomos, Archibishop, 135
Church of Cyprus, 95, 98, 99
Churchill, Winston, 83-4, 86;
  his views on Corfu, 42;
  on Crete and Cyprus, 43, 46
Clerides, Glafcos, 6-8, 11-13, 70,
  135;
  acting President, 10, 36, 69;
  favours an independent unitary
  state, 30;
  and refugees, 120
Clifford, Clark, 74-75
Colonels, the Greek, see Makarezos,
  Papadopoulos, Pattakos, also
  junta
Colonial Office, 82-3, 85-6
Committee of Missing Persons, 140
Commonwealth, 98, 126
Communists, 3, 8, 13, 64, 100,
  101, 103, 121
Concert of Europe, 40;
  effectiveness of, 40, 52
Congo, later Zaire, 46
Constantine I, King of Greece,
  43, 84
Constantine II, King of Greece, 101
Constantinople, 83
Constitution, 1, 2, 6, 21, 31, 44,
  45, 91, 133-4
Corfu, 41
Corsica, 42
Crete, 21, 40, 41-2, 52, 84
  comparison of with Cyprus, 38-9,
  46, 52
Crimean War, 42-4
Cuba, 63
Curzon, Lord, British Foreign Sec-
  retary, 42
Cyprus Army, 1, 20
Cyrenaica, 87
Czechoslovakia, arms imported
  from, 8, 67

Davies, Rodger, US Ambassador,
  11, 54;

meets Sampson, 69
  murdered, 70
Defence, (British) Ministry of,
  85-6
de Cuellar, Javier Perez, UN Secretary-General, 14, 15, 127;
  his 1983 proposals rejected, 15;
  holds 'proximity talks', 16, 78,
  135, 141;
  and 'summit talks', 16, 141-2
de Gaulle, Charles, 100
Democratic Centre Union, 18
Democratic Rally, 13, 15, 135-6
Denktash, Rauf, 11, 12, 16, 78,
  127, 130, 139, 140;
  arrested, 6;
  talks in Beirut with Clerides, 7;
  reaches agreement on guidelines
  with Makarios, 12, 74;
  with Kyprianou, 13, 76;
  elected President by Turkish Cypriots, 13;
  rejects de Cuellar proposals, 15;
  US contacts with, 66
Dhekelia, 28
Derwinski, Edward, 79
Development Plans, 117
Disraeli, Benjamin, 43-4
Dodecanese Islands, 146
Dominican Republic, 62

Eastern Mediterranean, 53, 56,
  70, 72, 87-8, 104, 126
Eastern Question, 126
Ecevit, Bulent, Turkish Prime Minister, seeks British co-operation, 9;
  sends ultimatum to Greece, 10, 69
Egypt, 83, 88, 152;
  occupied by Gladstone, 44, 83
Eisenhower, President Dwight, 58
Elections, Parliamentary, in 1970, 8;
  in 1973, 9;
  in 1978, 12;
  in 1983, 14
Emergency Action Plans, 109,
  117, 118
enosis, 1, 4, 5, 7-9, 31, 57, 62,
  64, 84, 101, 136;

favoured by Greek Cypriots, 21, 42, 44;
and by some Labour ministers, 86;
achieved by Crete, 39, 52;
and by Corfu, 42;
renounced under Zurich-London agreements, 44;
'double *enosis*', 63, 94, 101;
Makarios' attitude to, 30, 100, 101-2.
EOKA (National Organisation of Cypriot Fighters), 21, 44, 69;
and Makarios, 99, 100
EOKA-B, 33;
formed by Grivas, 9;
proscribed, 9;
works for *enosis* with Greek junta, 67
Episkopi, 11, 33, 35
Estia, Athens newspaper, 8
Ethnarchy, 99, 100-102, 104
European Community, 153-4
Evdokas, Dr. Takis, 7, 18
Evren, Gen. Kenan, President of Turkey, 141
Evros, River, 5

Falkland Islands, 90, 91
Famagusta, 10, 11, 35, 142;
incidents at, 3, 5, 28
Finland, 60
Ford, President Gerald, 71, 78
Foreign Office, 85-6
France, 39, 59, 128, 148, 154

Gaza, 26
General Assembly, 14
Geneva, conferences in, in 1964, 4, 62;
in 1974, 10, 49
Geneva Declaration, 10, 70
Georgadjis, Polykarpos, Minister of Interior, 30;
attacks St. Hilarion, 3
murdered, 8, 33, 103;
and fighting in Limassol and Polis, 24;
favours *enosis,* 30

Germany, 39, 43, 59, 84, 128, 148, 154
Ghizikis, Phaidon, President of Greece, 9, 10
Gladstone, William, 44, 83
Gobbi, Hugo, 13-14
Great Britain, 3, 9, 16, 39, 41, 44, 46, 55, 57, 82-3, 93, 138;
believed to favour amendment of Cyprus constitution, 21;
and danger to British citizens, 10, 22, 92;
and Joint Truce Force, 23;
strategic interests, 82, 85;
annexes Cyprus, 84;
supports US policy, 141
'Great Greek Island', 39
Greece, 1, 4-6, 10, 21, 44-5, 55, 57, 66, 70, 78, 85, 101, 104, 126-7, 138, 145, 147, 149
calls on Makarios to form government of national unity, 9;
withdraws from military participation in NATO, 11, 70, 72;
offered Cyprus in 1915, 42, 84;
and obligations under Treaty of Guarantee, 49;
denounces importation of Czech arms, 67;
regarded as 'friendly but unstable' 87-8;
defeats Communist rebellion, 88;
relations with Turkey, 136
Greek Americans, 57, 74, 77
Greek Army, in Cyprus, 1, 3, 4 6, 61, 138;
officers killed at Famagusta, 3;
connections with EOKA-B, 9;
resists Turkish invasion, 10;
and the Joint Truce Force, 23-26;
and the National Guard, 30
Greek Cypriots, 3, 8, 10-12, 14, 16, 21, 24, 29, 64, 100, 101, 117, 119, 126, 129, 131, 135;
attitude to Zurich and London agreements, 1, 45;

Port Said, 44
Portugal, 73
Prem Chand, General, commanding
   UNFICYP, 36
Progressive Front, 18
Provisional Turkish-Cypriot Ad-
   ministration (PTCA), established
   1964, 6, 66;
   planning for, 22

Reagan, President Ronald, 75, 77,
   79, 138, 141
Refugees, 11, 13-4, 47, 72, 106-24,
   131, 132;
   relations with political parties,
   121-2
Republic of Cyprus, 14, 16, 24,
   47, 78, 93, 100-2, 141;
   established by treaties, 1, 44;
   authority repudiated by Turkish
   Cypriots, 4;
   governmental reshuffle, 9, 67;
   consent required to deployment
   of UNFICYP, 46, 59;
   relations with US, 55, 66, 79;
   federal structure considered, 79;
   rejects Nimetz plan, 95;
   its international status, 128, 137;
   economic measures of against
   Turkish Cypriots, 129, 133
Ridgway, Rozanne, 79
Rolandis, Nikos, Foreign Minister,
   15, 135
Russia, 39, 41, 44, 82

St. Hilarion, 3, 28-9
Salisbury, Lord, British Prime Min-
   ister, 42
Samos, 146
Samothrace, 146
Sampson, Nikos, 24, 28, 69, 95;
   proclaimed President, 9, 34;
   resigns, 10, 36, 69;
   and Nicosia fighting, 22
Sandys, Duncan, 23
San Francisco, 52
Saudi Arabia, 152
Security Council, 3, 9-11, 16, 24,

45-6, 50-2, 137, 142
Serbia, Greek treaty obligations
   to, 43, 84
Seychelles, 96-7
Sisco, Joseph, 69
Sovereign Base Areas, 20, 58, 88-91,
   93, 127;
   provision for in Zurich and Lon-
   don agreements, 1;
   give shelter to Makarios, 34, 92
Spain, 73
Special Relief Fund, 109
Spinelli, Pier, 26
Suez Canal, 83, 87-8
Supreme Constitutional Court, 1
Sweden, 60, 153
Syria, 84, 151-2

Thant, U, UN Secretary-General, 3
Thimayya, General Subayya, commanding UNFICYP, 31
Thrace, 138, 149;
   Turkish reinforcement of, 65
Thucydides, 41
TMT (Turkish Defence Organization), 4, 31
Treaties of Alliance, of Establishment, of Guarantee, 1, 2, 3,
   10, 45;
   special nature of treaties of guarantee, 48-9;
   obligations of guarantor powers,
   49, 90-2;
   and UN Charter, 50, 92
Troodos Mountains, 30, 97
Truman Doctrine, 57
Tuomioja, Sakkari, 4-5
Turkey, 1, 3-6, 10, 15-16, 21,
   44-5, 52, 55, 57, 66, 82, 84-5,
   104, 126-8, 131, 136, 145-9;
   military aid to by US, 11, 13,
   73-5, 77-9;
   recognizes British annexation of
   Cyprus, 84;
   risk of war with Britain, 92;
   commitment to Cyprus, 132
Turkish Air Force, 2, 35;
   intervenes at Kokkina in 1964,

171

The Pilgrim's guide to

DEVON'S
CHURCHES

Published in the UK by Cloister Books
The Old Deanery, The Cloisters, Exeter, Devon EX1 1HS
ISBN 978-0-9558962-0-0

First edtion 2008

Design: Krystyna Hewitt
Production: Anno Domini Publishing, Hertfordshire, UK

Printed and bound in Singapore

PREVIOUS PAGE: St Michael de Rupe, Brent Tor
OPPOSITE PAGE:
TOP LEFT: Witheridge, St John the Baptist; TOP RIGHT: Exeter, St James – open air service;
BOTTOM LEFT: North Devon location map: © Crown Copyright and/or database right.
All rights reserved. Licence number 100048101
BOTTOM RIGHT: Oreston (Plymstock), Church of the Good Shepherd

The Pilgrim's guide to
DEVON'S
CHURCHES

The location, history, architecture and stories
of Devon's 618 Church of England churches

With historical text by Canon Professor Nicholas Orme
Introduction by Dr Michael Langrish, Bishop of Exeter
Foreword by Dr Rowan Williams, Archbishop of Canterbury

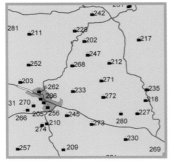

CLOISTER BOOKS

Thank You!

In addition to the main contributors to this book, The Most Revd Rowan Williams, Archbishop of Canterbury; The Rt Revd Michael Langrish, Bishop of Exeter; Canon Professor Nicholas Orme; The Very Revd Jonathan Meyrick, Dean of Exeter, we would like to thank the hundreds of authors from our churches who contributed text, without whom this book would not have been possible. In addition, our special thanks are due to The Churches Conservation Trust which cares for ten of the churches in this book and which has been extremely helpful to us in its production.

We would also like to pay tribute to our team of voluntary photographers:

Keith Burton
Julia Dallen
John Nelmes
Nick Shutt
Louise Skinner
Andrew Stevens

We are particularly grateful for the dedication and time given by Marian and Richard Gilpin, in collating all the gazetteer text and indebted to all those who have made contributions both large and small, including: John Allan, Mark Beedell, Oliver Blackmore, Tom Cadbury, Jan Croysdale, John Dobson, Peter Gee, Janet Goddard, Krystyna Hewitt, Peter Horlock, Sally Kimmis, Sara Knaggs, John Mapson, Ed Moffatt, Mark Nightingale, Graham Rowland, Penny Sexton, Susan Skinner, Alistair Sutherland, Allen Van Der Steen, Exeter Cathedral Library, The Royal Albert Memorial Museum & Art Gallery and Torbay Council.

Cloister Books

CONTENTS

FOREWORD

by The Archbishop of Canterbury

'Devon, glorious Devon' is not glorious only because of a very special blend of natural beauties; it has a truly glorious heritage of parish churches – and, more important, the history of countless Christian communities that goes with this. From the earliest days of Christianity in Britain, the West Country has provided a succession of great figures of faith, from Boniface and Aldhelm through to the modern age.

The present Diocese of Exeter, now celebrating eleven hundred years of existence, can also (in virtue of many centuries of common ecclesiastical organisation) claim a share in the great inheritance of Celtic Christianity in Cornwall – though the Diocese of Truro now stands proudly having reclaimed the ancient independence of the Church in the Duchy. Christians in contemporary Devon can rightly be grateful for the cloud of witnesses surrounding them from their past and praying silently with them today.

And today the Diocese continues the same work that Aldhelm and Boniface knew, the work of bringing good news to an entire community – a community now much more varied than ever, including many growing centres of population and the great urban and maritime complex of Plymouth as well as the immemorial villages and market towns and the scattered moorland settlements. That sharing of good news today involves all kinds of new experiments – what we have come to call 'fresh expressions' of the Church's life – but it is still focused upon the mystery and the gift of Christ that first stirred the people of the region to celebration and sacrifice all those centuries ago in the 'Age of the Saints'. The visible reminders of continuity in the service of this mystery can never be ignored or overlooked. They stand to tell us of the faithfulness of God throughout our history – the open door of Christ's love, set in the midst of our human life once and for all, calling every generation.

That is what this book witnesses to – God's faithfulness. I hope and pray that, as you read and look at the pictures of the great heritage of this diocese, something of that faithfulness will come across and speak to you of God's promise to you personally, and God's willingness to be there for you and for all the human family today. May God bless the Diocese of Exeter in its work and witness, and all of you who pick up this excellent guide to its story and its message.

+ *Rowan Cantuar:*
Lambeth Palace
Passiontide, 2008

LEFT: St Petroc, Exeter (Central).

INTRODUCTION

by The Bishop of Exeter

In 2009 the Diocese of Exeter is celebrating the 1100th anniversary of the founding of a separate Bishopric for Devon, with its centre first at Crediton and then, since 1050, in the city of Exeter. In the following pages you can read something of the story of the past eleven centuries as well as catching glimpses of the church and parish life as it is to be encountered today.

Putting this book together has been a very exciting project, involving many people right across the diocese. So, inside you will find a colour photograph of every church and worship centre, with a brief article on each one. The photographs were taken by a team of voluntary photographers; each church was invited, through its churchwardens, to write a paragraph telling the story of that church, its architecture, its history and, perhaps even more importantly, something about its mission and ministry now. There are also short chapters on the history of the Church, on understanding Devon's churches, and on the relevance, symbolism and meaning of church furnishings.

Sadly, over the course of 1100 years, the Christian Church has allowed itself to become divided into different denominations. However, whilst this book deals with the parish churches of the Church of England I very much hope that Christians of other backgrounds will find here parts of their own story and one that we still share.

Whoever you are, whether a parishioner, a visitor or someone with their roots here in Devon, I hope that you will find that this book is for you, and that it will help you to a better understanding, and therefore a greater enjoyment, of those churches which have for so long been such an important part of this county's life.

Above all, I hope that in these pages you will find what for Christians gives meaning and richness to life itself – and that is the reality and love of God. Of course, God is to be found everywhere, not just in our church buildings. Nevertheless, many people enjoy visiting churches and come away not just having seen a beautiful or interesting building, but also sometimes with a sense of a real spiritual encounter and an awareness of the presence of God.

I very much like the description of Devon's churches by one writer, as places of 'poetry, intimacy and prayer'. I do hope that this book will help you to discover this for yourself.

+ *Michael Exon*
Exeter
2008

LEFT: *St Mary the Virgin, Down St Mary.*

ST PETER'S CATHEDRAL: ITS LIFE AND HISTORY

by Jonathan Meyrick
Dean of Exeter

As Professor Orme says elsewhere in this book, the earliest recorded Christian church in Devon was in Exeter. It was in existence at the beginning of the 5th century. It was to be another 650 years before a cathedral church was established in the city.

Much of the history in the mid-Saxon period is unclear. By the beginning of the 8th century Devon was being administered ecclesiastically from Sherborne in Dorset. Within 200 years, it became clear that this was too big an area and Devon was given a 'pro temps' solution via Bishop Asser. It appears from John Hooker in the 16th century that early in the 11th century, towards the latter period of Bishop Asser's time, there may also have been bishops based in Tawton. Hooker's speculations were discredited in the 19th century, though, and there is no reference to them in the Handbook of British Chronology's definitive list of British Bishops.

However that may be, within five years the centre of the diocese was clearly established at Crediton under Bishop Eadulf. In just under 150 years, the centre had moved to Exeter. Bishop Leofric, who began his episcopate at Credition administering the Church in Devon, was now also given the Church in Cornwall to care for. He was enthroned in a Saxon church dedicated to St Mary and St Peter. Nothing of this building remains, but it is likely to have been a stone church, replacing a wooden, originally monastic, building that had been burnt by the Danes in 1003. Leofric gave the care of his new cathedral not to monks but to secular canons, who were required to follow a rule of life and be his 'family'.

The third bishop, William Warelwast – a nephew of the Conqueror – began a new cathedral around the year 1112. Whilst the date of its commencement is not certain, we do know for sure that its high altar was dedicated on 21st November 1133. The College of Canons still meets on that day and an anniversary service is held – directly tying the present life of the cathedral with the moment when the early-12th-century building began to be used for worship. The Saxon monastery church was left to decay, although the new church retained the dedication to St Peter.

From Gilbert Scott's restoration in the 1870s, we know there was a five-sided apse at the east end of this cathedral, which stood at the step up to the present presbytery. The West End was approximately where the present one is and we can picture the look of the whole from the surviving towers, which still stand to the north and south of the present building. They are both solid and graceful, with Romanesque lines and decorations softening their four-square strength. Their positioning at either end of the crossing is unique in England and then, as now, they allowed for a view through from east to west. If the building progress continued at the same rate we can assume (say Vyvyan Hope and John Lloyd in 1973) that the Norman cathedral building was complete by 1180, some 50 years in total.

The Norman cathedral was initially looked after by a chapter of twenty-four canons led by a Precentor and a Treasurer. They would have done so as the bishop's immediate family and his influence would have remained strong. The Precentor held the senior position within the chapter.

Leofric left one very significant new element in the cathedral's make-up: his library of books. Most of these went to form part of Thomas Bodley's library in Oxford, one of the premier libraries of the country. Despite that, a library has continued at the cathedral and now contains the remnants of Leofric's gift (the Foundation Charter of King Edward the Confessor and the Exeter Book, a collection of Anglo-Saxon riddles and poems). It also houses the only surviving regional Domesday collection and a variety of collections from the 17th, 18th and 19th centuries, as well as more modern theological works.

RIGHT: St Peter's Cathedral, Exeter: choir and organ with nave beyond

By the early part of the 13th century, it had become clear that the bishop needed a 'deputy' in the running of the cathedral. In 1224 William Brewer was elected bishop. He had previously been the cathedral's precentor and would therefore have known of the growing difficulties. With the support and encouragement of the archbishop, he had added a dean to the cathedral's Foundation in order to achieve this. He also added a Chancellor to act as secretary and lecturer in theology. He gave to the new dean, Serlo, the churches of Braunton, Bishop's Tawton (with its two chapels) and Colaton Raleigh. He also gave him the house that had been the Archdeacon of Totnes'. The present dean is housed in a house once belonging to the Archdeacon of Barnstaple and which more recently housed the suffragan bishops of Crediton. Some things don't change!

The dean presided at chapter meetings, with, until 1967, the precentor always acting as the senior canon.

Since 1967, that responsibility has always resided with the longest-serving canon residentiary.

Bishop Brewer also gave land from his own garden for the construction of a chapter house. The present building is clearly a mixture of the original Early English building and a 15th-century rebuilding of the upper part and the east window. The cathedral Fabric Rolls of 1412-13 confirm that the house was in ruins, presumably following a fire.

Bishop Walter Bronescombe, bishop in the second half of the 13th century, embarked on a grand rebuilding of the cathedral. Probably inspired by the new Salisbury Cathedral in 1258 (the year he became bishop), he decided that he wanted one of those and dusted off his sledgehammer. The 'new work' was started in the early 1270s, at the east end. The cathedral was temporarily divided into two whilst the work was done, so its worship could continue. The side-chapels in the quire were re-glazed in 1279, the high altar rededicated on 18th December 1328. The final reference in the Fabric Rolls to this rebuilding concerns a pinnacle on the west front dated 1376-7. The whole project therefore took just over 100 years. It is in a remarkably

RIGHT: St Peter's Cathedral, Exeter, from the north west.

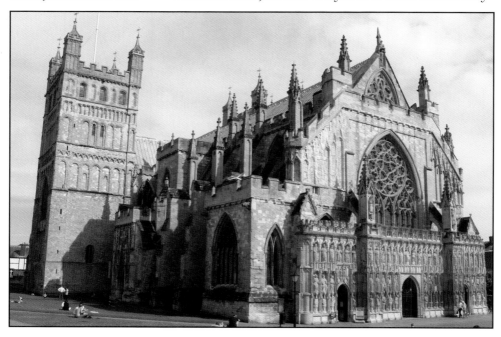

homogenous style: Decorated Gothic. The twin towers enable the nave roof to soar through to the east end uninterrupted, making it the longest Gothic vaulted ceiling anywhere. The present archbishop has described it as the cathedral which makes him smile. On a sunny afternoon, it is breathtaking.

Like all cathedrals, it now operates under a Constitution and Statutes, which changed at the turn of this century. The chapter remains its governing body, chaired by the dean, the head of the Foundation. The dean is also a member of the bishop's staff, retaining the old 'family' link with the bishop. The chapter is enlarged to include up to four non-residentiary members, at least three of whom are lay. In addition to the wider College of Canons, which contains the archdeacons, suffragan bishops and a number of parish priests from the diocese (prebendaries) and now lay canons, the Foundation has a new body: the Cathedral Council. This acts to keep a friendly – but critical – eye on the cathedral's governance. It gives advice to the chapter, and would alert the bishop if it felt a problem was emerging.

For many centuries, musicians have been part of the Foundation too. There are currently a Director of Music, an Organist and an Assistant Organist with responsibility for the Girls' Choir, twelve men singers and up to 40 choristers. There are paid staff in administration, in the vergers' department, in the shop and refectory, and in the care and maintenance of buildings and grounds. There are also hundreds of volunteers in the life of the cathedral, some of whom are also part of the regular worshipping congregation.

The Cathedral Foundation today, as in Leofric's time, understands its function to be the church at the centre of the diocese. It exists for the glory of God, for the bishop, clergy and people of the diocese, for the city and the county, and increasingly for those who find in it a touchstone to seek for God in a hectic and secular world.

A CHURCH OF TWO THOUSAND YEARS

by Canon Professor Nicholas Orme

How things began

We owe a lot to the Romans. They started to join together what are now England and Wales. They built many of our towns and roads, and introduced us to reading and writing. And it was under them that Christianity came to our island, inspiring groups of believers and the building of churches. By about AD 400 there was a church in Exeter – the earliest recorded in Devon.

Shortly after 400, Roman rule faded away. The British people of the South West, the Dumnonii, formed their own kingdom; Devon is the modern form of its name. But Christianity did not die; instead it grew stronger. The local kings and nobles were Christian, and there were priests and monks although we know little about them.

In the 600s the Anglo-Saxons began to reach Devon, and their leaders, the kings of Wessex, gradually conquered it. Anglo-Saxons settled in the area, and the British Devonians adopted English speech and customs. The Anglo-Saxons had been converted to Christianity by this time, so there was no break in the history of the Church.

Christianity brought Devon into European culture and society. As early as the 680s St Boniface, an Anglo-Saxon boy linked nowadays with Crediton, went to school in a monastery at Exeter before becoming a scholar and missionary in Germany. Soon afterwards, in about 705, St Aldhelm, another leading scholar, was made bishop of Sherborne with responsibility for the Church in Dorset, Somerset, and 'dire Devon' as he jokingly described it. By the 890s this area was too big for one

The landscape of Devon is characterised by hundreds of churches (St Edward, Shaugh Prior, LEFT), each of which has left an indelible print on the history of the county and the life of the community, to the present day.

bishop to look after, so King Alfred appointed his Welsh friend, Bishop Asser, to take care of Devon and Cornwall from a base in Exeter. Asser is Devon's first recorded bishop.

When Asser died in 909, Devon was given a permanent bishop, and Cornwall gained one a little later. At first the bishops who followed Asser worked from Crediton, where the Church owned a country estate, but as Exeter grew in size and importance it was decided that they should return there and also take charge of Cornwall. This happened in 1050. The first bishop of Exeter was Leofric, and he established Exeter Cathedral, which has been the cathedral of Devon ever since. Cornwall regained a bishop in 1877.

Boniface, Aldhelm, Asser and Leofric were our founding fathers. They are men whom we can still get to know from their books. Boniface was a linguist and letter writer, Aldhelm a poet and scholar, Asser the biographer of King Alfred and Leofric a book-collector. They remind us that, over 1000 years ago, Devon was not a backwater but home to leading scholars of the day.

Parish churches

The earliest churches in Devon, up to the 900s, were minsters. They were staffed by groups of clergy: sometimes monks, sometimes clergy who lived in private houses and might be married. The minsters lay well apart in places like Axminster, Hartland, Plympton, Stokenham and Yealmpton, because the population was still small and scattered.

During the 900s, smaller churches were built to serve new villages or lords' estates. We call these 'parish churches'. They were staffed by a single clergyman, known as the rector or vicar. Some of the minsters duly turned into parish churches, and by the 1100s there were churches of this kind all over Devon, in town and country alike, just as there are today.

Parish churches are one of Christianity's most important and lasting creations. Nearly all that existed in Devon in 1100 still survive, and more have been founded in modern times. The parish is the district belonging to the church, whose people were originally expected to support it in return for the care it gave them. From the 900s down to 1936, farmers had to pay tithes to the clergyman – one tenth of their produce, or the value in cash, to provide him with his living.

Clergy and people gathered in church for worship on Sundays and festival days. There was usually a wish to have as large and beautiful a church as possible, so all the churches of the 900s were rebuilt later on, sometimes more than once, especially in the 1100s, the 1400s and the 1800s. Since parishes varied in size and wealth, however, there was (and is) no such thing as a standard church.

Small country parishes had modest churches, as can be seen today at Brentor or Honeychurch. Prosperous towns like Barnstaple, Cullompton, Honiton and Tiverton acquired big and splendid ones, because wealthy gentry or merchants helped to finance the building. In the 19th century, when England was rich with the profits of industry and trade, other large churches were built in Torbay and Plymouth.

Today our churches often seem like millstones round our necks. It takes so much of our time and money to run them. Nevertheless the effort is worthwhile. Parish churches are the Church's best advertisements: attracting attention with their spires and towers and bells. They still inspire affection from people, even people who do not come to church. We cannot exist without them; one could say that there is not so much a Church of England as an England of churches.

Religious houses

Devon's biggest church is the cathedral. Since it became one in 1050, it has been run by a community of clergy spending time in the worship of God. Nowadays there are only half a dozen clergy, but in the Middle Ages there were as many as sixty. These clergy were (and are) not monks but canons and priests, living in separate houses. The 'close', the area outside the cathedral that contains their houses, still looks like a village set around a green.

About two dozen more large churches in Devon were staffed by groups of clergy in the Middle Ages, roughly between the 1000s and the 1500s. Two were smaller versions of the cathedral: Crediton and Ottery St Mary. Others were monasteries like Buckfast Abbey, Hartland Abbey and Tavistock Abbey. Monks, as their clergy were called, also gave their lives to worshipping God, but differed from the cathedral clergy in other ways. Monks had no personal possessions. They ate together in a refectory, slept in a dormitory and shared the monastery's books and other goods. Monastery buildings were set closely together, like those of a modern school or college, usually around a four-sided cloister. We tend to think of monks as scholars and inventors: producing books, writing histories and drawing beautiful pictures. Few did so, however. Most did not work in the fields and none taught children, as we also imagine, although they gave food to the poor.

In the early 1200s St Francis of Assisi in Italy felt that monks did not come close enough to the life of Jesus and his disciples. Francis founded the friars, who lived in groups like monks but travelled about like the disciples to work among the people: preaching and hearing confessions. Friars had no lands or income like cathedrals and monasteries. They lived from donations, like a modern charity. They took education

seriously, because only educated men could preach well and teach the Christian faith. There were four friaries in Devon: two in Exeter and two in Plymouth, and these were important centres of learning and pastoral care.

At their peak there were two or three hundred monks and friars in Devon. Three nunneries catered for women at Canonsleigh near Tiverton, Cornworthy near Dartmouth and Polsloe near Exeter. Nuns were fewer in number than monks or friars, however, and did little except pray, not having yet developed the work with schools and hospitals that nuns did in later centuries.

The world of the religious houses is a world we have largely lost. They have left us only a few ruins, some archives, and a handful of books. In their own day, many people valued the work they did. But this work stopped abruptly at the Reformation, and although a few monasteries and nunneries were founded again in Victorian times, they have never become as central to Church life as they were in the Middle Ages.

The Reformation and afterwards

Between about 1530 and 1560 the Reformation changed the Church in Devon, as it did throughout England. Its changes were unusual in being very large, relatively quick, and carried out by kings, queens and parliaments, not by the Church itself. England ceased to recognise the pope as head of the Church. The Church of England was established under the rule of the king or queen. Monks, friars and nuns were abolished, and the government took their property. Services in the parish churches changed from Latin to English. Statues and paintings of Christ and the saints were removed, and churches were made to look plainer. People were encouraged to read the Bible in English, and to pray to God directly, not through saints. Rectors and vicars were allowed to marry. These changes were controversial. In 1549 the arrival of the 'Book of Common Prayer', containing the services in English, caused an uproar in Devon. Men from Sampford Courtenay began a revolt, which was joined by protesters from Cornwall. The rebels attacked Exeter but failed to capture it, and in the end the government brought up troops to defeat them. Many rebels were killed in battle or executed.

The Reformation also had its supporters. Some of these suffered too, because they called for change when it was not allowed. Thomas Benet was burnt in Exeter in 1532 for supporting the new beliefs, as was Agnes Prest in 1558. Others emigrated from England: Reformers under Mary Tudor, Roman Catholics under Elizabeth I.

In Elizabeth's reign (1558-1603), however, efforts were made to persuade people of the rightness of the Reformation as well as simply enforcing it. Two scholars from Devon, John Jewel and Richard Hooker, wrote influential books to explain what the Church of England was and stood for. Jewel argued that it was based on the Bible and the beliefs of the early Church, freed from the corruptions of later times. Hooker added that God had given us not only the Bible but the power of reason. The Church of England was based on reason too.

For a time, during the reign of James I (1603-25), there were fewer disputes and most people accepted the Church as it was. Then, in the 1630s, controversies arose again. Some, known as Puritans, thought that the Church was still too Roman Catholic. Others, led by William Laud, the archbishop of Canterbury, wished to make worship in churches more beautiful, and criticised some aspects of the Reformation. Disputes between the two sides helped bring about the Civil War, which broke out under Charles I in 1642.

The Civil War caused a major disruption to the Church. The winners of the war, the Puritans, tried to reform it further but they did not succeed in the long term, and when Charles II was restored as king in 1660, the old Church too was restored. Many of the Puritans now left (or had already left) the Church to form churches of their own: Baptists, Quakers, Congregationalists and Presbyterians. At first the government of Charles II persecuted these people to make them return to the Church of England. But this policy failed, and in 1689, under William III, they were allowed to worship in their own churches. This permission was not extended to Roman Catholics for another century.

BELOW: The broken reredos in the Chapel of St Saviour, Exeter Cathedral. It was deliberately damaged during the Reformation because of dislike of its religious imagery.

From countryside to town

The 18th century, the Georgian period, was a quieter time for the Church. Giving freedom of worship to the Puritan 'dissenters', the Free Churches as we now call them, had a soothing effect. The countryside (Devon was still largely rural) prospered, and the clergy gained more from tithes. They often held their parishes for long periods, as you can see from the lists of rectors and vicars in parish churches. The Georgian Church has come to be regarded as dull and even lazy. This is unfair. It started some of the changes that we link with Victorian England. More new churches were being built than at any time since the early 16th century, with different layouts inside. Parish church dedications (to St Mary, St Peter, All Saints and so on) came back into use after being forgotten since the Reformation. Unfortunately, mistakes were made when they were restored, so that many today are not the original ones.

Religious revivals took place, especially through the work of John Wesley, a clergyman of the Church. He visited Devon frequently between 1739 and 1789, at first arousing violent protests from mobs, but preaching with striking effects on those who heard him. At Plymouth, 'The fear of God seemed to spread itself over all, so that they received what was spoken as the word of God.' Wesley's followers became known as the Methodists. In the end they built their own chapels and chose their own ministers, but they have always had close connections with the Church of England, and for a long time some people attended services at both church and chapel.

The Methodists marked a quickening of changes in the Church and society, which continued during the 19th century. England experienced the Industrial Revolution. Plymouth became a large city. Seaside resorts developed, especially around Torbay. All the Devon towns grew in size, and by 1900 most Devonians were townspeople, not country dwellers. How people thought about religion began to change too. The 19th century saw the rise of two new movements in the Church: the 'Evangelicals' and the 'Tractarians' (later known as 'Anglo-Catholics'). Very roughly speaking, Evangelicals stressed Bible reading and preaching, while Tractarians tried to bring people to God through careful and beautiful worship. These changes caused new tensions. Tractarians were accused of coming too close to Roman Catholicism, and Evangelicals to the Free Churches. The bishops of Exeter had difficulty keeping the two sides in order. Bishop Philpotts caused a national sensation by trying to stop the Evangelical clergyman George Gorham from becoming vicar of Brampford Speke in 1847, but in the end

OPPOSITE PAGE: An early free-church chapel: Loughwood Baptist Chapel, Dalwood, c. 1700.
BELOW: The exterior of the Chapel.

ABOVE: Brampford Speke church, centre of the 'Gorham controversy', 1847-50. Later, Gorham rebuilt the church.

Gorham won. Later bishops were equally unsuccessful in trying to discipline the Anglo-Catholic churches of Plymouth.

Yet the tensions were also creative. Each side inspired people's faith, and led them not only to build churches but to found schools and do social work. Priscilla Lydia Sellon organised a community of women to work among the poor of Plymouth and Devonport. Starting in 1848, she established an orphanage, a hostel for boys, a refuge for girls, a home for old sailors, six schools, a soup kitchen and much, much more.

Modern times

The Victorians had great religious successes. But the Church of England was winning a smaller percentage of support from a larger population. Many people now belonged to other Christian Churches, and far more did not belong to a Church at all. The Victorian poet Matthew Arnold compared the surging sea of faith in the Middle Ages with 'its melancholy, long, withdrawing roar' in his own day.

This feeling of decline increased in the 20th century. Statistics showed that fewer people were going to church or believing in Christianity. The Church's resources grew less. Tithes came to an end in 1936, and there were fewer Church members to give money. Clergy in the countryside no longer looked after a single parish but two or three or several. People began to talk of a 'post-Christian era'. While the statistics are true, they are also misleading. Was there ever a 'sea of faith'? At all times in the past, religious writers and Church leaders have despaired about the religious apathy and wickedness around them. The death of religion in the 20th century has also been much exaggerated.

Christianity is always a missionary faith. Its members are always dying, and new ones need to be found. The Church in Devon has never stopped recruiting members, even if it has not succeeded in attracting everyone. And the 20th-century Church moved on in fresh and vigorous ways. Worship became more varied than it was even in the 19th century. Today you

BELOW: Bishop Michael with children from Feniton (VA) Primary School.

may choose to worship from the Book of Common Prayer with the 'Authorised' ('King James I') version of the Bible and traditional hymns. You may attend a modern-language service from 'Common Worship', with modern Bible translations and modern hymns and songs. You may go to informal 'Family Worship', or reflective worship with meditation and 'Taizé' songs, or a service of healing. Or you may join a house group for study, prayer and friendship.

A vast amount of new religious material is being produced in Devon alone: songs, prayers, films and presentations. Leadership in the Church is spread more widely. Women have been ordained as priests since 1994. Lay people help govern the Church and lead services, many of them ordinary members of the congregation.

Christians of different kinds have closer links. The old suspicions and hostilities between the Church of England ('Anglicans'), Roman Catholics and the Free Churches have given way, if not always to agreement, to respect and goodwill for each other. Anglicans and Free Churches co-operate in training their clergy and ministers in the South West Ministry Training Scheme. Anglicans and Catholics jointly run a secondary school in Torbay.

The Diocese of Exeter has established vigorous links with the diocese in Cyprus and the Gulf, and Thika (Kenya); with the Roman Catholic Diocese of Bayeux-Lisieux and the Church in Melanesia.

The Church of England continues to work for the good of people as a whole. It is sometimes said that it works more for its non-members than for its members! It runs and supports hundreds of schools in Devon. It sends chaplains to the armed forces, hospitals and prisons. It invites everyone to be christened, married or buried. It provides Christian teaching, clubs for young people, centres for the homeless and help for the elderly.

The story of Christianity in Devon is both long and complicated, because it covers two thousand years and millions of people. Every generation remakes the

ABOVE: Live music at the front of the Cathedral during a 'Life on the Beach' outreach event.

Church to some extent, and yet what we believe and do as Christians is essentially as it was in Victorian and Georgian times, at the Reformation, throughout the Middle Ages, and under the Roman Empire, right back to the time of Jesus.

UNDERSTANDING DEVON'S CHURCHES

by Canon Professor Nicholas Orme

Undo a Russian doll, and you find a smaller doll, and a smaller one inside that. Take them all out, and you have a row of dolls. A parish church is the same. If you study it carefully, you can take apart the layers of its history. Even a Victorian church will contain a couple of layers, and if the building is medieval, you may see as many as six. A church can teach you not only about its own history, but about the history of England: religious history (Christianity) and social history (how people lived and thought).

Churches from 1066 to 1300

Nearly all Christian churches face east, the direction of the sunrise, where people in biblical times imagined God as living. By about 1066, the date of the Norman Conquest, most churches were built in two parts. The eastern, smaller part was the **CHANCEL**. This was where the priest said the services, and he had to keep it in repair. In it, near the east wall, was the

LEFT: A large city church: St Andrew, Plymouth.
RIGHT: A small rural church: St Mary, Honeychurch.

ALTAR (a stone table), at which he celebrated mass (or communion), using bread and wine. Further west were seats for him and his clerk. Other important people, like the lord of the manor and his family, might also have seats there.

West of the chancel was the **NAVE**, a larger area. This was the place for lay people, the congregation, and they were responsible for its upkeep. At first there may have been little furniture, so that they often stood or knelt on the floor, but seats are mentioned in Devon as early as 1287. Services were in Latin, and the congregation were expected to watch them and say their own private prayers, not to join in saying the words or singing. Even their view of the service might not be very good, because chancel and nave were often separated by a wall with a single open archway within it.

Churches from 1300 to 1550

By about 1300 churches were being extended or rebuilt to make them bigger. The space between the chancel and the nave was opened up, so that there was no wall between them. However, because the chancel was regarded as very holy, it was screened off by a new kind of barrier: the **ROOD SCREEN**.

The rood screen ran across the church from north to south. It was usually made of wood and still exists in some churches. The lower parts were panelled up to about 1.25 metres. Above the panels were open arches, and over the arches a canopy. The canopy supported a gallery, reached by a ladder or by a staircase in the church wall (the **ROOD STAIR**). On the gallery was a large statue of Christ on the 'rood', meaning 'cross', which is why we talk of rood screens.

Between about 1300 and 1550 all churches had such screens. This meant that the church was not one big room, but a group of rooms. Behind the screen was the chancel, where the service was said. In front of it was the nave, where people watched the service. Many churches had side chapels, which were private areas for the gentry or for guilds of parishioners. The porch was another room. Weddings took place there, and the baptism service began there before the baby was taken inside the church to be dipped in water in the **FONT**.

RIGHT: The fine late-medieval roodscreen at St Andrew, Cullompton.

The font was placed near the church door, because baptism brings a new member into the church.

By the 1400s seats were becoming common. Congregations paid to have the whole of the nave filled with benches (known as **PEWS**). Medieval benches often had their ends carved with scenes of everyday life or the objects associated with Christ's crucifixion (crown of thorns, nails and ladder).

People's seats in church reflected their social status. This was true from the Middle Ages down to recent times. The gentry sat in the chancel or a side chapel. The wealthier townspeople or farmers took the front pews in the nave, while servants and poor people went to the back. In country churches seats were often linked with houses, and you sat in the seat of your house. In towns people sometimes paid rents for seats, and only those at the back were free for the poor.

A medieval church service was not meant to teach you anything. It was a ceremony in beautiful surroundings, with statues of saints, wall paintings, and stained-glass windows. It was an experience, in which you were forgiven, healed and blessed. Priests rarely preached sermons, but by the 1400s many churches had a **PULPIT**: a high box reached by stairs. During the service the priest went into the pulpit and read aloud the 'bead-roll'. 'Bead' means 'prayer', and parishioners could have their names written on the bead-roll for a small sum of money. The names were read and prayed for every week.

Churches from the Reformation to the 1830s

Between 1538 and 1560 the Reformation drastically changed the insides of churches. The stone altar in the chancel was replaced by a wooden table to remind people of Christ's last supper with his disciples. Statues and paintings were removed or whitewashed, and new visual aids – the Lord's Prayer and the Creed on big boards, and the **ROYAL COAT OF ARMS** – were displayed instead.

The rood screen usually remained, minus the statue of Christ. But the priest moved from the chancel to a **READING DESK** at the east end of the nave, from which he led the services. The church became a single space, not a group of rooms. Nearly every service happened in the nave. The chancel was only used during part of the communion service, and that service took place only about four times a year. Baptisms and weddings happened entirely in church, not in the porch.

Services were now in English. They were lessons rather than experiences. There were readings from the Bible and prayers that taught you about God and how to behave. The clergy were encouraged to use the pulpit for preaching sermons. The church became like a schoolroom, with the priest as teacher and the congregation as the pupils.

Church services did not change much between the 1560s and the 1830s, but some alterations were made to the insides of churches. In the early 1600s there were attempts to make them more reverent and

ABOVE: St Mary, Molland, north aisle. It is filled with seating typical of 17th- and 18th-century churches.

beautiful. The communion table was fenced off with **ALTAR RAILS**, and stained glass was reintroduced into some windows. Pulpits grew larger during the 1600s and 1700s as preaching became more important. The old narrow benches were often replaced by more comfortable seats with doors, sometimes known as 'horse-box' pews.

As rood screens decayed, some were removed to make the church more open inside. Music in church became more popular, and a **GALLERY** was built at the west end of the nave to house musicians and sometimes a choir. Their members led the congregation in singing psalms from the Bible in rhymed translations, like 'The Lord's My Shepherd, I'll not Want' (Crimond).

The Victorian era, 1837-1901

The pace of change increased in the 1830s, roughly when Queen Victoria's reign began in 1837. English people developed a love of the Middle Ages, and the art and architecture of those times. They began to dislike the plain comfortable churches of the Georgian period, and to want a more ancient and beautiful setting for services. At the same time they shared the Georgian liking for a church that was one open room, without barriers.

The Victorians' view of churches owed a lot to their love of the theatre. They saw the chancel as a stage where the service should happen. They raised the chancel floor by half a metre or so, with steps leading up from the nave, instead of the chancel being level with the nave as before. They sometimes removed the remaining rood screens, so that people in the nave could see the chancel clearly.

The priest often moved back to sit in the chancel and led the service from there once again. The choir left the west gallery (which was usually destroyed), and joined the priest in the chancel, wearing coloured robes. Communion services (centred in the chancel) became monthly or weekly, and many churches replaced their communion tables with stone altars like medieval ones. In the nave, the horse-box pews made way for simpler ones like those of the Middle Ages.

ORGANS had sometimes existed in medieval and Georgian England, but they became almost universal in Victorian times. One skilled organist was more reliable than a group of amateur musicians, and the organ had greater volume and a variety of sound. **HYMNS** – original religious poems – replaced the old rhymed psalms. Hymns had begun to be popular in Georgian England, and the Methodist chapels made much use of them. Now they became part of church services too.

Not every church was the same inside. It was harder to change an old church than to start afresh with a new one. There were also differences between churches that were 'high-church' (those of the 'Tractarians' or 'Anglo-Catholics') and ones that were 'low-church' (or 'Evangelical'). 'High' churches reintroduced medieval features like a **CROSS** and **CANDLES** on the altar, images of Christ or the saints, and coloured vestments for the clergy and their assistants. 'Low' churches had none of these things, but they still tended to follow medieval fashions in how they were designed and decorated.

The 20th century

During the first half of the 20th century, Victorian tastes continued to spread through Devon churches. Crosses, candles and vestments gradually became common everywhere, and were no longer thought of as 'high-church'. Then, in about the 1960s, a new and different era of change began to affect churches, a change that followed changes in society.

People no longer went to church because they were expected to go, or had nothing better to do. They went because they wanted to. They tended to be better educated and, in a more democratic society, they regarded themselves as equal. Families went to church together, rather than parents going to church and children to Sunday School at a different time and place. Churches responded to this change by involving the congregation in services more than before. Altars were moved away from the east wall of the chancel, and sometimes down the chancel or into the nave, to bring the priest and people closer together. The congregation was encouraged to do more in the services: reading lessons, leading prayers, playing music or organising

LEFT: *Twentieth-century church art: the east window (Christus Surrexit) at St James' Church, Exeter (1956).*

presentations. Services became more informal and there was more moving about, partly to include children and meet their needs. This sometimes led to changes in the seating. Pews seemed too solid and awkward. They were sometimes replaced by **CHAIRS**, which were easy to move.

Modern churches are social spaces as well as sacred spaces. There is often a kitchen or an area where refreshments are served after services. There may be areas for visual displays: children's work, school photographs, or exhibitions about a current issue or a charity that the church supports.

A thousand years of change

Churches have not always been the same. They have been differently furnished and used in different periods. The simple early medieval churches grew into churches that were groups of rooms with various uses. These churches were highly decorated and gave you a religious experience. The Reformation turned the church into a single space, and taught you in a plain schoolroom. The Georgians made churches more open and comfortable, and the Victorians made them more like theatres. In modern times churches have become more democratic and informal. All of these changes tell us about changes in society outside the church.

Hardly any churches have managed to hide their past altogether, unless they have been completely rebuilt. So, when you look round a church, you will generally see traces of previous times and fashions. The building, and perhaps the rood screen, may come from the Middle Ages. The Reformation brought the whitewashed walls and plain windows. The Georgians built big pulpits and galleries; the Victorians raised the chancel and made the church more decorative again. There may be tombs and monuments, from medieval knights and ladies through Tudor and Stuart gentry to the word-filled tablets of the 1700s and 1800s. Christianity does not change in its basic beliefs, but churches and people vary in how they are Christian. They always have done.

FURTHER READING

There are two good one-volume histories of the Church in England: S. Gilley and W. J. Shiels (eds), *A History of Religion in Britain* (Blackwell, 1994), and A. Ward (ed.), *Not Angels but Anglicans* (Canterbury Press, 2000). On Devon in particular, see N. Orme (ed.), *Unity and Variety: a History of the Church in Devon and Cornwall* (University of Exeter Press, 1991, still in print). Many periods of Devon Church history, with maps, are covered in R. Kain and W. Ravenhill (eds), *Historical Atlas of South-West England* (University of Exeter Press, 1999). A complete guide to church architecture in Devon can be found in B. Cherry and N. Pevsner, *Devon* ('The Buildings of England', Penguin Books, now Yale University Press, 1989); and one to church dedications in N. Orme, *English Church Dedications* (University of Exeter Press, 1996).

The best books on particular periods usually cover England in general. They include, for the Middle Ages, J. Blair, *The Church in Anglo-Saxon Society* (Oxford University Press, 2005), and R. N. Swanson, *Church and Society in Late Medieval England* (Blackwell, 1989). A. G. Dickens, *The English Reformation* (2nd edn, Batsford, 1989), is well balanced by Eamon Duffy's delightful *The Voices of Morebath* (Yale University Press, 2001), which focuses on a Devon parish. For the 17th and 18th centuries, see S. Doran and C. Durston, *Princes, Pastors and People: the Church and religion in England 1529-1689* (2nd edn, Routledge, 2003), and J. Walsh and others, *The Church of England c.1689-c.1833* (Cambridge University Press, 1993). G. W. O. Addleshaw and F. Etchells, *The Architectural Setting of Anglican Worship* (Faber, 1948) explains how churches were used between 1550 and 1948. O. Chadwick, *The Victorian Church* (A. & C. Black, 1966) says a good deal about Devon. Most of the 20th century is covered in A. Hastings, *A History of English Christianity 1920-1990* (3rd edn, SCM Press, 1991), and G. Davie, *Religion in Britain since 1945* (Blackwell, 1994).

LEFT: *St Mary, Molland; with visual aids typical of the 17th and 18th centuries: the Royal Arms and the Ten Commandments.*

GAZETTEER OF CHURCHES

Dividing the county into ten areas, colour coded and each with a map, the gazetteer lists all of Devon's Church of England places of worship, broadly in alphabetical order by place name. A short description of the church and its history is given for each entry.

People today think that church dedications are ancient, but many in use today are 18th and 19th century inventions. For more information, see 'Further Reading' (p41): *English Church Dedications*, N. Orme. Spellings, too, have changed over time and the book reflects current usage.

The OS grid reference for each church can be found in the index at the back of the book.

Lundy Island

NORTH DEVON

TORRIDGE

MID DEVON

EAST DEVON

EXETER

WEST DEVON

TEIGNBRIDGE

TORBAY

PLYMOUTH

SOUTH HAMS

LEFT: Holy Cross, Crediton.

EAST DEVON

Combining a section of the World Heritage Coast, with its attractive seaside towns, and unspoilt countryside with numerous villages and hamlets, East Devon has 93 Anglican churches and chapels, most of which are open during the day.

1 Alfington, St James & St Anne
Grade II

Described as 'A Victorian gem at the end of a country lane' this church was built in 1849. The Architect was William Butterfield, the famous Victorian ecclesiastical architect. Of particular interest is the stained-glass window over the altar designed by Augustus Pugin. The most famous incumbent was John Coleridge Patteson, who eventually became the first Bishop of Melanesia and was martyred on the island of Nukapu. A monument at the back of the church commemorates his life and work. This village became a separate ecclesiastical parish in 1881, and it is now part of the Otter Vale Team.

2 All Saints, All Saints
Grade II*

Consecrated in 1840, a daughter church of Chardstock, it became a parish church in 1998. Originally built at a cost of £1211.7.4 with a 51ft-high belfry containing a single bell. The church's so-called 'mean' chancel was extended in 1890 by 14 feet providing a larger vestry and an organ loft. The pulpit was moved to the north, the east window to the west and a new east window installed. The Ten Commandments tablets were added in 1858 and the texts around the arches in 1861. The church maintains close links with the school and is a vital part of this scattered community.

3 Awliscombe, St Michael & All Angels
Grade I

The church belonged to Wells Cathedral by 1200 but has always been in Exeter diocese. Each successive century has contributed enhancements from its era to the structure or fabric, resulting in the prayerful, welcoming building we have today. Notable features are the Beer stone carved screen, the Last Supper window and a curious double opening porch. Our weekly congregations aged from 0 to 90 are only one aspect of Christian life in the parish: situated in the geographical centre of Awliscombe village, the church is central to most of the local social fabric, maintaining a symbiotic relationship throughout the parish whilst looking to the future.

4 Axminster, St Mary the Virgin
Grade II*

On a bluff above the River Axe, the fine 13th-century tower dominates a small market-manufacturing town. A two-storey porch leads to a four-square, gracefully columned nave and a long, dignified chancel. For a millennium, every age has left its mark, and, occasionally, its treasures, to delight the visitor's curiosity: now ambitious future schemes are proposed. On Thursdays, a busy market sweeps across Minster Green to the walls of our church, expressing its place at the heart of the community. This much-loved building is in constant use for spiritual leadership of the town, frequent music events and by townspeople from a toddler group upwards.

5 Axmouth, St Michael
Grade I

The village has deep historic roots dating back to when the Romans landed in the Axe Estuary to embark upon their conquest of the south west. There are medieval wall paintings within the church which reflect historic and maritime connections. St Michael's is part of the Undercliff Mission Community with St Peter and St Paul, Uplyme. We are a traditional, open evangelical church, attracting members from across the region. Great emphasis is placed upon expository Bible teaching in a pattern of worship which integrates with Uplyme. The principle service takes place every Sunday, alternating Holy Communion with non-sacramental services which are always lay led.

6 Aylesbeare, St Mary
Grade II*

Early records mention a Norman building built of red stone. The 15th-century church has a tower with six bells, low diagonal buttresses and embattled parapet. The first recorded vicar was Gregory in 1261. The ancient porch door opens with a latch string. The nave has a black and white wagon roof. Steps show evidence of a rood loft. The light church has some stained glass and a First World War memorial to soldiers and a VAD nurse. Extensive repairs to the south aisle in 1840 and a new roof in 2004 reflect a generous continuity. The Mothering Sunday Service tradition of children handing posies to mothers continues.

7 Beer, St Michael
Grade II

This church was built in 1877 by Hayward of Exeter in Early English/Decorated style, replacing an old chapel. It consists of nave, chancel, north and south aisles and transepts, vestries and north-west tower. The furnishings, including the choir stalls, pulpit and font are contemporary with the construction of the church. The clock is of the early 18th century with a later escapement, and there is a bell of the early 15th century. The east window of 1889 is by Ward & Hughes.

8 Bicton (East Budleigh), St Mary
Grade II*

Lady Louisa Rolle built St Mary's in 1850 in memory of her late husband Lord John, and having done so had the adjacent medieval church of Holy Trinity reduced to a designer ruin with the south east corner rebuilt by Pugin as a handsome mausoleum. With the Rolle estate now dismantled, St Mary's finds itself spectacularly situated within Bicton Park Botanical Gardens. The thousands of visitors who enter the church every year from the park find a rare Victorian gem, untouched by modernisation, aglow with brilliantly coloured glass. A tiny congregation maintains the church for them with a cheerful, prayerful welcome.

9 Brampford Speke, St Peter
Grade I

This church, first recorded in about 1100, was largely rebuilt in 1852, but its earlier shape can still be traced: a chancel and nave, a later south chapel, and the surviving western tower of the 15th century. The church became nationally famous through the 'Gorham controversy' of 1847-1850: the long drawn-out attempt by the Bishop of Exeter to prevent the appointment of G. C. Gorham, an evangelical clergyman, as vicar. Today we are a lively country parish with a variety of services, including a well-supported family service, 'Service with a Smile', on the third Sunday of every month, and a range of social activities and celebrations of other special occasions. Come and see us some time!

EAST DEVON

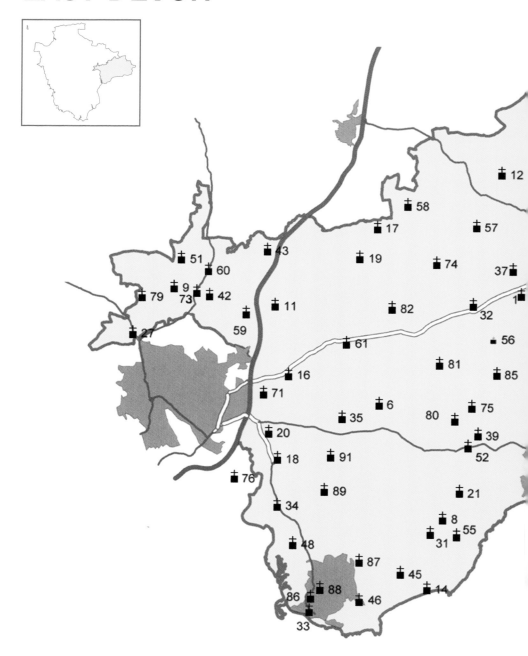

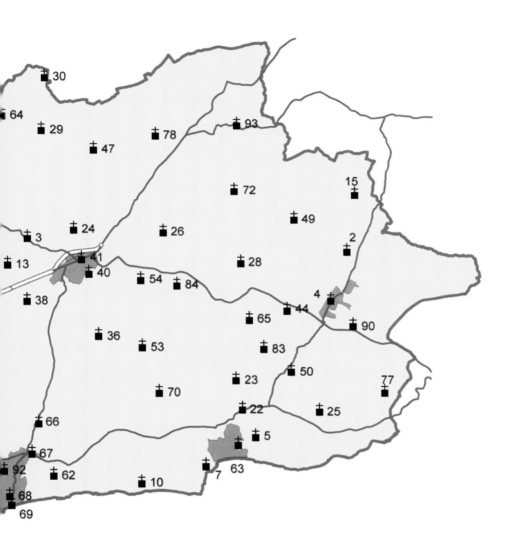

EAST DEVON: LOCATION OF CHURCHES

47

10 Branscombe, St Winifred
Grade I

The Norman tower is four-square, with slit belfry openings. It contains a priest's chamber, with small window overlooking the altar. The nave is mainly Norman, overlooked by the Millennium Cross. The church was enlarged during the 13th and 14th centuries, with transepts, extended nave and chancel. The fine oak gallery is Elizabethan. The chancel screen of 1660 evokes a style of a Devon farm parlour. There is a three-tier pulpit, rare in Devon. The tomb of Joan Wadham (d. 1583) is in the north transept. Her son Nicholas founded Wadham College, Oxford. The church is central to active village life, maintaining strong links with the C of E primary school.

11 Broadclyst, St John the Baptist
Grade I

This is a large Perpendicular church with Somerset-type tower using volcanic trap and Bere dressings. The main arcade was erected c.1400. The north aisle and decorated style window and sedilia appear to be remnants of a previous church. The tower is 16th century. It has arms of Henry VIII and the Chudleigh family. There is a large Jacobean monument to the first Sir John Acland (1613), also a monument to Edward Drew, who died in 1662, legal officer to Elizabeth I. The oak internal rooms (2007), are used for outreach activities. The church is prominent in the village and is developing its work as part of the Clyst Mission Community.

12 Broadhembury, St Andrew Apostle & Martyr
Grade I

Dedicated by Bishop Bronescombe in 1259, but the present church dates mostly from the 15th century. In the nave are two 14th-century windows, and a fine 15th-century window opened to give light to the pulpit, with sculpted figures of flying angels inside and of a man and woman in mediaeval headgear on the outside. The 15th-century font is enriched with figures – St Peter, St Paul, John the Baptist, a bishop and archbishop. These figures are reproduced on the millennium kneeler tapestries at the communion rail, embroidered by the WI. The chancel and tower were restored in the mid-19th century. Regular worship, both Prayer Book and Common Worship. Close links with school and parish.

13 Buckerell, St Mary & St Giles
Grade II*

This church is of medieval origin with the 'revel' being held on the first Sunday in September, St.Giles' day. The simple structure of the main building dates back to 1319 but many changes followed over the centuries. The tower was added later to replace a bell turret. The nave has a wagon roof and the chancel has been refitted. The original stonework is hidden under roughcast but the stone would have come from Buckerell's own quarry, long since exhausted. The church clock is of particular interest. Its age is uncertain; once a one-handed clock it is driven by weights and pulleys.

14 Budleigh Salterton, St Peter
Grade II

This church was consecrated in 1893, designed by G. F. Prynne in Early English form. Nave, chancel, lady chapel, north and south transepts. Walls limestone; tongue and groove barrel-vaulted roof. Interior carvings Beer stone, columns of Ashburton marble flank the pillars. Chancel has a 1931 reredos, choir stalls of dark oak, and nine mosaic panels of New Testament scenes. A unique pulpit in filigree brass represents a net and fish in reference to fisherman, St Peter. 1942 bomb damaged north aisle, roof and all glass. Fine organ is the result of amalgamating Worcester Cathedral Nave organ with original. Worship is a mixture of traditional and modern. We make every effort to cater for all ages.

15 Chardstock, St Andrew
Grade II

In 1155 it was given by Gilbert de Percy to Salisbury Cathedral and became a Peculiar under the jurisdiction of the Dean. It was rebuilt by Canon Charles Woodcock in 1863-1864; only the south wall and former porch remain. The Victorian church consists of nave, chancel, north and south aisles and transepts and a west tower with a ring of six bells dated 1868 and an 18th-century clock bell. The internal fittings are contemporary with the rebuild with the exception of a Jacobean pulpit, the Bowditch Hatchment and Estmond Memorial. It is home to a faithful and friendly congregation and caters for a variety of liturgical tastes.

16 Clyst Honiton, St Michael & All Angels
Grade II*

The first church on this site was probably built in the 12th century and the original font dating from around 1170 is still in use. Today's church dates from the 15th century, but although much of the basic fabric appears to be medieval, the church is essentially the result of a thorough restoration in 1875, when nearly all the detail was replaced. Some fine marble memorials remain from an earlier period. The embattled western tower houses eight bells. A small but very welcoming and well-loved church situated in the heart of the village, opposite the local church school, and just beyond the runway of Exeter International Airport!

17 Clyst Hydon, St Andrew
Grade I

The earliest fabric of the church dates back to the 15th century, the south aisle was added a century later, and the north aisle was built in the 19th century by the Huyshe family, who had the living here for many years, and have their family genealogy recorded in the east and north-east windows. The western tower dates from the 15th century, but underwent major reconstruction c.1658, following a fire. The box pews were built by the village schoolmaster's son, William Hole, in 1832, at a cost of £130. The church has a small but welcoming congregation, and provides a range of worship styles to suit different tastes.

18 Clyst St George, St George
Grade II

The chancel dates from 1300 and the tower and nave from about 1420. Extensively rebuilt between 1851 and 1857 from foundation level by the Victorians, this church was destroyed by enemy action on 31st August 1940. Restoration began in 1950 and the present church was rededicated on 4th July 1952. There is a very good ring of 6 bells. A previous rector, H. T. Ellacomb, 1790-1885, on finding his bell ringers too drunk to ring for divine service, devised the individual chiming mechanism now used throughout the world. In 2002, to mark the 50th anniversary of the earlier restoration, further work was undertaken to enable disabled access and lavatory facilities.

19 Clyst St Lawrence, St Lawrence
Grade I

The present church building, notable for its tall tower and short nave, dates back to the 15th century, being a rebuilding of an earlier structure. The font remains from the previous building and is thought to date from about 1200. The church contains a fine chancel screen of 15th-century origin with 20th-century paintwork and an incised slab which has been dated prior to 1275. Within the grounds can be found a preaching cross which is reputed to have been damaged during the Prayer Book Rebellion of 1549. The church is well supported by the community and there are bi-monthly evening services.

20 Clyst St Mary, St Mary
Grade II

Parts of the church date from the 13th and 15th centuries. Transepts were added in 1818, and lengthened in 1870; the building was reordered and reoriented in the 1890s. The church is cruciform in plan, with a west tower. Internally, there are three stained-glass windows of high quality. The organ was installed in 1938, and the three bells date from 1430, 1485 and 1674. In the churchyard there are some listed monuments and a fine cedar tree. In 1991 the church was extensively damaged by a fire, following which some reordering took place and the choir screen, altar and pulpit were removed.

21 Colaton Raleigh, St John the Baptist
Grade II*

Built in 1226, the church consists of a nave, chancel, north and south aisles, south transept, reservation chapel and west tower. The north arcade and the font are 13th century and are the oldest surviving parts of the building. The tower is 15th-century and two of the six bells date back to this period. An active team ring regularly. Restoration was carried out in 1875 under the architect R. M. Fulford. Inside, there are interesting examples of rare sgraffito work carried out at the time of the restoration. A small, welcoming, group of people worship here every week. The services vary between Holy Communion, evensong BCP and family services.

22 Colyford, St Michael
Grade II

A small church built in 1889 in the Arts and Crafts style by R. M. Fulford, originally intended as a private chapel. Comprises nave and chancel in one, south transept, south-west porch and north vestry. There is a bellcote over the west gable. The interior is of red and yellow brick with stone dressings. The oak reredos of 1891 has a relief of Bartolommeo's 'The Entombment' in an elaborate surround. This, along with the pulpit, lectern, font and chancel screen, is part of the original furnishings of the church.

23 Colyton, St Andrew
Grade I

The church is mainly of the 15th and 16th centuries, but there is some 12th-century work in the tower base and chancel. An important feature is the west window, installed as plain glass in the 15th century, but re-glazed in the 19th with stained glass. The octagonal lantern sitting atop the Norman tower, in which is a ring of eight bells, is an impressive sight. A fire in 1933 caused extensive damage, but that revealed a Saxon cross now standing in the church. The two brass chandeliers each holding thirty-six candles were bought in 1796. The church is in the centre of the town and plays an important part in the community.

24 Combe Raleigh, St Nicholas
Grade II*

St Nicholas Church, Combe Raleigh dates mainly from the early 15th century although the list of rectors dates from 1260. The nave piers are of Beer stone and the walls of 'dressed chert'. The nave and aisle have Devon wagon roofs. The 14th-century tower has an unusual stairwell and stair turret. The south door is also very old and unusual: it is formed of two leaves hinged in the middle. The church is one of the only two public meeting places in the village and provides a venue for a variety of activities, both secular and religious. These range from concerts and carol services to flower festivals and Easter Egg hunts.

25 Combpyne, St Mary the Virgin
Grade I

Set in the valley of Combpyne St Mary with Rousdon it serves the combined parish, and is a gem much appreciated by the local community and visitors. With possible Saxon origins, the church dates from 1240; renovations occurred in the late 19th century and 1950-1951. Notable are the tower's 13th-century arch, the unusual saddleback roof ', the 13th-century Beer stone font, the triptych of the Last Supper and a remaining rood staircase. Two of three bells date from 1400 and historic murals include a ship, perhaps drawn by a 14th-century seafarer; the pews come from St Pancras. The church has community use, including concerts, and services are weekly.

26 Cotleigh, St Michael
Grade II*

Coteleia is recorded in the See of Crediton in 909 and in the Domesday Book. The north aisle, nave and tower were built in the 15th and 16th centuries of stone and rubble. All columns, arches and windows are made of Beer stone. The nave has a 15th-century ceiled wagon roof consisting of six bays of moulded ribs and purlins, with four leaf motifs and shields under each truss. The box pews were changed to the existing oak pews in 1911. The 15th-century stone font is carved with several designs. The tower has a ring of six bells, the tenor weighing 7cwt. The churchyard has two chest tombs.

27 Cowley (Newton St Cyres), St Anthony

This chapel of ease was founded in 1868 on the benefaction of William Gibbs of Tyntesfield. Built of limestone and in a medieval Gothic style, it consists of nave, chancel, south vestry, north porch with bellcote over the chancel arch. The oak reredos was the work of Harry Hems and was given in memory of the Merivale family of Barton Place. The altar cross was presented by Lady Florence Cecil in 1936 and came from Bishop Cecil's chapel at Barton Place. Historically, Cowley belonged to the parish of Brampford Speke, but the chapel was transferred to the parish of Newton St Cyres in the mid-20th century. There is a weekly Eucharist – 4th Sunday excepted.

28 Dalwood, St Peter
Grade I

This church was restored in 1875. It was extended by 3ft on the south wall, the box pews were ripped out, the gallery taken down and the carved oak screen removed. There are traces of medieval glass in the east window. The two bosses overhead symbolise where the civic power ceased and the ecclesiastical power began. We have six fine bells hung in an iron frame. We have an enthusiastic band of ringers. The pulpit is Jacobean and looks as if it was at one time part of a 'double-decker'. The crudely cut wording exhorts us to 'Walke as Children of Light'. The church plays an important part as a centrepiece for this vibrant village.

29 Dunkeswell, St Nicholas
Grade II

The first real church was consecrated in 1259, the local abbey maintaining it. A later church was rebuilt in 1818 and 1868, in Early English style. Poor workmanship and vibration from US Navy aircraft led to the tower's demolition in 1947; replaced in 1954, its bells were rehung in 1959. Interesting are the Norman font, with its scaly elephant and figures, the six corbels depicting the Simcoe sisters, the US Navy memorial plaque for 187 officers and men and its donated organ, the east window and the WI village map. There are close links with its sister churches and the Methodists and a rolling plan for further linking.

30 Dunkeswell Abbey, Holy Trinity
Grade II

Mrs Simcoe and daughters planned the building of 1842, in lofty, puritanical style, and gave its endowment. Standing on the abbey church site, it served a separate parish until 1959. Features are the Simcoes' designs, tiles from the original abbey floor, the coffins of founder, William Brewer, and his wife and much Simcoe memorabilia of the General's time as the Lieutenant-Governor of the Province of Upper Canada, 1791-96, and at Wolford Lodge. The church lies in a peaceful, green area among remains of the original abbey; much of the abbey stone was incorporated in the new building, looked after by a caring community. There is at least one service there every month.

31 East Budleigh, All Saints
Grade I

A church has stood here since Saxon times and still faithfully serves this small rural community today. The building we now see is mostly 12th and 15th-century. Our 16th-century carved oak benches are quite remarkable. Carved by villagers depicting the occupations of those times, all of them are secular without a single sacred emblem. Some mythical beasts are thought to have been carved by sailors returning from America with Drake or Raleigh. The 15th-century wooden ceiling shows some wonderfully restored and re-gilded bosses. Our most famous son, Sir Walter Raleigh, was born in the village in 1552. The Raleigh pew can still be found in the nave.

32 Escot, St Philip & St James
Grade II

The church can be easily missed, lying as it does amidst green fields and approached by a track from the old A30. Built in 1840 by Sir John Kennaway, surrounded by an immaculate churchyard, it is surprisingly spacious, with a wonderfully peaceful atmosphere, consisting of simple nave and chancel lit by lancet windows. Although the interior is plain, the reredos with its Gothic pinnacles and mosaic inlay is immediately noticeable. Two windows on the south side are of exceptional interest, installed in the late 19th century, and designed by the distinguished artist Henry Holiday. Now part of the Otter Vale Ministry, the small, welcoming congregation enjoys worship every Sunday.

33 Exmouth (Littleham-cum-Exmouth), Holy Trinity
Grade II

High above the town of Exmouth, the tower of Holy Trinity has been a landmark for travellers and sailors for nearly two hundred years. Drastic restoration was needed by 1905 and in 1992 extensive re-ordering resulted in the building we have today. This Victorian church supplies most of our parish and outreach needs under one roof. The ground floor houses the church, offices and coffee bar and is fully compliant for the needs of the disabled, including a lift to the first floor where a large hall with full catering facilities and toilets are sited with a further smaller hall on the second floor. All this without compromising the beautiful interior.

34 Exton (Woodbury), St Andrew

The original church was a winnowing barn given to Exton by Lady Rolle in 1864. On 30th September 1960 this building was destroyed by flooding. A new church of brick and tile construction was completed by 1962, built above flood level. In 2004 the church was reordered with the help of Mr Plant – the sanctuary was redecorated, the pews replaced by padded chairs and the seating area carpeted. Lighting is from four decorative chandeliers. Music is provided by a Bevington Chamber organ. Weekly services are held in the morning but the service on the first Sunday is in the evening.

35 Farringdon, St Petrock & St Barnabas
Grade II*

Rebuilt in 1870-1871 by William White. Comprises a nave, narrow chancel, north aisle, north transept, vestry, south porch and west tower with a shingled spire. Contrasting colours of stone are used throughout, and being of one building phase the style is consistent. The interior is of stencilled red brick, with the most elaborate designs in the chancel. The Beer stone font is Norman. The nave floor includes several reset 17th-century ledger stones, and there are Minton tiles in the chancel showing symbols of the Evangelists. The oak altar is decorated with painted stencilled designs similar to those on the walls.

36 Farway, St Michael & All Angels
Grade II*

The list of Farway rectors dates from 1340 but a smaller church stood here long before that date. Built of local flint stone, the church has three Norman pillars. The chancel has two 18th-century monuments and a stained-glass window dedicated to the Revd Thomas Putt. An apple tree grown in local orchards is named the 'Tom Putt'. The north aisle was rebuilt in 1628 and in the side chapel, the 'Prideaux chapel' is a monument of Sir Edmund Prideaux who died in 1628. The 15th-century tower holds six bells. The original peal of three was increased to six in 2001 and re-hung in a new frame.

37 Feniton, St Andrew
Grade II*

This is a warm and friendly church dating mainly form the 13th and 15th centuries with links to c.1066 when the Malherbe family took possession. The last Malherbe built the south aisle upon marriage in 1549, decorating the capitals with his 'n' her arms. We have a functioning six-bell tower, a beautiful rood screen, c.1550, a rare stone cadaver in exceptional condition, c.1500, and a Henry Holiday east window (1878) with a central panel of Christ, thought to be unique. Some pews are 17th-century; others have ends expertly carved c.1905. We have contemporary links with Melanesia through Bishop John Coleridge Patteson, born in Feniton Court in 1827 and martyred in 1871.

38 Gittisham, St Michael
Grade I

The earliest mention of the church is when the first recorded rector was instituted in 1279. The church is built of dressed flint, cement covered and is in the Early English and Perpendicular styles. There is a tower at the west end with a clock and five bells. The interior breathes the atmosphere of the 18th century with the box pews, installed in 1715, wagon roof and the collection of hatchments and a Georgian west gallery, first used on Good Friday 1701, having been built by Sir Thomas Putt. In the south aisle, there are several memorials, particularly one to Henry Beaumont who died in 1591 and another to Sir Thomas Putt and his wife.

39 Harpford, St Gregory the Great
Grade II*

This 13th-century church, comprising a nave, a north aisle and a chancel, was faithfully restored in the 1880s. Of particular interest are the font, the leper squint and the rich variety of stained glass. The 15th-century west tower houses a peal of bells, which are rung on most Sundays. Augustus Toplady, author of Rock of Ages, was vicar in 1766. Two lines from the hymn are engraved on the base of the churchyard cross, which was erected in 1778 as his memorial. The Book of Common Prayer is used for every Sunday service, its traditional liturgy drawing most members of the regular congregation to Harpford from nearby villages.

40 Honiton, St Michael & All Angels
Grade II*

Dating originally from 1406, St Michael's is the original parish church of Honiton. It is now a chapel of ease under the patronage of St Paul's Honiton, but continues to be used for Eucharist and Evensong services as well as for weddings and funerals. The church is unusually built as a perfect rectangle, which accounts for its fine acoustic qualities. It was badly damaged by fire in 1911 but was restored and re-dedicated in 1912; in 2000 furnishings from the Allhallows Chapel at Rousdon were moved to the church to form the Allhallows War Memorial Chapel.

41 Honiton, St Paul
Grade II*

Built on the site of the old Allhallows School Chapel, St Paul's was dedicated by the Bishop of Exeter in 1838. Designed by Charles Fowler, a Devon architect, the church is built in a Norman style with rounded arches and using local stone; the 104ft bell tower is a conspicuous landmark in the town. The church benefits from a modern organ built by Kenneth Tickell, which is much appreciated by visiting organists. The church is very active in the community and acts as the parish church, hosting a number of civic services. The musical tradition in St Paul's is very strong and the church also offers a number of services and outreach sessions.

42 Huxham (Poltimore), St Mary the Virgin
Grade II*

The original 14th-century church was entirely rebuilt in the 19th century – the chancel in 1864 by Hayward, and the nave in 1871 by Ferrey. It is a small building, comprising nave, chancel, south porch and west bellcote. The font is Norman, set onto a 19th-century base. There are fragments of medieval glass in the chancel windows, and a medieval piscina in the south chancel wall. The timber screen is possibly 15th or 16th-century, although may be even earlier.

43 Killerton (Broadclyst), The Holy Evangelist (Proprietary Chapel)
Grade I

The Chapel of the Holy Evangelist was built in 1841 by Sir Thomas Acland, 10th Baronet (1787-1871) as a place of worship for his family and the tenants and workers on his estate. The seating is like that of a college chapel: the congregation facing one another across the central aisle. In years gone by, everyone had their own special seat with children ranged on benches across the chapel. Killerton House is now owned by the National Trust. The chapel lies in the parish of Broadclyst and is still used occasionally for worship. It is open to visitors who explore the estate.

44 Kilmington, St Giles
Grade II*

The body of the church was rebuilt in 1861-1862. It had become dilapidated since earlier work was carried out in 1832. The tower is original and dates from the end of the 15th century. Two lancet windows in the sanctuary (one depicting our patron saint) date from an earlier church prior to 1288. The oldest monument in the church is that of the Southcott family on the north wall. A royal coat of arms from the time of Charles II is on the ceiling and there is a hatchment above the west door. A stone in the south churchyard marks the site of a mass grave of warriors who died fighting the Danes in 937.

45 Knowle (Budleigh Salterton), St John
Licensed for worship in 1893.

46 Littleham cum Exmouth, St Margaret and St Andrew
Grade II*

The original parish church for Exmouth, has been at the centre of the community since 1236 and remains so today. The chancel dates back to the 13th century, the nave and tower to the 15th and the Drake family added the north aisle in the 16th century. Lady Nelson is buried in the churchyard and there is a memorial to Emily and Mary Peel, daughters of former Prime Minister Sir Robert Peel. Today, this spirit-filled church serves the village of Littleham through daily prayer and mission. It has a heart for the community and actively supports cross-denominational outreach initiatives in Exmouth as well as various overseas missions.

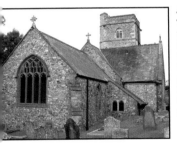

47 Luppitt, St Mary
Grade I

The early 14th-century cruciform building stands on the hill overlooking the village, and is believed to have been built by Sir John Carew of Mohun's Ottery. The tower and porch were probably added in 1500. The early Norman carved stone font and pillar piscina predate the building. The tower has eight bells, three of which were recorded in 1553. The chancel was rebuilt in 1890, and the oak seats, pulpit and furniture were installed in 1923. Regular worship includes an all-age family service, morning and evening Holy Communion, and Evening Prayer. On the 5th Sunday the parishes of the benefice unite for worship. There are strong links between church and community.

48 Lympstone, Nativity of the Blessed Virgin Mary
Grade II*

A Norman font recalls an early church, first documented in 1228, whose rector in 1275 was Henry Potel. In 1409 Bishop Edmund de Stafford consecrated the church, rebuilt in local red sandstone; the tower and three bays of the north aisle arcade and the chancel arch remain. A further rebuilding 1863-1864 under Edward Ashworth demolished much of the church, including richly coloured wall and roof paintings, but it retains historic traces and is much loved by locals and visitors. Worship each Sunday is traditional; every month there is a family service with a worship band. The Primary School worships in church twice a week.

49 Membury, St John the Baptist
Grade I

The present building incorporates work of every century from the 12th to the 20th, proof of continual existence of Christian worship on the site. The tall tower of the church, which is slimmer and taller than most Devon churches, can be seen from many vantage points and dominates not only the village but the surrounding countryside. The belfry contains six bells and there is a very keen group of ringers. The church forms part of the Axminster group of five churches, with services every Sunday including a family service which involves young people from the village, plus frequent special occasions which attract all age groups throughout the year.

50 Musbury, St Michael
Grade I

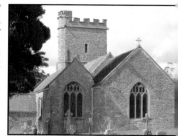

This church dates from the 13th century. It has been much altered, and extensively rebuilt and re-ordered in the 19th century. It contains many monuments; the most striking one commemorating the Drakes of Ashe, dates from 1611 to 1646 and consists of three couples kneeling, a very rare arrangement. The granddaughter of Sir John and Lady Drake, the last of the couples commemorated, was Elizabeth, mother of the first Duke of Marlborough, born at Ashe in 1650. A fine organ supplied by Bevington in 1870 was restored in 1990. There is a peal of six bells dating from 1785, regularly rung. The clock dates from 1729. Services are Prayer Book and Common Worship.

51 Netherexe (Rewe), St John the Baptist
Grade I

This church is designated as a chapel of ease. The church stands in the corner of a field and is very small, consisting only of chancel and nave with continuous roof, south porch and vestry. It is thought a church stood here in Saxon times. On the south side of the chancel there is a piscina with trefoil arch and on the north side a credence table. The font is said to be Norman with square bowl scalloped beneath and on the base. The church holds five services a year, including the major festivals of Christmas, Easter, Whitsuntide and Harvest.

52 Newton Poppleford, St Luke
Grade II*

A church has stood in the centre of this village in the beautiful Otter Valley for over 700 years. Most of the church was rebuilt in the 1870s: only the tower is ancient. More recently the village has grown and the interior of the church rearranged to be warm and welcoming. The church is still at the centre of the community's spiritual life, with lively Sunday worship and children's teaching. There are several home groups, an after-school club, a teenage group, and meetings for regular prayer and Lent courses. Christians are also at the heart of many of the societies that help the village to be a vibrant and caring community.

53 Northleigh, St Giles
Grade II*

St Giles dates from the 14th century (nave and chancel) with the north aisle, chapel and tower added in the late 15th century. Pew ends, pulpit and chancel screen are beautifully carved oak from the 15th century. The four bells, regularly rung, form the only complete pre-Reformation set in Devon. The parishioners and village residents of Northleigh have engaged in a major renovation in 2007. They are justly proud of a medieval treasure which is open every day to all, which welcomes visitors and community of all ages every Sunday for worship, and which reflects a commitment to the spiritual welfare of all whom it serves.

54 Offwell, St Mary the Virgin
Grade I

St Mary's is a small rural church located in the middle of the village. Of 13th-century origin, the chancel arch and south window were certainly built about 1200. The roof is ceiled so what is above the ceiling can only be implied by the close spacing of the roof trusses as being earlier than the15th century, when there was a major rebuild. The interior is of great beauty, enriched by 18th-century box pews, the 1724 pulpit (added to in 1784) and part of the painted rood screen which came from St Mary Major in Exeter, demolished in 1970. Edward Coppleston, Bishop of Llandaff, restored the church in about 1840.

55 Otterton, St Michael & All Angels
Grade II*

William the Conqueror granted Otterton Manor to the Abbey of Mont St Michel, Normandy and priory and abbey were built in the 12th century. After 1415 the priory fell into ruin. The church served Otterton until 1870 when it was demolished and the present church built on the site in one year. The bell tower was left in situ unusually at the east end. The new building is of Beer stone, marble pillars and woodwork all supplied by the Rolle estate, with a reredos of Caen stone from Normandy. It is well supported by the local community and the school, and has a small faithful congregation in this large building.

56 Ottery St Mary, St Mary the Virgin
Grade I

This grand collegiate church was built substantially in its present form in the early 1340s by Bishop John de Grandisson and was modelled on Exeter Cathedral. The church dominates the small town of Ottery St Mary (the birthplace of Samuel Taylor Coleridge) and is acknowledged to be one of the finest parish churches in the country. It also features one of the oldest surviving mechanical clocks in the country. We are a friendly church with weekly traditional and all-age worship services giving variety with the aim of meeting our mission statement, 'to know God better and to make God better known'. We form part of the Otter Vale Team.

57 Payhembury, St Mary the Virgin
Grade I

Building began in the 12th century, but it was substantially added to in the 15th. The church is built of Beer stone and was restored by the Revd George Messiter-Terry in 1897. A richly carved and painted screen extends across the nave and aisle dating from 1450. The chancel roof is decorated with twelve bosses and twelve musical angels. The church boasts some of the oldest glass in Devon. There are six bells with an enthusiastic team of bell-ringers. The church stands at the heart of the village. There are strong links with the primary school, an all-age monthly service, and a small but welcoming congregation.

58 Plymtree, St John the Baptist
Grade I

At the heart of the community, this building dates from the 14th century, and has a tower with six bells. There is a magnificent carved 15th-century rood screen complete with original paintings on the panels. On the north side are unusual Tudor windows. Many wooden pews have medieval carved ends. The outside of the tower includes a rare statue of the Madonna and Child. A splendid yew tree has been recorded as over 1100 years old. The church is used regularly for a variety of worship styles as well as by the village primary school and for ecumenical services. It is a haven of beauty, tranquillity and peace.

59 Poltimore, St Mary the Virgin
Grade I

Poltimore has long been linked with the Bampfylde family and Poltimore House. Its parish church was built in 1390 by John Bampfylde, from red sandstone and volcanic trap. The entrance on the north side is along a cobbled path dated 1743. There is a priceless rood screen c.1520 with delicate Renaissance carving. Four diamond-shaped canvases, with armorial bearings, hang in the church. The six bells, cast in 1723, all have founder's initials and dates. The church is valued by the community, though the number worshipping regularly is around 20. Linked with the Raddon Team and Stoke Canon Benefice it forms a Mission Community, sharing services and extending a warm welcome.

60 Rewe, St Mary the Virgin

Dates mainly from the 15th century – the nave and north aisle are of c.1450 and the north transept and chancel are of 1495, built by Sir Nicholas Wadham. The tower was rebuilt in 1810 after being struck by lightning, and the building was restored in 1867-1868 by Sedding and Ashworth. The screen is 15th century and was painted in 1870, along with the pulpit, aumbry, and 1631 almsbox to match the redecoration of the chancel at this time. There is a good set of medieval pew ends, one recording the marriage between Wadham and Seymour. The stone font is also of the 15th century.

61 Rockbeare, St Mary with St Andrew
Grade II*

A small, light village church, with west tower, north aisle wall and aisle arcade of grey ashlar and medieval, and south and east walls of red sandstone. Much rebuilt in 1887-1889 by Hayward and Tait. It has a wagon roof with bosses; west gallery with Elizabethan parapet over Second World War Memorial; Perpendicular west doorway with fleurons around arch; stained-glass window in chancel by Louis Davis 1928. There is a very rare lectern with pelican feeding young. Attractive higher lychgate 1890. Lower lychgate 1962. Our small elderly congregation meet twice a month, but are hoping to reach out more into the village now we are part of the Clyst Mission Community.

62 Salcombe Regis, St Mary & St Peter
Grade II

A massive Norman pillar, carved stonework and doorway mark a 12th-century origin, extending into a 13th-century south aisle, chancel and arcades, and a 15th-century vestry. 20th-century additions include a bell-ringers' gallery and a 'Whistler' triptych. An extensive burial ground is still in use, with planned enlargement into a Garden of Rest. Congregations for the two Sunday services are drawn from a wide area, extending well outside the parish boundaries, as is common in the Sid Valley Team. Teas in the churchyard on summer Sundays are a strong attraction to residents and visitors alike.

63 Seaton, St Gregory
Grade I

Situated in a large churchyard half a mile from the sea, St Gregory's has been much altered over the years, with parts dating from the 13th, 14th, 15th, 18th, 19th and 20th centuries. It comprises nave, north aisle, chancel, south chapel, vestry, south porch and west tower. The interior was restored in 1860 by Ashworth, and then again in 1901 when the roofs were renewed and the internal fittings updated. The pulpit, font and clergy desk by H. Hems date from this time. At the west end of the church there is a gallery, which was installed in the 19th century. There are a number of monuments in the church.

64 Sheldon, St James the Greater
Grade II

This delightful church nestles in the tiny village of Sheldon in the Blackdown Hills. It dates from the 13th century, replacing an existing church. The bell, stolen in 1981, was a testimony of the endurance of the Christian faith in the parish of Sheldon over five centuries. The church is frequently visited by architectural enthusiasts as it has a beautifully carved rood screen and an ancient font with a carved wooden canopy. St James the Greater is the centre of a small community and remains a tranquil, quiet place for churchgoers and visitors.

65 Shute, St Michael
Grade II*

The earliest record of the church refers to the foundation of a chapelry of Colyton Church during the 13th century. Originally built in the Early English architectural style the building was considerably enlarged during the Hanoverian period of the 15th century when the Lady chapel was added and again in the early 19th century, with the addition of the north aisle. A treasured possession is a former barrel organ built by Ebenezer Blackwell in 1757. This instrument was formerly housed in Shute Barton, now a National Trust property adjoining the churchyard. Worship is largely traditional with a monthly family service, frequently lay led, and well attended.

66 Sidbury, St Giles & St Peter
Grade I

St Giles has one of only six known Saxon crypts in the country and architecture covering all periods to the present day, including a tower c.1150, eight bells and a needle spire reaching 95ft. Stepping inside through the two-storey porch the nave, aisles (c.1190) and transepts have barrel vaulted ceilings dated to the 15th century. At the west end, a gallery c.1620 with a fine organ and a font c.1450. The chancel has several ancient memorials. Note the five exceptional Kemp windows. We are part of the Sid Valley Mission Community with services to suit varying preferences and strong links with the C of E School.

67 Sidford, St Peter

The foundation stone was laid in 1866 by Stephen Cave, MP for Shoreham. The initial building was completed and consecrated in September 1868. Originally built as a chapel of ease, it was licensed to hold services in 1868 by the Bishop of Exeter but not fully licensed until 1943. Built of red brick with bath stone facings it is in imitation of the Early English style. There is a clerestory over the nave arches. We are part of the Sid Valley Mission Community with services to suit varying preferences and have a hall attached which provides outreach to the community.

68 Sidmouth, All Saints
Grade II

Begun in 1837 to be a centre for low church worship in the town, the church continues in the Evangelical tradition, playing a full part in the life of the Sid Valley Team. Although very plainly decorated with many pews, there is a certain beauty to its austere simplicity. There are plans for a complete renovation of the interior in 2008-2009 to enable the church to be the centre of vibrant worship for the new century, helping us to fulfil our vision to be a biblical church with a heart for God for all the generations in the town.

69 Sidmouth, St Giles & St Nicholas
Grade II*

The tower and columns in the north aisle are all that remain of Sidmouth's medieval parish church recorded in 1174. In 1858 a major rebuild created the spacious church of today. Rich stained glass is a major feature: the west window was presented by Queen Victoria and the east window by the Earl of Buckinghamshire. A small piece of medieval glass representing the wounds of Christ is preserved in the Lady chapel. Open daily, many find the church a haven of prayer and peace. The church fosters links with the civic life of the town and welcomes its many visitors, especially at the Sunday Eucharist which draws a large congregation.

70 Southleigh, St Lawrence
Grade II*

Of Norman origins and with a 15th-century tower, the church was mostly rebuilt in the 19th century. Restored in 1880 by Hayward, it consists of nave, chancel, west tower, south aisle, vestry and porch. The south entrance is a rebuilt Norman doorway. Internally all of the furniture and fittings date from the 19th century, some with Gothic decoration. The prayer desk, choir stalls, lectern and pulpit are all oak, and the pews are pine. In the churchyard there are four listed tombs made of Beerstone ashlar dating from the 17th and 18th centuries.

71 Sowton, St Michael & All Angels
Grade I

Believed to be fourth church sited here, the current building is partly medieval and partly Victorian Gothic Revival. In 1845 it was largely rebuilt of Heavitree stone at the expense of John Garratt of Bishops Court, under architect John Hayward. He kept the old northern arcade with its carved capitals, one showing the pomegranate of Aragon and the Tudor rose. The interior remains virtually unchanged to this day. It features stencilled walls and roof in the chancel and a variety of good stained-glass windows by Thomas Willement. The tower contains a clock and eight bells. Now part of the Clyst Mission Community, it offers twice-monthly evening services.

72 Stockland, St Michael and All Angels
Grade I

Stockland church shows evidence of an earlier 12th-century building with Norman Romanesque arches surviving on the south wall of the chancel and a 13th-century lancet window in the Broadhayes Chapel. However, most of the church, including the 100ft tower, was rebuilt in the 14th century with the addition of a north aisle in the 15th century. The six bells date from 1603. A small building at the south west entrance to the churchyard was known as the Church Ale House. Stockland Church is part of a mission community and regularly joins with the other churches for a united service. The weekly worship includes a monthly Family Service.

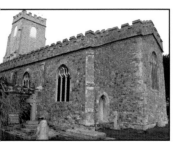

73 Stoke Canon, St Mary Magdalene
Grade I

The church is set in a graveyard where wildflowers, trees and bulbs make a peaceful setting. The tower is 15th-century, but the nave, south porch and chancel were rebuilt in 1835 by Mason. This resulted in an aisle-less building, with the interior of the church a simple, light, 'preaching box'. The building was further restored in 1875 by Ashworth. The tower contains a ring of six bells, the earliest dating from 1641. The font may be pre-Conquest. There are some medieval bench ends. Substantial roof repairs have recently been undertaken and a major but sympathetic reordering is in the pipeline to allow wider and more flexible use of the building.

74 Talaton, St James the Apostle
Grade I

The beautiful village church is noted for its early 15th-century tower, with statues of saints and of the Virgin and Child. The tower houses a peal of six bells, still in regular use, two of which date back to the 15th and 16th centuries. Despite 19th-century restoration to the north and south aisles, and rebuilding of the chancel, the original roof survives as a fine example of an early wagon roof. The original rood screen, in beautifully carved oak, still divides the nave from the chancel. We are a welcoming church with one goal and two objectives: to glorify God, to know Christ and to make him known.

75 Tipton St John, St John the Evangelist
Grade II

This 'church on a hill' was completed in 1839 and the village primary school was built in the grounds. Strong links with the school have been maintained and there is also an active church youth group. The typically Victorian church is stone-built and simple in design, with a gallery at the west end. A particular feature of the church building is its stained-glass windows: one is a copy of Holman Hunt's painting 'The Light of the World'. Services range from informal family worship to traditional Evensong and the church organises many social events. Congregational members are involved in most aspects of village life.

76 Topsham, St Margaret
Grade II

Overlooking the Exe Estuary with magnificent views towards the sea and the Haldon hills, the church was rebuilt in 1873 to a design by Edward Ashworth. The 14th-century tower remains (with six bells) and also the Norman font and some memorials going back to the 16th century. The church has a strong choir and musical tradition and is currently planning to install a fine Nicholson organ from a redundant church in Plymouth. The Children's Church is popular with young families in the town and we aim to serve all ages in the community, with events and activities at the back of the church and in the adjoining church rooms.

77 Uplyme, St Peter & St Paul
Grade II*

Uplyme Church is part of the Undercliff Mission Community with Axmouth St Michael. We are a lively, open evangelical fellowship which puts great emphasis upon Bible teaching and outreach. We have very strong links with our neighbouring church school. The church's worship and mission are largely administered by lay people and we are enriched through having a breadth of ages and traditions within the fellowship. Although proudly in Devon, the village has strong links with neighbouring Lyme Regis and the heritage coast. Come and visit this beautiful area and, if you call at Uplyme church on a Sunday, you are guaranteed a warm welcome!

78 Upottery, St Mary the Virgin
Grade II*

Set in the picturesque Otter Valley, this church stands at the centre of Upottery. The chancel can be dated c.1150. It is built in the Perpendicular style with the tower added soon after 1400. The 18th-century tower clock was installed by A. Cleak of Bridport in 1794. Four bells were originally installed in 1553. These were replaced in 1818 with five bells, the sixth being hung in 1897. A local artist designed the stained-glass Millennium window. There are several memorials to the Addington family. The church has strong links with the community and offers a wide range of services and activities to both young and old.

79 Upton Pyne, Church of Our Lady
Grade I

Set on a north-facing hill the original church probably dates from the early 12th century when the manor was granted to a Pyne. The church was consecrated in 1328 and partially survives in the fabric of the chancel. The tower has statues that were carved in the cathedral workshop in 1349. The Victorians did much to the interior, but on the south wall two 16th-century canopied tombs commemorate the Larder family. Behind the altar a copy of a Jean Jouvenet painting of the Last Supper draws one to Holy Communion; lay-led services are well supported. The Raddon Team looks to become a Mission Community in 2009.

80 Venn Ottery (Tipton), St Gregory
Grade II*

This charming little village church is thought to have existed in 1095. The red stone Norman tower sits on Saxon foundations. A calamitous fire in 1780 destroyed the thatched rood, and much of the church, and it was not properly rebuilt until 1882, by the Victorians. Many of the beautifully carved medieval pew ends survived the fire, including one representing Pope Gregory. Augustus Toplady (author of 'Rock of Ages') was vicar from 1766-1768. The congregation is very welcoming to visitors, and support a sung Eucharist and a traditional Communion, both once a month, together with a number of special services.

81 Westhill, St Michael the Archangel
Grade II

Built in 1846 by Sir John Kennaway, and designed by the architect Mr Wollaston, St Michael's is in the Early English style. The roof is varnished oak, the lancet-headed windows are filled with stained glass and there is a small bell tower. The pulpit and font are of carved stone. A short history, written in 1987, is available in the church. Within the Otter Vale Team, St Michael's is a lively, growing village church, which aims to provide services and activities for many traditions and ages. Current details and a map can be found on the website. Our vision is to be a church 'Bringing Jesus Christ to our Community'.

82 Whimple, St Mary
Grade II*

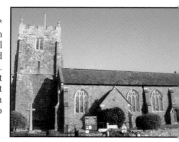

Built in the Perpendicular style and dating from the 15th century, the church was substantially altered in 1845 when a south aisle was added and the chancel extended. It has medieval tracery, carved bench ends to the nave pews and 19th-century box pews in the aisles. There is a 16th-century octagonal font. Incorporated in the tower screen are eight painted panels which it is thought formed part of a rood screen. The squat tower contains six bells, the oldest dating from the 15th century. We are a friendly and outgoing church with a variety of services and activities. We have one goal and two objectives: to glorify God, to know Christ and to make him known.

83 Whitford (Shute), St Mary at the Cross

Built of red brick in 1908 as a daughter church to St Michael's at Shute, it was originally designated as a mission church for the village of Whitford. There is photographic evidence held of the construction and records of fundraising methods, one of which involved collecting cards filled with 120 pennies. Prayer Book Holy Communion Services are held once a month with special quarterly services celebrating specific events in the church calendar year. Musical accompaniment is by an American organ. A bellcote at the west end houses two bells.

84 Widworthy, St Cuthbert
Grade II*

A little gem of a church – 14th-century – set in beautiful countryside outside the village of Wilmington off the A35. The list of rectors dates from 1274. The font is l5th-century. It has a remarkable collection of monuments, starting with a knight, Sir William Prouz, dated l329, in his armour, the monument to Alice Isaack, 1685, with its original paintwork, and many marble monuments to the Marwood family from the l700s. St Cuthbert's serves a friendly, supportive community very ready to welcome all. There is a service every Sunday morning. The church is open daily between 9am and 6pm but closes in winter at 4.30pm.

85 Wiggaton (Ottery St Mary), St Edward the Confessor — *Grade II*

The church was built in 1893 after local fundraising and the generosity of two landowners ensured that the church was debt free. The simple but impressive design provides a good atmosphere for services and is adaptable for other community uses. The church was described in the parish magazine in 1893 as forming a striking feature in this picturesque hamlet. Our present mission, with the full support of the Otter Vale Team Ministry, is to take God's message to as many in our community as we can and to play our full part in the team mission. The building has been and continues to be at the centre of the community in Wiggaton.

86 Withycombe Raleigh, All Saints

Built in 1896-1897 during the incumbency of Godfrey Pierre de Putron, there is a memorial tablet in his memory. The church was built on reclaimed land from the estuary. It has a full-length arcaded nave with north and south aisles, north and south transepts, a choir and an apsidal baptistry. A tower was added in 1907. Specifically built for ceremonial practices of the Anglo-Catholic movement within the Church of England, the Blessed Sacrament has been reserved continuously since 1925, and daily mass is celebrated. All Saints is part of the Withycombe Team Ministry. It is active within the life of the town and community and reaches out to people of all ages.

87 Withycombe Raleigh, St John in the Wilderness — *Grade II**

The present building, probably the third on the site, is c. mid-15th-century, Perpendicular in style, although substantially rebuilt in the 1920s-1930s, and re-ordered, to provide modern facilities, in 2001. Historic features include a 15th-century green man, and a unique pair of roof bosses commemorating the uncrowned king Edward VIII. Surrounding is an extensive churchyard. The church serves a densely populated suburban area of north Exmouth, within the parish and team of Withycombe Raleigh. Of a modern catholic tradition centred on the Eucharist, St John in the Wilderness has a lively, active and mission-oriented church community, reflecting the local population in comprising people of a wide range of age and background.

88 Withycombe Raleigh, St.John the Evangelist — *Grade II*

This church was built in 1864 to meet the pastoral and spiritual needs of the expanding population of the area. The church was designed by Ashworth to seat 700 people; the interior has been altered over the years and is now a light, warm and welcoming place of worship for all ages. The most notable features are the stained glass by nationally known designers and manufacturers. The tower contains a full ring of twelve bells. In 1972 Withycombe Raleigh became a large Team Ministry with three churches. There are close links with the community including the local primary school and Community College. The Parish Eucharist is the main act of worship each Sunday.

89 Woodbury, St Swithun — *Grade I*

This church occupies a site of Christian worship dating from early times. Mention is made in the Domesday Book of a manor called 'Wodeberie'. The present church was built in the Early English style in the 13th century. It comprised a chantry, nave, and chancel with 16th-century screen and porch. An 84ft tower was added in 1409. The fine east window contains glass reputed to have come from York Minster. Embroidered kneelers worked by the ladies of the congregation to designs from the Revd Keble Martin's 'Concise British Flora'. A choir of twenty and a peal of bells rung each Sunday confirm continuing Christian worship in Woodbury today.

90 Woodbury (Axminster), Holy Cross

About 1850, Lady Tullock built this church and a school for the hamlet of Woodbury. In 1929, administration passed to the Church of England and it is now part of the Axminster parish. Curiously, the congregation retains the right to maintain the building as they see fit. It is an attractive building of random flint; the outside pointing is gradually being restored to the original lime-based type. The church's aim is to persuade more senior 'lapsed' churchgoers to resume their faith. The atmosphere is always welcoming, the services change seasonally between traditional and contemporary styles and the social life is strong. The congregation is flourishing.

91 Woodbury Salterton, Holy Trinity   *Grade II*

Dates from 1843-1844 and was a gift of Miss Marianne Pidsley of Greendale. Some of the stone used to build the church came from the medieval tithe barn at Woodbury. It comprises nave, chancel, south porch and north-east vestry. The interior of the church is tall, and has an arched-brace roof with kingposts. The chancel arch of Heavitree stone was originally painted to resemble Beer stone. The chancel was refitted in 1899 but the remainder of the fittings are contemporary with the construction of the church, including the box pews. There is a west gallery beneath which there is a modern kitchen and WC facilities.

92 Woolbrook, St Francis of Assisi   *Grade II**

The first building for worship in the parish was a mission church affectionately called the 'Tin Tabernacle' that stood at the junction of Woolbrook Road and Core Hill. The current church, dedicated on the 16th May 1931, was consecrated on 29th January 1938. In 1957 the magnificent stained-glass east window was built by G. B. Cooper-Abbs as a gift in memory of Edward Percy Green. The new porch was added in 1967. The parish of Woolbrook was authorised by the Queen in 1979. St Francis has a strong Anglo-Catholic tradition and the Eucharistic service forms the centre of worship at the church.

93 Yarcombe, St John the Baptist   *Grade I*

Predominantly of 14th-century date, the church dominates the upper Yarty valley. Of that period are the clergy stalls, which incorporate carved panels representing saints and the Virgin and Child, whilst the pulpit contains linenfold carving from Buckland Abbey, erstwhile home of Sir Francis Drake. The hatchments relate to the Elliott-Drake family and the royal arms are those of George III. Nearby is the Jacobean altar table and high in a north transept window is a stained-glass representation of a 14th-century pedlar. Of the following century is the finely carved stone font. The church offers a range of services, modern and traditional; visitors always receive warm welcomes.

EXETER

Exeter describes itself as the regional capital, and is home to both the Cathedral and Devon County Hall, as well as the University, Regional Development Agency and the national headquarters of the Met Office. Described as one of the liveliest cities in the southwest, it also boasts a further 29 Church of England places of worship, ranging from the ancient to Christian communities meeting today in schools.

94 Alphington, St Michael & All Angels
*Grade II ***

The present Perpendicular church built of local stone stands on the site of a much older building. The west end of the church, rebuilt at the close of the 14th century, was improved in 1477. Further restoration took place in 1877 and after the fire of 1987. Of particular note are the Norman font, described as one of the finest in the county, and a highly regarded ring of eight bells. Although worshippers are requested to remove their pattens (clogs) before entering the church, those that do enter will be warmly welcomed and find an active, outward-looking church which aims to serve its local community and communities further afield.

95 Beacon Heath (Whipton), Holy Trinity

Modern brick-built church, constructed in 1993, set in the middle of a large housing estate. It is on the former site of the Devon County Show Ground. Worship was previously held for many years in Beacon Heath School.

96 Countess Wear, St Luke

St Luke's was erected as a chapel of ease for Topsham in 1838, not even sporting a churchyard, let alone a chancel. Fifty years later the church became a parish church and six years later a fine chancel was added. So marked the development of the parish church through very generous giving. Today we enjoy, and use, the fine qualities of the cabinetmaker, carpenter and glazier. The pews are of English oak and wonderfully carved. The stained glass is from a renowned London studio and there is a well-maintained churchyard. Today, this small church serves a growing community and one which still follows very generous habits.

97 Exeter (Central), St Stephen
*Grade II**

St Stephen's has stood close to the Guildhall on Exeter High Street for more than 1000 years. In 1086, the Domesday Book records that the building belonged to the Bishop of Exeter. All that survives from this period is the crypt, a low-vaulted Romanesque design. During the Commonwealth, St Stephen's was sold to one Toby Allen, who used the crypt as a stable. In 1660, the parish was re-established and the church restored. The octagonal neo-Gothic font appears to date from the early 19th century. Although damaged, St Stephen's survived the blitz in 1942, was refurbished in 1972, and today continues to host lively church services, exhibitions, concerts and community activities of all kinds.

EXETER

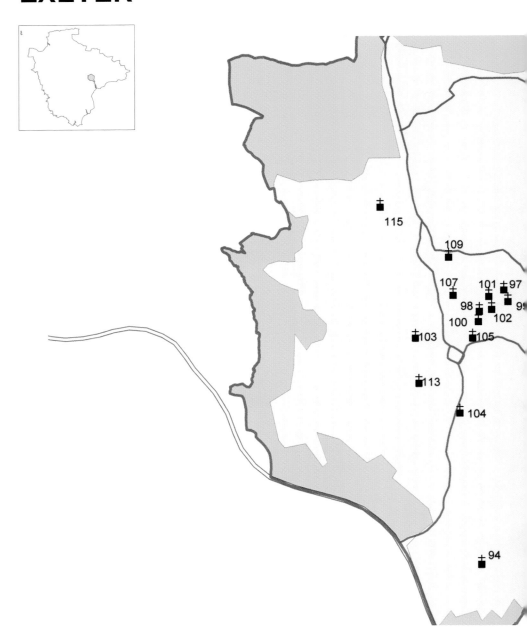

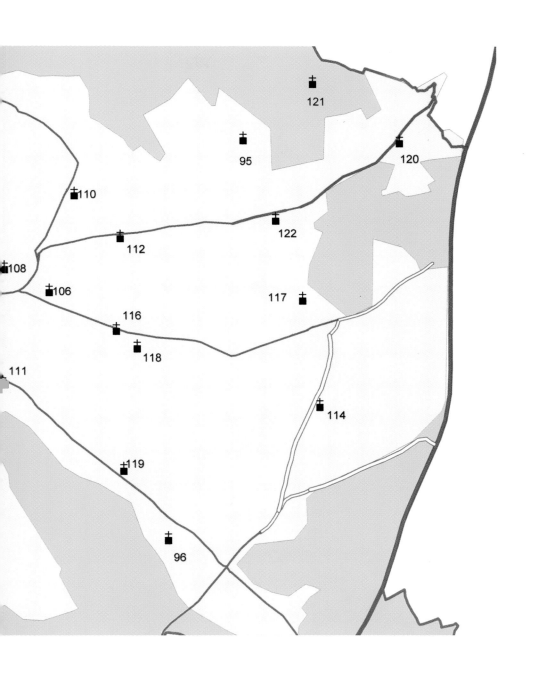

98 Exeter (Central), St Mary Arches
Grade II*

With its unique Romanesque nave-arcade, St Mary Arches is both the most conventional and the prettiest of Exeter's surviving medieval churches. Once a much larger building with an imposing tower, it now consists merely of nave and side-aisles. It was modified in the 15th century and had chantry chapels until the Reformation. During the Commonwealth (1649-1660), the stained glass, altar-rails, font and other furnishings were removed, only for the church to be handsomely refurnished in the later 17th century. For much of its history, it was a church of some civic importance and today still contains memorials of city mayors. It is presently used as offices for a non-denominational evangelical church.

99 Exeter, St Martin
Grade II*

THE CHURCHES CONSERVATION TRUST

Having escaped both Victorian refurnishing and the Second World War bombing which severely damaged other Exeter churches, St Martin's has kept both its medieval simplicity and its 18th-century charm. The first church on this site was consecrated on 6 July 1065 by Bishop Leofric; some of the original masonry remains in the walls of the nave. Early in the 15th century the church was enlarged and remodelled. In the 18th century it was completely refurnished. Unusual stone reredos and oak altar rails were installed, as was the gallery at the west end and the box pews. An elaborate 18th-century monument commemorates Philip Hooper, the benefactor who donated the reredos.

100 Exeter (Central), St Olave
Grade II*

Founded in late Anglo-Saxon times, this church is dedicated to St Olaf, a Christianised Viking king. All that remains of the original church is possibly the small square tower, very unusually standing in the sanctuary. The church was largely rebuilt towards the end of the 14th century. The single medieval bell was inscribed in Latin, meaning By my lively voice I disperse all that is harmful. Further large-scale modifications took place in the 15th century. It was declared redundant during the Commonwealth period and served a variety of uses before being restored. In Victorian times, it was refurnished and came under the influence of high church revival, a tradition that continues today.

101 Exeter (Central), St Pancras
Grade II

Situated in the old 'British Quarter' of the city, St Pancras stands on possibly one of the most ancient Christian sites in Britain. The present building is first recorded in 1191, from which period dates the font. What we see now largely belongs to the 13th century. Since the Reformation, St Pancras' has intermittently been closed and dilapidated for long periods. In the Second World War, it was a haven for worshippers whose own churches had been damaged or destroyed. Today, Holy Communion is celebrated regularly and, as the church is open each weekday, it still provides an opportunity for peace and quiet.

102 Exeter (Central), St Petrock
Grade II

The largest and most central of Exeter's surviving ancient churches, it originally lay in the most prosperous commercial and residential part of the town and was famous for its charitable concern for the poor. Its history of development is complex and it has been enlarged, especially in the 15th and 16th centuries, to accommodate growing congregations. Radically remodelled in the 1820s and with further work in the 1880s, the church also houses one of the lightest peals of six bells in the country. Today, on the cathedral side, is an agency serving some of the needs of the socially deprived. The rest of this interesting church can be visited by prior arrangement.

103 Exeter, Emmanuel

The current building was consecrated in October 1900 and replaced an earlier tin construction. It is in the early Perpendicular style and built of Babbacombe limestone with dressings and window traceries in Bath stone. There are a number of stained-glass windows, most notably those at the east and west ends. A small community of regular worshippers celebrate the Eucharist on the 3rd and 4th Sundays of the month, while on the 2nd Sunday there is a service of Prayer & Praise led by lay people. The 1st Sunday is reserved for the St Thomas & Emmanuel Team Eucharist, every three months or so held at Emmanuel.

104 Exeter, St Andrew

St Andrew's began as a daughter church of St Thomas. The first building was destroyed by enemy action during the Second World War. The congregation continued to worship in the adjacent church hall in Willeys Avenue. The present building in Alphington Road was built in the 1960s and the design taken from boat-building in Scandinavia. The east window is dominated by a gilded cross. The lower part is in clear glass permitting a view of the church from outside. It is a district church within the St Thomas and Emmanuel Team Ministry. As well as the Sung Eucharist on Sunday there is a monthly service of the ministry of healing.

105 Exeter, St Mary Steps   *Grade II**

Opposite the site of the west gate of Exeter. Its irregular shape was dictated by the neighbouring streets and buildings, and its unusually pronounced differences in floor levels were determined by the steeply sloping site. The present building dates mainly from the 15th century. The tub font is Norman. The chancel fittings, including the east window, date from the 1960s. The tower clock dates from 1619. The dial with the sun and five stars rotates, with the sun pointing to the hour. The figures are often called Matthew the Miller and his sons. The fine screen originally belonged to the now demolished church of St Mary Major.

106 Exeter, St Matthew Newtown

St Matthew's kept the 125th anniversary of its dedication in September 2007, and as was locally reported "since 1882 has provided a haven of prayer and worship". Robert Fulford, the architect, encouraged by the then Bishop Frederick Temple, was asked to build a "church of beauty". Its massive structure belongs to the Victorian Catholic Revival. St Matthew's, within the East Exeter Group Ministry, is developing an exciting plan for the re-ordering of the back, for use by a variety of groups. St Matthew's is in the area of Newtown – aptly reflecting the call of Christ's community here to be his 'New People' looking to the future with hope and faith.

107 Exeter, St Michael & All Angels Mount Dinham   *Grade II**

Stands north of the Longbrook valley, its 230ft spire dominating river, rail and city. Consecrated in 1868, a daughter church of St David, it was the generous benefaction of Tyntesfield merchant William Gibbs (recumbent effigy) and shares the mount with John Dinham's almshouses. A model church of its day, its furnishings survive largely unchanged, but with the marks of inter-war Anglo-Catholicism – high altar, statutes, Stations of the Cross from Oberammergau. Its worship is in keeping: traditional sung mass, eastward position, plainsong. Sharing outreach with St David's it contributes grand music, vespers and benediction, weekday observances and a monthly lecture.

108 Exeter, St Sidwell

Regarded as the most ancient Christian site in Exeter, in medieval times St Sidwell's became a major site for pilgrims, who came to the shrine of Exeter's own saint, St Sidwella (Sativola in Latin). Where St Sidwella was martyred, according to legend, a spring gushed from the ground. There have been five churches built on this site, the earliest being in Saxon times. The present structure, built in 1958, replaced the fine fourth church that was destroyed in the catastrophic Exeter blitz of 1942. St Sidwell's was re-ordered in 1999 to house a thriving Community Centre, accommodation units, the Mothers' Union Diocesan Offices and a chapel that is used for worship on Thursdays.

109 Exeter, St David
Grade II*

It stands in its ancient graveyard north of the old city since at least 1100. The present church (1900) is by W. D. Caröe, his best work – with an unusual squat tower (eight bells). The interior is spacious and light with high-quality wood and stonework. The original furnishing, from font (with ancient predecessor and spire-like cover) to altar, reredos and grant organ, is varied only by a moveable nave altar. Here, modern-language Parish Communion is the centre of a life including extra worship, children's work in church and three schools, Exeter College, much lay ministry, a weekly soup kitchen and a parish link in Kenya.

110 Exeter, St James

The church is situated at the hub of three main residential areas, about a mile from the city centre. The original St James' was destroyed during the Second World War. The present church was consecrated in 1956. It is brick-built in a traditional design with architectural references to Santiago de Compostela. It has a high altar, a lady chapel and two side chapels. The baptistry is at the west end. The interior is airy and so designed that natural light enhances the architectural features. We aim to be a place and people of welcome and nurture to all, and have a wide range of outreach activities for young, old and in-between.

111 Exeter, St Leonard
Grade II

The first church was built on this hill site soon after 1100, as part of the manor of Exminster. By 1800, it was the smallest parish in Devon, with 26 houses and 133 inhabitants. In Victorian times the rapidly growing Exeter suburb needed a much larger building, and the fourth church was built between 1876 and 1886. After a fire in 1989, the interior was completely re-ordered, and a large church centre added alongside, to serve our diverse congregation, now one of the largest in Devon. Our first church plant was in 2003; we are praying about a second plant.

112 Exeter, St Mark

Alongside the busy Pinhoe Road in the east of Exeter lies the handsome red-brick structure of St Mark's. Inside, symmetry and order, together with the peal of ten bells, the music and the worship, speak of other rhythms of life. Built in 1936, the architect was Ernest Hooper, and within the interior the fine reredos is by Herbert Read – a protégé of Harry Hems. Among recent projects is the introduction of open coffee mornings on Wednesdays, as a sign of welcoming all to this gathering space. In addition to the lively, weekly Family Eucharist, there is a monthly lay-led Evening Prayer, an indication of the ministry of all at St Mark's.

113 Exeter, St Thomas the Apostle
Grade II*

The first St Thomas, built in 1261, was a chapel at the west end of the new bridge across the Exe. A church was first built and consecrated on the present site in 1412. The vicar, Robert Welshe, was arrested and hanged from the church tower in the 1549 uprisings. The building was burnt down in 1645 in the Civil War. Rebuilt soon after, it was extended with a new chancel and transepts in 1828. The magnificent lectern dates from the end of the 14th century. It forms a Team Ministry with Emmanuel and St Andrew, which together serve a large part of the area west of the Exe.

114 Exeter, Trinity (St Leonard)

Trinity Church is an Anglican evangelical church that was planted from St Leonard's Church, Exeter in September 2003 and, thanks to God's faithfulness and goodness, we have continued to grow. We have a large church family with an active children's programme. We benefit from a strong emphasis on Bible teaching and seek to share the good news of the Gospel with those we meet, especially those living in the area of Clyst Heath. Lay members of the church are active in teaching and leadership and we encourage all church members to be fully involved in the work of the church. For further information, please visit our website.

115 Exwick, St Andrew
Grade II

This listed building was consecrated on 26th September 1842 as a chapel of ease to St Thomas, Exeter and built in the Gothic Revivalist style. The then vicar of St Thomas was responsible for this build. The entire roof is richly decorated in stencil work, using Catholic Revivalist symbolism with much use of gold leaf, now very dirty. The mosaic work which forms the reredos to the high altar, by Antonio Salviati, (19th century) incorporates sheet gold as a feature of his works. The floor tiles are Puginesque, some covered with carpeting. The church, currently under pastoral review, has Sung Eucharist as its main act of worship.

116 Heavitree Livery Dole, St Clare
Grade II

The almshouses were rebuilt in Puginesque medieval style in 1849 by Lord Rolle of Bicton and have recently (1980) doubled in size with the westward addition of more grey-brick houses. Lord Rolle restored the red sandstone chapel, first documented in the 1430s. It is a very simple aisle-less building with dagger tracery in the east window, but otherwise notable only for the 17th-century altar rails and fragments of medieval glass introduced in 1849 from Bicton. It still serves its purpose ministering to the almshouse residents. Holy Communion services are held weekly on Thursdays, and also at Easter and Christmas. Although the chapel is small it is often full at these services.

117 Heavitree, St Lawrence

Built as a chapel of ease in 1957, St Lawrence (named after the bombed city church) is now a district church in the Heavitree Team. A church/community hall, St Lawrence hosts: Guide and Scout sections, a dance school, dog training, Townswomen's Guild, mother and toddler group, and senior citizen tea parties in order to serve Christ in the people of the community. St Lawrence serves the housing estates west of Middlemoor which have no other community facility. As a worshipping community our heart is the Family Mass on Sunday with a Sunday School we call Seekers. Our style is informal; our teaching scriptural, traditional and fully sacramental.

118 Heavitree, St Michael & All Angels *Grade II*

A church with medieval origins, St Michael & All Angels was rebuilt in 1844-1846. The tower was added in 1890, and the chancel extended in 1893. It consists of nave, chancel, north and south transepts, west tower and south porch and is of white limestone with slate roofs. Internally, notable features are the medieval piers, which were re-used from the old church, the elaborately carved alabaster reredos by George Gilbert Scott, which was moved from the cathedral to the church in 1939, and fragments of the screen from the medieval church. The peal of eight bells was installed in 1897. An ancient yew tree stands in the churchyard.

119 Heavitree, St Paul (Burnthouse Lane)

St Paul's is part of the Heavitree Team Ministry in Exeter. The building was erected in the 1950s with people being asked to contribute "bricks". As a result local people feel a sense of "ownership" and they support local coffee mornings, etc. The previous church on this site, named St Loyes, was a wooden structure, and this is still being used as the church hall. At present there are plans to redevelop the whole of the present site, church, church hall and burnt-out vicarage and to build affordable housing and a worship and community centre. Regular Sunday services are held, also Monday Mass and services for special occasions.

120 Pinhoe Hall Church

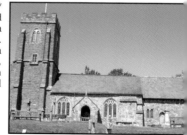

John Bradford, vicar at Pinhoe 1844-1863, was responsible for the building of the hall church in 1850. It was known as the parish schoolroom and used as a school from 1850 to 1877 when a new school was built in the village, although from time to time in subsequent years it was used to relieve overcrowding in the school. The hall was licensed for divine service in 1863 and became known as the mission church. In 1928 it was licensed for celebration of Holy Communion. It continues to be used for an early service of Holy Communion on Sundays and for community activities during the week.

121 Pinhoe, St Michael & All Angels *Grade II**

Situated on a hill facing the Exe estuary, this 15th-century church once had a white clad tower and was a landmark for mariners. There was probably a wooden Saxon church on the site that was burnt by invading Danes in 1001. The oldest part of the church is the font with its Saxon base. The screen is a fine example of 15th-century work and the carving of the Poor Man of Pinhoe, representing a parish beadle in the time of Queen Anne, is one of only two in the country. Worship at this small, welcoming church varies from traditional to contemporary. There are active pastoral links with the community.

122 Whipton, St Boniface

The church is situated in a residential area of the suburb of Whipton, a couple of miles from Exeter city centre. Built of brick in 1955-1958, with a bell tower on the south side, this building is traditionally cruciform and the architect was Macmillan Scott. It became the parish church of Whipton after the closure of All Saints in the 1980s. Some of the furnishings from All Saints are included in this building. The church is light and airy and consists of a large nave, north and south aisles, sanctuary and Lady chapel, vestries and children's room.

MID DEVON

Devon's 'Heartland' with lively market towns and peaceful villages, set amidst the area's beautiful hills and valleys. At the heart of these communities, you can explore 79 Anglican churches in the area, many of which have a long and interesting history.

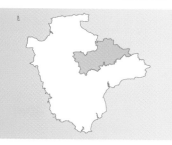

123 Ash (Halberton), Ash Thomas Chapel

Small Victorian church comprising nave, chancel, south porch and north vestry.

124 Ashill (Uffculme), St Stephen   *Grade II*

Built of red brick in 1882 to designs by Devon architect R. M. Fulford as a chapel of ease with attached hall. This small church consists of nave, chancel and south porch. No tower, but a bellcote at the east end of the nave. Internally there is a low chancel screen, with all fittings dating from the late 19th century. The east window dates from 1904, with all other windows containing the original patterned glass of 1882. The village congregation at Ashill is small but faithful and welcoming. Worship is largely traditional with a more family-oriented service once a month. There is also an active youth ministry.

125 Bampton, St Michael & All Angels   *Grade I*

The earliest part of the present building, the nave south wall, is thought to date from the 12th century, the base of the tower dating from the 13th and the chancel from the 14th century. The north aisle was added by Thomas Bourchier in the 15th century, with pillars and arches of white stone from Beer. The memorial window was constructed in 1921. The pulpit is 16th-century. The sundial c.1586 is the oldest recorded in a church in Devon. The rood screen dates from c.1450; in 1812 it was moved to the chancel arch and subsequently returned to its original position in 1938.

126 Bickleigh, St Mary   *Grade II**

Dating from at least the 12th century, St Mary's stands overlooking the picturesque village of Bickleigh. The church was consecrated in 1268; the oldest object is believed to be the font, which is considered to be a late 12th-century Norman design. The 13th-century tower, chancel and nave were enlarged in the 15th century by the addition of the present south aisle, separated from the nave by four ornate arches. The post-Reformation tomb of the Carew family is among the finest in Devon. The church is small but welcoming and has strong links with both the village and the local school.

MID DEVON

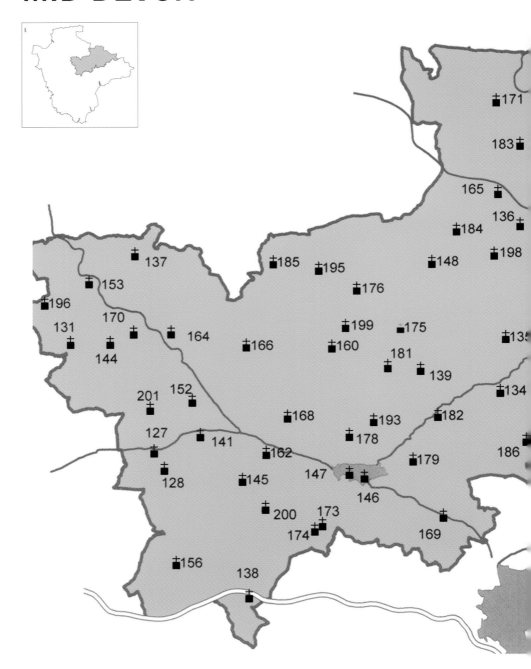

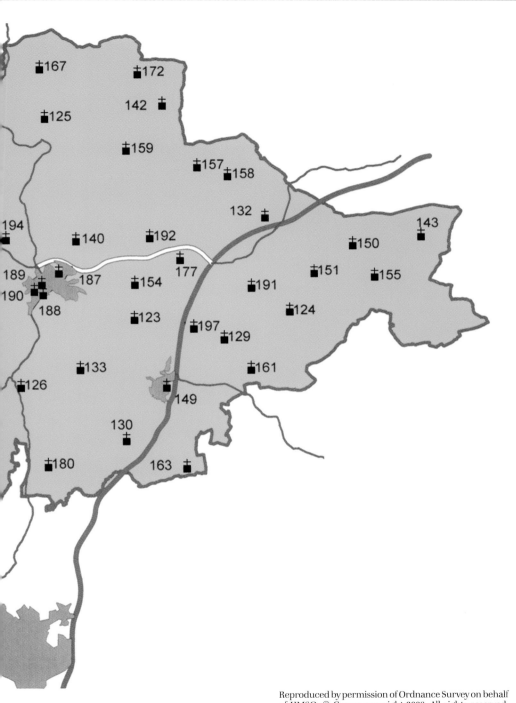

MID DEVON: LOCATION OF CHURCHES

127 Bow, Church Room
Licensed in 1911

128 Bow (Nymet Tracey), St Bartholomew   *Grade I*
There was a church here during Norman times but the present building dates from 1170, being added to during the 13th century. The church interior was much changed in the 17th century, renovated in 1859 and again in 1889, when the original pews and gallery were removed. The interior of the church has therefore been much changed but retains a tranquillity and sense of peace. We hope that visitors will leave with an understanding of the oneness of all things, a recognition of the faith of the Christian men and women who have worshipped in this place for many centuries and a greater awareness of our Maker and Redeemer.

129 Bradfield (Uffculme), All Saints   *Grade II*
Built in 1874, All Saints Chapel replaced one at Bradfield House, destroyed by fire An older font outside the chapel carries a dedication dated 1854: "Love lives on and hath the power to bless." Worshippers have included wounded soldiers in the Second World War and children with learning difficulties, resident at the house. In 1970 the chapel was stripped and taken over by Uffculme Trust. In 2000 services restarted and, through generous donations from local people and businesses, the bells returned and pews and electricity were installed. Particular features are the stained-glass windows, Walrond family memorials and unique wooden crosses bearing the names of families wiped out in the plague.

130 Bradninch, St Disen   *Grade II*
Originally dedicated to St Denis, Bradninch's parish church became popularly known as St Disen's in the 19th century. Mainly 15th-century and early 16th in date, with earlier stonework surviving in the chancel, it was restored in the 19th century when the nave and aisles were heightened. The nave piers have floriated capitals and include, opposite the south door, a green man. The pride of St Disen's, however, is its 15th-century rood screen. The 52 painted wooden panels include depictions of the temptation of Eve, the Annunciation and the Christ child. Worship is largely traditional but with a contemporary, informal, monthly family service together with other special services and events.

131 Brushford, St Mary the Virgin   *Grade II**
Set high above the Taw, isolated at the end of a narrow lane, this is one of the smallest Devon churches. Although restored in the 19th century, the Norman origins of nave and chancel are still visible in its north window and in the undecorated south door. The tower, with shingled top and low slated spire, is a Tudor addition. Internally, the most striking feature is the screen. Dated 1520, the linenfold panelling below and delicate tracery above are probably the work of an immigrant Breton craftsman. Serving a tiny rural parish, a traditional service is held, generally on the first Sunday of each month.

132 Burlescombe, St Mary the Virgin
Grade I

This church was built late in the 13th century with stone from the local quarry at Westleigh, with dressings of Ham and Beer stone. Aisles were added in the 15th century. The north aisle is linked with the Ayshford family to whom two interesting wall memorials are dedicated. The chancel screen was part of an original rood screen. In the chancel there is an altar tomb dedicated to Nicholas Ayshford. The font is octagonal. The tower contains five bells by Pennington 1637-1640 with a treble added in 1909. The tower was rebuilt in 1637. Services are many and varied and we have strong links with Burlescombe C of E Primary School.

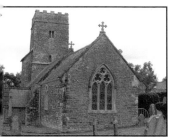

133 Butterleigh, St Matthew
Grade II*

The tower is all that can be seen of the 13th-century church, which was re-consecrated in 1319. It contains three bells, one of which was cast in about 1485. The nave, chancel and aisle were rebuilt in 1861 with pews for about 120. The 13th-century font and piscina remain and a poor-box, carved, painted and dated 1629. There are memorial plaques and windows to local benefactors and past rectors. One window is by Morris & Co. The church is always open from 9.30am to dusk. Services every Sunday are sensitive to the needs of the old and the young in the parish and in the wider world.

134 Cadbury, St Michael & All Angels
Grade I

Probably the second church on this site, the present building of Cadbury church is mainly of 15th-century origin and lies on the high ground between Tiverton and Crediton. The most notable features include a panel of medieval painted glass depicting the crucified Christ, the Norman font, a dedicated carved stone reredos and a screen of glass and carved wood at the rear of the church. The tower houses six bells, two of which are medieval. Recently, Cadbury, which gives its name to the deanery, has become one of the eleven churches in seven parishes forming a Mission Community, looking forward to more lay-led services in addition to those led by the priesthood.

135 Cadeleigh, St Bartholomew
Grade I

St Bartholomew has borne witness to the Christian faith for many hundreds of years and continues to welcome those who climb the hill to Cadeleigh. A modest but enthusiastic congregation shares its love for the building with the wider community who come to mark life's major events. The church boasts a monument to the Leach family dating from the 17th century, said to be the largest in a parish church in Devon, a statue of St Anthony and his pig in a niche on the tower and a fine peal of six bells. With God's help the church will be the physical sign of his presence for many years to come.

136 Calverleigh, St Mary the Virgin
Grade II*

This church was built in the reign of Edward III, in about 1337. Though the nave and tower (with six bells) were built during the 14th century, the south aisle, as it is today, was not built until the early 16th century. The church, set in tranquil woodland, is a haven for wildlife, with a pond at the bottom of the churchyard. The congregation is a small, faithful and welcoming one, of all ages and with a good community spirit, holding varied weekly worship including traditional, family, youth and lay-led services and an annual open-air service. There is also a choir and a bell-ringing team.

137 Chawleigh, St James
Grade I

The first recorded priest of the church was Richard de Grangiis in 1279 but the present building is almost entirely a 15th-century structure, considerably embellished around 1840. The rood screen extends across the nave and aisle and is a delight to the eye but the intricate carving does tend to separate the small choir and organist from the rest of the church. A local band ring the bells hanging in the tapering tower, the Local Ministry Team, small choir and regular organist all help to maintain welcoming weekly Sunday morning services. This, together with various other activities, gives a Christian presence in the village.

138 Cheriton Bishop, St Mary
Grade I

This church is of Norman origins, with a 13th-century chancel and 15th-century nave, north aisle and tower. The south wall and the porch were rebuilt, along with the restoration of the interior in 1884. Internally, there are the remains of a fine medieval screen with painted figures, a Norman font, a 16th-century pulpit, royal arms to George II, and a case containing alabaster figures found when the south wall was rebuilt. The chancel ceiling with its carved oak bosses dates from the 13th century. The north aisle windows include fragments of medieval glass, and some medieval benches also remain.

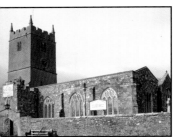

139 Cheriton Fitzpaine, St Matthew
Grade I

The church is Perpendicular in style. The nave and chancel date from the 14th century with the tower (now with a ring of six bells), north and south aisles and porch added in the 15th century and an 18th-century vestry. Restoration took place between 1883 and 1885 and a servery and children's area were created in 2000. There are wagon roofs with carved bosses. There are 19th-century reredos, wooden pulpit, octagonal stone font and a 20th-century nave/chancel screen, tower screen and organ. Together with the Methodist Church, St Matthew's maintains a Christian presence in this mid-Devon village with mid-week and Sunday services and a developing youth programme.

140 Chevithorne, St Thomas
Grade II

The manor of Chevetorna is mentioned in the Domesday Book, and remained part of the Tidcombe Portion of the old parish of Tiverton until the 19th century. St Thomas's was originally a chapel built in 1843 by William Rayer, rector of the Tidcombe Portion, and became a parish church in 1884. This rural parish (now incorporating Cove) retains close links with Tiverton, and forms part of the proposed Tiverton Mission Community. Knightshayes Court lies within the parish, and the Town Leat (a stream given by Countess Isabella of Devon in the 13th century as a free water supply to Tiverton) flows through it.

141 Clannaborough, St Petrock
Grade II*

The church, with an unusual raised churchyard, occupies a site which was used in early Christian times. The parish, six miles long, spans two hills but lacks any village, the church being close to The Barton mentioned in the Domesday Book. Records date back to the 13th century but the present building is of simple 16th-century style, of nave and chancel with a western tower, the oldest part, housing eight bells rung from a frame. The interior was greatly restored in 1858-1859 by Selina, a member of the Wreford family, resident for three centuries at The Barton. There is some lovely stained glass and since there is no electricity, all services are candle-lit.

142 Clayhanger, St Peter
Grade II*

The west tower probably dates from the 13th century, but the remainder of the church was rebuilt in 1879-1891. It comprises west tower, nave, chancel, south porch and north-east vestry. The 19th-century rebuilding involved re-roofing, a new chancel arch and renewal of windows. The ceiling of the porch probably dates from the 15th century. Internally, the chancel fittings, including poppy-head choir stalls, date from the 19th-century restoration. In the nave there is a 17th-century wooden lectern, and a 19th-century pulpit. The font is Norman. There is a good set of early-16th-century carved bench ends displaying various motifs. The bells date from 1611, 1740 and 1749.

143 Clayhidon, St Andrew
Grade I

Built almost 800 years ago, Clayhidon Church stands on one of the highest points in the Blackdown Hills from where there are extensive, wonderful views. Internally, there is an effigy reputed to be that of Ralph de Hidon, the first recorded rector of the parish. From that time there have been architectural changes to the building until the millennium. The churchyard is at its most beautiful in spring when the ground is covered in wild daffodils growing among the twelve chest tombs, eleven of which are listed. An enthusiastic team of ringers ring the six bells. There is a warm welcome to the weekly services and to the Church Room, next door, with its own history.

144 Coldridge, St Matthew
Grade I

The majority of the building dates from the 15th and 16th centuries, although there are remnants of an earlier building, including a Norman font. The chancel was restored in 1877, the remainder of the church in 1897. It comprises nave, north and south aisles, chapels, choir, sanctuary, west tower and south porch. Internally, there is a fine medieval oak screen and the remains of an unusual parclose screen, thought to be the work of French craftsmen. The pulpit is also an example of excellent carving. The bench ends are of various ages, some of them carved. There are a number of medieval Barnstaple floor tiles depicting roses, lions and pelicans.

145 Colebrooke, St Andrew
Grade I

The church is situated in a commanding position overlooking Copplestone, Coleford and Penstone. The earliest known reference to the church occurs in the 12th century when Bishop Bartholomew of Exeter claimed the patronage from Henry II. The church was substantially restored in the late 14th and 15th centuries. The tower contains six bells dating from 1553. The Copplestone Chantry Chapel or aisle is surrounded by a very beautiful 16th-century screen completed most probably by a Breton carver. The carved vicar's seat carries the Copplestone family arms and the font with a notable cover both from the 15th century. Worship is largely traditional but includes a well-supported family-orientated service once a month.

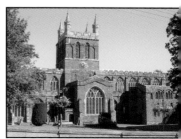

146 Crediton, Holy Cross
Grade I

The Christian community in Crediton traces its roots back to St Boniface who is believed to have been born here c.680. Eadwulf became the first bishop here in 909 and a cathedral was built which remained until 1050. A substantial Norman minster was built in the 12th century, which became a collegiate church where a college of canons was resident until the Reformation. The church was largely rebuilt in the 15th century. Simon Jenkins calls it 'a church of all the arts' and it boasts a fine Harrison & Harrison organ and a recently recast peal of twelve bells. The church is open daily and further information can be found on the website.

147 Crediton, St Lawrence Chapel — *Grade II*

This ancient chapel was originally linked with a hermitage and a leper hospital. At the Reformation, the chapel was stripped of its land and roof and nothing is known of its fate until the 19th century when the shell was repaired and divided into cottages. It was purchased in 1921 by Mrs Drake, who restored it in memory of her husband and gave the chapel to the Governors of Crediton Church. It was used as a school chapel until 1993 and has recently been restored with a new floor and heating. There is a communion service on Wednesdays and the chapel is used for Sunday evening services and art exhibitions.

148 Cruwys Morchard, Holy Cross — *Grade I*

Parts of the fabric of the nave and chancel date from the early 14th century, and the tower was partly rebuilt after a fire of 1689. Restored in the early 19th century, when a vestry was added and some of the box pews were altered. It comprises nave, chancel, west tower, south aisle and porch. The interior was refurbished after the 1689 fire, and an almost complete set of good 18th-century fittings remain, untypical for Devon, including a Classical chancel screen, and pews named after the local farms whose tenants or owners contributed to the restoration. The churchyard contains a number of listed tombs and a revolving lychgate.

149 Cullompton, St Andrew — *Grade I*

A large church comprising nave, chancel, west tower, north and south aisles, vestry and south porch. Parts date from the 15th century, the 100ft elaborate decorated tower was built in 1545-1549, and the south 'Lane' aisle was begun by John Lane, a cloth merchant, in 1526. The buttresses of this aisle are decorated with symbols of Lane's wealth – ships and cloth shears. The nave and chancel have elaborate timber ceilings with angel corbels; the Lane aisle is fan-vaulted. The west gallery was inserted c.1630. There was a major restoration in 1849-1850 under Ashworth, when the chancel was also rebuilt. The 15th-century screen is one of the longest in Devon.

150 Culm Davey, St Mary's Chapel — *Grade II*

The people of Culm Davy have been worshipping here for at least 500 years. It is within the parish of Hemyock but designated a chapel of ease as it enabled inhabitants of the hamlet to avoid the hard and frequently flooded walk to St Mary's The small flintstone building was extensively reconstructed around 1850 with only the porch and inner doorway now displaying medieval workmanship. It is surrounded by a charming churchyard, whose gravestones record a recurring pattern of local names. The chapel continues to provide the focal point for the community, with Harvest and Christmas drawing capacity congregations. There are services every 2 weeks (BCP) to which all are welcome.

151 Culmstock, All Saints — *Grade II**

This church consists of nave, north and south aisles (the latter formerly the chapel of the Blessed Virgin Mary), chancel and tower. The chancel is the oldest part, probably 13th-century. The walls are of Blackdown chert rubble masonry. The tower has three gargoyles and uniquely, a yew growing in its top. Above the tower arch is a royal coat of arms painted in 1810. The original stone rood screen is now repositioned behind the altar as a reredos. This building contains fine 19th-century window glass and is noted for its excellent acoustics. Our worship is an equal mix of Common Worship and Book of Common Prayer.

152 Down St Mary, St Mary the Virgin
Grade I

There has been a church here since the 12th century. Of that original building, only the sandstone tympanum over the south doorway and the north sanctuary stonework remain. The present tower was built in the early 15th century to replace one blown down by a storm. The nave arcade, piers and font are also 15th-century. In 1870 the north aisle walls were rebuilt. The rood screen is a faithful copy of the mediaeval original, and carved by a father and son living in the village in the late 19th century. Services are held every Sunday and there is active lay involvement in the worship and life of the church.

153 Eggesford (Wembworthy), All Saints
Grade II*

A small and isolated church, restored and much rebuilt in 1867. Some older fabric remains at the east end, the tower dates from the 15th century. Comprises nave, chancel, north aisle with mortuary chapel, north porch and west tower. The interior dates mainly from the 1867 restoration, including the tiled floors, altar rails, choir stalls and pulpit. Seating includes some 18th-century box pews. The north aisle contains the family box pew of the Earls of Portsmouth, which now contains the organ. The font is Norman, restored in 1919. There are two significant 17th-century monuments to the Chichester family, and a large 18th-century monument to William Fellowes in Italian marble.

154 Halberton, St Andrew
Grade I

The church stands on the site of an earlier Saxon church. It is built of red sandstone, and exhibits many characteristics of the Decorated style of the 14th century. Of particular note is the fine and massive rood screen (c.1420), a rare and interesting survivor of the ravages of the Civil War. There is a square 12th-century Norman font, and a beautifully carved 15th-century pulpit. The tower houses six bells, rung regularly by our own ringers and visiting teams. Each month Sunday worship includes Sung Communion, Matins, Holy Communion (Book of Common Prayer) and a family service held jointly with the Methodist congregation.

155 Hemyock, St Mary
Grade II*

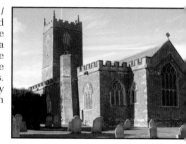

This church occupies a central position in the village, alongside Hemyock Castle. The first written record dates from the year 1268, but it is obvious that parts of the building are much older. Originally the church had a spire on top of the tower, but it was removed in the late 1600s. The bell tower does house a tuned peal of six bells dating from 1552. Inside the building, the bowl of the font dates back to 1200. The southern aisle was formally a chantry dedicated to St Katherine. The church is the centre of an active church community serving the very socially active and friendly village, and welcomes all comers.

156 Hittisleigh, St Andrew
Grade I

This church is of Norman origins, with a late 13th-century nave and chancel. The tower dates from the late 15th century, and the north aisle is of the early 16th century. The majority of the windows to the nave, chancel and aisle are also 16th-century. There were restorations in 1914, in 1926 when the box pews were removed, and in 1967 when the church was re-roofed. The flagstone floor in the nave includes several 16th-century and 17th-century ledger stones. The font is Norman, with zig-zag carvings. Two of the old box pews remain in the north chapel; all other furnishings are late 19th or early 20th-century.

157 Hockworthy, St Simon & St Jude
Grade II*

The church dates back to at least the 12th century, the list of incumbents beginning in 1173. The tower is medieval, the rest being built in 1864. The architect, Charles Greenway, is commemorated in one of the stained-glass windows of which there are several good examples. The Newman family were vicars or patrons from 1852-1948. There is a little ornamentation and no surviving monuments from the original building. Holy Communion and Matins are held every month with a well-attended family service every other month. The church is also involved with other local bodies in running village fetes and other social events and supporting the rebuilding of the village hall.

158 Holcombe Rogus, All Saints
Grade I

The south aisle dates from the mid-13th century and the remainder from the 14th century. The north aisle roof has an unceiled wagon roof with 60 curved matched beams bearing carved bosses and angels. The Court pew is surrounded by a screen surmounted by medallions representing Old Testament scenes carved c.1620 reputedly by a Dutch refuge from Topsham and is of national importance. The Bluett Chapel has two very fine 17th-century monuments with reclining figures. The chancel floor, pews and pulpit date from the 19th century. The oldest of the fine peal of six bells dates from the 16th century. The church has an active congregation and weekly services.

159 Huntsham, All Saints
Grade II*

The church was built in the 13th century and altered in the 1430s. Situated in the head of Lowman Valley in the Devon countryside. Built of local stone and oak from the Huntsham estate. The organ, in memory of Charles Troyte, and font in memory of Fanny Troyte. The tower clock was installed in 1912; three bells date from 1552 with another three added in 1866 and two more in 1874; the first peal by Devon ringers on eight bells in 1875. In 2004, the eight bells were remodelled and rehung by the Whitechapel Bell Foundry, the seventh being one of the original three bells; treble new President's bell in 2004.

160 Kennerleigh, St John the Baptist
Grade II*

A small church comprising nave, chancel, west tower, north aisle and south porch. The tower, nave and chancel are 14th-century; the north aisle is 15th-century and the church was thoroughly restored in 1847-1848. In 1920 the three original bells were removed and melted down to cast the present light carillon chime of eight bells. Internally, there are fragments of medieval glass in the sanctuary lancet window, and a much-restored 15th-century north aisle wagon roof, and 16th-century chancel roof. The fittings and furnishings are all Victorian, although the vestry screen includes a length of 16th-century carved oak cornice, possibly from a rood screen.

161 Kentisbeare, St Mary
Grade I*

The church at the heart of the village was built in the 13th century on the site of an older Saxon building, and was added to over the next two centuries. The chequer pattern tower is the only example in Devon, built of white Beer stone and a rare cinnamon brown variety of red sandstone from Upton. The 15th-century screen is the glory of the interior; it was probably a prototype of a class called Herein found all over Devon. It has notable Perpendicular windows and fine stained glass. The tower holds a peal of six bells, the earliest dated 1616. Our worship ranges from traditional to contemporary.

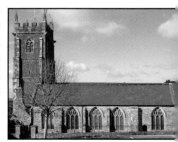

162 Knowle (Down St Mary), St Boniface Proprietary Chapel   *Grade II*

This church in the North Creedy Team was formerly the village school but was dedicated by the Bishop of Crediton in 1953. It is the only church in the large team that provides kitchen and toilet facilities within the building and it also boasts a car park. There is a Garden of Remembrance dedicated by the Bishop of Crediton in 2003. That was also the year when an embroidered reredos was erected and blessed. Beautifully crafted by a parishioner it portrays the Benedicite from Morning Prayer. The church also serves the nearby village of Copplestone. The worship is contemporary and there is great emphasis on providing a warm and loving welcome and fellowship.

163 Langford (Cullompton), St Andrew   *Grade II*

A combined cottage and mission chapel, formerly a single house. It dates from the 17th century, possibly incorporating older work. Constructed from cob, plastered, with a thatched roof, it is of two storeys. The chapel is in the former parlour and is open to the roof. It was licensed for worship in 1937.

164 Lapford, St Thomas of Canterbury   *Grade I*

The present church on the foundations of a Norman church dates from the 15th century when the north aisle was added. The vestry was added in 1869 and the chancel rebuilt. In 1871 the porch was rebuilt with further renovations in 1888 and 1955 when a new reredos was installed. It comprises nave, chancel, west tower, north aisle, vestry and south porch. Impressive interior, with a 15th-century wagon roof to the nave, and late-15th-century rood screen, amongst the finest in the county. Most of the seating is 15th-century oak benches, of two distinct types. Other furnishings date from the 19th century, including the Beer stone pulpit and font.

165 Loxbeare, St Michael & All Angels   *Grade II**

The church building is Norman with some Victorian modifications. The stubby tower is a distinguishing feature as is the 17th-century pulpit and 'Apprentices' seat' which may be pulled out from the side of the pew. Mystery surrounds the stone carving on the Norman entrance. 'ALIMA RECIT OMU' could refer to the name of the Mason or the Ailmer family who held lands locally in Saxon times. As a parish in the Exe Valley (now commended as a Mission Community) we enjoy a variety of worship styles: Family Services, Praise Services and Family Communion. We include a teaching programme, home groups and Christianity Explored courses.

166 Morchard Bishop, St Mary   *Grade I*

This is a large church comprising nave, chancel, north and south aisles, west tower, vestry and south porch. Of medieval origins, rebuilt in the mid-15th century, the chancel was refurbished in the late 17th century and restored in 1887-1891. Internally, the nave has a high hammer beam roof of late-19th-century date, but incorporating some older timbers. The east window contains 18th-century stained glass. There is a fine late-17th-century oak reredos, and the mahogany altar rails date from 1768. The late-15th-century rood screen is very fine and sumptuously decorated. The choir stalls and pews are late 19th century, but probably include some earlier timbers. The Beer stone font dates from 1848.

167 Morebath, St George
Grade II*

The tower possibly dates from the 13th century, the north aisle is 15th-century, and was restored and parts rebuilt in 1874-1875 by Butterfield. It comprises west tower, nave, chancel, north aisle, vestry, and south porch. There is a complete set of early-15th-century granite windows to the north aisle. The Butterfield restoration included new roofs to nave and chancel, new font, benches, pulpit and altar rails. Internally, there is a late medieval ceiled wagon roof to the north aisle with moulded ribs and carved foliage bosses. The fittings are mostly by Butterfield except for a 20th-century reredos and a co-eval altar. The best Butterfield fitting is the polished marble font. The church is now famous through Eamon Duffy's book *The Voices of Morebath*, about the parish during the Reformation.

168 Newbuildings (Sandford), Beacon Church

This church was built in 1875 as Newbuildings School and was at one time 'licensed for divine service'. The school closed in 1935 but some of the old desks were retained and it became a chapelry of Sandford parish. It was lit by gaslight until the recent installation of electricity. As its name suggests, the church offers commanding views. The chapel serves a congregation mainly connected with farming and Harvest is a great event. In recent years a Nativity has been set up in the outbuildings before Christmas and a dawn Eucharist has been held at Easter. A communion service is held on the fourth Sunday of every month.

169 Newton St Cyres, St Cyr & St Julitta
Grade I

The church, built of warm Posbury stone, stands on a bluff, overlooking the thatched cottages nestled below. The oldest part is the 15th-century tower, with its clock (1711) and inside an eight-bell peal (1733 on). The interior has beauty, simplicity and light. The nave was rebuilt in the 15th century while the north aisle was added in the 16th, both surmounted by a wagon roof with carved bosses. Of the many tributes to parish life, the largest are a fine monument to Sir John Northcott (1632) and a rare royal arms of James II. The church has various styles of service, a strong musical life and expanding mission community role.

170 Nymet Rowland, St Bartholomew
Grade I

St Bartholomew's is a small church in rustic surroundings. Like many others, it is of Norman foundation, was extended in the 15th century and altered, not too seriously, in Victorian times .It has a peaceful interior of simple charm, with a Norman font. Our chief glory is the 15th-century wooden arcade. Hewn from solid oak, its columns and arches are a great rarity and this is the finest example in Devon. A small but loyal congregation attends services every Sunday of the year and the church is full for the Harvest and Carol Services. There are regular chamber music concerts in aid of church funds.

171 Oakford, St Peter
Grade II

Dating from the 13th century (the earliest recorded rector is 1260), the church has a medieval tower with eight bells, the main building is lofty and light, being rebuilt in 1838 after a disastrous fire. The stained-glass windows are noteworthy, the east window dates from 1875, the west designed by Keaton, Butler and Bayne, the Spurway window by the American, Arild Rosencrantz, and the chancel window designed by Heywood Sumner. The Spurway memorial is dated 1692. The organ was built by J. R. Mortimore of Tiverton in 1841. The congregation is small and welcoming. Traditional, Common Worship or family services are held each week.

172 Petton, St Petrock
Grade II

This was rebuilt in the Norman style, replacing an earlier church on this site c.1840. The two small bells in the bellcote hung in the earlier church date from 1320. They rank with Haccombe, two bells at Bulkworthy and one at Petersmarland, among the oldest six bells in Devon. The oak pews have doors and the "cartwheel" west window has stained glass commemorating Queen Elizabeth's Silver Jubilee in 1977. The embroidered gold altar frontal likewise celebrates the Queen's Golden Jubilee in 2002. The services, twice a month, are traditional, plus the major festivals, where a good congregation for a small church can be expected.

173 Posbury, St Luke
Grade II

The chapel was built in 1836 at a time when the Governors of Crediton Church were concerned that numbers for Sunday services were too great for the parish church. It is a proprietary chapel under the patronage of the Shelley family. Today the chapel serves a gathered congregation who enjoy the peaceful setting of the chapel in a beautiful valley and the Prayer Book Communion services which are celebrated on the first and third Sundays of each month. Posbury is situated to the south west of Crediton on the Devonshire Heartland Way and next to Posbury Clump, a former stone quarry listed as an SSSI for its unusual volcanic rocks.

174 Posbury (Crediton), St Francis Proprietary Chapel
Grade II

This is the chapel of the Franciscan Servants of Jesus and Mary and is not open to the public.

175 Poughill, St Michael & All Angels
Grade I

Though its rectors are known back to 1278, Poughill has mostly escaped the history books. The present building is 15th-century and the architecture typical with some remaining box pews and wall paintings. There is a ring of six bells reckoned "the sweetest peal in Devon", enthusiastically enjoyed by the local band. Together with the village hall, the building is at the centre of community activity and has regular attendance twice a month from a below-average age group. Popular memory links Poughill with the cuckoos which are "set free from the church tower at Poughill, Devon, in time for Witheridge Fair", *The Times* 1937.

176 Puddington, St Thomas à Becket
Grade II*

Parts date from the late 15th century, but the church was thoroughly restored in 1837 by Bowden, including rebuilding of the nave and chancel and addition of north aisle and south porch. It comprises continuous nave, chancel, north aisle, west tower and south porch. Internally, the ceiled wagon roof to the nave was extensively restored in 1838 but possibly includes some older reused timber. Chancel includes 18th-century black and white marble chequer floor. Most of the furnishings are 19th-century, including a mahogany altar rail on gilded Gothic-style iron supports. The Gothic-style oak choir stalls incorporate a high-quality 17th-century oak bench. The oak pews are from 1838 but incorporate some late-15th/early-16th-century bench ends.

177 Sampford Peverell, St John the Baptist
Grade I

This church, which was substantially rebuilt in the 13th and 19th centuries, has renewed itself over the past twenty years. Belying the overwhelming Victorian appearance of the building itself, members of the congregation, encouraged by the rector, have begun to look into fresh ways of worship and to engage the village in looking outward to world problems and their Christian solutions. Within the village itself, relations with Methodists, which were always good, improve daily. Together with other parishes in the team, the church is actively working within the thrust of Moving on in Mission and Ministry towards self-supporting status.

178 Sandford, St Swithun
Grade I

In the early 16th century this former chapel of ease was considerably enlarged in the Late Gothic style and all that remains of the earlier Saxon building is the tower base. Pews were added and Tudor carpenters carved their magnificent pew ends depicting imagined animals and natives of the New World. 100 years later the local squire added a west gallery for children from the poor house. This gallery houses the organ and choir. In Victorian times the church was further enlarged and restored so that over 600 people could attend services. We meet every Sunday for the sung Eucharist. The music of voice, organ and bells remains central to our worship.

179 Shobrooke, St Swithun
Grade II*

Set half-a-mile outside the village. Externally a medieval church, probably of the 13th century – the earliest recorded rector is of 1259 – built of local Raddon red stone, mainly in the Perpendicular style. Fine 15th-century tower with peal of six bells at west end. The north aisle is 14th or 15th-century, the south aisle and porch added in 1880 during typical Victorian "restoration", including new raised roof, which left little of the original interior. Some good 19th-century stained-glass windows. Fine cob wall in churchyard, recently restored, and ancient "holy well" in nearby lane. Services every Sunday, alternately Book of Common Prayer and Common Worship.

180 Silverton, St Mary the Virgin
Grade I

Set in the middle of the village, this delightful parish church was restored and the two westernmost bays rebuilt in 1860 followed by further restoration in 1880. The tower is battlemented with corner pinnacles and buttressed. The south and north aisle consist of four bays each with a porch occupying the westernmost bay of the south aisle. Replacement nave roof bosses were carved by local man Mr Jack Perrin following roof repairs in 1957. The organ pipes were moved to the gallery in 1972 and the space vacated used to set up the Lady chapel dedicated to St Anne. Services range from traditional to contemporary, including a monthly family service.

181 Stockleigh English, St Mary the Virgin
Grade II*

The church, which is Early Decorated, of dates 1300-1370, includes a 14th-century nave and chancel. It was restored and much beautified between 1878 and 1883. The church has a medieval font and over the south door painted arms to one of the early King Georges. This was badly damaged by fire and has now been splendidly restored. Lighting used to be by bottled gas. The system is still in place, possibly requiring only minor work for full restoration. The church has recently been fitted with new locally made lighting chandeliers and heating.

182 Stockleigh Pomeroy, St Mary the Virgin
Grade I

Stockleigh Pomeroy is a very small parish, nestling under the Raddon Hills. The Norman doorway is all that is left of the church built by the Pomeroy family, who added a north aisle in the 15th century. The church, surrounded by ancient cottages, is plain and unassuming, but boasts an interesting set of Renaissance bench ends. Services are held each Sunday, some of which are taken by retired clergy from the Crediton area. There is a keen congregation, whose members work hard to support the life of the church, which provides a deeply loved spiritual and social centre for the parish.

183 Stoodleigh, St Margaret
Grade II*

St Margaret's Church was probably first built in Norman times near the manor house known as Stoodleigh Barton. The first recorded incumbent was installed in 1264. In 1879 extensive restoration took place. Although enlarged and restored at the end of the 19th century, the church still has much of its 15th-century original construction intact. The yew tree, which is reputed to be over 1000 years old, was possibly planted when the church was built. There is a peal of six bells. The nave has an original wagon roof with bosses decorated with faces. Today, we have a small and welcoming congregation with a family atmosphere and a service every Sunday.

184 Templeton, St Margaret
Grade II

St Margaret's was built in the late 13th century for the Knights Templar returning from the Holy Land, hence the name Templeton. It started as a chapel attached to Witheridge. It fell into disrepair and was beautified in 1740. However, within a hundred years it was in need of major repair again. In 1878 this work was completed. The building is now in good decorative order. It is situated in the middle of the village and serves a rural community of about 110 people. The parish of Templeton is in the Exe Valley Group of churches. There are usually three services per month and a toddler service once a quarter.

185 Thelbridge, St David
Grade II*

Dating from the late 13th century, the first recorded priest is Sir William de Thellebrigge, instituted rector on 2nd May 1280. The present building was largely restored between 1871 and 1873 and, whilst it retains some 14th-century features, it is described as largely 15th-century. Set amid the rolling mid-Devon countryside, the gargoyles set at each corner of the tower present an intimidating feature peering ferociously down on all who enter the church. Frequent visitors appreciate the quiet and peaceful atmosphere of this country church, which is always open. A traditional monthly Eucharist, Morning Prayer and additional services are held throughout the year.

186 Thorverton, St Thomas of Canterbury
Grade I

Now part of a Mission Community formed in 2006, this spacious church, with attractive stained-glass windows, dates from early medieval times, although with subsequent development. The oldest remaining parts are the porch, notable for its stone carvings, and tower containing a ring of 10 bells, which attracts ringers from far and wide. There are a number of finely carved pews and a striking eagle lectern. An active, all-age congregation participates in a variety of worship, in which music plays an important role. Church members play their part in the village community and its primary school, including holding an annual Church Week and Arts Festival.

187 Tiverton, St Andrew

St Andrew's was designed and built by Alan Rome in 1971 as a flat-roofed rectangular edifice of rusticated red Devon cast stone, with an eastern apse and a screened narthex. It is lit by large windows occupying most of the south wall. The large altar is of cast conglomerate, and the wooden side altar has figures carved by members of Blundell's School workshops. The font, pews and organ came from redundant churches in nearby Cove, Exeter and Blackburn respectively. Prior to 1971, a mission hall church, which opened in 1959, served the newly defined parish in the developing eastern part of the town. Services are mainly modern Eucharistic.

188 Tiverton, St George
Grade I

Described as the county's best 18th-century town church. A 'Wren' design, work started in 1713, though it was not completed and consecrated until 1731. It is constructed in Ham Hill stone, having three aisles with vaulted plaster ceilings. A gallery, running along the north and south walls, was extended to include the west side in 1841. The east end stained-glass window, installed in 1845, depicting St Andrew, was copied from Wells Cathedral. The large extension, added in 1969, is much used during the week for church and community activities. Sunday morning worship is contemporary, with children's and youth teaching running concurrently in the extension and other nearby accommodation.

189 Tiverton, St Peter
Grade I

Overlooking the River Exe adjacent to Tiverton Castle, a church has stood here since 1073 or earlier. It has a Norman north door and imposing late-medieval tower with eight bells. The ornate chantry chapel was built by local merchant John Greenway in 1517. The organ is by Christian (1696). In the nave there is an impressive brass chandelier given in 1707. The interior and windows are Victorian or later. The north transept houses a collection of 17th-century books and pamphlets presented by the Revd John Newte in 1715 (view by appointment). It has been a place of worship for centuries, changing to meet the needs of the 21st century.

190 Tiverton, St Paul
Grade I

The parish church of Westexe, St Paul's was built under the patronage of Ambrose and Caroline Brewin, son-in-law and daughter of John Heathcoat, and consecrated in 1856. The building, which has excellent acoustics, is of local red Devon sandstone, in the Decorated style of the 14th century. The peal of six bells was recast in 1976 from the original chiming five. In 2001, St Paul's joined with St George's, to create a united benefice. In the evangelical tradition, St Paul's has regular mid-week services in addition to two each Sunday. It has always been the "factory church", and seeks to continue to reach out, and preach the gospel.

191 Uffculme, St Mary the Virgin
Grade II*

St Mary's Church has origins in the 12th century but the earliest architectural features are 13th or 14th-century. Significant expansion and modifications, including the addition of the spire, were made in the Victorian era under the noted Devon architect John Hayward. Unlike many churches the resultant main worship space is almost square. The 67ft screen, dating from the 15th century, is the longest in Devon and has been partially restored to show the original colouring. Uffculme is a close and active community and the church congregation is correspondingly warm and participative. Services are varied to be as inclusive as possible and to accommodate a range of worship preferences.

192 Uplowman, St Peter
Grade II*

This church was erected in the 15th century on the site of an earlier church built by Walter Stapeldon, Bishop of Exeter, 1307-1326. The present church was built by Lady Margaret Beaufort, Countess of Richmond, mother of Henry VII. The south aisle was lengthened with the addition of a small chapel/chantry founded by one of the Courtenay Family whose initials "PC" are seen over the niche between the choir and the south aisle. Delightful stained-glass windows include memorials to the Revd S. Pidsley, Mr Commissioner Bere and the fallen from the wars. War plaques and records of past rectors are displayed.

193 Upton Hellions, St Mary the Virgin
Grade I

Overlooking beautiful countryside and built of local masonry and volcanic rock, St Mary the Virgin has an original Norman doorway. The tower has remaining medieval plaster, an embattled parapet and rare, original Devon bell-frame (c.1500). Originally housing three bells made by Exeter Medieval Foundry, two were removed in 1769. Inside there is a 13th-century font; intricate stained-glass window; 17th-century alabaster prie dieu; unusual zodiac tiles behind the altar; and ancient roof bosses in nave wagon roof and Tudor south aisle. The lychgate was erected in 1894. Linked ecclesiastically with Sandford in 1928, this wonderful church holds services four times a year, plus celebratory worship. Current restoration plans involve stabilising the stained-glass windows.

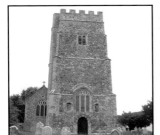

194 Washfield, St Mary the Virgin
Grade II*

Washfield parish is a triangle of glorious countryside directly north west of Tiverton. St Mary's church stands at its centre. A rector is recorded in 1266 and the present building dates mainly from the 15th century. The screen of 1624 carved with rustic classical foliage replaces a rood screen destroyed at the Reformation. It encloses the chancel and the pew of the Worth family, who owned much of the parish from the early Middle Ages until the 1880s. In 1964 Washfield joined one of the earliest group ministries; this is now the Exe Valley Team. Worship is offered nearly every Sunday by a faithful congregation on behalf of a lively community.

195 Washford Pyne, St Peter
Grade II*

A small and remote church rebuilt in 1882-1884 by R. M. Fulford, apart from the base of the tower, which is of the 15th century. Described as "characteristically inventive" by Pevsner, it comprises nave, chancel, south transept chapel, west tower with low broach tiled spire, south porch, and vestry. The tower is Perpendicular, the rest is late-19th-century Gothic with Arts and Crafts elements. Internally, the Gothic-style choir stalls and pews are of oak, the Gothic chancel screen was the gift of Charles Comyns Tucker (d.1922), and the Gothic-style oak pulpit the gift of Elizabeth Bragg (d.1910). An elaborately carved oak lectern. All of the carved work is by H. Hems.

196 Wembworthy, St Michael
Grade II*

Is of medieval origins, with some parts early 16th-century; tower of 1626, porch of 1849, the majority rebuilt in 1868 and restored again in 1902 by Harbottle Reed. It comprises nave, chancel, north aisle with east chapel, west tower, and porch on west end of nave. Perpendicular style throughout. The porch has a tiled floor which contains encaustic memorial tiles to the Revd Peter Johnson (d.1869) and his wife Gratiana (d.1845). Both the nave and north aisle have ceiled wagon roofs which though much-restored in the 19th century still retain good deal of early-16th-century carpentry. The chancel has a 19th-century painted stone reredos. The pulpit is 17th-century, restored in the 19th century. 19th-century Beer stone font.

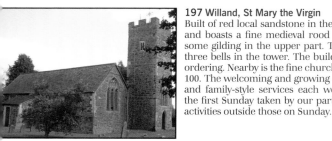

197 Willand, St Mary the Virgin
Grade I

Built of red local sandstone in the 14th century, this small church seats 100 and boasts a fine medieval rood screen decorated in ancient colour with some gilding in the upper part. There are two stained-glass windows, and three bells in the tower. The building is being prepared for a proposed re-ordering. Nearby is the fine church hall constructed in 1986 which also seats 100. The welcoming and growing congregation is served by both traditional and family-style services each week with a joint Communion service on the first Sunday taken by our part-time vicar. There is a full range of other activities outside those on Sunday.

198 Withleigh, St Catherine
Grade II

Built by the Carpenter family, and opened in 1847 as a chapel in the parish of Tiverton. The site was formerly that of a medieval chapel of ease, the remains uncovered during excavation for the present building. Extensively repaired and modernised in the 1960s, with lowered ceiling, strip lighting and a new vestry. The organ is an historically interesting instrument, having some unusual features. A parish from 1886, and now one of nine in the Exe Valley Team. St Catherine's is a community church. It has weekly services, and seeks to care for the members of the community who all regard it as theirs.

199 Woolfardisworthy East, St Mary
Grade II*

Though on an ancient site, the present church was rebuilt in 1842 of local stone and paid for by the rector, aided by a church rate of 1s/6d (7.5p) for three years. A study of the monuments gives a correct impression that money and leadership came mainly from the rectory family. The tower is probably older than the rest of the building and the three bells are, being dated from the early/mid 18th century. Some of the woodwork is probably from the previous building. Worship is largely traditional with monthly services of Eucharist and Evensong. We have an annual pattern of united services with our friends from other denominations.

200 Yeoford Chapel (Crediton), Holy Trinity

This chapel was built in 1891 by W. Dart of Crediton, founder of the local company Dart & Francis. The land for the church building was given by Sir John Shelley of Shobrooke Park. The church is constructed of cavity brickwork with a purple slate roof and consists of a nave, vestry and north porch. The interior is simple, with a stone font contemporary with the construction of the church. There is a bell turret at the west end clad with wood shingles.

201 Zeal Monachorum, St Peter
Grade II*

Parts date from the 12th and 13th centuries, much rebuilt in the 15th and early 16th centuries, with major restorations of 1850-1853 and 1907-1912. It comprises nave, chancel, north transept, south aisle, west tower and south porch. Internally, nearly all of the fittings are c.1913, including the altar rail, choir stalls and benches, and chancel and parclose screens. The pulpit is a First World War memorial. The font is Norman. There is interesting stained glass; the east window by Hardman (1851), the south window of the chancel is also mid-19th-century and includes a representation of the Virgin and Child by Clayton and Bell. Most of the rest of the glass is early-20th-century by Drake.

NORTH DEVON

North Devon has a distinctive character and spirit and this is certainly reflected in its churches and their people. In every bustling market town, quiet village or along the beautiful and at times dramatic coastline, you will find one of 84 of our churches, faithfully witnessing to the Christian story in each generation.

202 Arlington, St James
Grade II*

Set within the grounds of Arlington Court, St James was largely rebuilt in the 1840s, with the tower added in 1899. With a nave, chancel, south transept and west tower, all of the internal fittings date from the 19th century. The Chichester family, who owned Arlington Court, are commemorated in a number of monuments in the church, including that of Rosalie Chichester (d.1949), who bequeathed the house to the National Trust. The fortnightly congregation is tiny and elderly – reflecting the small community – and the worship traditional. This large church, dominated by Chichester family memorials, was literally built around a family and lifestyle that has now vanished.

203 Ashford (Pilton), St Peter
Grade II*

The first recorded vicar of Ashford, a Domesday Saxon settlement, was instituted in 1269. A new church was built around 1332, of which part of the tower and two bells remain. The font is late Norman, and the original bench ends 16th-century. The church was largely rebuilt in 1852, when much fine Jacobean panelling was added. Ashford is a very small parish – only 359 acres, with about 100 households. Because the village has no pub, school or shop, the church tries to act as a centre for village life, offering music, coffee and lively friendship every Sunday, and hosting special events in the tiny church hall throughout the year.

204 Atherington, St Mary
Grade I

Dating from the 15th and 16th centuries, and restored in the 1880s. Consists of a nave, chancel, north aisle, south transept, porch and west tower. Internally, much of the early fabric survives, including the font. The screens are of particular interest; that between the aisle and chancel retains its loft of c.1530-1540. The chancel/nave screen is said to have come from the chapel at Umberleigh House. Some of the pews date from the 17th century. There are also a number of important monuments. A small but very welcoming church in the heart of the village. Services include morning and evening Communion, and an informal monthly all-age service.

205 Barnstaple, Holy Trinity
Grade II*

The substantial Somerset style tower is clearly visible on your approach to Barnstaple. Originally constructed in 1842, the church and tower suffered significant failures, and the church was rebuilt in 1868 with the tower believed to have been reduced in height at this time. Major refurbishment is planned for 2008. Our church is a major feature of town life, with a welcoming weekly service plus many other prayer, worship, outreach and social events to serve the community and the margins in the town. The Scout troop that meets in the church hall were the first in Devon, established there in 1908.

NORTH DEVON

238
237
239
207 223
27
255
246
242
285
281
211
228
202
247
225
232
214
213
252
268
212
234
203
27
262
233
206
231 270
272
241
205 256 245
240
266
210
273
283
274
236
257
209
221
277
204
27
220
216

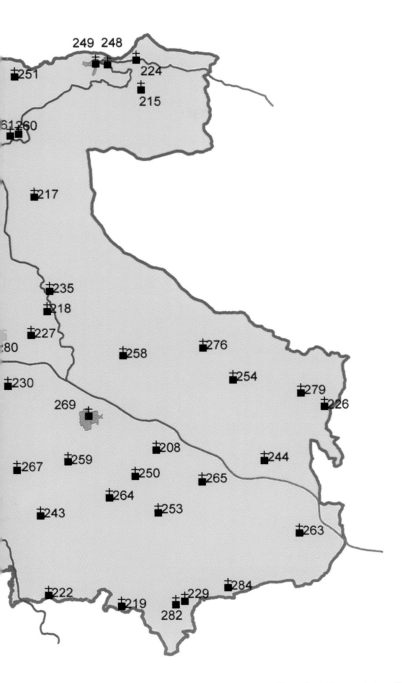

206 Barnstaple, St Peter & St Mary Magdalene
Grade I

Built in 1318 and restored by Sir Gilbert Scott in the 19th century, the church is crowned with a twisted lead spire. It nestles in the heart of bustling Barnstaple at a pedestrian crossroad. It shares its site with the 15th-century St Anne's Chapel, once the Grammar School and now a museum. Interior treasures include fine 17th-century wall monuments, a medieval chasuble and a fine organ. The Sunday Sung Eucharist is the core of the church's life. On weekdays the church is open and used, for daily worship, for peace and quiet and prayer, and for a wide range of church and community activities.

207 Berrynarbor, St Peter
Grade II*

This beautiful church, with a magnificent tower, has evidence of Saxon, Norman and early English Perpendicular styles of architecture. The statues in the tower were removed during the Reformation, but there are some examples of 16th-century monuments in the church itself. The font is in a Norman style, and the south aisle was probably added to the 12th-century building. The lychgate is next to the site of the church house, which was demolished some time ago. The six bells in the tower are rung regularly before Sunday worship. There is a short history and description on paddle boards for visitors to the church.

208 Bishops Nympton, St Mary the Virgin
Grade I

A church was built on the present site in the 12th century; it was rebuilt in the 15th century, restored in 1603 and extensively restored in 1869. The church comprises a nave, chancel, south aisle, lady chapel, vestry, organ chamber and beautiful 15th-century tower some 120ft high, accentuated by flood-lighting. The font is Norman and we have some commemorative stained-glass windows. Above the vestry door is a 15th-century wooden statue of St James the Apostle. Of our four services a month, one is held jointly with the Methodist chapel. We have close ties with the local Primary School and hold a Summer Club for the Oakmoor Group children every year.

209 Bishops Tawton, Herner Chapel
Grade II

Built by Charles and Beatrice Chichester and consecrated as a chapel of ease in 1888. Evensong (according to the Book of Common Prayer) is held on the second Sunday in the Month between May and September.

210 Bishops Tawton, St John the Baptist
Grade I

Our church, built on the site of a medieval chapel, was completed in 1882. Over the years numerous improvements have been made, including a south doorway, choir vestry, brass eagle lectern, stained-glass memorial windows and a Bath stone pulpit. Application has been made to re-order the church by replacing pews with chairs. We are friendly, warm and welcoming and hold a good variety of formal and informal services. Our Sunday School is thriving, also the Early Bird service with breakfast, and we have a choir and music group. We have missionary links with Zimbabwe and Japan, and locally support people with special needs.

211 Bittadon, St Peter
Grade II*

Baring Gould's *Devonshire Guide* (revised 1949 by Ronald Hicks), having noted that it is one of the smallest in the county rather, unfairly states "it contains nothing of interest, save the ancient font". Despite this there are several interesting memorials – to Edward Pointz 1691, Henry Ackland 1675 and also to the Chichester family. The murals behind the altar (the Resurrection and St Peter) were the work of Alan Gladwell, who lived in nearby Burland House, in 1937. Both church (rebuilt 1883) and churchyard are lovingly cared for by the few who live in the parish. There is a monthly Communion and packed church for Harvest and Christmas Carols.

212 Bratton Fleming, St Peter
Grade II

With sections dating from the 14th and 15th centuries, St Peter's was very heavily restored in the mid-19th century, following the collapse of the tower onto the nave in the early years of that century. The church consists of a nave, chancel, north aisle, south porch and west tower. Spring provides visitors with a churchyard covered in masses of daffodils. St Peter's became an Anglican-Methodist church in 2007 when the two congregations formally joined together to worship under one roof. Services include Holy Communion (Anglican and Methodist) and a less formal monthly all-age service. The church is active in the community, having numerous links with many village organisations.

213 Braunton, St Brannock
Grade I

The site of the present 13th-century church has known Christian worship since early times. Important features include a wagon nave roof with medieval bosses, early Norman font, Jacobean pulpit, medieval pews and a 120ft broach spire dated as one of the oldest in the country. The earliest feature is a Saxon burial stone. We have an important civic role in the community, which was founded by our patron saint, St Brannock. The church is open daily for visitors and prayer. Sunday and midweek Eucharists are supported by lay-led daily Morning Prayer. House groups, children's work, pastoral teams, an emerging Fresh Expression group and social events are part of an active church life

214 Braunton, Saunton St Anne

This chapel was built by two benefactors as a chapel of ease in 1896, partly to serve the growing local populations and partly to replace an earlier chapel at Crow, on the Taw estuary, that had been on a pilgrim route until it was overwhelmed by sand in the 18th century. The stones were quarried from the sea cliff at Saunton. The stained-glass windows by Mary Lowndes were installed at the east end in 1906. The chapel is in a delightful, wooded setting, adjacent to the North Devon Coast Path. It provides a peaceful haven for visitors. Services are conducted each Sunday, with Morning Worship following the Book of Common Prayer.

215 Brendon, St Brendon
Grade II

The church stands in an isolated position high up to the west of the village. The nave, chancel and south porch were built in 1738, the tower rebuilt in 1828, and the whole church was restored, and the north aisle, north transept and vestry added, in 1873. Internally, the fittings date mostly from the late 19th and early 20th centuries. There is an elaborately carved wooden reredos, altar rails and carved choir stalls, all from the early 20th century by Brendon carpenter, John Floyd. The carved wooden lectern is by Joseph Totterdell of Brendon. The stone font dates from the 12th century, with a 19th-century cover.

216 Burrington, Holy Trinity
Grade I

The building of Holy Trinity began around 1150. The oldest feature is the Norman font, which has now served for 32 generations. The north wall and part of the tower are 13th-century with improvement and enlargement in the 15th century. The slightly later chancel screen is exceptionally fine. The heavy oak porch door reveals shot marks, possibly from Cromwellian muskets. We are a small hill village and have recently had considerable difficulty in meeting running costs, but a vigorous fund-raising campaign is now underway, which gives us great hope for the future.

217 Challacombe, Holy Trinity
Grade II*

Originally dating from the 12th century, the church was rebuilt in 1854. Situated in the old manor of Barton Town, it is away from the centre of the village, which migrated to lower in the Bray Valley. It consists of nave, chancel and west tower. The latter boasted of being one of the wettest in the country, with ferns growing on the inside, until it was traditionally rendered in the 1990s. The bells are chimed by a one-person mechanism, and the 100-year-old organ is still pumped by hand. Services are held fortnightly, and the church is well supported by the village community, especially through the annual sheep-dog trials.

218 Charles, St John the Baptist
Grade II

Set high on the hill at Charles, the church was built for and serves a small rural community. Reputed to be built on the site of a Celtic chieftain's fortress, the present building dates from the 11th century but was largely restored in 1875. The east window is a memorial to R. D. Blackmore, who spent many holidays with his uncle, the rector. Our faithful and welcoming congregation joins with the local Anglican and Methodist churches for worship and is active in all aspects of the community. Worship is mainly traditional for the twice-monthly services. In addition, there are special services and community activities, including a popular summer local history exhibition.

219 Cheldon, St Mary
Grade II*

This small and unpretentious country church comprising nave, chancel and tower with four bells dates from the 16th century and is built in Perpendicular style. Noteworthy in the interior are the font (12th-century and certainly from an earlier church), the bench ends, the pulpit (probably late-17th-century) and, most remarkably, in place of a screen, two stands supporting mid-18th-century coats of arms, one of which displays three creatures identified as badgers, or possibly bears. The monthly celebration of Evensong attracts congregations of up to twenty, filling the church.

220 Chittlehamholt, St John the Baptist
Grade II

Built in 1838, this church stands outside this small village, adjacent to the manor house. Designed by R. D. Gould of Barnstaple, it is a fine example of his work and a typical Victorian church. Inside it has a central aisle and stained pine pews. Seven large lancet windows with lancet triplets at the east and west ends, together with pale plaster walls and white ceiling, provide a very spacious and pleasing effect. Services range from traditional to contemporary and the small friendly congregation bear witness in the life of the community with monthly drop-in lunches, publication of the local news-sheet, a study group and a thriving affiliated youth club.

221 Chittlehampton, St Hieritha
Grade I

Widely referred to as "the cathedral of North Devon" with its own unique saint, the beautiful late-15th, early-16th-century church of Saint Hieritha with its magnificent 114ft decorated tower watches over the village of Chittlehampton. Hieritha, or Urith, a Celtic maid, converted by Glastonbury monks, was martyred when her faith was blamed for a life-threatening drought. A lively church, with a variety of styles of services and social activities designed to reach out to our community in keeping with our vision statement: "Reaching Upwards, Reaching Outwards". We are also linked through the diocese with Gatura parish in Thika Diocese, Kenya. See our website for information about us and our church family.

222 Chulmleigh, St Mary Magdalene
Grade I

Outstanding features include a Norman carved roundel over the south porch, a 15th-century font and magnificent Perpendicular four-stage tower. Continuous nave and chancel, with full-length north and south aisles, wagon roofs with carved bosses and angels, elegantly carved 16th-century rood screen, extending across the nave and aisles, surmounted by 17th-century wooden statues of the four evangelists. Substantial restoration between 1879 and 1881, finely carved pews and pulpit added. A notable collection of 19th- and 20th-century stained glass. A recent flourishing innovation is our "fresh expressions" of church – the Beacon. This and St. Mary's offer a wide spread of contemporary to traditional worship.

223 Combe Martin, St Peter ad Vincula
Grade I

This beautiful church has a magnificent tower, rising to 99 feet, and eight bells rung weekly. The church was probably built over an original Saxon building and is now in the Early English Perpendicular style, with the north aisle leading to a chantry chapel, built in about 1333. The parclose screen is beautifully carved and superior to the rood screen, which contains Tudor paintings of the twelve Apostles and Jesus, in the nave, while also featuring lady saints on the "women's" side of the church. Alongside the font of 1427, there is evidence of medieval wall paintwork. There are two Green Men. Guides and leaflets are available for visitors.

224 Countisbury, St John the Evangelist
Grade II*

The parish of Countisbury includes Lynmouth and the church dates from 1796 but is on the site of earlier churches. The churchyard contains memorials from this earlier period. The church was built without an architect using local labour: names still familiar in the area Slocombe, Lock, Fry and Crocombe. The earliest entry in the register is 1607 and the current burial register was started in 1813. Most of the crew of the epic launch of the Lynmouth Lifeboat of 1898 are buried here. The church is open every day and on Sundays during the summer an interdenominational Candelit Epilogue is held.

225 Croyde, St Mary Magdalene
Grade II

The church opened in 1874 as a mission church to assist those parishioners unable to travel comfortably to the parish church in Georgeham. It was also used as an Infant School, a Sunday School and a night school during winter months. Even then, Croyde was a popular seaside resort and the church provided a valuable facility for visitors. In 2001 the pews were replaced with chairs, carpeting was laid and other furniture renewed to enable the building to be used for additional purposes as well as regular Sunday services. It houses summer exhibitions, marriage courses, church retreats and parish meetings. A new bell was donated and hung in 2002.

226 East Anstey, St Michael
Grade II*

Probably dating from the 16th century, although on the site of an earlier church, it was substantially rebuilt in 1871 at a cost of £800. The oldest detail is the doorstep of the south door, probably part of an old Norman lintel with zig-zag pattern. The broad-based square embattled tower, the south porch and the window between predate the rebuilding. There were four bells in 1553. In 1905 the old tenor bell was recast into two smaller bells and currently there is a ring of five. The yew tree outside was brought from the parsonage pear orchard in 1832. The credence table column is from the old rood screen.

227 East Buckland, St Michael
Grade II

The tower probably dates from the 15th century, but the remainder of the church was rebuilt with a chancel in the position of a north aisle in 1862-1863 by R. D. Gould. It comprises west tower, nave, chancel and south porch. The porch has an 18th-century sundial by T. Berry. Internally there are unplastered stone walls, and painted royal arms over the south porch doorway. All of the furnishings date from the 20th century.

228 East Down, St John the Baptist
Grade II*

East Down is first recorded as a parish church in 1260. The present building was the local manorial chapel, dating back to the 13th century, prior to becoming the parish church by gift in 1469. Numerous additions, alterations and refurbishments have taken place over the centuries. The screen is of particular note and is a fine specimen of 15th-century craftsmanship, which was carefully restored in 1925. The tower is the oldest part of the building and still shows signs of a "bullet" hole, on the east side, from a skirmish in the Civil War. Within the churchyard lies a rare example of a church house of the same period as the church. A small, friendly church in lovely rural surroundings.

229 East Worlington, St Mary
Grade II

Although originally dating from the 12th century, only the late Norman entrance arch and one window of the original wooden spired church remain. The church was substantially rebuilt through the generosity of its patron, the Earl of Portsmouth, in 1879 with a new tower containing a ring of six bells, four of which date back to 1727. These bells were refurbished and rehung in 2006 with the aid of a Heritage Lottery Fund grant. Weekly worship is shared with St Mary's, West Worlington through the Little Dart Team Ministry and a Local Ministry Team, as is mission in, and the pastoral care of, this active little rural community.

230 Filleigh, St Paul
Grade II*

Rebuilt in 1732 by the Fortescues of Castle Hill, but incorporating some fabric from the old church; remodelled in 1876-1877 by Clark of Newmarket. It comprises west tower with spire, nave, transepts, south aisle and apsidal chancel. Originally built in a Classical style, but Victorian remodelling converted the church into the Norman style. The interior is dominated by memorials to the Fortescue family. The elaborate chancel roof was painted by Lady Susan Fortescue c.1880. The marble font is dedicated to Georgina, Countess Fortescue, as are the six chancel stained-glass windows. Many of the other windows are in memory of the Fortescues, and there are also many monuments to the family.

231 Fremington, St Peter
Grade II*

Our beautiful parish church dates back to the 13th century. St Peter's, however, is not a museum, but is home to a friendly and living church. Much dedicated work has been done over recent years to breathe new life into this house of prayer, so that today people of all ages – praise God, in growing numbers – come to worship God and to grow in faith, fellowship, and fun (you may find puppets giving the occasional sermon!). Our prayer is that more and more people may discover within the walls of St Peter's the joy of a living and personal relationship with our Lord and Saviour, Jesus Christ.

232 Georgeham, St George
Grade I

First recorded in 1231, then in 1261 as Ham St George. 13th-century remains include a knight effigy, font and crucifixion scene. 14th-century remains are the tower, piscina and quatrefoil window. Most arches are 15th-century. In 1762 radical Romanesque-style changes were made. Major restorations in 1876 altered most windows, enlarged the vestry and installed a new font, pulpit and the current seating. The organ was installed in 1881. There is a fine peal of eight bells, the oldest dated 1748. Services are held weekly. The ecumenical Mission Community has strong links with St George's House Christian activity centre, Christian Surfers UK, the local Baptist congregation and the village school.

233 Goodleigh, St Gregory
Grade II*

Originating from the 15th century, the church (excluding tower) was later deemed unsafe and in 1881 was demolished and rebuilt. The church now consists of nave, chancel, south aisle and original tower (housing six bells). Several interesting monuments have been preserved; these include the royal arms, dated 1788. Sunday worship is shared with the Methodists (with whom there is a Covenant). Junior Church meets weekly, other than during school holidays and on the third Sunday of each month when there is All-Age Family Worship. The village school uses the church regularly.

234 Heanton Punchardon, St Augustine
Grade I

The original building having been destroyed by fire in 1285 (arson suspected; parish priest involved!), the present church dates largely from the 15th century. Situated on top of a hill, it commands superb views over the Taw and Torridge estuaries. The bell tower is topped by pinnacles, which lean outwards to resemble a crown. The spacious interior is light and has a fine screen. The churchyard contains the graves of airmen killed during the Second World War. The church has a lively approach to worship, using different styles to suit all ages and backgrounds. Evangelism plays an important part in church life and activity and a very warm welcome is assured any visitor.

235 High Bray, All Saints
Grade I

Located on the fringes of Exmoor, we are overlooked by Bronze Age burial sites and in turn look down to a valley where Romans lived and worked. There was probably a church on this site in Saxon times but most of the present stone building dates from the 15th and early 16th centuries. You may come to look at the Norman font, the curious column capital with its rope and face decoration or even the sensational wildflowers in the spring. But to us this church, together with our friends at the chapel in the village, represents a continuing tradition of spiritual life in this community of which we are the proud stewards.

236 Horwood, St Michael
Grade I

The horn-shaped Norman piscina is unique. The pew ends show folk art symbols of the Passion of Christ, figures of saints and local coats of arms. The 17th-century lead-glazed chancel floor tiles of lions, flowers and birds are made from local Torridge clay. In the Lady chapel are a 15th-century alabaster effigy of Elizabeth Pollard and a wonderful memorial cross, made from artillery and cartridges brought back by a villager from the Great War. The Horwood Mermaid is carved on a column. The treble bell (Bristol 1370) is one of the dozen oldest bells in Devon.

237 Ilfracombe, Holy Trinity
Grade I

Standing on the site of a Saxon church, the Norman church was enlarged to its present size in 1322 and the tower incorporated inside the building. It has one of the finest wagon roofs in the west country, dating from the 15th century and richly carved with bosses, corbels and figures. The sanctuary roof dates from the 19th century. Note the gloria or celure, the panelled roof over where the rood screen once stood and the restored (1889) clerestory. The windows are of particular interest – by Hardman, Williment, Ballantine, Kempe. Very much a 'civic' church for the community. The men and boys' choir lead the (traditional) Sunday Eucharist.

238 Ilfracombe, St Philip & St James
*Grade II**

During the mid-1800s a level site in the harbour area was given and the parish church raised £2,434 for a daughter church to serve the growing quayside community. The cornerstone was laid on 1st May 1851 being the feast of St Philip & St James. With £4,000 spent, lack of funds brought the building to a standstill. Mr W. Stone, of Bristol, whilst on holiday, provided the £1,500 to complete the roof. The service of consecration took place on 10th June 1857. Since that time it has been a spiritual home for thousands whose evangelical witness has left a profound impression on the lives of an ever-growing and ever-changing community.

239 Ilfracombe, St Peter
*Grade II**

Victorian and Edwardian pioneers, recognising the need for another church to serve Ilfracombe's growing population, instructed a nationally known architect, G. H. Fellowes-Prynne, to design what was to become a daughter church to Holy Trinity. Although vestries, chapels, west porch and upper part of the tower were never completed, what the congregation got for their £6,749 3s 6d was the striking building you see today. The church, consecrated on 10th December 1903, has always reflected the Anglo-Catholic or high church tradition of the C of E. Sung Mass on Sundays and a resource for the 500 children from the nearby C of E Junior School.

240 Instow, All Saints' Chapel

Built in 1936 as a memorial to his wife by the architect, Napier Orphoot, this small white Adriatic chapel is resplendent with Art Deco and Byzantine features. The roof timbers were taken from an old ship of the line, HMS Revenge, launched in 1859 and broken up in Appledore. It is situated within the village and has a garden, grounds and car parking space. There are proposals to adapt its use to present needs. Until recently, it has been used for early morning Communion and Evensong or BCP Communion in the evenings. It is open daily for contemplation and prayer.

241 Instow, St John the Baptist
Grade I

A Celtic foundation church set high above Bideford Bay. The tower rises to 54ft. Notable features are the Norman font, 1547 pillars and wagon roof, and memorials including Humphrey Sibthorpe d.1797, first Oxford Professor of Botany, John Downe d.1640 and the Clevlands of Tapeley Park, patrons. The church was restored in 1875. The bells date from c.1553. The organ was built by a craftsman from France, Cavaille-Coll. There is a communion service on Sunday and a regular Family Service. We meet for coffee and fellowship in the church room. Parishioners are involved in many community activities. We edit and distribute the Parish News to 1000 households every month.

242 Kentisbury, St Thomas
Grade II*

The church is understood to be dedicated to St Thomas and was first mentioned in the Deed of 1275 when Hamilton de Heanton was appointed rector. The Wolf family were the founders of the church and on the south wall of the church there is a tablet which mentions them. Restoration of the church was carried out from 1873-1875, when the north aisle was added, the chancel enlarged and the chapel extended. The work was carried out by E. Dolby of Abingdon for the absentee rector and patron – the Revd Thomas Openshaw. Today there are services held twice a month and the congregation is relatively small.

243 Kingsnympton, St James
Grade I

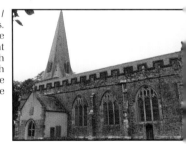

There has been a place of worship on the site for over a thousand years. The north wall of the building dates from Saxon times. When one enters the church by the south porch the threshold is part of the shaft of an ancient granite Celtic cross. The word "Nympton" is derived from "nemet" which meant "a sacred grove". The church is famous for its rood screen, which is deemed to be among the finest in Devon. Worship takes place in the church every Sunday and is a mix of traditional and modern services. The congregation is 'all-age' and growing.

244 Knowstone, St Peter
Grade II*

Lying on a slope overlooking the 16th-century public house, the church dates principally from the 15th century, although the south doorway is said to be Norman. The west tower and the north aisle are rendered. It comprises west tower, nave, north aisle, chancel and south porch. Internally, there are 18th-century Communion rails, a 19th-century pulpit incorporating parts of a former screen, two windows with stained glass by Drake, and 19th-century tiled floors, raised and fielded panelled benches, and font. The painted royal arms date from 1724. There are monuments to John Culme (d.1791), Philip Shapcote (d.1690), and a wall monument to the Froude family, including Revd John Froude (d.1852).

245 Landkey, St Paul
Grade I

The site of the church, associated with St Kea, an early Celtic saint, is on the side of a deep valley. The present church was built of local stone in the 15th century in the Perpendicular style, with a tower with battlements, and it was restructured in the mid-19th century. The font and three beautiful effigies date back to the 13th century and there is a hagioscope from the south aisle. Today the church is active with a growing congregation, a very active Mothers' Union and regular services are held on Sundays, Wednesdays and festivals.

246 Lee, St Matthew

Grade II

St Matthew's (or St Matthew's & St Wardrede's), one of the few churches built during the reign of William IV, was consecrated in 1835. This little gem seats 90 at a push, with a musicians' gallery, fine Jacobean carved oak woodwork (a gift from the old manor house but fitting perfectly in the much later church), and fascinating Victorian wall decorations of various Christian emblems. St Wardrede is an obscure figure, possibly a Celtic saint who came to preach the gospel here as far back as the 6th century. Today our flourishing church is at the heart of the village community, faithfully serving our resident population and our many visitors.

247 Loxhore, St Michael & All Angels

Grade II*

Probably over 700 years old, and located in peaceful surroundings to the north of the village, this small and attractive church saw major 15th-century and Victorian restorations. Beneath a wagon roof with flower and leaf bosses, arch-less wooden piers separate the nave and north aisle. The chancel has an unusually narrow two-light east window, and the octagonal font a decorative 16th-century cover. There are interesting 17th-century memorials to the Carpenter and Hammond families. The refurbished peal of six bells is rung from the ground floor of the tower at the west end. The small but faithful congregation, characterised by strength of fellowship, gathers for worship in a traditional setting.

248 Lynmouth, St John the Baptist

Grade II

This is the daughter church of St John the Baptist, Countisbury. The church was built by local craftsmen in 1869 to serve the flourishing small resort of Lynmouth as a chapel of ease. At the turn of the century the south aisle was added, then the belfry as a memorial to the First World War. In 1952, when Lynmouth was devastated by floods, there was considerable loss of internal items but little structural damage. The United States Air Force, which had been stationed nearby during the Second World War, presented the new oak vestry as a memorial to those who died, and their names are recorded on the plaque on the vestry wall.

249 Lynton, St Mary the Virgin

Grade II*

St Mary the Virgin is situated in an area of outstanding natural beauty overlooking the sea with spectacular views of Countisbury headland. The tower is 13th-century, the nave was rebuilt in 1741 and there were a series of Victorian and Edwardian restorations and rebuilding between 1868 and 1905. The building is considered to be one of the finest examples of Arts and Crafts architecture in Britain. The church provides a sense of stability and historical continuity for the community, and offers a ministry of prayer and hospitality for the many tourists who visit the area. The parish includes a daughter church, St Bartholomew, in Barbrook.

250 Mariansleigh, St Mary

Grade II*

"Remote and unvisited" is the Shell Guide's verdict on Mariansleigh. But the reward for the intrepid is a small gem of a parish church. A first glance yields little of immediate interest, but a closer look shows that there are odd pews and furnishings. The interior was completely burnt out by a fire in 1932, and the church then benefited from a sort of "jumble sale" from other churches which gave us their casts-off. The result is pleasing, all enhanced by the clear light flooding into the church. There is a superb east window (1954) depicting The Last Supper.

251 Martinhoe, St Martin
Grade II*

The site of the present church was that of a chapel serving the families of Martinhoe Manor, recorded in the Domesday Book. The date of this chapel, built within the dimensions of the present chancel, is believed to be Saxon. There was substantial rebuilding in Norman times, although the form recognisable today was not completed until about 1200. James Hannington, who became the first bishop of Eastern Equitorial Africa, was curate at Martinhoe before joining the Church Missionary Society. Today, this beautiful church is a wonderful house of prayer for visitors exploring the hidden treasures of Exmoor. It is loved and maintained by a small number of devout worshippers.

252 Marwood, St Michael & All Angels
Grade I

The first recorded rector was Thomas Payne in 1263. A good deal of the first 13th-century church building erected at this time remains. Most of the present church is 15th-century and comprises a nave, chancel, tower, north aisle and south chapel. There are unsealed wagon roofs throughout and the remainder of the 16th-century screen and pew ends have interesting carvings. The beautiful neighbouring Marwood Gardens also attract visitors. The church uses various styles of worship to suit all ages and backgrounds. It has a lively Sunday School, a real heart for outreach and community occasions and draws people in with a warm welcome.

253 Meshaw, St John the Baptist
Grade II

Set in the heart of Meshaw village, St John's is a quiet and peaceful place of worship in rural north Devon. The earliest Christian worship is recorded in 1263, the parish register commences in 1580. The church was rebuilt in 1838, and comprises a nave and bell tower, and a beautiful stained-glass window in the sanctuary depicts the life of Our Lord. Significant benefactors were the Karslakes; several family members are interred here. As part of the Little Dart Team of 13 parishes, we have a small but loyal congregation served by clergy and our own Local Ministry Team, sharing worship twice monthly.

254 Molland, St Mary
Grade I

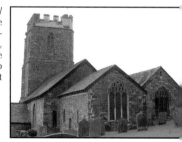

As with so many north Devon churches, this dates back to c.1300. Over the centuries, the church has grown: the tower and north aisles are early 16th-century. The church is famous for its complete Georgian interior: box pews, (some four-square) and three-decker pulpit, all dating from about 1740. There are magnificent, wall-mounted memorials of the 17th and 18th centuries to the Courtenay family, former lords of the manor. The church is always kept unlocked: come and visit.

255 Mortehoe, St Mary
Grade I

Situated above the village square, St Mary's has been at the heart of this community since Norman times. The chancel, west end and belfry were added around 1275. South and north transepts followed in 1307 and 1500, when a new south entrance was also built. Victorian alterations included the removal of the gallery and the addition of much beautiful stained glass. Notable features include six bells, the barrel roof, a magnificent mosaic on the chancel arch, fine carved pews, and the tomb of William de Tracy. With our sister parishes in Lee and Woolacombe we share worship, pastoral care and a vision for the needs of the community we serve.

256 Newport, St John the Baptist

Built on the site of a medieval chapel, the church was consecrated in 1829 as a chapel of ease for the community of Newport within the parish of Bishops Tawton. The parish became independent in 1847, at which time the building was in urgent need of repair. The current building was completed in 1882, and fronts directly onto the highway. It consists of a nave, chancel, north aisle, vestries and north porch and is built of local limestone. A 1960s church hall is linked to the church by way of a covered walkway. It is well used for a variety of activities.

257 Newton Tracey, St Thomas à Becket   Grade II*

In 1139 Henry de Tracey was given the ownership of Barnstaple and probably built a small chapel for his Newton Tracey tenants. Soon after, the Traceys chose to dedicate it to Thomas à Becket, then England's most recent saint, and the earliest evidence of a church is the 12th-century font. Built mainly of ham stone the church has a bell tower, nave, chancel, north aisle and south porch. The chancel area is Early English. The earliest recorded rector, Walter de Tawstocke, was instituted in 1282. Today some pews have been removed and it is planned to use the church as a centre for the community as well as for services.

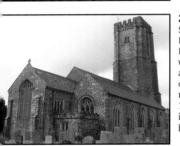

258 North Molton, All Saints   Grade I

Situated above the village square, the church dates from the late 15th century. It was altered internally in c.1844, 1876-1883, and then restored in 1886-1890. It comprises nave, north and south aisles, south porch, chancel, vestry and west tower. Notable features internally include the fine 15th-century screen across the nave and aisles, 15th-century parclose screens between aisle chapels and chancel, the 17th-century panelling to the chancel, reredos with royal coat of arms (James I), late-17th or early 18th-century Communion rails, 15th-century octagonal wooden pulpit and Beer stone font. The organ was installed between 1876-1883. There are also a number of fine monuments both in the church and churchyard.

259 Nymet St George, St George   Grade II*

Dates mainly from the 15th century, with a tower of 1673. The church was restored and partially rebuilt in 1882 by Harbottle. It comprises nave, chancel, north aisle, west tower, south porch and vestry. The tower is interesting for its date; constructed of hand-made bricks which were made in the parish by J. Moore, who was paid £22 5s 4d. Internal features include the 19th-century commandment boards and tiling incorporating the symbols of the evangelists; the pulpit, lectern, reading desk and chancel seats which were all memorials of 1880; and the font which is 15th-century. The 19th-century nave benches carefully incorporate medieval fragments. There are a number of 18th- and 19th-century monuments.

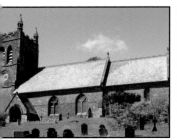

260 Parracombe, Christ Church   Grade II

Christ Church is set in Parracombe village to the north west of Exmoor National Park and continues a tradition of Christianity dating from Saxon times. Completed in 1878 it replaced the dilapidated 12th-century church of St Petrock. The tower contains the original 17th-century bells. Not only the centre of worship, Christ Church is home to a thriving youth club and closely linked with the successful local C of E Primary School. The view from the porch over the steeply sloping churchyard and Heddon Valley includes Holwell Castle, a Norman motte and bailey. There are frequent visitors and many remark on the tranquil beauty found here.

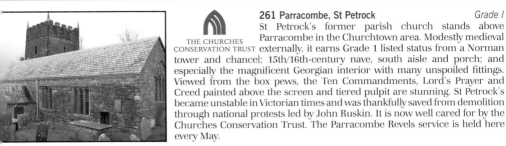

261 Parracombe, St Petrock — Grade I

St Petrock's former parish church stands above Parracombe in the Churchtown area. Modestly medieval externally, it earns Grade 1 listed status from a Norman tower and chancel; 15th/16th-century nave, south aisle and porch; and especially the magnificent Georgian interior with many unspoiled fittings. Viewed from the box pews, the Ten Commandments, Lord's Prayer and Creed painted above the screen and tiered pulpit are stunning. St Petrock's became unstable in Victorian times and was thankfully saved from demolition through national protests led by John Ruskin. It is now well cared for by the Churches Conservation Trust. The Parracombe Revels service is held here every May.

262 Pilton, St Mary the Virgin — Grade I

Athelstan founded Barnstaple's oldest church, as a minster, later a priory, in the 10th century. The present church dates from 1259. The altar is Elizabethan and the altar rail, with a rare book seat, is Jacobean. A beautiful, partly restored, rood screen, c.1430, separates chancel from nave. A carved font cover and pulpit adorned with rose and iron hand are fine examples of 15th-century work. Today we have good links with our church school and the very supportive local community. Presently we are working with fellow churches to form a viable mission community.

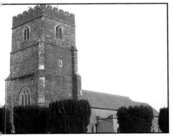

263 Rackenford, All Saints — Grade I

The earliest reference to this church is 1239 although the present building is mainly 15th-century; however, the arch for the south door is 14th-century. Another feature to admire is the great west arch. The church is a small and ancient building of stone in the Early English style, consisting of a chancel, nave of four bays, aisle, south porch and an embattled tower containing six bells; the font is of the reign of Henry II. Part of the Exe Valley Group, Rackenford Church holds weekly services including the popular monthly Family Service involving children's activities. All festive occasions are well supported by the local community.

264 Romansleigh, St Rumon — Grade II

The church, dedicated to the Cornish St Rumon, was rebuilt in 1868 to Ashworth specification, replacing a 14th-century building, which had lost its spire in a storm in 1703, and was now in a state of decay. The present bell chamber, housing three original and three donated bells, was rebuilt on what remained of the 14th-century west tower in 1887. A Saxon font, replaced with a more ornate one in 1869, still remains in the church. The shaft of a medieval preaching cross stands in the churchyard. Services of Holy Communion and Morning Prayer on first and third Sundays of each month. The church is used for other events.

265 Rose Ash, St Peter ad Vincula — Grade II*

A church has been in this beautiful setting in the village green since the 12th century. Its claim to fame perhaps lies in the Southcomb family, members of whom were rectors for 273 years, ending with Edmund Southcomb as recently as 1949. Three stained-glass windows and several wall-mounted memorials are dedicated to the memory of members of the family and pews bear inscriptions acknowledging their donation by Southcombs. A notable churchwarden was John Tanner Davy, who brought the Mark Masons to Devon and started the Devon Ruby Red herd of cattle. A small but welcoming church, it holds four traditional services each month.

266 Roundswell Church, Barnstaple

Roundswell Church is a partnership of Anglican, Baptist, Methodist and United Reformed churches working together to extend the Kingdom of God. We meet in the community centre at Roundswell each Sunday morning. We are a family church and our worship is contemporary in style. As a church without walls we seek to engage in mission wherever we can. Most of the church are members of our small groups, meeting together for worship, fellowship and mission. We desire to be a church in which people encounter Jesus, his love, and his power as we gather together to worship and serve him.

THE CHURCHES
CONSERVATION TRUST

267 Satterleigh, St Peter   *Grade I*

In 1995 the Churches Conservation Trust took over the responsibility for this delightful little church, accessed through the farmyard at Satterleigh Barton. It is mainly 15th-century with nave, a wooden bellcote and a south porch leading to a remarkable medieval door. The font is 15th-century. The wooden lychgate is a memorial to those who lost their lives in the First World War. The regulations of the Trust allow services to be held six times a year, usually when there is a fifth Sunday in the month, in the form of a Matins service. This tiny church's services are very popular and the church is often full.

268 Shirwell, St Peter   *Grade I*

Parts of the church are over 760 years old: the tower, chancel arch, priests' door to the vestry, and 12th-century font. See also the rare wooden arch, hewn from rough timber, by the north transept. Six bells are rung weekly from the ground floor, where a plaque to the memory of Robert Bellringer has been located. Round-the-world sailor, Sir Francis Chichester, is buried to the right of the south porch and opposite are two 1500-year-old yew trees. Recent reordering has provided excellent social and refreshment areas for regular congregation and community use. This active church is focussed on youth work and outreach.

269 South Molton, St Mary Magdalene   *Grade I*

Set in a large churchyard in the town centre, this large church dates mainly from the 15th century and was restored in the 19th century. It comprises nave with clerestory, chancel, north and south aisles, transepts, west tower and south porch. The tower is 107ft high and until 1751 was topped with a spire. The aisles were widened in 1825-1829 and the windows enlarged. Features internally include the fine 15th-century stone pulpit, octagonal stone font and tower screen of 1903 which is made of marble, Caen stone and mahogany. There is much Victorian and Edwardian stained glass, some by Hardman. There are also good 18th-century wall monuments.

270 Sticklepath, St Paul

The church was built in 1955-1956 to serve the new parish in west Barnstaple. The original 1935 multipurpose building to the rear is now the hall. Light oak pews flank a central aisle leading from a rose-marble font, past a brick pulpit into the raised chancel. Above the altar is the main feature of the interior: a large stainless steel cross, enclosing illuminated coloured glass. There are six stained-glass windows, donated by families of previous members. A friendly church offering a wide variety of worship, and welcoming to all ages. Working in partnership with other local churches, groups and organisations has always been a focus of its community-based ministry.

271 Stoke Rivers, St Bartholomew

Grade I

A wide grass path leads to this simple little church, built high on a hill overlooking farmland and Bideford Bay. It was built in the 15th century in the Perpendicular style and remains unaltered. The pulpit is made of the original Renaissance carved bench ends. The font and its cover are original, and surrounded by medieval tiles, probably made in Barnstaple. There is a Cromwellian Chest, a "bobbin" chair, a George III coat of arms, and the north wall retains the 15th-century windows. We have a small, friendly congregation, with services held twice monthly. Our regular coffee mornings and concerts give the local people their only social meeting place.

272 Swimbridge, Holy Name (Gunn Chapel)

Grade II

Gunn church, or chapel of ease (together with a stable which still exists), was built on part of a field known as Gunn Field. It was opened for divine service by Dr Temple, then bishop of the diocese, on 7th August 1873 and during the 48-year incumbency of the Revd 'Jack' Russell. The Church of the Holy Name is built of local stone and is a simple design, being a single room containing a nave and a sanctuary with an adjoining meeting room separated from the chancel by a folding oak screen. A beautiful east-end stained-glass window depicts "Faith, Hope, and Love": virtues that the congregation try to express in their daily lives.

273 Swimbridge, St James the Apostle

Grade I

At the heart of the village of Swimbridge stands the parish church of St James with its medieval spire, one of three in north Devon. The stone-built church, which has grown and been added to over the centuries, contains splendid ornate carved woodwork from the 15th century. The screen and unique Renaissance font and the medieval stone pulpit stand out. Restored in Victorian times it was the parish church of the Revd John Russell, the famous parson who bred the Jack Russell terrier. He is buried in the churchyard. The church continues to change and adapt to serve its community welcoming visitors into its beautiful and peaceful atmosphere.

274 Tawstock, St Peter

Grade I

The nave aisles, tower, transept and chancel are 14th-century (c.1340) and changes to the roof, walls and the insertion of the windows were made in the 15th century (c.1480). In the Tudor period (c.1540) the chancel chapel was added and in the 17th century the porch was built. The current mission and ministry of this beautiful church is to care for the people of the parish, especially their spiritual needs, to help in their journey of faith, deepen their relationship with God and to offer support during important family milestones.

275 Trentishoe, St Peter

Grade II*

Probably one of the smallest parish churches in the diocese. It serves the small hamlet of Trentishoe and shelters in the side of a hill, with plain glass east end windows which provide stunning views of Exmoor National Park. It is a good walk away from the Coastal path, and can be reached by sign-posted country roads. The church has a minstrels' gallery at the west, tower, end, with a hole cut through to allow the bow of the viol to pass through. The chancel predates the only written evidence of the church, and may well go back to pre-Norman times. The two bells are rung before the monthly service.

276 Twitchen (North Molton), St Peter
Grade II

A small church on the edge of Exmoor. Although a church on this site is first mentioned in 1340, the present building was much rebuilt in 1844 by Hayward, except for the west tower, which dates from the 15th century. It comprises nave, one-bay chancel and west tower. The chancel fittings, which date from 1916, include the Communion rails, and carved wooden altar. The oak reredos of 1938 was carved by Herbert Read of Exeter. Other fittings date mainly from the 19th century and include a late-19th-century vicar's desk, chair and wrought-iron reading desk, the pulpit, mid-to-late-19th-century pews, and the stained glass. The restored font originally dates from the 12th century.

277 Umberleigh (Chittlehampton), Church of the Good Shepherd

This small painted timber church is situated in a small churchyard without burials. It is of simple plan, consisting of nave, chancel, porch and vestry. The interior is plain, with plastered walls and ceilings and plain timber benches.

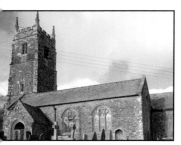

278 Warkleigh, St John the Evangelist
Grade II*

A path through a farm, leading to a lychgate, invites you to this medieval church and churchyard, which has beautiful views of the north Devon countryside. The south aisle retains its 15th-century roof with carved bosses. The chancel was rebuilt in 1850 and the nave was re-roofed in 1867 to match the rebuilt chancel. The west tower houses a fine peal of six bells, two of which date from 1553. The tower and church were restored in 1883. Warkleigh with Satterleigh is a scattered, lightly populated parish. Services are evangelical and are held fortnightly, alternating between Communion services and family services. The atmosphere is friendly and visitors are most welcome.

279 West Anstey, St Petrock
Grade II*

One of only 18 churches dedicated to this Celtic saint, its nave and chancel date from 1319, the tower from 1450. Restored in 1879 by the London architect William White. Some interesting internal features remain, including a decorated tub-shaped Norman font c.1150, predating the building. Several richly carved oak pews c.1530 and an early polychromed screen in the tower arch. Fragments of medieval stained glass are noteworthy. The tower possesses an unusual set of eight tubular bells installed in the 19th century. Set deep into the southern edge of Exmoor, this picturesque church serves a lively rural community, part of the Oakmoor group of seven churches; worship is regular and traditional.

280 West Buckland, St Peter
Grade II*

The list of rectors goes back to 1261 but only the west tower and the priest's door remain of the original church. The tower supports a fine set of bells and is buttressed to the Victorian church built in the 1860s. Today, the church with a 15th-century font, a south aisle and marble-covered circular pillars that support the vaulted Victorian roof make this a country church that can hold 130 people. The congregation is small but faithful and welcoming. Services are held on three Sundays a month and there are links with the local community that ensure a Christian presence at the heart of the village.

281 West Down, St Calixtus
Grade I

The first recorded priest is Gervaise de Creditone in 1272. The nave dates from about 1320. The church is of a cruciform plan with a tower at the west end. The chancel was rebuilt in 1675, and the tower dismantled and rebuilt in 1711-1712. Considerable restoration took place in 1874 when the chancel walls were raised and new roofing and seating installed. The south transept has a slanted, arched opening, or "squint", allowing a view of the alter. In the north transept is an effigy of Sir John Stowford, Knight; it is one of the few effigies made of oak still remaining in the country. A friendly village church that tries to engage with the local community. Services alternate with Eucharist, Morning Prayer and one family service a month.

282 West Worlington, St Mary
Grade I

The church is situated on the side of a hill overlooking the picturesque Little Dart river. The 15th-century church with its unique spire of wooden shingles has a large churchyard surrounded by Grade I thatched cottages which are astride the road which leads down the steep hill to East Worlington. The church has recently undergone a major repair programme to restore the floor and panelling of the interior. The bells have also been refurbished recently and are rung on a regular basis. Services are held on the second and fourth Sunday of each month.

283 Westleigh, St Peter
Grade I

With a list of vicars going back to 1297 the present spacious and welcoming building dates from about 1300. The original cruciform plan was extended to include a north aisle in about 1500. There is an embattled 15th-century tower with a peal of bells dedicated in 1882, increased from four in 1553. Interesting internal features include a substantial Early English font, carved medieval pew ends, some very early north Devon floor tiles and monuments to the Cleveland family of Tapley. The organ was installed in the late 18th century. There is a service every Sunday including a shortened informal family service.

284 Witheridge, St John the Baptist
Grade II*

Built about 1428, but with some remains of Early English and Norman features, the building contains many notable features. These include a stone font and pulpit, a squint, many stained-glass windows, a peal of eight bells and a statue of the patron saint. Historically it was the centre of the Anglo-Saxon Hundred. In the year 2000 we had an area at the back of the church refurbished and made it into a kitchen area which includes toilet and hand-washing facilities, a facility much appreciated by our parishioners and where new and old blend well together The church is open during daylight hours.

285 Woolacombe, St Sabinus
Grade II*

In the wake of the late-Victorian explosion in mass tourism, Woolacombe, once a tiny hamlet, needed its own Anglican church. St Sabinus (named after a 5th-century Italian bishop) was designed by Caroe, built of local red sandstone, and consecrated in 1912. The spacious, well-proportioned interior, with its varied and unusual stained glass, is adaptable for all kinds of worship and social events. As well as the main Sunday Communion service, St Sabinus holds a weekly toddler service, and a Wednesday coffee morning/drop-in. The congregation offers a warm welcome to our many seasonal visitors; the church is open every day for all to experience its peace and beauty.

PLYMOUTH

Plymouth, with the largest population centre in Devon, nestles in an area of outstanding natural beauty, with the Dartmoor National Park to the north, the natural harbour of Plymouth Sound to the south and the rivers Plym and Tamar on either side. The churches are responding to changing needs of their wider communities and a significant number, out of the 37 churches serving the city, are being rebuilt or remodelled for the 21st century.

286 Crownhill, The Church of The Ascension · Grade II

This church was designed by Robert Potter, its foundation stone being laid by Princess Alexandra in May 1956. Dedicated by Robert, Bishop of Exeter, in December 1958, this building has made a notable contribution to 20th-century church architecture. It was among the first churches to have free-standing altars and its design enhances the spirit of prayer and worship. The windows in the east wall were designed by Geoffrey Clarke and the ciborium over the altar painted by Robert Medley. Today we minister to a growing population. Our worship is both traditional and contemporary, with links to the Church in Malawi.

287 Devonport, St Aubyn · Grade II*

It was built in 1771 in the Classical style as a church for the expanding dockyard, with the chancel added in 1885. Consists of a nave and galleried aisles under one roof, chancel, and west tower with octagonal spire. Internally, the fittings include late-19th-century square-ended oak pews and an octagonal oak pulpit. The round-headed windows are typical of the period; there is stained glass to the east window, otherwise there are plain leaded windows with rectangular panes. At the time of going to print, there are exciting plans to retain a worship space at the east end of the building, and provide a community library in the remainder of the building.

288 Devonport, St Barnabas

The original church was built in 1886 and served the parish faithfully for over 100 years. It became clear, however, it was unsuitable as a place to serve the wider community, and it was demolished in 2002. A new church building was created out of the original church hall and a modern place of worship and community centre was opened in 2003, incorporating the original war memorials. St Barnabas is now united with St Michael's as a single benefice, and we have a worship style suitable for all ages that is relevant to life in the 21st century. More details can be found at our website.

289 Devonport, St Bartholomew

Built on the site of 'Outlands', the birthplace of Captain Robert Falcon Scott, the church was opened in 1959, funded under the Government war reparations scheme. Its angled windows reflect some of the thinking that went into the design of the then new Coventry Cathedral, and the modern stained glass spectacularly lights up the east wall on a sunny day. The church is bright and airy and warm, serving the parishes of Milehouse, which includes Central Park and Plymouth Argyle's football ground. The church hall next door is a much-valued resource for the local community, used by charities, youth and special interest groups and children's parties.

290 Devonport, St Boniface

One of the new Plymouth churches, St Boniface has been built on the site of the former church hall and the innovative design on two floors has a worship space and large foyer on the ground floor whilst below there is a large space for both parish and community events. Stained glass is a major feature as the former church had glass designed by Father Charles Norris from Buckfast Abbey in the 1960s, and includes one spectacular window of Christ that spans both floors.

291 Devonport, St Budeaux   *Grade II**

Set in a stone-walled churchyard, surrounded by trees overlooking the magnificent Tamar Valley, this parish church still looks from the outside like a traditional village church. Completed in 1563 (it is claimed with old stones from a previous building), the marriage of Francis Drake (1569) is one of its claims to fame. It was also the focus of battles in the Civil War. The inside reveals much history, with extensive monuments to wealthy families. It now serves the not so wealthy families of St Budeaux, in a community which has grown enormously since those early days, and provides space for traditional and modern styles of worship for all ages.

292 Devonport, St Mark Ford

As this book is being put together the builders are just going on site to provide a new building. The parish wishes to have a flexible building on a small site and the design incorporates some stained glass from the old building. The parish has a commitment to the local community and it is hoped that this will be enhanced by the new building, due for completion in 2009.

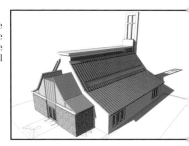

293 Devonport, St Michael

The original church was built in 1845, but destroyed in April 1941 during an air raid. The church was restored and reopened in 1953 but the quality of workmanship was poor, which meant that the church became impossible to maintain. After many years of prayer and planning, the church family, recognising the importance of a Christian presence in the area, decided on the total demolition and redevelopment of the site. The result is that a new place of worship will open in 2009, including memorials and stained glass from the previous church buildings. St Michael's is a welcoming, Bible-based congregation of all ages showing God's love in word and deed.

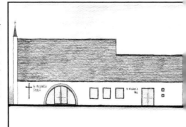

294 Efford (Plymouth Emmanuel), St Paul

Completed in December 2007, on top of a hill overlooking the River Plym Estuary, this new church and community hall lies at the heart of Efford. Designed to provide as much for the needs of everyone in the neighbourhood as for the worship of God, it replaces a 1960s church built on this post-war housing estate with funds for the replacement of St Paul's Devonport, destroyed in the blitz. The new building incorporates panels from the huge coloured glass window designed at Buckfast Abbey, which was such a distinctive feature of its predecessor. A novel, modern design of cross enhances the front face of the tower.

PLYMOUTH

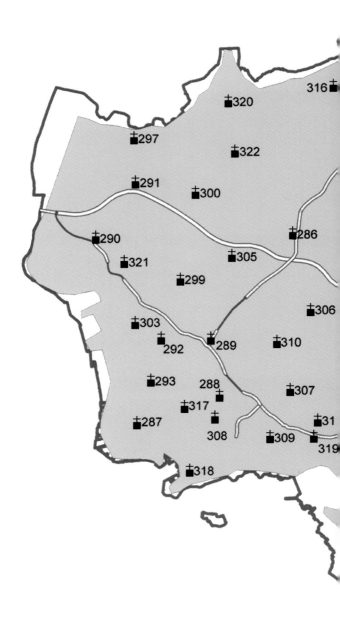

316

320

297

322

291

300

286

290

305

321

299

306

303

289

310

292

293

288

307

317

31

287

308

309

319

318

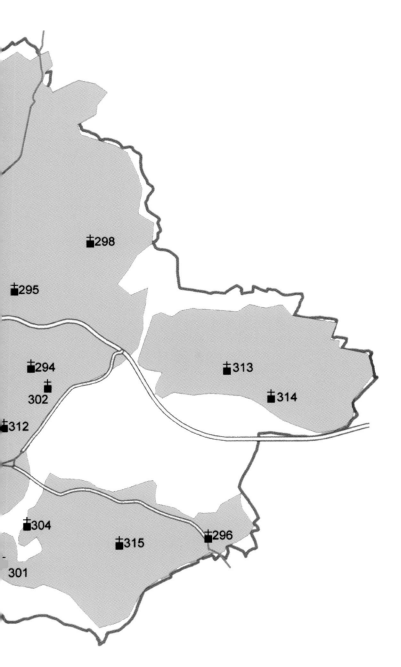

295 Eggbuckland, St Edward the Martyr
Grade II*

Until 1939, Eggbuckland was a small country village. Following the expansion of Plymouth to the north, it became part of the city. The church dates from 1430, the granite font having survived from that period. Barrel roofing was installed early in the 20th century. An attractive reredos of Portland stone commemorates Queen Victoria's Golden Jubilee and an oak rood screen, pulpit and organ screen date from the early 1900s. New oak pews were added later, carved by the sisters. St Edward's is a Bible-based teaching and praying church for all ages of the community.

296 Elburton, St Matthew

St Matthew's history goes back to 1915 when a mission hall provided a distinctively evangelical Anglican church for the area. The present church was built in 1923. The interior is open with exposed limestone walls and roof timbers. Recent additions in 2006 provide modern facilities for our increasing congregation. We are a welcoming church of all ages and try to maintain a family-friendly feel by catering for all in our activities and teaching. Our services reflect a range of styles but our emphasis throughout is on seeking to understand and apply God's word. There is an active youth and community ministry reaching out into the local community.

297 Ernesettle, St Aidan

One of the new Plymouth churches, St Aidan's opened in late 2007 and it is designed to enable a flexible use of the building for small and large church services as well as being configured for community use, which is an important part of the parish's work in this area of Plymouth. The new building retained the large window of St Aidan from the old building.

298 Estover, Christ Church

High on a hill in north Plymouth, amid three large housing estates, Christ Church is unique in Devon. Part of a modern community centre complex comprising multipurpose church, coffee bar and community halls, the church is an ecumenical venture between Roman Catholic, Anglican, Methodist, Baptist and United Reformed traditions. The side chapel boasts a fine stained-glass window made by monks at Buckfast Abbey. The building opened in 1980, refurbished and updated in 2006. Strong links exist with local schools. Communion services are held twice a month, Junior Church meets weekly. Sunday services vary from traditional to interactive multi-media. We actively seek ways of sharing God's love with our community.

299 Ham, St James the Less

Built in the late 1950s, with the foundation stone being laid on 15 March 1958 by the Revd W. T. Trelawny-Ross. Built of red brick and consists of nave, chancel, north transept, Lady chapel, vestry and sacristy. The worship space is light and airy. The church hall is connected to the church and partitioned by way of a folding screen.

300 Honicknowle, St Francis

St Francis' Church was built in 1939 as a mission centre to serve the local area of Honicknowle. It became a parish in 1956 when the post-war estate was built. The church is post-war modern comprising a church and two halls. In 2006 the parish joined with those of St Aidan in Ernesettle and St Chad in Whitleigh to form the Budshead Group of parishes. Two new priests to serve the new Group took up appointment in 2008. The main form of worship is the Eucharist which is celebrated every Sunday and during the week. Mission outreach to the families and to the elderly in the community is growing.

301 Hooe, St John the Evangelist   *Grade II**

Overlooking the Plymouth suburb of Hooe, St John's was built in 1855 to the designs of William White in a simple neo-Gothic style. Next to the church is the church hall (formerly the village school), also designed by White and well used by the community. The church contains a memorial chapel that commemorates local residents who died in war as well as service personnel from the now closed RAF Mountbatten. The land for the church was donated by Lord Frederick Rogers, a keen supporter of the Oxford Movement and friend of John Keble, and the style of the weekly worship, low Anglo-Catholic, still reflects this.

302 Laira, St Mary the Virgin   *Grade II*

Laira St Mary was consecrated on 2nd July 1914. The church is built on an elevated site above one of the main roads into Plymouth city centre. It is constructed of granite with sandstone mullions and tracery to the windows under a slate roof. There is a small tower housing eight tower bells. Inside, we have a fine stained-glass east end window. The font is of Cornish Polyplant stone. Our worship is of the Anglo-Catholic tradition with the Eucharist celebrated on Sunday and Wednesday mornings. The church is very involved with the local community and enjoys good links with the local schools.

303 North Keyham, St Thomas

One of the new Plymouth churches. After many years of being in a vast Victorian building the parish now meets in a new small, elliptically shaped church building on the site of the garage of the former vicarage. The two buildings now form a space which enables the parish to serve its community in a sustainable way

304 Oreston (Plymstock), Church of the Good Shepherd

The Church of the Good Shepherd is the daughter church of the parish church at Plymstock. It is a little church by the sea. The building probably started off as a mission hall built by the local fishermen. It then became a church school, until a chancel was added and the church dedicated in 1886. The Good Shepherd has very much the feel of a village church and the church family come from the local community. There is a sung Eucharist each Sunday morning (aided by a new organ!) and mid-week services. The 'Little Lambs' (an under 5's group) and an After School Club take place weekly in the church hall.

305 Pennycross, St Pancras
Grade II

The church and font date from 1482. Extended and rebuilt in 1820, it is cruciform in shape and in Gothic, Perpendicular style, with moulded barrel ceilings and a ribbed vault in the chancel extension. A lively, welcoming, Bible-based church, providing a range of worship styles, from traditional to contemporary (with music group). Sunday young people's groups and midweek home groups help people of all ages grow in faith. We reach out to the community through Youth Clubs, Mums & Toddlers and through "Start" and Alpha courses for those enquiring about faith. Chaucer Café Church is a "Fresh Expression of Church" in an estate in the north of the parish.

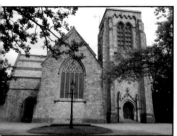

306 Plymouth, Emmanuel
Grade II

The original chapel, built to serve the village of Compton Gifford, some 200 souls, and licensed in 1836, soon proved inadequate to cater for the growth of the population. Betsy Revel, widow of the late incumbent, offered land to build a church, to be named Emmanuel after his Cambridge college. In 1869 the first cornerstone was laid by the vicar of Charles Church, consecration occurring in 1870. In 2007 a project is under way for a wing to be extended out from the north of the church, so great has been growth over the last few years, necessitating urgent enlargement of facilities now totally unable to cope with all present needs.

307 Plymouth, St Matthias
Grade II

Located in the North Hill area of Plymouth, St Matthias was built in 1887 by Hine and Rodgers. It was paid for by Mrs Watts in memory of her husband, Matthias Watts, and its prominent tower is a feature of the skyline in this part of the city. It comprises nave with clerestory, chancel, north and south aisles, south porch, transept, vestry and west tower. Features of the interior include the pulpit and font of Devon marble by Hems, the 1891 reredos by Fellowes Prynne, and the stained glass by Fouracre & Watson, including the east window of 1890.

308 Plymouth, St Peter
Grade II

Located in Wyndham Square, St Peter's has had an interesting history. It was built as a Nonconformist chapel in 1830, licensed as an Anglican church in 1848, and was largely rebuilt in 1880-1882 by G. Fellowes Prynne, whose father was the vicar. In 1906 the tower was added. The church was badly damaged in the Blitz, and restored in the 1950s by F. Etchells. Further change has occurred over the last few years, with a large fabric restoration project, followed by substantial internal reordering, both for liturgical purposes and to make the building suitable for use by the wider community, and fit for purpose in the 21st century.

309 Plymouth, St Andrew
Grade I

The city centre church of Plymouth, dating largely from the 15th century, was severely damaged in the Blitz and famously restored under the watchword Resurgam after some years as a garden church. Reconsecrated in 1957, the magnificent stained-glass windows are designed by John Piper. Among many famous people associated with the church are Catherine of Aragon, Francis Drake and Captain Bligh. The active congregation has the desire to live for, worship and proclaim Jesus Christ in the life of the city and beyond, with a special concern to minister to the civic and commercial life of the city and to those in need.

310 Plymouth, St Gabriel
Grade II

Situated in the suburb of Peverell, St Gabriel is one of seven churches planned for the Plymouth suburbs in 1906. Built by W. D. Caröe, the nave was completed in 1909-1910, the chancel in 1924, and the north east chapel in 1954-1955. It comprises nave, chancel, aisles, transepts, north east chapel with bell turret, and porches. Internally, the reredos is by one of the Pinwell sisters of Ermington, the font is by Caröe, and the 17th-cetury altar rails are from Lostwithiel St Bartholomew's. The stained glass depicting English saints was designed by Caröe. The St Oswald window in the south aisle is a war memorial of 1918 by Kempe & Co.

311 Plymouth, St Jude
Grade II

Founded in 1875, St Jude's has always been an innovative church. Heating was installed in 1879, the spire in 1882, the first hall in 1888, a porch in 1895, the 'new' electric lighting in 1901 and a second hall in 1905. Always outward looking, the church once more looks to a new generation with plans finalising during 2008/9 for its 'Next Era' building project. Many missions and missionaries have started here and their heart for the young has a similar pedigree: paid youth ministers for more than 13 years, a Pre-school for more than 40 years and Boys' and Girls' Brigades for over 100 years – the BB founded here in 1902.

312 Plymouth, St Simon
Grade II

Situated in the Mount Gould area of Plymouth, the church was designed by H. Reed and constructed at the beginning of the 20th century. It is built of local limestone. It consists of nave, chancel, north and south aisles, north porch with bell chamber over, organ chamber, and vestry. The west end of the church was not completed until the late 1950s. The pulpit of 1908 is of uncarved coloured marble, and there are rich chancel furnishings with some woodwork by the Pinwell sisters of Ermington. Some of the stained glass is by Kempe & Company.

313 Plympton St Mary, St Mary Blessed Virgin
Grade II*

Standing in the grounds of an Augustinian priory that was founded in 1121, the present church dates from 1311. The tall granite tower is a visible sign of the historical and continuing worshipping community. Features within the building include the Strode memorial (1637) and a canopied tomb of a Courtenay. The Parker memorial in the chancel tells the sensitive story of the death of a young child. Today, visitors often comment on the warm welcome offered and the sense of a friendly and caring community. Daily worship, a weekly parish Eucharist and a wide range of social and pastoral activities characterise the life of the parish today.

314 Plympton St Maurice, St Maurice
Grade II*

The church was constructed in the 14th century in the Perpendicular style with some remodelling and restoration over the years. The wagon style roof has a slate covering. The interior of the church is ornate and consists of chancel, nave with north and south aisles and south porch. A tower housing eight bells is at the west end. A memorial to Sir Joshua Reynolds, the famous 17th-century portrait painter, who lived in the village, is located in the north aisle. The church, which has followed the Anglo-Catholic tradition over many years, is at the heart of the community. The recently refurbished church community hall provides facilities for everyone to use.

315 Plymstock, St Mary & All Saints
Grade II*

This church dates mainly from the 15th century and comprises nave, chancel, north and south aisles, south porch, vestry, and west tower. Internal features include the round Norman font of red sandstone, chest made up from 16th-century panels, fine late medieval carved oak rood screen restored in the 19th century, including some remains of original paint, and a fine 17th-century pulpit. There are two fine 17th-century monuments to the Harris family of Radford in the south aisle chapel, an 18th-century black and white marble monument to the Harris family, and a 19th-century monument to the Hare family of the Retreat. The stained glass includes the east window which is a Pre-Raphaelite Te Deum of c.1880.

316 Southway, Holy Spirit

Created as a parish in 1971 and formerly the daughter church of St Mary's, Tamerton Foliot, the links have been re-established with the formation of a Mission Community between the two churches. Built in stages from the 1960s and finally consecrated in 1989, the church's two stained-glass windows were designed at Buckfast Abbey, depicting the links with the Holy Spirit. The church and its hall are used by a wide range of community groups of all ages; services reflect this diversity catering from traditional to contemporary in both liturgy and music.

317 Stoke Damerel, St Andrew with St Luke
Grade II*

The oldest part of the building is the oblong tower dating from the 15th century while other parts of the ancient church have been incorporated into the present day interior. With the growth of the dockyard in the early 18th century the church was enlarged to accommodate the large number of worshippers. The north and south aisles were added in 1715 and 1750 respectively, making the building unusual in that it is wider than it is long. Current efforts are underway to develop the modern parish centre as a focus of outward-looking mission activity, including remodelling the interior of the church to enhance worship and participation.

318 Stonehouse, St Paul
Grade II*

Located on Durnford Street, St Paul's was built in 1831 by John Foulston, with the east end extended in 1890 by Hine & Odgers. It was built of Plymouth limestone rubble in a Gothic style. It comprises aisle-less nave with west gallery and central west tower with a slightly wider chancel at the east end. The interior is light and airy, and contains a late-20th-century meeting room and facilities at the west end under the gallery. Fittings include an octagonal marble font and panelled pews to gallery, otherwise there are later pitch-pine fittings. The church stands in a little altered late-Georgian street which has been regenerated in recent years.

319 Sutton-on-Plym, St John the Evangelist
Grade II

The church designed by Benjamin Ferrey, was consecrated in 1855 for a parish that had been created several years before. The pulpit retains its Victorian decorations but other such features have been lost. Nevertheless, the high altar reredos, with its depictions of the Crucifixion, Resurrection and Ascension, help provide a beautiful and peaceful shrine beside the busy highway. The Lady chapel was rebuilt in the early 1950s. There is a window in honour of Our Lady, Star of the Sea, which includes a fishing vessel, very relevant since the fish market relocated to join other industry in the parish. The renovated tower will proudly beckon worshippers for many years to come.

320 Tamerton Foliot, St Mary
Grade II*

The village stocks, a 17th-century sundial, 15th-century font and roof bosses, 14th-century effigies, memorials spanning the 17th to 20th centuries and a board listing vicars from 1283 to the present day, are all to be seen in this church, which dates architecturally from the 13th century. Altered and enlarged, with north and south aisles rebuilt in Victorian times, the church has a peal of six bells which call to worship for services at least twice every Sunday. Services are both modern (CW) and traditional (BCP) and an active choir, Sunday School, house group, Toddlers Group, and Luncheon Club are evidence of a Worshipping, Working and Witnessing community.

321 Weston Mill, St Philip

This church was completed in 1913 to designs of N. Alton Bezeley. It is built of local limestone. The apsidal sanctuary constructed of reinforced concrete. The large stained-glass east window by Charles Norris was added in 1963. It is in a mosaic style depicting St Philip.

322 Whitleigh, St Chad

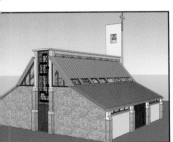

The 1950s church building has recently been demolished to enable a new, smaller but more flexible facility to be built on the same site.

SOUTH HAMS

The South Hams is a landscape of contrasts, from high wild moorland to wooded river valleys and tidal estuaries. It is an area of traditional farming, market towns and villages. It boasts some of the most beautiful beaches the country and the whole area is served by 74 Church of England churches.

323 Ashprington, St David
Grade I

Custodians of the past with our eyes on the future, St David's aims to offer witness, commitment and support to our village and beyond. Of Norman origins, all that remains from this period is a fine 12th-century font. Apart from this, the west tower is the earliest part of the church, dating from the 13th century. The remainder of the church was rebuilt some 200 years later and restored again in mid-Victorian times. Internally, the parclose screens, pulpit, lectern, reredos and other woodwork and carvings in the chancel are the work of Herbert Read and mainly date from the period 1890 to 1910.

324 Aveton Gifford, St Andrew
Grade II*

Originally dating from the 13th century, the church suffered major bomb damage during the Second World War. It was rebuilt from 1948-1957 with the tower completed in 1970. It is of a cruciform plan with an aisleless nave and crossing tower. Internally there is a 14th-century font and a stone altar. There are a number of memorials, including that to the Revd Vaughan (d.1847), who was vicar for 57 years. A friendly church, welcoming all ages. Activities include: choir, music group, hand bell-ringers, youth club, and Congo missionary link. We have a strong link with the village Primary School. Worship ranges from contemporary to traditional.

325 Avonwick, St James
Grade II

This is a proprietary chapel built in 1878 at the total expense of Mr and Mrs F. J. Cornish-Bowden of Black Hall and is still maintained by their descendants through a family trust and by the generosity of a regular congregation. The church is in every way self-supporting but consistently supports other causes. Since its dedication it has been a blessing and a source of spiritual refreshment to very many within the community and further afield. This living church seeks at all times to reach out to all, and all who worship here are welcomed into the fellowship of the Lord whom we seek to serve.

326 Beesands (Stokenham), St Andrew

This chapel of ease, sometimes known as a mission room, was erected in 1883, adjacent to the beach in the fishing village of Beesands in Start Bay. This was by subscription, the vicar at the time being the Revd J. C. Carwithen. The font is dedicated in memory of seven lives lost by enemy action in the village on 26 July 1942. Two of the seven were a two-year-old child and Phyllis Wrath, a nineteen-year old home on leave from the army. Regular worship takes place in this peaceful chapel and is frequented by visitors who find it a place of peace. Teas are provided at weekends to raise money for repairs.

327 Berry Pomeroy, St Mary
Grade I

The church was rebuilt in the 15th century, possibly by Sir Richard de Pomeroy, and was restored in 1878-1879. It comprises nave, chancel, north and south aisles, south porch, and rendered west tower. Internally, the nave is wide with 15th-century arcades with leaf frieze capitals, some bearing benefactors' names. There is a fine 15th-century rood screen, and parclose screen with original colour. The font is 15th-century. The majority of the remainder of the furnishings are Victorian. There are a number of monuments including that to Sir Richard Pomeroy and his wife (1496), and the Revd John Prince, vicar of St Mary's and author of The Worthies of Devon, first published in 1701.

328 Bickleigh (Glenholt), St Anne

This church was built in 1956 by members of the parish. It was extended in 1995 and again in 1999. The original part of the building is constructed of stone, which is rendered, with the later parts in brickwork. The church hall forms part of the church building, and kitchen and toilet facilities are provided.

329 Bickleigh Down School, St Cecilia

St Cecilia was originally just called School Church, and developed on the new, and ever-growing, housing estate at Woolwell where it was felt a place of worship more central to the community was needed as the parish church was several miles away down country lanes. A monthly service supported by the other congregations moved into the more suitable St Cecilia's hall, which was built when the school expanded. This became a happy home for the new worshipping community and a good name for them to adopt. Through various phases the congregation has grown into a weekly thriving community with a thriving liturgy and half of the congregation are children.

330 Bigbury, St Lawrence
Grade II*

The entrance path continues from an imposing gateway into Bigbury Court Farmhouse, formerly the manor house. There was a church here in the 12th century, the oldest part now standing being the tower – with commanding views over Bigbury Bay. Church contents include a Norman font, brass effigies from the 15th century and stained-glass windows with coats of arms of families involved in local affairs. The most recent acquisition is the ship's bell from *HMS Bigbury Bay*. This is often rung at the start of services, to which all are welcome. The church is open every day and our aim is to provide a Christian presence in all aspects of village life.

331 Blackawton, St Michael
Grade I

The church building is 14th-century, on the site of an earlier church. There is a Norman font, a Tudor rood screen and a modern meetings room. In the church is the tomb of Richard Sparke, whose bequest of a bread dole for the poor of the parish is still distributed each week. This church is the only place of worship in the village and welcomes everyone. There is a morning service every Sunday, monthly mid-week services and choral Evensong. Services are usually Communion (sometimes followed by healing ministry) or informal lay-led morning worship. The Christian festivals and the rural year are celebrated with special services.

SOUTH HAMS

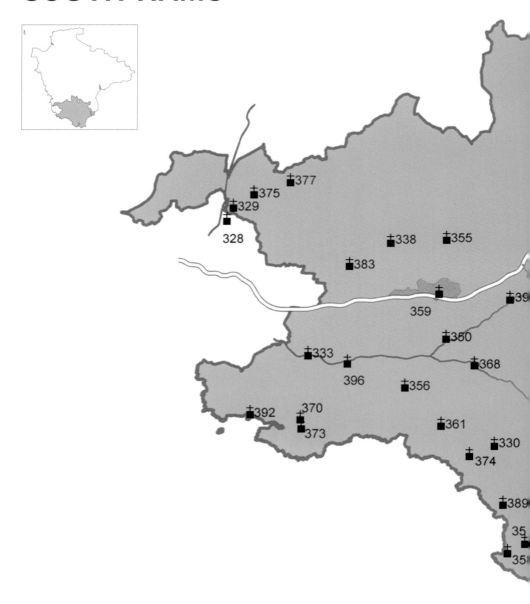

✝377

■375

✝329
■
328

✝338   ✝355

✝383

359   ✝
■

■39

✝350

✝333   ✝350
396   ✝356   ✝368

✝392   ✝370
■373

✝361

✝330
✝374

■389

35
✝
35

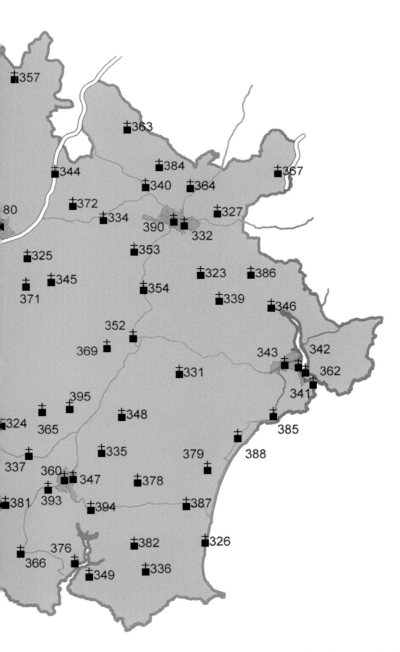

SOUTH HAMS: LOCATION OF CHURCHES

123

332 Bridgetown (Totnes), St John the Evangelist   *Grade II*

This church was built c.1832 as a chapel of ease to Berry Pomeroy. It is in a Gothic style with a large north tower and built of squared granite rubble with freestone dressings. The stained-glass east window with original stone tracery is by P. Tysoe. Gutted by fire in 1976, it was rebuilt within the original shell in 1980. At this time, the building was substantially remodelled and reordered, including the provision of additional floors to provide a mezzanine level and meeting areas, toilets, kitchen, etc. The building is used extensively by the community during the week for secular activities.

333 Brixton, St Mary   *Grade I*

The church is Perpendicular in style, built in the 15th century but with the tower a hundred years older. Entrance is via a south porch; the interior consists of a nave, with an outlying aisle each side – originally leading to a chapel at the east end of each of them. The church underwent mid-Victorian restorations, and the windows and some fine oak carvings date from that time. There are six bells which ring merrily. Services of worship are traditional and contemporary; we have a small but active congregation which supports a great number of Christian links both at home and abroad. The doors are open all hours.

334 Brooking (Dartington), St Barnabas   *Grade II**

Our charming chapel of ease is set back from the A385 at Tigley Cross and provides a sanctuary of peace and quiet. It was completed by a local family, the Champernownes of Dartington Hall, in 1855 in the high-Victorian style reminiscent of Pugin. The 120ft spire forms a distinctive landmark. The two grey Dartington marble pillars to be found in the nave were shown at the Great Exhibition of 1851 and admired by Queen Victoria. The church, which lies at the heart of a small community, is open daily and supported each Sunday morning by a loyal and friendly congregation who from time to time put on concerts and organ recitals.

335 Buckland Tout Saints, St Peter   *Grade II*

There was a chapel of ease here in 1426, associated with Buckland House and used by the family and staff. By 1683 other parishioners also attended, but by 1782 it was recorded that "This chapel had long lain in ruins." It was rebuilt on its present site in 1778 by John Henry Southcote, the then owner of Buckland House, to serve the family and staff and the villagers of Goveton and Ledstone. A service is held every Sunday and the four Country Services are celebrated through the year. Service times are displayed on the church and village noticeboards, in the Link, and are also available on the web site.

336 Chivelstone, St Sylvester   *Grade II**

The only church in the country dedicated to this 3rd-century pope is set in deep country almost within the farmyard of Chivelstone Barton. It was originally a chapel of ease to Stokenham. The church consists of nave, chancel, north and south aisles, west tower and south porch. On the south door is a sanctuary knocker. The pulpit is unusual, being carved from a single block of wood – the centre section of the screen (which dates from the 15th century) was dismantled in 1979 and restored in the workshop of Herbert Read of Exeter. The services are traditional with a service for children once a month.

337 Churchstow, St Mary the Virgin
Grade II*

A church had been established at Churchstow by the time of the Domesday Survey of 1070 and was owned by Buckfast Abbey. On 17th December 1703 the chancel was struck by lightning and later rebuilt. The lofty tower, complete with 87 steps, can be seen from a wide area and holds six bells which are regularly rung. The church contains a barrel roof and a 13th-century font with a squared bowl dating from around 1170. The pulpit is made from Jacobean oak. With traditional and contemporary worship, this friendly church welcomes all ages and has strong ties with the local community.

338 Cornwood, St Michael & All Angels
Grade I

St Michael's overlooks the village of Cornwood and the southern edge of Dartmoor. It is first mentioned in the bishop's register in 1257, although the main body of the church is 15th-century and boasts a fine carved Jacobean pulpit. St Michael's has been at the centre of family life in this parish for more than 600 years and continues to offer a range of services both traditional and modern, from The Book of Common Prayer said Communion to a more informal Fresh Expressions of Worship for younger and less traditional folk. We have a strong link with the village school and a warm welcome for all.

339 Cornworthy, St Peter
Grade I

The granite pillars of the nave supporting limestone and granite arches help date this Grade I listed church from about 1350-1375, and part of the screen may also date from the 14th century. The Norman sandstone font is all that remains from an earlier building. The box pews and pulpit are Georgian and the tower, rising in three diminishing stages, houses a peal of six bells. It is a simple but beautiful and light little church, welcoming to all who worship or visit. Church activities often involve the community at large. We are part of the Totnes Team Ministry, and the Eucharist is celebrated at least once a week.

340 Dartington, St Mary the Virgin
Grade II*

The church, apart from the tower, was moved from Dartington Hall to its present site in the 1870s under the architectural supervision of John Pearson and was consecrated in 1880 by Frederick Temple. The medieval granite font is the oldest part; and the pulpit (around 1500) was restored in the early 1800s when Newman and Keble preached here. There is also a fine screen (part 15th-century). St Mary's holds at least one service every Sunday as well as many baptisms, weddings and funerals and is proud of its welcome, music and breadth of worship. It sees itself very much as a part of the village and Hall Trust community.

341 Dartmouth, St Petrox
Grade I

The church is situated by the river mouth. There is reference to it in a title deed pre-dating the Norman Conquest and another in 1192, when it was maintained to give a light at the harbour entrance. This appeared to have been abandoned by 1332, when two priests were licensed to celebrate in the chapel of St Petrox. There is further reference to the chapel in 1425. In 1641 the church was practically rebuilt, including the tower and two arcades. Internally there are three brasses, all dated during the early 1600s. The church is generally open during the summer period. Services are held on Sunday evening during the summer and at festivals.

342 Dartmouth, St Saviour
Grade I

After a long argument between the Bishop of Exeter and the Abbot of Torre, the original chapel was dedicated by Bishop Brantyngham on 13th October 1372. The church, originally dedicated to Holy Trinity, but popularly known as St Saviour's, consists of a square tower, nave and chancel with north and south aisles and two chapels in the transepts. You enter through one of the finest doors in England, dated about 1340, but refurbished in 1631. The rood screen is from 1480 and is in good condition, as is the stone decorated pulpit of 1490. There is a varying pattern of Sunday services, including Sung Evensong.

343 Dartmouth Townstal, St Clement
Grade I

St Clement's is the mother church of Dartmouth, built well away from the river. It may well stand on the site of an even older Anglo-Saxon or Celtic church. It is mentioned in ecclesiastical records in 1200, when it was granted to the Abbot of Torre. Beneath the window in the south transept is a deep recess containing a recumbent effigy in Purbeck stone. The altar is unique and dates from James I. The tower of red sandstone is visible for miles around. Services are held on alternate Sundays at 11am and the children's Anchor Club is based here. Reordering work is due to start in 2008. The church is not always open.

344 Dean Prior, St George the Martyr
Grade I

This is a delightful 14th-century building, located next to the A38 Devon Expressway between Buckfastleigh and Rattery; offering a warm welcome and an atmosphere of friendly fellowship and quiet, spiritual reflection. The St George's flag flies proudly above the bell tower, with a 'Devon six' bells. A small inscribed window pane commemorates the incumbency of the poet Robert Herrick. See our informative website. Sunday services are held with a range of modern hymns, readings from the King James Bible and Holy Communion from the Book of Common Prayer. Pull-off parking bay at the front and parking at the rear.

345 Diptford, St Mary
Grade I

The first recorded rector occurs in 1226. The church was reconsecrated in 1336 after much new building, which included the fine tower and broach spire. The church and steeple are constructed mainly of local soft slate rubble. The building was restored in 1870, when many windows were replaced. The interior is in good order and has a fine barrel roof and an interesting screen. Diptford has an active village life centred around the church, primary school and various community activities. There are well-supported regular Sunday services, catering for all ages in our community.

346 Dittisham, St George
Grade I

The first church on the site was rebuilt in c.1333; it was enlarged in the 15th century, restored in 1846 under the direction of Pugin, and again in 1883 and 1924-1925. It comprises nave, chancel, north and south aisles, south porch, vestry and west tower. Internally, the chancel has a trefoil-headed piscina (possibly 14th-century), and a sedilia immediately to the west. There is an early-15th-century rood screen across nave and aisles, with painted figures in the wainscotting. The red sandstone font is Norman, and the pulpit is of painted stone. The organ of 1879 is by H. Halmshaw. The five bells were cast in 1802 by Thomas Mears of London.

347 Dodbrooke, St Thomas of Canterbury
Grade I

Built in the Perpendicular style, mostly 15th-century, the church retains a striking rood screen. The Lady chapel features a beautifully sculpted pieta. Another fine feature is the font, which is Norman, being flat and square of the table-top type. The fine roof of the south aisle has many elaborately painted bosses. On the outer wall of the church there is a sundial dated 1763, bearing the Latin inscription Lex Dei, Lux Die, "The Law of God is the light of day". The church retains its high church traditions which are much loved by the worshippers, both young and old, who regularly attend Sung Eucharist, held every Sunday.

348 East Allington, St Andrew
Grade II*

The church was built around 1268 forming part of the Fallapit estate owned by Squire Fortescue, but having been neglected during the 18th century, the new owner, William Cubitt, restored the building. The rood screen dated 1547, the carved pulpit and the alabaster reredos behind the high altar are of particular interest to the visitor. For over 700 years, the life of the church has gone on in this quiet country parish and today it encompasses the whole village with the youngest attending Sunday Club. A range of services provides a clear message, a strong choir and an all-inclusive form of worship where everyone is warmly welcomed.

349 East Portlemouth, St Winwaloe
Grade II*

Parts of the church date from the later 12th to early 13th century. The tower was added between 1400 and 1450, followed shortly by the side aisles and porch, and other changes were made to bring the church into the Perpendicular Gothic style. It contains a beautiful late-15th-century rood screen with 26 paintings of saints. A recent ground-penetrating radar scan showed a buried wall across the nave, suggesting the present church was developed from a smaller, possibly 10th-century building. St Winwaloe was a Breton saint who died in 532. The church is open all day to visitors, who are very welcome to its Sunday and Thursday morning services.

350 Ermington, St Peter & St Paul
Grade I

Today's building was begun in the 11th century. The spire is famous for being crooked: the result of using green timber in its construction. When it was hit by lightning in the 19th century it was rebuilt in stone but with the crookedness retained! During the incumbency of the Revd W Pinwell at the end of the 19th century, the church was restored. The beautiful carvings were made by the Pinwell sisters who went on to provide carvings for many other churches in Devon and Cornwall. Today the church lies at the heart of the community and welcomes all Christians to worship.

351 Galmpton (Malborough), Holy Trinity

Built 1866-1867 to replace the old church of St Andrew's at South Huish. The site was given by the Earl of Devon and the architect was Richard Coad, a pupil of Gilbert Scott. Early English style with lancets in the chancel and plate tracery in the nave. The tower is buttressed with a pyramidal cap. The 14th-century font, and four of the six bells came from the old church, parts of the two 15th-century alabaster retables also came from South Huish. A welcoming church with Common Worship Communion Services on three Sundays, with a Morning Service on the third Sunday of each month.

352 Halwell, St Leonard
Grade I

Halwell was one of four burghs, with Exeter, Lydford and Pilton, set up by Alfred in the 9th century for defence against the Danes and it had its own mint. Stanborough Camp, an Iron Age fort, and Halwell Camp are in the parish. The latest church to be built on this ancient site is a late-15th-century building with a fine Ashburton stone tower, housing six bells cast in 1763 – still regularly rung. Halwell is now in the Diptford benefice, drawing strength in sharing services, youth groups and fundraising. The church is used for Parish Council meetings, charitable lunches, the Harvest Supper, the children's Christmas party and fundraising activities.

353 Harberton, St Andrew
Grade I

St Andrew's Church in the village centre replaces a Saxon or Norman church, of which only the font remains. The nave's barrel roof, completed about 1370, has 80 carved bosses. The rood screen, coloured and gilded, and the stone pulpit are 15th-century, though the pulpit has replacement German statues and the screen was restored in the 19th century. The late-19th-century alabaster and mosaic reredos depicts Christ enthroned. The stained-glass windows are memorials. The tower houses six bells. A weekly Communion and other services ensure the church serves the community; we belong to a benefice of six parishes.

354 Harbertonford, St Peter
Grade II

The church of St Peter's is in the centre of the village. It was endowed by Mrs Anthony of Great Englebourne and was dedicated in 1859. The plan of the church is a significant change from the medieval plan form. The roof construction includes a dramatic star-shaped scissor braced over the crossing, and there is fine stained glass in the sanctuary. A small congregation meets weekly for worship and is keen to reach out and welcome new members; it is regularly used by the village school and a doctor's surgery. The church enjoys being part of a larger benefice.

355 Harford, St Petroc
Grade I

This small, simple moorland granite church dating from the 15th century was restored in 1880 and 1921. There is a Tudor porch and font and an old Saxon font, also an altar tomb with brass effigy of the 1563 Speaker of the House of Commons. The 1920 oak choir stalls, pulpit and organ front carved by Violet Pinwell of Ermington. Royal arms of 1728. Pleasing early-20th-century stained glass. Sharing clergy with Ivybridge, we enjoy a weekly service and occasional concerts, and the church and the small rural community are mutually supportive. St Petroc's open-door policy, welcoming many passing visitors throughout the year, is an important part of the church's mission.

356 Holbeton, All Saints
Grade I

This 15th-century cruciform church crowned with a 120ft spire stands sentinel like a cathedral over the village below. A fine eastern lychgate leads the visitor to the south porch, through an impressive Tudor doorway, richly carved and embossed, into a spacious stately interior. A splendid array of craftsmanship includes carved oak bench ends, screens enclosing chapels and an intricately carved stone pulpit detailing evangelists in its panels. There is a Norman font and a Victorian font of coloured marble. A magnificent east window depicts the Ascension of Christ. A friendly church used by the community, which it endeavours to serve. A variety of worship is offered and visitors are always welcome.

357 Holne, St Mary the Virgin
Grade I

Our church is medieval, part 13th-century, with 15th-century additions. The church's part-rendered exterior hides a hidden gem of peace, tranquillity and beauty, with a profound atmosphere of prayerfulness. Our most obvious treasure is the fine medieval rood screen whose gilded tracery and richly coloured paintings of forty saints is being carefully conserved. More recent 'saints' of Holne include Charles Kingsley, born and baptised in Holne in 1819, and Archbishop Michael Ramsey, who often joined the congregation during holidays here. Loved and used by the locals for worship, all-age workshops and special events, the church is kept open during the day for all who wish to visit.

358 Hope Cove, St Clement

This is the smallest church building in Woodleigh Deanery and designated as a chapel of ease, having a simple nave with the altar table beneath an arch in the wall behind. A single bell hangs beneath the roof cross, because it was once the village school. Situated overlooking the sea with views to Bolt Tail and across Bigbury Bay this is a popular church for holidaymakers as well as local people who seek a quiet haven of peace and tranquillity. A service of Holy Communion is held on the first and third Sunday of each month.

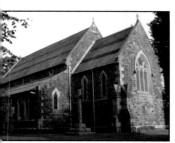

359 Ivybridge, St John the Evangelist

Built in 1882, by Hine and Odger of Plymouth on land given by Lord Blachford, the church reflects the late Victorians' renewed interest in medieval principles of design and ornamentation. The stonework is varied and modestly decorative: local limestone with granite quoins and buttresses and dressings in Bath and Portland stone; inside, columns of polished Ashburton marble. There is a fine oak screen, a handsome oak altar and retable all by Herbert Read of Exeter. The retable has a good example of a late Victorian Pre-Raphaelite nativity scene. St John's has an atmosphere of peace and prayerfulness much valued and commented upon by our many visitors.

360 Kingsbridge, St Edmund King & Martyr
Grade I

The parish church and burial ground were consecrated in August 1414, but a chapel on the site had already been serving the community for at least a century. The building retains many 15th-century features, including the screens, the font and the porch. Restorations and improvements were made in the early 20th century and major repairs to the roof have been completed. There is a central bell tower with a peal of eight bells and a three manual pipe organ. The prominent position of this large church in the town makes it ideal as a place of worship for locals and visitors, civic services and as a venue for concerts.

361 Kingston (Ringmore), St James the Less
Grade II*

This church dates from the 14th and 15th centuries, with a major restoration in 1893 by Sedding. It comprises nave, chancel, west tower, south porch, south chapel and north aisle. The south chapel has a squint to the main altar and aumbry. The interior fittings and monuments are mainly from the late-19th-century restoration – a panel in the porch records that £30 was given in 1892 towards re-seating and repairs. Exceptions are the 15th-century octagonal font, the priest's seat formed from medieval bench ends, and a late-18th-century memorial slab to Frances Stephens, aged 11 months. There is a medieval ring of four bells, now augmented to six.

362 Kingswear, St Thomas of Canterbury
Grade II

The earliest church on the site dates from 1170, though now only the tower is of significant age the rest having been rebuilt in 1847. The dedication to St Thomas was probably as a response to the wave of devotion which followed his murder in Canterbury Cathedral. There may, however, be a more personal link through one of the monks who served here when the chapel was dependent on Totnes Priory for its priests. Many continental pilgrims made use of the church on their way to Canterbury. Today we are a small but dedicated community of worshippers (part of the Brixham Team) who welcome visitors enthusiastically.

363 Landscove, St Matthew
Grade II*

This strikingly pretty Victorian church with a steeple was designed by Pearson of Truro Cathedral fame. In 1851 the Champerdown family of Dartington Hall gave the church, school and vicarage to the village where they owned the slate mine below the fields. This is a completely unaltered Victorian gem set in an attractive churchyard where the coachman Harry Baskerville, who showed Conan Doyle round Dartmoor, is buried. Visitors enjoy the old vicarage garden-nursery and tea room next door, and the views over the field and village below.

364 Littlehempston, St John the Baptist
Grade I

This pretty church stands on a grassy knoll above a tiny river and the railway. Approach from the Tally Ho Inn and church cottages, and cross the "pound" between the gates where horses stood during services. The church built in the time of Bishop Lacy (1420-1455) has a Norman barrel roof and font, and a wall painting survives in the parvis room above the porch, as do delightful stone figures of two knights and a lady in the church. The colourful rood screen was altered in Victorian times when pews and the magnificent Speechley organ were added. A committed community supports this church in its worship and maintenance and welcomes visitors.

365 Loddiswell, St Michael & All Angels
Grade II*

The tower, nave and chancel date from the 12th century, enlarged in the 15th century by south aisle, porch and priest room. The church was restored in 1866, and a new organ by Dicker installed. A stained-glass window above the altar depicts Christ Blessing Little Children. A north chapel window contains eight shields of Earls of Devon. Top lights are Tudor badges, portcullis, Tudor rose, fleur-de-lis and pomegranate, personal emblem of Queen Catherine of Aragon forbidden by Henry VIII after 1530. Six bells were hung in 1857. Today we seek to be a presence in and a part of Loddiswell's living, working, caring community and a worshipping home for all ages.

366 Malborough, All Saints
Grade I

The church, known locally as the Cathedral of the South Hams, can be seen from miles around. It was founded c.1200. The south porch has a fine vaulted roof, while the bell tower and spire are 13th-century and there is a fine example of a late Norman font. Although substantially reconstructed in the 15th century, and again in Victorian times, its beautiful sense of spaciousness remains unspoiled. Today, the active congregation is working hard to keep the church at the heart of village life. The renovated kitchen, within the body of the church, helps to make it a great place for concerts and other events held locally.

367 Marldon, St John the Baptist *Grade I*

A place of worship for over 600 years, structurally little changed since 1520. Memorials mark a history of service to parishioners and wider outreach by seafarers, merchants, and farmers from Gilberts of Compton to present-day Christians, actively involved in community life, working closely with the C of E school. Inside, enjoy light and colour, read "The Good Samaritan" in stained glass (backwards!), notice the leaning pillars, each with a different decoration, and spot the Green Man over the font. Open all day, offering a place of peace, prayer and renewal to villagers, tourists and way-marked trail walkers.

368 Modbury, St George *Grade I*

A prominent site overlooking the town and a fine tall broach spire ensure this church is a landmark near and far. It comprises a three-bay arcade, the masonry arches and piers separating north and south aisles dating from c.1300, transepts containing elaborately carved tomb recesses of the Decorated period, and a chancel with aisles leading off through 15th-century granite arches and east window were restored c.1860, the south porch in 1965. Today's church welcomes all ages with traditional and modern music, from organ and worship group. There is daily prayer, strong mission support, home groups, youth work, and a church car park.

369 Moreleigh, All Saints *Grade I*

Dating from c.1265 this modest-sized church consists of a porch, nave, chancel and west tower. It is situated well outside the village possibly because it is said to have been built in a farmyard, as a penance, by a knight who killed the Rector of Woodleigh in a duel. His tomb can be seen embedded in the south wall and only half within the church. Other features include a Saxon font and three bells, which are among the very few remaining which were cast in Exeter. The church welcomes all who come to join in worship which is both traditional and contemporary.

370 Newton Ferrers, Holy Cross *Grade I*

A church presence is recorded since 1084 – making it one of the oldest foundations in Devon. The present building, dating from the 12th century, was extensively remodelled in the 1880s by the Yonge family. Interesting features are a fine tower screen incorporating medieval bosses, a red granite and alabaster font, a 12th-century tomb lid, ancient stocks and barrel roof with two bends visible when looking from nave to high altar. Cyclamens planted in the churchyard by the Yonges bloom in spring and autumn. The church, which is open daily, lies at the heart of Newton Ferrers and maintains strong links with the primary school and community. Worship ranges from traditional to modern.

THE CHURCHES
CONSERVATION TRUST

371 North Huish, St Mary *Grade I*

The church (dedication unknown but said to be St Mary) was dedicated by Bishop Grandisson on 15 June 1336. Like the neighbouring church of St Mary Diptford, it has a medieval spire. The body of the building is probably early-14th-century work, enlarged in the 15th century by the addition of a south aisle. The granite font is dated 1662. The church is now in the care of the Churches Conservation Trust. Three services are held each year: Rogation Songs of Praise, Carols by Candlelight, and Remembrance Day. North Huish ecclesiastical parish has now been joined with St Mary's, Diptford.

372 Rattery, St Mary the Virgin

Grade I

The 11th-century church of St Mary the Virgin at Rattery stands on a prominent hill in this rural parish and its spire can be seen from many miles around. The interior of the church is very distinctive and is decorated with 19th-century sgraffito plaster work of an Italian design giving the church great colour and warmth, much appreciated at Christmas and Harvest Festival. Worshippers enjoy the hospitality of the 11th-century Church House Inn next door, which housed the original builders of the church. There is an active ministry to young families and to the people of the parish as a whole which covers a large area in South Devon.

373 Revelstoke, St Peter

Grade II*

The church was built in 1880-1882 by Charles Baring, who later became Lord Revelstoke. He offered to the village of Noss Mayo a completely new church within the village. It is a magnificent example of Victorian Gothic architecture. The woodcarving and the stained-glass windows are particularly notable. The patronage of the church passed to the Bishop of Exeter in about 1890. This church is part of the united benefice with Holy Cross Church at Newton Ferrers and All Saints Church at Holbeton. The church plays an active part in the social life of the village. Services include a Eucharist service twice a month with a family service also twice a month.

374 Ringmore, All Hallows

Grade II*

This church dates mainly from the late 13th or early 14th century, but with some remains of 12th-century work. It was restored in 1862-1863 and later, by the Revd F. C. Hingeston-Randolph, incumbent for more than 50 years. It comprises nave, north transept, chancel with north chapel, and tower with octagonal stone spire on the south side of the nave over the porch. Internally, the plain chancel arch has wall paintings above, said to have been discovered by the incumbent's restoration work in the 19th century. The rood screen and organ case are painted, and are probably Victorian. The chancel roof of 1915 is in memory of F. C. and M. J. Hingeston-Randolph.

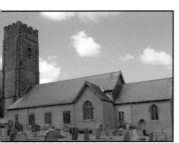

375 Roborough (Bickleigh), St Mary the Virgin

Grade I

The church consists of a nave and chancel in one, north and south aisles, west tower, south porch, and vestry. The 16th-century tower is the oldest part of the building, with the rest of the building dating from 1838 and 1882. The tower contains six bells, which were restored and re-hung in a new metal frame in 1937. Internal features include the fonts of the 12th and 16th-centuries, the former of crude tub shape with zigzag carving. The sanctuary was re-designed in 1964 with gifts from Lord and Lady Roborough of the striking east window, reredos, granite altar, sanctuary paving and communion kneelers.

376 Salcombe, Holy Trinity

Grade II

Holy Trinity was built between 1841 and 1843. Its English design of nave and two side aisles lit by tall lancet windows gives a light and airy feel. The church has many fine features including a richly carved pulpit and carved stone font with wooden canopy. These were carved by the Revd William Pinwell and given as gifts in 1844. The Lady chapel has a stone altar. Extensive plans are in hand to carry out alterations and improvements within the church. The worship is largely traditional, with an excellent choir and organist and a welcoming friendly congregation. Holy Trinity is now part of the Salcombe and Malborough with South Huish Benefice.

377 Shaugh Prior, St Edward
Grade I

Situated on the edge of Dartmoor, the church dates from the 15th century, and was not heavily restored in the 19th-century. It was built of stone rubble with granite dressings and a granite ashlar tower. It comprises nave, chancel, north and south aisles, tall west tower and south porch. Internally, the furnishings are mainly from the 19th century, with the exception of the interesting 16th-century font cover (which was found in a farm building and restored in the 1870s by H. Hems) in the form of a two-storeyed lantern-shaped octagon with a conical top. The chancel roof has some 15th-century carved bosses, and there is a medieval altar stone at the west end.

378 Sherford, St Martin
Grade I

The recorded history begins in 1073, but the church we see today is mostly 14th-century with nave, two aisles and a projecting chancel. A feature of the church is the chancel screen where there is original painting visible, believed to have been executed by monks from the chapels of Domesday manors. It was removed during the war as Sherford was evacuated for D-Day rehearsals at Slapton Sands. The pulpit contains carving from the roof loft, dismantled by order of Queen Elizabeth I. We are actively engaged in the local healing ministry and have a small but dedicated following; the church offers a mixture of worship and visitors are always made very welcome.

379 Slapton, St James the Greater
Grade I

Situated in the centre of the village, the church has stood here for over 650 years. The high altar was dedicated in 1318, though there is reference to the church in 1292. The chancel and two of its windows are 14th-century, of Early English style. The nave and aisles are later by about 75 years. There is a parvis chamber above the porch, a Jacobean cover to the font, an achievement dated 1766 and a fine rood screen. The tower contains a light ring of six bells. The church is involved with the community and events are well supported by the village. There is a service every Sunday.

380 South Brent, St Petroc
Grade I

The church is dominated by its Norman tower, the base of which holds the oldest part of the church thought to date from Saxon times. There is a fine Norman font. During the 11th century the Saxon building was enlarged to form a cruciform Norman church, the present tower being at the centre. Later, during the 11th to 14th centuries the church was further extended to the present building. St Petroc's prides itself on being the church of the whole village. There are both BCP and Common Worship services but we equally enjoy hosting baptisms, marriages and burials for anyone who lives here.

381 South Milton, All Saints
Grade I

Bishop Bronescombe of Exeter issued a licence for a chapel on the site in 1269. The porch and south wall are the oldest parts, followed by the nave, transept, and in the 14th century, the tower and north aisle. The font is unusual and thought to be pre-Norman. The medieval screen has been restored leaving the original paintings of the Saints. An 18th-century reredos now stands at the back of the church. There are memorials to the Roope, Prideaux and Elliot families. The six bells date from 1766. There is lay participation in worship: leading services, intercessions, readings, and administering the chalice. We have a weekly house group and links with Adumasa in Ghana.

382 South Pool, St Nicholas & St Cyriac
Grade I

After rebuilding, the church was dedicated in August 1318. It was extended in the 15th century and carefully restored in the 19th. The font is Norman with decoration similar to that in Dittisham Church. The screen dates from about 1480 and has fine carving and retains most of the original paintwork. There is an Easter sepulchre on the north side of the altar with the tomb and effigy of Thomas Bryant who was rector (1501-1541). In the south transept is a memorial to Leonard and Joan Darre and their family. She was the daughter of the Lord Mayor of London at the time of the Spanish Armada (1588). Services are held every Sunday.

383 Sparkwell, All Saints
Grade II

Built in 1859 and designed by Roger Elliot, architect of Plymouth, in the Early English style. It is a rural parish on the southern edge of Dartmoor being under the patronage of the Dean and Canons of Windsor. Much of the interior of the church was designed by the Revd Ernest Geldart and Mr Edmund Sedding. The church is of a broad tradition with an open-hearted, open-minded, open-door policy. The services range from Book of Common Prayer and Common Worship to Creation Centred Spirituality. There is a lively congregation consisting of locals, visitors and an adjoining (VA) School.

384 Staverton, St Paul de Leon
Grade I

In April 1314, Bishop Walter Stapledon visited Staverton and was not impressed by what he found. The present church dates from the edict which followed, although the lower parts of the tower may survive from the earlier building. The bells were recently restored and are now rung by an enthusiastic team of ringers. The lower parts of the screen are medieval and the loft was added by Harry Hems after 1889. There is a service on most Sundays. All are welcome. The music is always good and on special occasions, such as the Carol Service, is outstanding. The lovely churchyard is a mass of snowdrops and daffodils in the spring.

385 Stoke Fleming, St Peter
Grade II*

Used as a navigation mark to find the mouth of the River Dart, the tall tower of this 13th-century church has a ring of six bells and a fine clock. Near the 800-year-old Norman font is an effigy of the foundress, Lady Elyenore Mohun. The 14th-century brass of John Corp and his granddaughter, is the second oldest in Devon. The pulpit, carved in 1891 by Violet Pinwell then aged seventeen, displays 60 animals and four Bible scenes. Gloriously hand-stitched kneelers depict many of the houses in the village. In a united benefice with Blackawton and Strete, we are a live and welcoming church.

386 Stoke Gabriel, St Gabriel
Grade I

Standing above the River Dart, worship is thought to have taken place here for 1000 years. St Mary and St Gabriel's has a 13th-century Norman tower, was rebuilt in the 15th century and restored in the 1850s. The church has a fine carved rood screen and pulpit, painted medieval panels, three 14th-century pew ends and a magnificent yew tree in the churchyard. The nearby Church House Inn is still owned by the church. Part of a united benefice with Collaton St Mary, regular services, both Prayer Book and Common Worship are held, and the church aims to show the love of God to all parishioners.

387 Stokenham, St Michael & All Angels
Grade I

The church is beautifully crafted. It has a wealth of medieval features – double piscina, decorated capitals, Green Man and rood screen – exemplifying its provenance as the hub of a vibrant community. Its history, both ancient and modern, repays study. Archaeological digs have produced fascinating evidence of the medieval and prehistoric past. The church overlooks both fishing and farming communities of Start Bay. In 1943, it was the meeting place for the evacuee villages of the D-Day rehearsals. "Exercise Tiger" is commemorated each year by service veterans. Today, the church is helping to create the new Start Bay Benefice of nine churches, reaching out to a new community of churchgoers.

388 Strete, St Michael
Grade II

This church, formerly a chapel of ease, was built in 1836 by T. Lidstone in the Perpendicular style at a cost of £850. It became the parish church in 1881 when Strete was formed into an independent parish. It comprises nave and aisles under one roof, small sanctuary with vestry in the north east angle and west tower. The interior fittings and furnishings date predominantly from the church's construction, including the timber arcades. The lectern, reading desk, Communion rail and carved wooden reredos are original but the altar is possibly later. The carved wooden octagonal pulpit is dated 1887. The stained glass includes the east window dated c.1860-1870.

389 Thurlestone, All Saints
Grade II*

The original 12th-century red sandstone font survives. The present 13th-century church was extended in the 15th century. Woodwork includes the tower arch screen, the high altar crucifix from Oberammergau, the lady chapel altar with carved fragments from an ancient rood screen, the pulpit with figures of St Augustine and St Chrysostom and chancel roof bosses with passion emblems. The magnificent stained glass is modern except for a small lancet window by the high altar. A Royal Marines' tablet records its Second World War association with the church. Our mission is to be a worshipping body serving the living God in the parish and beyond. Worship ranges from traditional to contemporary.

390 Totnes, St Mary
Grade I

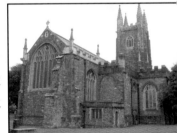

The red sandstone tower of this 15th-century church dominates the town and surrounding countryside. Entering by the carved original wooden south porch doors, there are four aisles (one 19th-century), a chancel and two side chapels. Important features include a unique carved stone screen, pulpit and font, an oak wagon roof, brass candelabrum and Father Willis organ. The 1636 cross-aisle civic pews confirm close, continuing links with the town and adjacent Guildhall. Led by a team rector (eight churches), this internationally visited church is open daily and widely used for prayer, worship and cultural activities. A far reaching, exciting renewal project is now supported by Friends of St Mary's.

391 Ugborough, St Peter
Grade I

The earliest written record of St Peter's is from 1121. The nave and supporting arcade were built before this, possibly on the site of an earlier church. The ornately carved north aisle timber bosses include symbols of St Eloy and St Brannock, and a Green Man. There is a splendid late-Norman font, a two-storey porch and an unusual 17th-century stone pulpit. A brass of a lady of the early 16th century graces the north transept. The rood screen, completed in 1422, is decorated with 32 painted figures of c.1525. Worship is both traditional and modern, and aims both to support older worshippers and encourage the younger generation.

392 Wembury, St Werburgh
Grade I

The church is Perpendicular in style, 14th century on a Norman foundation which replaced an earlier Saxon church, and consists of a main nave, south aisle, and north transept with a square turreted tower at the west end. All internal woodwork is of beautifully carved oak, including the roof beams, choir stalls, pulpit, lectern, parclose screen, reredos and pew ends. The church also contains several interesting monuments and stained-glass windows. It is open during the day, year-round, to cater for the many visitors using the South West Footpath, which passes adjacent to the church and has excellent views across the Bay to the Eddystone Lighthouse.

393 West Alvington, All Saints
Grade I

There is evidence that a church has stood on the site since 909. The present fine building is Early Perpendicular and was remodelled in the 15th century. The remains of the earlier 13th-century stonework can be seen by the piscine. The whole church was extensively restored in 1867 and now consists of tower, with belfry, nave, two aisles, parts of the beautiful original rood screen, a chapel set apart for the Ilbert family, chancel and a vicar's vestry added in the 19th century. We are a friendly and welcoming church with a variety of services to accommodate the old and the young and we have a strong link with the local primary school.

394 West Charleton, St Mary
Grade II

Dedicated in the 14th century, the church was restored in 1850. This was when the screen and rood loft were removed, and the Caen stone font, reading desk and pulpit were installed. The south transept window, installed during the 1970s, shows Mary looking very young with uncovered black hair. Nearby is a portable altar constructed in 1944 using oak from a bombed house on the Normandy bridgehead. Six bells housed in the 15th-century tower are rung regularly. During each month, Holy Communion is celebrated on two Sundays and every Wednesday, Evensong is held once, and there is one family service when we try to involve the Charleton C of E Primary School.

395 Woodleigh, St Mary the Virgin
Grade II*

The church building is the usual cruciform shape including a west tower with five bells, two dating from 1640. On the north side of the chancel there is a fine Easter sepulchre (c.1500) and a beautiful memorial tablet, in a pre-Raphaelite style, commemorating the blind wife of the Revd Frederick Sanders, a former rector (1898). The octagonal font is of granite; there are several interesting stained-glass windows and memorial tablets. The church was restored in 1890 and again 100 years later. The church is the only community building in Woodleigh and is used for a variety of village activities, not just church services.

396 Yealmpton, St Bartholomew
Grade II*

"The most amazing Victorian church in Devon" (John Betjeman). There is a 1500-year-old standing stone and a Saxon font from the original wooden building. This church dates from c.1225 – memorials, brasses and tower stairs survive. It had a total Anglo-Catholic revival rebuild, 1849-1852, by young William Butterfield with local Kitley marble altar, screen, font, and striped pillars. The collapsing tower was rebuilt in 1915 with an appeal in the name of "Old Mother Hubbard". Enthusiastic ringers summon to worship (six bells from 1779). There is a warm welcoming congregation; strong village, school, ecumenical links; lively musical eucharistic celebrations, all-age worship; concerts and recitals. Open daily, proclaiming God's hospitality.

TEIGNBRIDGE

Teignbridge - between Torquay and Exeter and the eastern part of Dartmoor – is made up of coastal resorts, beautiful varied countryside, wild moorland, and busy market towns. The 70 Anglican churches all reflect something of the community they are here to serve and warmly welcome visitors.

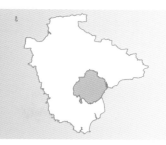

397 Abbotsbury, St Mary the Virgin
Grade II*

This church was built from 1904-1906 by E. H. Sedding in free Perpendicular Gothic style. Cruciform in plan. The central east window dates from the 15th century and was transferred from St Mary's Chapel, Highweek Street. It has curvilinear star-shaped tracery found in other local churches and is surrounded by badges of the Yarde and Ferrers families. The exterior of the nave is dominated by flying buttresses. Internally, there is an ornate rood screen and elaborately carved reredos. The piscina and pulpit are also from St Mary's. Other fittings include an eagle lectern, and good original four-light wrought-iron chandeliers. There is some stained glass to the east window and aisles; other windows have cobweb-pattern leading.

398 Abbotskerswell, Blessed Virgin Mary
Grade II*

The church is approached through a lychgate, believed to be the oldest dated example in England (1603). The chancel dates back to the 13th century but a church has probably existed on this site since the 10th. A typical Devon 15th-century screen divides the nave from the chancel, which is dominated by a statue of the Virgin Mary, revealed during the Victorian restoration, but unfortunately damaged before its presence was realised. Our worship encompasses both the traditions of 1662 and contemporary praise. We are always looking for new ways to bring the church and community closer together and combine our harvest thanksgiving with a Beer and Food Festival.

399 Ashburton, St Andrew
Grade I

Dating from the early 15th century with a 92ft tower, Ashburton was restored in 1882-1883 by G. E. Street. It consists of a nave, chancel, north and south chancel chapels, transepts, aisles, north porch, vestry and west tower. Internally, there are two fine 18th-century brass candelabras, an oak reredos of 1928 by Herbert Read and a pulpit by Harry Hems. There are also a considerable number of monuments. We are active within the life of the town community, are open to all and support various local groups. St Andrew's and several moorland parishes form a Team Ministry and it has links with the Church in Kenya.

400 Ashcombe, St Nectan
Grade I

Dating mainly from the 13th century, with a 16th-century north aisle, restored in the 19th century. The church consists of nave, chancel, north aisle, south transept and west tower. The 13th-century tower houses three bells supported on the oldest basically unaltered medieval bell frame in the country. There is a gilded timber eagle lectern of 1735 and an unusual set of 16th or 17th-century benches with carved bench ends. The windows contain fragments of medieval, 17th, and 18th-century glass. Our aim is to bring together this community and others connected with the parish in the worship of Christ, and the maintenance of all that supports this.

TEIGNBRIDGE

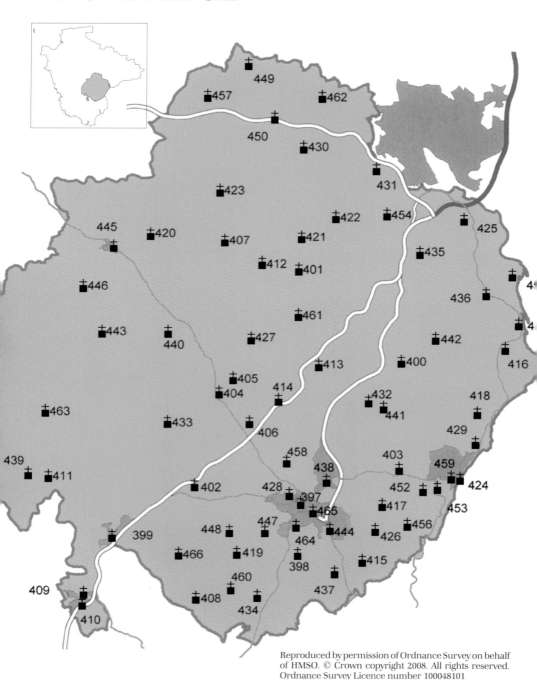

449
457
462
450
430
431
423
422 454 425
445 420 435
407 421
446 412 401 436
443 461 442 416
440 427 400 418
463 405 413 432 429
404 441
433 414 406
439 458 403 459
411 402 438 452 424
428 397 417 453
448 447 465 456
399 464 444 426
466 419 398 415
409 460 437
408 434
410

THE PILGRIM'S GUIDE TO DEVON'S CHURCHES

401 Ashton, St John the Baptist
Grade I

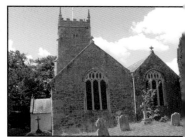

With its striking setting in the beautiful Teign Valley, Ashton Church is much loved by local people and has a growing congregation. Dating from the early 15th century, this church has important paintings, woodwork and stained glass. Notable features are the 15th-century rood screen, the Jacobean pulpit, medieval bench ends, and a well-preserved wall painting showing the mass of St Gregory. There are remains of medieval stained glass in many of the windows, a number of monuments, and royal arms of 1735. Our frequent visitors appreciate these and the deeply peaceful atmosphere. A monthly Eucharist plus frequent special occasions attract all age groups throughout the year.

402 Bickington, St Mary the Virgin
Grade I

This church dates from the 15th century, with an early-16th-century north aisle, and late-19th-century south porch and vestry. The church was restored in 1883-1884 by Christian of London and R. M. Fulford of Exeter. It comprises nave, chancel, north aisle, west tower and south porch. Internally, the nave and chancel have cornices of intertwined vine leaves, against which are angels holding shields. The fittings include an octagonal granite font, of the 15th-16th century, restored in 1883-1884 by Harry Hems of Exeter. The choir stalls, altar table, lectern and credence table are also by Hems. Monuments include a stone tablet of 1689, and several 17th-century floor tomb slabs.

403 Bishopsteignton, St John the Baptist
Grade I

This lovely church nestles into Haldon Hill, one of the ancient beacon hills in England. The original church, which is mainly Norman on Saxon foundations, was built in 1130 but almost at once the nave was extended, leaving the tower midway along the south wall. In 1815 a spire topped the present tower, at the west end of the church, but in 1863 it was removed and the tower itself raised by another 10ft. Today it is used as an entrance but the arch to the original west door can be dated back to 1130, and decorative work in the door arch indicates influences from even earlier Celtic and pre-Christian days.

404 Bovey Tracey, St John
Grade II*

In 1849 the Revd Charles Leslie Courtenay was appointed vicar of Bovey Tracey. This was the year of his marriage to Lady Caroline Summers, who was the daughter of the Earl Summers and a maid of honour to Queen Victoria. Shortly after his arrival Father Courtenay, inspired by the Oxford Movement, not only decided to build a new vicarage, but also a new church. This church, to be dedicated to St John the Evangelist, was to serve as a chapel of ease to the parish church of Sts Peter, Paul & Thomas. The consecration and dedication of St John's took place on Thursday 16th June 1853 by Henry Phillpotts, Lord Bishop of Exeter. Later, St John's became a parish in its own right. To this day it maintains the catholic faith of the Church of England.

405 Bovey Tracey, St Peter, St Paul & St Thomas
Grade I

There has been a church in Bovey Tracey since Saxon times. The present building was begun as an act of penance by the de Tracey family for William de Tracey's part in the murder of Thomas Becket. It has a particularly fine medieval screen dating from 1470. Today a lively congregation of all ages meets here, with a range of services from quiet and traditional with choir and organ to lively and contemporary worship with the music group. For further details see our website.

406 Bovey Tracey Heathfield, St Catherine

St Katharine's church was originally a small chapel built along from the Heathfield cottages built for workers in the pottery clay pits of Heathfield. Along with a small school room it served a handful of houses. After the Second World War, as Heathfield expanded onto the old US Army base, a new tin Tabernacle church was built on the old base site. In 2003 this was sold and the funds poured into a new school and worship centre in Heathfield. Alas, a slip in spelling has left the new school and centre as 'Catherine' but nevertheless a smouldering faith still maintains the sacramental presence of Christ in Heathfield.

407 Bridford, St Thomas Becket   Grade I

One of the six churches of the Teign Valley Group, Bridford Church is much loved by residents and visitors alike. Building began in the late 15th century on the site of a 13th-century chapel, this Perpendicular style, granite-faced church has Tudor rose and pomegranate roof decorations, indicating its construction in the reign of Henry VIII and Katherine of Aragon. Most striking is the eight-bay richly carved rood screen, with figures defaced by Cromwell's soldiers, and at the back panels covered with extraordinary paintings. The broad Anglican tradition is represented at services enjoyed by a small but loyal congregation who welcome all comers to our monthly Eucharist and on other occasions.

408 Broadhempston, St Peter & St Paul   Grade I

Set in the circular graveyard, once a Neolithic village with five roads to it, this church is approached through an arch which was the gate to the village. The original Saxon building dedicated to St Petroc was replaced by a Norman one in 1400. The Monks Retreat Inn housed the builders who gave us a church with interesting stones in the floor, a splendid rood screen restored by Harry Hems in the 1890s and many medieval features. There is a splendid modern embroidery in the side chapel. This is a fine church with welcoming worship and congregation.

409 Buckfastleigh, Holy Trinity   Grade II*

Holy Trinity Parish Church is the oldest church in Buckfastleigh, lying on the south eastern edge of Dartmoor. It is spectacularly sited high up on the edge of Bulley Cleaves quarry, with the spire a distinctive landmark. The church dates from the 13th century. Its first vicar was Wolvan whose patrons were the abbot and convent of Buckfast. It is now in ruins after a devastating fire in 1992, although the tower has been restored. The church register dates from 1602. English Heritage recorded that a thorough restoration was made in 1844-1845 by John Hayward of Exeter, a leading Gothic Revival church architect, which included new roofing.

410 Buckfastleigh, St Luke

Is modern, completed in 2002 and replaces Holy Trinity, situated on the hill outside the town and severely damaged by fire in 1992. The basic shape of St Luke's is hexagonal, with a large sanctuary for the Lord's Table. A side chapel and coffee lounge adjacent to the main area with a large hall underneath and additional facilities make a versatile, useful building. The font, believed to be Norman, came from Holy Trinity, and the adapted stained-glass windows in the prayer chapel are from the old St Luke's. We aim to be inclusive, far-reaching, innovative, biblical, informative and educational; also seeking to reach out to the community.

411 Buckland in the Moor, St Peter
Grade II*

Dates from the 15th or early 16th century. It comprises nave, chancel, north aisle and transept, south porch, and west tower. The church was much restored in 1907-1908. Interior fittings include the Norman font, rood screen with painted figures on the lower panels and black and white figures on the reverse, the early-18th-century wooden pulpit, and royal arms of George II. On the walls of the north aisle there are 19th-century slate tablets, carved with the Creed and Ten Commandments. A photograph displayed in the church shows box pews removed during the restoration of 1907-1908; parts of these may survive in the panelled dado that now lines the nave, aisle and transept.

412 Christow, St James
Grade I

Christow, meaning 'St Christina's holy place', sits on the western slopes above the River Teign. St James' Church at the heart of Lower Town dates from the 15th century, built of local granite in the Perpendicular style. Inside, the most striking features are the three-dimensional painted plaster coat of arms of 1682, the chancel screen and a square Norman font. The burial crypt of the Pellew family of Canonteign lies beneath the chancel, which is adorned with their memorial stones. The elegant tower houses eight bells regularly rung by a dedicated and competitive team. Sunday services range from traditional to informal, attracting all ages throughout the year. For visitor and worshipper, a warm welcome is assured.

413 Chudleigh, St Martin & St Mary
Grade I

Dates from the 13th century with subsequent additions and restorations. Mainly built in Perpendicular style, with nave and chancel (with hagioscope), substantial west tower and large north transept, arch-braced roof, and broad longitudinal rib. Stained-glass windows from mid 19th century. The rood screen has 20 painted panels depicting apostles and prophets, each with a verse. The 1897 stone drum pulpit is corbelled out from a flight of stone steps. The font comprises a large polished 19th-century granite bowl and an older Purbeck marble stem. The weekly worship includes family-orientated and traditional services reflecting the church's role at the heart of a growing community.

414 Chudleigh Knighton, St Paul
Grade II

The building dates from 1849 and is an early work of Sir George Gilbert Scott. It is a simple cruciform building without aisles in an Early English style. It is believed to be the only flint-clad church of its type in Devon. Furnishings are complete and largely original, although the organ has been relocated to the gallery. The east window is of stained glass by Harry Stanners, 1962. The church building is a focal point in the village and is valued by the wider village community. Christians of all denominations contribute both to the life and worship of the church. Holy Communion services alternate with family services.

415 Coffinswell, St Bartholomew
Grade I

Nestling in this picturesque village, the simple 12th-century church contains interesting medieval and later features. The 70ft tower of red sandstone (stucco clad by the Victorians) was built c.1220 and houses a ring of six bells, the earliest dating back to Henry VII. The north aisle was added in the late 1400s, where now stands the shifted Norman font of Beer stone. Pews were removed in the mid-1990s, creating a much-used meeting and children's area, enlarged when the original ringing chamber was reinstated in the year 2000. Services are held each Sunday and our church continues to serve and care for its community.

416 Cofton, St Mary
Grade II

The church dates back to the 13th century but it was restored and reopened in 1839. It serves the villages of Cockwood, Dawlish Warren and Cofton. It is small and intimate with a friendly fellowship and being in a holiday area is particularly welcoming to visitors. Our worship has a strong emphasis on teaching and the building of discipleship. Services alternate between Holy Communion and Morning Worship. Mid-week activities include a Bible study group, a fellowship for older people, an Alpha course and social events. We are affiliated to Dawlish, and work with the other main churches of the area and are strong supporters of Fair Trade and aid to the Developing World.

417 Combeinteignhead, All Saints
Grade II

A fine Norman font testifies to the existence of a church here in the 11th century, though the building is first mentioned in registers for 1250. The fine carved oak rood screen dates from c.1450, while the Elizabethan carved bench ends in the north transept are considered among the best in the country. Extensive restoration work occurred in the 19th century. There is a peal of six bells, one of which is an Alphabet Bell, bearing marks of the medieval bell-founders of Exeter. A small, but faithful, congregation welcomes locals and visitors to Sunday services, while this rural church enjoys popular children's services each month.

418 Dawlish, St Gregory the Great
Grade II*

Originally built in Saxon times, this church was rebuilt in 1875, using grey limestone ashlar with Bath stone dressings. The tower is of red sandstone and is believed to have existed before 1438, and houses a peal of eight bells. In 1984 the narthex was built, providing a ground floor reception office and toilets. A stairway leads to the upper floor with a kitchen, a large meeting room, used for various activities, and the Sunday School. St Gregory's aim is to offer a witness to the people of Dawlish through its various services and through work in local schools and its youth club. We offer a warm welcome to all.

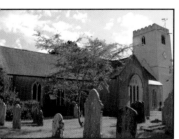

419 Denbury, St Mary the Virgin
Grade I

This beautiful church dates from 1291 and is cruciform in shape. Its beauty lies in its simple yet well-ordered interior. The east window depicts Jesus' baptism, crucifixion and ascension and is very fine. There is a wooden medieval screen in the north transept which came from Dartington's old church and the screen in the south transept was crafted by a villager in 1988. The 62ft tower houses five bells, the oldest from 1631, and also contains a clock dated 1730 which only has one hand. The musicians' gallery supports the villagers' millennium tapestry, which is well worth seeing because it depicts all aspects of Denbury village.

420 Doccombe Chapel (Moretonhampstead)
Grade II*

Set in a farmyard, Doccombe Chapel opened as a place of worship in 1878. The original building was a barn belonging to the Gregory family who paid for the conversion helped by public subscription. The ministry was shared by the rectors of Moretonhampstead, Dunsford and Hennock until 1926 when Moretonhampstead took sole responsibility. Today, the chapel holds one Communion service a month as well as, most appropriately for this special place, Harvest Thanksgiving and a Carol Service. Although it is not consecrated several baptisms have been performed and recently two Doccombe residents were married under a special license.

421 Doddiscombsleigh, St Michael
Grade I

Built around 1450 incorporating some Saxon masonry, then significantly restored in the 1870s, St. Michael's was too hidden in the wooded tributary valley to the River Teign to attract the attention of the Roundheads. The wonderful medieval stained glass, including a Seven Sacrament window, survived and is now a national treasure. Even today the entrance is elusive, but worth finding to note the unusually shaped and varied stones of the walls and tower, handsome foliage capitals inside and the glorious view of Haldon. The fine bells are rung by an enthusiastic team. A monthly Eucharist plus services on special occasions throughout the year – and for all a warm welcome is assured.

422 Dunchideock, St Michael & All Angels
Grade I

Nestling in the lee of Great Haldon, and surrounded by farmland, St Michael & All Angels dates from the late 14th century and was significantly restored in the late 19th. The restored rood screen is of great beauty, deeply and richly carved, and there are notable roof bosses and bench ends. There is a striking memorial to General Stringer-Lawrence, who is also commemorated by the triangular tower on the hill known as Haldon Belvedere. A scattered village, Dunchideock has a strong sense of community and people are very proud and supportive of their parish church. Sunday services range from traditional to informal and, for visitor and worshipper, a warm welcome is assured.

423 Dunsford, St Mary
Grade I

Built c.1450 incorporating stone remains from 1260, then significantly restored in 1846, St Mary's stands prominently at the heart of this picturesque village in the beautiful Teign Valley. The massive timbers under the gallery came from Powderham estate, while the imposing tomb in the north east belongs to the Fulford family who go back to Richard I's reign and still live at Great Fulford. The striking roof bosses in the chancel include the Star of David and a Jewish seven-branch candlestick. A strong competitive team ring regularly with enthusiasm. Sunday services range from traditional to informal, attracting all ages throughout the year. For visitor and worshipper, a warm welcome is assured.

424 East Teignmouth, St Michael the Archangel
Grade II

There has been a church on this site since before 1044. The Saxon church survived a French invasion in 1690 and was demolished and rebuilt in 1823. The tower was added in 1887, and eight bells hung in 1897, celebrating Queen Victoria's Jubilees. The Lady chapel was added 1925 and a chapel of remembrance in 1932. In 1992 the west end was modified to provide narthex rooms for social occasions, meetings, crèche, Sunday Club and other groups. The church hosts choral and classical concerts for the benefit of the wider community. We are part of a team of six churches and known as a happy and welcoming church.

425 Exminster, St Martin of Tours
Grade I

The building, at the heart of the community, dates from the 14th century and is constructed from locally quarried red sandstone. It consists of chancel, nave, south aisle, south porch and a 70ft west tower containing a peal of eight bells. The barrel-vaulted ceiling of the lady chapel, dated to 1633, is notable for its 16 moulded panels of the apostles and evangelists. Worship embraces a pattern of services, including both traditional and modern. A wide range of groups and activities throughout the week cater for all ages. Redevelopment has led to an increase in the local population, so St Martin's continues an active outreach to the community.

426 Haccombe, St Blaise
Grade I

Nestling close to Haccombe House, an ancient seat of the Carews, Lercedekenes and de Haccombes, this simple sandstone building houses some remarkable treasurers. Built in 1233 and enlarged in the 14th century, later restorations have retained its character. Among adornments from the 13th and 14th centuries are fine effigies (including that of the crusader founder and an unusual alabaster heart burial effigy), rare floor tiles and glass window lights. The following three centuries contributed particularly Flemish glass windows, an imposing Courtenay family effigy and brasses. Ornate Georgian stonework is seen in the screen, pulpit and reredos. The weekly services in this rural church adhere to the Book of Common Prayer.

427 Hennock, St Mary
Grade I

There has probably been a church on this site for over a thousand years, and the worshipping community today both draws from this and looks to serve God in the future. The old name of the village was Hainoc, as mentioned in the Domesday Book. The first Saxon church was most likely of oak timber, and the present font, which is late Norman work about 1170, is from this era. The oldest part of the church is the tower, built in 1250, the rest, including the screens and ceilure, about 1450. The wonderful old rood screen contains 44 panels with pictures of saints. The congregation is small but welcoming.

428 Highweek, All Saints
Grade I

Consecrated in 1428 and restored in the late 19th century it was a chapel of ease to Kingsteignton until 1864. The chancel was rebuilt and extended in 1892, and the south aisle was lengthened in 1892. There are an aisled nave with chancel, south porch and west tower. Internal features include the Ten Commandments flanking the east window; restored 15th-century wagon roofs to the aisles; the 15th-century font; and brass eagle lectern. Memorials include that to Walter Wemyss Leslie, d.1863, by Pickering of Carlisle and Elizabeth Hocombe d.1780. The stained glass is mainly of the late 19th century, apart from some medieval stained glass in the top of a north window.

429 Holcombe (Dawlish), St George

The church, built in 1867, was originally the village school (but with the provision for worship on Sundays). The school ceased in the 1870s, and in 1893 the building was enlarged by the addition of a chancel, sanctuary and organ recess. In the mid 1930s choir stalls, a pulpit and pews were installed. The organ was installed in 1939, and the church was consecrated in 1945. A new choir vestry and small meeting room and kitchen were built in 1981.

430 Holcombe Burnell, St John the Baptist
Grade II*

Although Christian worship at the site of the present church preceded the Norman period, a more permanent building was then erected, parts of which remain. Much of the present building dates from the late 15th century, when the adjoining Barton was acquired by the Tudor politician, Sir Thomas Dennis. These include the tower and arcades of the main aisle, the mullioned windows and clear glass, the font and the rare Easter sepulchre. The church was restored in 1843-1844. The 16th-century altar chest (probably Spanish) and the organ are from Culver House. There are six bells. Although some way from the village of Longdown, services are held every Sunday.

431 Ide, St Ida
Grade II

Bishop Leofric set up the first church in Ide soon after 1057. No trace exists. The next church which follows was built during the period 1253 to 1291. All that remains of this second church is the base of the tower. The third parish church was really an enlargement of the second. The fourth and existing church was consecrated by the Bishop of Exeter on Friday 19th September 1834, the tower being all that is left of any previous churches. Dedicated to St Ida of Herzfeld in Germany whose great-grandfather was Charles Martel. She was canonised in 980 on 26th November.

432 Ideford, St Mary the Virgin
Grade II

There has probably been a church here for over 1000 years. The bell tower (14th-century or earlier) and the nave and aisle (14th and 15th-century) are the oldest surviving parts. A Saxon connection is given added weight because in 1850 a carved lintel was dug up dating from 1050-1100. This was incorporated into the 'new' building and can be seen outside, on the south wall of the chancel. In 1990 Ideford became part of the Haldon Team Ministry and a major project to replace the present flooring, seating and heating was launched in 2006, completion due in 2008. We now embark on developing our Mission Community.

433 Ilsington, St Michael
Grade I

The first written record of St Michael's is dated 1187; it is today a mainly 15th-century structure. It is one of the finest examples of Dartmoor churches with two chapels either side of the chancel. A richly carved rood screen leads to the nave separated from two side aisles by 10 granite arcades, supported on slender pillars. The two Devonshire barrel roofs joining in a central boss make up a spectacular roof. Many other features include medieval bench ends and a 14th-century piscina. In the churchyard there are ruined remains of the manor house. Close links with two church schools and parish organisations ensure the church remains a living symbol of centuries of faith.

434 Ipplepen, St Andrew
Grade I

This large light church is at the centre of village life in every way. Its 14th-century tower dominates the village and holds an ancient clock and a peal of eight bells. The third building on this site, it is mostly 14th-century with carved and decorated 15th-century rood screen and pulpit and Beer stone font. Traces of the earlier buildings remain, including some Norman carving. The high altar, consecrated in 1318, is enclosed by oak rails dated 1724. St Andrew's has an active choir, well-attended traditional worship, and a monthly service for younger families. There is a website and a quarterly newsletter, and an active outreach with many social activities.

435 Kenn, St Andrew
Grade I

St Andrew's dominates the picturesque Kenn valley. The sandstone church with its buttressed tower is essentially a 14th-century structure, with a well-preserved medieval rood screen, the interior refurnished during the 19th century. The font, however, is Norman and a charter dated c.1150 refers to the church. A Saxon foundation is likely and the churchyard, with its old meadow flora and ancient yew, almost certainly predates it. The large hollow yew is probably in excess of 1500 years of age, indicative of an early Christian remnant marker. St Andrew's, which enjoys strong links with the local Primary School, remains a focal point for the village communities that it serves.

436 Kenton, All Saints
Grade I

Visitors to this lovely village are stunned by the size and beauty of the 14th-century church at its heart. An archaeological survey, prior to the major refurbishment of 2008, revealed walls of two earlier churches and the remains of a medieval bell-foundry. The magnificent screen, dating from 1455, was restored in the early 20th century in memory of one of the Courtenay family. The 15th-century pulpit, the Lady chapel, the Lumley memorial cross and the great reredos all have their own fascinating story. Today the church is the home of a growing and lively congregation where all ages are warmly welcomed and work together to show and proclaim the love of God.

437 Kingskerswell, St Mary
Grade II*

Situated on the ancient route between Newton Abbot and Torquay, Kingskerswell parish church stands in its own valley close to the ruins of the manor that it once served as a chapel. The building pre-dates 1301. Once a cuneiform building, it was enlarged in the 15th century. The tower contains six bells and the Diamond Jubilee clock for Queen Victoria. Little remains of the medieval glass and the choir screen has also gone. Some of the Victorian pews have been removed to create a refreshment area with kitchen at the rear of the building. The altar table is made of Devon oak and elm and represents the empty tomb on Easter Day.

438 Kingsteignton, St Michael
Grade II*

There has been a church here since the Saxon times. Bishop Walter Stapeldon consecrated the present building on 3 May 1318. Built of red sandstone, it was enlarged during the 14th century and the limestone tower added 50 years later. Extensive restoration took place in the mid 19th century. There is an interesting monumental inscription on the chancel floor. The fine organ is located under the tower and a second organ above the vicar's vestry. There are 8 bells. They have been rung for worship every Sunday since the end of World War II. The Parish Eucharist is celebrated each Sunday; evening services include Choral Evensong.

439 Leusdon, St John the Baptist
Grade II

Built of granite in 1863 by Charlotte Rosamund Larpent, St John the Baptist stands some 850ft above sea level on the edge of Dartmoor with a spectacular southern aspect towards the South Hams. It is part of the Ashburton and Moorland Team of churches. The architect created a welcoming and friendly building which enjoys the love of many in this scattered parish. Two lovely tapestries, made by parishioners as a Millennium project, hang at the west end of the church. With a wonderful acoustic, graciously carved reredos and an enthusiastic choir and organist, we warmly welcome visitors and walkers to our services, which are held each Sunday.

440 Lustleigh, St John the Baptist
Grade I

Standing in the centre of the village, the church was built in what is thought to have been a 5th- or 6th-century Christian graveyard. The earliest part of the church is the 13th-century chancel, remarkable for the beautiful rood screen, ascribed to the reign of Mary Tudor. The north aisle was added in the late 15th century; at its west end stand Datuidoc's Stone, certainly the oldest monument in the church, moved in 1979 to its present site from the floor of the south porch. Datuidoc was probably a Christian, buried in the already existing graveyard, where the stone was raised to his memory in about 550 to 600.

441 Luton (Ideford), St John the Evangelist — *Grade II*

Built in 1853 as a chapel of ease to the parish church of Bishopsteignton by the Revd W. R. Ogle, constructed of grey limestone, the church seats about 100. The east window commemorates Captain John Henry Rhodes, the chief benefactor. The west window was removed from Bishopsteignton Church and is in memory of the Revd W. Ogle. The church became a parish church before being made a chapel of ease once again when the parishes of Ideford and Luton were combined, although it remains licensed for weddings, baptisms and funerals. Monthly evening services are held, also festival services such as Harvest, Christmas, Easter and Mothering Sunday when the church is packed.

442 Mamhead (Kenton), St Thomas the Apostle — *Grade II**

Probably 13th-century or earlier in origin, with a 15th-century north aisle; south transept probably 13th or 14th-century but much altered, with a 15th-century tower. It comprises nave, chancel, west tower, south transept and porch, north aisle, and vestry. There were a sequence of 19th-century restorations; one before 1830 attributable to Salvin; reseating of 1854 by Mackintosh; and a further restoration of 1915. Fittings include the 1909 timber reredos carved with the crucifixion, the 1914 timber drum pulpit, the timber eagle lectern with memorial date of 1904, and the 19th-century font with a carved bowl. There are a number of monuments, and fragments of medieval glass in the chancel.

443 Manaton, St Winifred — *Grade I*

Situated below Manaton Rocks, St Winifred's dates from the early 15th century when the nave and chancel were built of granite in the Perpendicular style. The tower and aisles were added c.1500, the former housing six bells, two dating back to the 1440s. There are five stained-glass windows, the oldest glass dating from the 15th century and the most modern, a Brangwyn window, from 1929. The outstanding historical feature of the church is the carved, painted screen put up around 1500 and literally defaced in 1548 during the Reformation. St Winifred's is an integral part of a united benefice, has services every Sunday and home groups meeting throughout the year.

444 Milber, St Luke — *Grade II*

The origins of the parish lie in the post First World War period, with the construction of a temporary church in 1929. The Revd William Keble Martin famously had a dream about a church with three naves, relating his vision to his architect brother Arthur, who drew up plans for the present building. The foundation stone was laid in 1936, and the Lady chapel and south nave were completed; further work was not possible as the Second World War intervened. It was left to the Revd John Hammond to complete the task, the completed building being consecrated in 1963. In keeping with its origins, the parish maintains the orthodox catholic tradition.

445 Moretonhampstead, St Andrew — *Grade I*

St Andrew's stands on a magnificent site with its 90ft tower dominating the village – grandly austere with its staircase turret and four pinnacles; this was under construction in 1418. Inside the church the markings of a high pitched roof can be seen, evidence of a smaller church to which the tower was added. The porch stands out from the south wall, square and battlemented, with an upper chamber; on the east wall, the medieval holy water stoup is still intact. Although the church has suffered some Victorian 'restoration' the building retains the characteristics of a typical 15th-century Devon church, still beautifully cared for and well-loved.

446 North Bovey, St John the Baptist
Grade I

Situated among pretty thatched cottages and adjacent to the village green, parts of St John's date from the 13th century although the major part is 15th-century. There are barrel-vaulted ceilings over the nave and north and south aisles, and in the chancel, some ancient roof bosses, one showing three rabbits, their ears meeting and forming a triangle, symbolic of the Blessed Trinity. The 15th-century rood screen is of oak with panelling and tracery, and has figures of the twelve apostles carved into the entrance arch. The church, which is open during daylight hours, is well kept by a small but loyal group of parishioners and the churchyard is a peaceful sanctuary with views to Dartmoor.

447 Ogwell East, St Bartholomew
Grade I

The present building is mid-15th-century: it has a nave with rood screen, chancel, north aisle, family chapel, and tower with six bells. It was restored in 1886. Outside are two halves of an early carved Christian memorial stone to "Caocus Son of Peblig" a local chieftain who died around the year 500. These are built into the gables at the east and west end of the north aisle. We have mission links in Sudan, in Paraguay, with OM Ships and support Send a Cow and Fairtrade projects. St Bartholomew's is open each day. We meet for worship every Sunday morning and visitors are always welcome.

448 Ogwell West
Grade I

THE CHURCHES
CONSERVATION TRUST

Approached by winding, undulating lanes, West Ogwell has an atmosphere of remote obscurity which belies its closeness to Newton Abbot. The church stands on a knoll, with open views across the landscape, beside the former manor house built in 1790. It seems that the chancel and nave, which are of similar length, were built around 1300. A two-storey west tower was added to this cruciform building around 1400. Its exterior is severely plain but inside, apart from the medieval roof, 13th-century sedilia and a simple Jacobean pulpit, it is mostly late Georgian, with box pews, tiered benches in front of the tower screen and elegantly curved Communion rails.

449 Oldridge, St Thomas
Grade II

This quiet simple stone church stands in the garden of Oldridge Barton at the end of a lane running west along the ridge from Whitestone. The Cheriton family own the farm and care for the little church rebuilt in 1841. There had been a church on the site since 1100 and the font outdates the present church. The stained-glass window in the chancel commemorates Mrs Medley who was sadly killed returning to Exeter after the official rededication ceremony when the brakes on the hired carriage driven by the vicar failed on Nadderwater hill. Four services a year, weddings and christenings attract many outsiders, visitors as well as regulars.

450 Pathfinder (Whitestone), St John the Evangelist

Built on mobile home lines of Canadian Cedar Wood by Messrs Horton Brothers, it was erected in 1981. It is 36ft long with a transept north and south, and a vestry. The bell is outside but rung from within the church. The furnishings are the work of residents in the village. Altar, altar rails, credence table, reading desk, Methodist book table and all the hassocks are handmade. The cross on the east wall is handmade from Pathfinder oak. The heating is in the ceiling. There is one Sunday Holy Communion and one Evensong each month and Holy Communion every Thursday morning.

451 Powderham, St Clement Bishop & Martyr
Grade II*

A church was consecrated at Powderham in 1259, probably in the present north aisle. This was extended to include the nave and south aisle and the tower in the late 15th century. The sanctuary was extended in the 19th century in memory of the 10th Earl of Devon. Much of the stained glass is of this date. The church was occupied by Parliamentary forces during the English Civil War, when they besieged the castle, and they made holes in this door for their muskets, which were expertly repaired but may still be seen. There are six bells. All services are according to the Book of Common Prayer of 1662.

452 Shaldon, St Nicholas (Ringmore)
Grade II

This church was built c.1280 by the family of Stephen de Haccombe, probably on the site of a Saxon place of worship. As the hamlet of Ringmore grew, so did the church – by 32ft with a three-tier pulpit, unsightly galleries and a Saxon font. But Shaldon grew too and, when a new larger church was erected there, St Nicholas reverted to its previous size. Church architects agree that the east end wall is the original structure. It became a chapel of ease but remains in regular use for Sunday worship and is surrounded by a picturesque churchyard.

453 Shaldon, St Peter
Grade I

This church, consecrated in 1902, replaced the earlier, much smaller, parish church in Ringmore. The chancel and lady chapel contain beautiful coloured marble but are surpassed by the magnificent marble pulpit. Five figures stand on the rood screen and the unusual font is a marble statute of John the Baptist holding a clamshell. The Crown of Thorns is echoed in the tracery throughout the church. Rebuilt in 1985, the organ is acknowledged as one of the best in Devon. The church is regularly used for musical and other events, including by the Shaldon Singers, the Shaldon Festival, the local school and the Horticultural Society.

454 Shillingford, St George the Martyr
Grade II*

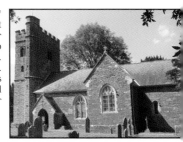

It is built of red sandstone, dating from the 14th century and set in a quiet rural situation. Originally the domestic chapel of the Shillingford family. Sir William Huddesfield, Recorder of the City of Exeter and Attorney General to Edward IV, purchased the lands, enlarged the church and erected the tower. The tomb of Sir William and his wife is on the north side of the chancel. The ancient door has a Sanctuary Ring in the centre. Much restoration was carried out in the mid-1880s. A small but welcoming church with varied forms of worship. Present aims are focusing on reaching out to the wider community and encouraging young people.

455 Starcross, St Paul
Grade II

Built in 1828, the church lies at the heart of the village. Set back from the Exe Estuary, it is a substantial building of stone consisting of chancel and nave (reputed to have the widest unsupported roof in Devon) with a small western turret. There are a number of interesting 19th and early-20th-century features. Each stone was shipped across the Exe Estuary, coming originally from a chapel in Exmouth. In 1987 the western gallery was brought forward and community rooms formed, providing a well-used parish and community resource. The lively and friendly village church (now part of the Dawlish group of churches) has weekly worship to suit all ages.

456 Stokeinteignhead, St Andrew
Grade II*

This delightful 12th-century church with its distinguishable wagon-shaped roof is set in the heart of the quaint village of Stokeinteignhead. The building originally consisted only of nave and chancel, the aisles being added during the 15th century. Interesting features include an original 600-year-old door, sandstone capitals of several saints including our own patron saint, St Andrew. Visitors will delight in the heart-shaped brass in front of the pulpit with its curious engravings that mark the grave of Elizabeth Furlong, whose family owned the Manor of Gabwell. There is a weekly Sunday Eucharist, growing Junior Church, choir and bell-ringers and a warm welcome.

457 Tedburn St Mary, St Mary
Grade II*

This welcoming church is situated in the old part of Tedburn St Mary, next to a donkey sanctuary, a mile from the centre of the village. It is unlocked daily except during January and February. The earliest part of the building, the Lady chapel, dates from the 13th century; the tower is a little later, the bells dating from 1736, the chancel 1868. There are strong links with the Methodists and together we organise annual Tent Services after the September Village Fair. We have varied services, one every Sunday; once a quarter joining with nearby parishes. The words over the entrance door are "Surely the Lord is in this place".

458 Teigngrace, St Peter & St Paul
Grade II*

This church was dedicated in 1787 by James and George Templer Esqs and the Revd John Templer Esq, vicar of Teigngrace, who demolished the earlier church and rebuilt. Restored in 1872, it comprises west tower, nave and chancel with equal north and south transepts and apse in Gothic style, with large Gothic timber windows. The interior is also Gothic, including an important 18th-century organ by Davis of London, a hexagonal limestone font, and the box pew of the south transept. The reordering of 1872 contributed the pews and Communion rails. There are a fine series of mural tablets, including those to Charles Templer (d.1786); to James Templer of Stover (d.1782); and to his wife Mary (d.1784).

459 Teignmouth (West), St James the Less
Grade II*

The Norman church dates from 1256. Originally built of stone in cruciform design with a red sandstone tower 54ft high, the oldest building in the town. The belfry ladder in the tower 22ft high kept in place by its weight. Still sound and strong after seven centuries. The church, apart from the tower, was rebuilt in 1821. It is one of few octagonal churches in England with a centre lantern 62ft high. There is a 14th-century reredos, a clock, bells and organ. St James' has always had close links with Bishopsteignton and East Teignmouth and this continues as all now form the Haldon Team Mission Community.

460 Torbryan, Holy Trinity
Grade I

THE CHURCHES CONSERVATION TRUST

This is a 15th-century building with an imposing tower. The white Beer stone arcades, the plastered walls and ceilings, and the uninterrupted light coming through the large windows of clear glass make a perfect setting for the screen, pulpit and altar table. It is all highly "atmospheric". The carved woodwork of the altar table is of exceptional beauty. The 15th-century seating is preserved, encased within early-19th-century box pews which all have brass candleholders. Holy Trinity is a redundant church maintained by the Churches Conservation Trust and there are only a few services a year. These are held at Epiphany, Easter, Trinity and Harvest.

461 Trusham, St Michael the Archangel — Grade II

Trusham Church is the oldest of the Teign Valley churches, being listed in the Domesday Survey of 1086 as belonging to Buckfast Abbe. The church in its present form was completed in the 15th century. The most notable features are the 17th-century Stookes monument and the 16th-century Staplehill monument. Also of interest are the 12th-century font and the piscina. In the tower, there are six bells, one of which dates from 1450. Located at the highest part of the village, our aim is to bring together this small rural community, putting a Christian presence at the heart of our village.

462 Whitestone, St Catherine — Grade I

Set high on south-facing hills this small 13th-century church has been a landmark for sailors entering the Exe Estuary for many centuries and is still privileged to fly the white ensign from its tower. Inside the plain granite pillars and sandstone arches complement the colours of the remaining front of a 17th-century west gallery embellished with the arms of bishops of Exeter. A tower with six bells, which are regularly rung, a leper's squint and some medieval glass in the windows are other significant features. We are a small, faithful congregation doing our best to reach out into the community and provide a ministry for all ages.

463 Widecombe-in-the-Moor, St Pancras — Grade I

Known as the Cathedral of the Moor, this church was built in the 15th century and the tower added in the 16th. Major repairs were undertaken to the tower in 2002. Of special interest are the roof bosses above the nave, and the remaining base of an ancient rood screen; also a vivid description of the lightning strike on the church in 1643, on a plaque under the tower. St Catherine's chapel provides a quiet place for prayer. The church's uncluttered interior, and acoustic qualities make it much sought after for concerts. Special Plough and Rogation services are held in due season as well as the usual range of services each month.

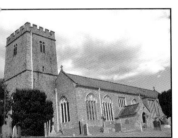

464 Wolborough, St Mary the Virgin — Grade I

A church has stood on the site for 1000 years and is mentioned in the Domesday Book; it originally served the now disappeared village of Uleborough. The church is a noble building, grade I listed in a Perpendicular style with tall pillars having differently carved capitals, it has an early 20th-century barrel roof. It noted for its magnificent medieval rood screen and fine peal of eight bells. The church is normally open for visitors on Sunday afternoons May-Sept. It serves a parish covering part of Newton Abbot and is a popular wedding choice. There are services every Sunday and visitors are always welcome.

465 Wolborough, St Paul's Newton Abbot — Grade II

This church was built to meet railway expansion in 1861. It is of a cruciform design and was enlarged in 1886. It is a light and airy building with a spacious interior reordered in 1977. A new hall and church complex was added in 1998. The church is open daily during office hours. It has a lively church community meeting every Sunday, and visitors are always welcome. Regular worship ranges from modern Fresh Expressions to more traditional Eucharist. We have mission links in Sudan, in Paraguay, with OM Ships, and a recent Youth Group visit to Uganda led to a partnership with a school and orphanage in Kampala.

466 Woodland, St John the Baptist

Grade I

This tiny church serving a farming community is well worth a visit. Built by villagers in 1499 it was unaltered till the near-perfect Victorian interior added the pews, screen, panelling, altar and a splendid barrel roof. The Norman font survives with other features around the nave. The rear wall has a pre-Reformation cope altered to be a frontal in that period, and other walls hold charity panels and monuments. The kneelers reflect village scenes and farming in all seasons. The hall across the small square has a very fine village tapestry. A small congregation keep the church to a fine standard and visitors are welcome to regular worship.

TORBAY

One of the more densely populated parts of 'old' Devon, Torbay – or the 'English Riviera' - is traditionally associated with the Great British seaside holiday with the coastal towns of Torquay, Paignton and Brixham, as well as lesser-known settlements, such as Goodrington or Babbacombe. There are 24 Church of England churches in 'The Bay', offering a varied experience of worship, architecture and history.

467 Babbacombe, All Saints
Grade I

Consecrated in 1867, All Saints was designed by the distinguished Victorian architect William Butterfield in the Gothic style, using local red sandstone with Bath stone dressings. It is regarded as one of his most important churches. A notable feature of the ornate interior is the use of a wide range of coloured marbles. Along with Butterfield's magnificent pulpit and font, All Saints boasts some fine Victorian and Edwardian stained glass. Built in an era when high-church ideals were being restored, All Saints maintains a strong catholic tradition in its worship to this day. A more informal children's service brings together some of the younger families in the parish.

468 Brixham, St Mary the Virgin
Grade II*

Built of local sandstone, with a tower of 104ft, boasting ten bells, and standing proudly in its immense churchyard one mile above the harbour, St Mary's is the ancient parish church of Brixham. Originally serving the agricultural community of 'Cowtown' it embraced the growing fishing community of 'Fishtown' until All Saints was built. The spacious lofty nave is filled with light from the many stained-glass windows and the simple interior resounds with six hundred years of prayer and devotion. Worship is centred on the Eucharist, and there is a fine organ in regular use. The church is accessible for wheelchair users, and the congregation is welcoming and inclusive.

469 Chelston, St Matthew
Grade II*

This church was built in 1896 and is regarded as one of the finest churches of the late Victorian era. It is of the catholic design in its features with the roof bosses stressing the sacraments and in its original plans there was to be a crucifix placed looking down the main street of the parish. St Matthew's is a warm church built in the local red sandstone and was needed because of the arrival of the railways in Torbay. St Matthew's has a unique set of stained-glass windows from the turn of the 20th century and a font with an unusual pulley system lid.

470 Chelston, St Peter (Queensway)

St Peter's was built in 1961 with the intention of serving the new housing estate established in lower Chelston. After some years of great success there were years of decline and it is now being revamped into a church community centre serving the lower Chelston area and the parish as a whole. It is typical of 1960s design. Its future use as a church centre has led to the church being redesigned as a multi-purpose area. A chapel is used for mid-week services. New building work will involve a large meeting room, kitchen, café and youth room. The latter will house a club of over 120 members.

TORBAY

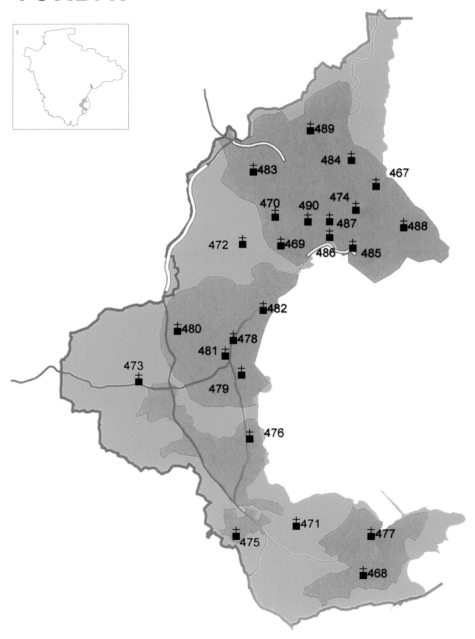

THE PILGRIM'S GUIDE TO DEVON'S CHURCHES

471 Churston Ferrers, St Mary the Virgin — *Grade II**

Worship at a Saxon cross was followed by a Norman manorial chapel, which was enlarged by manor tenants, Bozuns and Ferrers, who added a porch, parvise, tower, nave and north aisle. By 1480 the church belonged to the village and the Yardes had converted the original chapel to a Perpendicular south aisle. Major restoration work in 1864 was led by Lord Churston's family. The east window was given by Agatha Christie in 1957. Recent changes include modern utilities, a churchyard and, in 2002, the restoration of the cross. Six bells, the earliest 1440, summon to Sung Eucharist services and many weddings. The choir, flower arrangers and social gatherings are all active.

472 Cockington, St George & St Mary — *Grade II**

This church is set in the middle of Cockington Country Park. Dating back to 1069, it was built by the Normans and remained a private chapel despite its size until 1881, when it became the parish church of the newly constituted parish of Cockington. Some special features of the church are a Commonwealth bell, a pulpit which is thought to have come from a Spanish galleon beached on Torre Abbey sands at the time of the Armada, a much-admired screen (1917) and aisle pillars. Services are held here every Sunday and Wednesday and many weddings take place each year. The church is normally open during the day and is much visited.

473 Collaton St Mary, St Mary the Virgin — *Grade II**

This church was built in 1864-1866, designed by J. W. Rowell of Newton Abbot along with the village school and vicarage, for the Revd John Roughton Hogg of Blagdon, as a memorial to Hogg's daughter who died in 1864. The contractor was Harvey of Torquay; the carved work by Mr Jackman of Teignmouth. It comprises nave, chancel, south west tower, porch, vestry and organ chamber. The interior contains a well-preserved set of 1860s fittings and decoration, including a grand marble font with suspended cover, given by Miss Durant of Sharpham, carved by Earp to the designs of Bentley, and elaborate stone reredos, also by Bentley and Earp, with a sculpture by Phyffers depicting the Last Supper.

474 Ellacombe, Christ Church — *Grade II*

A moderate-sized town church (built 1868-1907), Christ Church is now the only church in a densely populated Urban Priority Area, other denominations all having re-located since 1945. Externally and internally unadorned, its broad 14-metre nave is roofed with an outstanding pine vault of great complexity; and the south aisle is supported on slender quatrefoil section cast-iron columns with Corinthian capitals. The small, energetic congregation has renovated the whole building over the past decade. In tandem with neighbouring St John's Torquay, it reaches out to the poor and populous parish they share. The contiguous parish hall is the nearest thing Ellacombe has to a community centre.

475 Galmpton (Churston Ferrers), Chapel of the Good Shepherd

A Vale Farm cider barn was sold on generous terms by Mrs Jane Tully to Churston Ferrers parish to be converted to a chapel of ease. Galmpton village had become more populous than Churston and both places needed a church hall. The conversion was carried out by parishioners, known as the 'Pick and Shovel Brigade', in nine months. Gifts for furnishing poured in and the Bishop of Plymouth dedicated it in 1961. It is in regular weekly use for Eucharist services, for Lent and study meetings, baptisms and funerals. The reredos paintings, copies of Fra Angelico angels, are by the daughter of the Revd H. F. Lyte. Above this peaceful little chapel is the hall.

476 Goodrington, St George

Designed by Sir Edward Maufe, architect of Guildford Cathedral, the foundations were laid in 1938. The choir, tower and transepts were consecrated on the 25th March 1939, the nave added in 1962. The transepts have been enhanced by spectacular stained-glass windows by Dom. Charles Norris of Buckfast Abbey and the west window depicts the imposing figure of St George, after whom the church is named. Open all day, Morning and Evening Prayer and the Eucharist are central to our daily worship. The Sunday liturgy includes traditional and contemporary music, with term-time Sunday School and monthly All-Age worship. A friendly church, we are open to God and open to all.

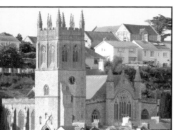

477 Lower Brixham, All Saints
Grade I

The present building is a late Victorian replacement for the original. In the early 19th century, when the fishing port of Lower Brixham was a new and raucous boom-town without its own church, the Church Commissioners paid for the first church on the site. The vicar, Revd Henry Francis Lyte, became famous for his pioneering pastoral work among the fishing community and for his hymns, especially 'Abide with me' which today is played each evening on a carillon. Our link with the fishing industry is still valued and we mark it in an annual Harvest of the Sea celebration.

478 Paignton, Christ Church
Grade II

This church was built in 1888 in the Gothic style. It was designed to seat a vast congregation and this is reflected in the sheer scale of the building. The bell tower was never completed, though the plinth remains visible. The original iron church of 1886 is still in use as the church hall. The interior of the church reflects the evangelical tradition that the church was built in and that it continues to reflect in its worshipping life. Christ Church continues the vision of the founders of the church, an evangelical church that seeks to proclaim the good news of Christ in its local community, with various services held every Sunday.

479 Paignton, St Andrew
Grade II

This is a fine late-19th-century aisled church built in a transitional Decorated/Early English style in the 1890s, extended in 1920 by W. D. Caröe. Large and spacious, it has always stood in the catholic tradition of the Church of England, to which the high altar, with its large set of six candles and crucifix, the lady chapel, with the Sacrament reserved in a lovely tabernacle, plus the statues of Our Lady and St Andrew, bear sufficient testimony. There is a Sung Mass each Sunday morning and a weekday Mass on Wednesday morning. Attempts are being made to increase the size of the congregation to a church which offers traditional catholic worship.

480 Paignton, St Boniface

This is a hall church dedicated in 1961 by Bishop Robert Mortimer. The sanctuary area is screened off from the hall with a glass screen and contains a marble altar which the bishop consecrated at the same time, and which has enclosed relics of St Vincent, martyr and the confessor Victorinus. There is a Sung Mass each Sunday with a Sunday School at the same time, and a weekday Mass on Tuesday morning. Set in the middle of a large housing estate, St Boniface witnesses to the importance of the Christian faith and its witness to God's love shown in Jesus. A new development is planned which would include a new church.

481 Paignton, St John the Baptist
Grade II

This church has Saxon foundations, some remaining Norman work (including the recycled west door, some pillars and the font) and a 14th-century porch; the nave is mainly 15th-century. Remarkable is the 15th-century stone screen of the Kirkham Chapel. The pulpit is a rare 15th-century one. Samuel Chapin was baptised and married in the church, then sailed as a Pilgrim Father to America and was one of the founders of Springfield, Massachusetts. The church has links with the Oxford Movement – John Keble was offered the living – and still stands in the catholic tradition. There is a daily Eucharist, and two main services on Sunday morning, one traditional, the other more informal.

482 Paignton, St Paul Preston

The church, erected in 1939 and the third on the site, is built in the Devonshire style with its lofty tower and barrel ceiling. The fittings by Wippells of Exeter include a finely carved reredos depicting the Emmaus Supper. A flight of steps leading up to "the chapel of the sea" is an interesting feature. The hall was added in 1969, and the meeting porch in 1990. An illuminated cross over the tower, "the Light over Preston", can be seen around the parish and out at sea, symbolising the mission of the church to those near and far. There is a broad spectrum of worship, a wide range of all-age activities, and firm community and overseas links.

483 Shiphay Collaton, St John the Baptist

The original building, completed in 1897, was the gift of the squire and intended primarily as a school, though suitable for use as a daughter church of St Marychurch at weekends. In the 1950s it was realised that Shiphay had become large enough to be an independent parish and the church was extended. Features include its bright interior, the beautiful west window and carved panels in the lady chapel and south aisle. Situated in the heart of Shiphay we aim to share the love of God within the community. Members work amongst the homeless in Torbay, run courses for those enquiring about Christian faith and a large children's work.

484 St Marychurch, St Mary the Virgin
Grade II

Originally built in 1856-1861 by J. W. Hugall, and then rebuilt in 1952-1956 after serious war damage, apart from the tower. Built of local grey limestone rubble with yellow sandstone dressings and a natural slate roof. It comprises nave, chancel, north and south aisles, and west tower. The 1950s rebuild is in a conventional Gothic style with a buttressed south aisle and traceried windows. There is a 12th-century font depicting a man on horseback with a bugle, a man with a dog, a man with a sword, a boar and dog, and a harp player. The pre-war rood screen remains; other internal fittings are post-war, and by Herbert Read of Exeter.

485 Torquay, St John
Grade I

St John's overlooks the harbour and fronts cliffs of the limestone from which G. E. Street constructed it (1861-1871) for the gentlefolk then wintering in Torquay. We inherit an architectural gem: stone vaulted chancel; Burne-Jones paintings; William Morris east and west windows; carved Caen stone, alabaster-framed reredos; Salviati Venetian mosaics; a rare immersion font; wrought iron parclose screen; minstrel's gallery; much Devon marble; a bishop's throne; a columbarium. A fine Walker organ complements congregational worship and public concerts. Our tower (1885) bears an illuminated cross which shines at night as a beacon to seafarers. Linked to Christ Church Ellacombe since 1990, we share their mission to populous and impoverished Ellacombe.

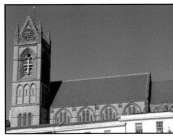

486 Torquay, St Luke
Grade II*

St Luke's overlooks the seafront in Torquay. An atmosphere of cheerful jubilation greets the visitor to this highly decorated church. The foundation stone was laid in 1861, and an interior with short iron columns was built. An apsed chancel roof depicts angels and the Benedicite. St Luke's flourished, but in troubled times in the 20th century there was a decline in attendance. In 1949 a young vibrant priest was presented to the living. His enthusiasm built up the spiritual life of the parish with such effort that it once again became one of the foremost churches in Torbay. St Luke's continues to offer varied forms of worship, traditional and contemporary.

487 Torquay, St Mary Magdalene (Upton)
Grade II*

This church was consecrated by Bishop Henry Phillpotts in 1849. The architect was Anthony Salvin and it was built in the Gothic Revival style. The spire rises 50m, dominating the skyline of Torquay. In 1855 an eight peal of bells was added and rung for the first time on Christmas Day. The new organ, built in 1880, was said to be one of the largest and most celebrated instruments in the south west. Railways had come and Torquay had become a very big tourist resort. Today the church reaches out to Torquay in Christ's name, seeking to meet, worship and grow in his presence.

488 Torquay, St Matthias (Ilsham)
Grade II*

150 years old in 2008, St Matthias' was designed in the Decorated style by Anthony Salvin, a leading exponent of the Victorian Gothic Revival. Among notable features are the carved alabaster reredos and pulpit, the oak 'Snelgrove Arch', the newly refurbished organ, and the stained glass in the east and west windows, the latter based on the Te Deum. The church is linked to the modern church centre, where activities extend from pre-school to senior citizens, counselling to dancing. We have close links with two church Primary Schools, and have a full-time youth worker. Our worship ranges from traditional to contemporary. We would love to welcome you.

489 Torquay, St Martin (Barton)
Grade II

Built during the Second World War, Saint Martin's has a well-maintained exterior and grounds, but the interior is truly splendid. The free-standing stone high altar bears witness to the centrality of the Eucharist in the life of the parish from the 1940s until the present day. An imposing canopy with a hanging crucifix over the altar adds to the grandeur. At the east end, behind the sanctuary, lies the lady chapel, tastefully reordered at the end of the last century. Both the church and adjoining hall are firmly at the heart of this large residential parish. The main Eucharist is on Sunday morning.

490 Torre, All Saints
Grade II

This church is in the original part of Torquay, called Torre, was designed by J. L. Pearson, architect of Truro Cathedral, and built as a daughter church to the ancient church of St Saviour. Agatha Christie's father was instrumental in its build; she was baptised here and she worshipped here. An item of interest is our beautiful Lady chapel. All Saints has always witnessed to the traditional catholic faith, as practised in the Church of England and the services are traditional. Outreach is active; our church school has 200 pupils; we have 100 annual baptisms and approximately 40 annual confirmations. We have a mass congregation of 200 and regular events and clubs.

TORRIDGE

Here, coast and countryside meet, including the tiny island of Lundy. From small village to bustling market towns, this area of North Devon has some spectacular views, notably across the Atlantic. Some of the 64 Anglican churches are dedicated to Celtic saints, such as Petroc or Nectan, typical of the north coast of Devon and Cornwall.

491 Abbots Bickington, St James   Grade II*

Often referred to as "the church in the farmyard", this smallest of churches is found at the end of a tree-lined pathway. The spire is just visible over the top of the tower which contains three bells. The east window has fragments of ancient stained glass. The nave is just 10ft wide and has seating for 22 worshippers. The other 22 sit in the transept. On the wall is a fine monument to Thomas Pollard who died in 1710 and who is buried beneath the altar. Although only around three dozen parishioners live in Abbots Bickington, the service register often records attendance at Festivals and special occasions as *church full*.

492 Abbotsham, St Helen   Grade II*

Abbotsham, 'the hamlet of the abbot', derives from the fact that originally the parish was under the care of the Abbey of Tavistock. Records show that there was an older church two miles away, but no ruins are left today. The Norman font with its cable moulding at the top and base was brought from there to the present church around 1280. One of the most interesting features of the church is the fine collection of bench ends dating from the 16th and 17th centuries. Some of these carvings were disfigured at the time of the Commonwealth. A small, well-maintained church with three traditional services on a Sunday.

493 Alverdiscott, All Saints   Grade II*

Alverdiscott means "Alfred's Cot", but goes back as a settlement to Iron Age times. The church is said to date from the 1400s. Rectors date from William of Brauntone 1297. Artefacts include font, holy water stoup, and porch door-case, all early Norman. In 1579, the north aisle was added by Richard Bellew. Here is an alabaster monument of Thomas Welshe, 10, who died in 1639. Restoration in the 1800s included removal of the rood screen and loft. An oak panel was added to the roof beam inscribed, "This is none other than the house of God, this is the gate of heaven". A small, friendly congregation. All visitors are welcome.

494 Alwington, St Andrew   Grade I

Its origins are unknown but there is evidence that a church has been on the site since the 13th century. At the corner of the tower is still the base of a 13th-century preaching cross that is a National Scheduled Monument. It is Grade I listed, with an elaborate, tall west tower with fine large gargoyles. The south aisle has high-quality masonry and fittings and is associated with the Pine-Coffin family, a member of whom has been patron since 1297. The church is acknowledged to be one of the most beautiful in north Devon with an ongoing and energetic ministry to a predominantly agricultural community.

495 Appledore, St Mary
Grade II*

Situated in the maritime settlement famous for shipbuilding, the church was built in 1838 to the typical Church Commissioners' plan to replace a chapel of ease to cater for the growing population of Appledore. The new church, built in a Gothic style, consisted originally of a nave, chancel and north and south aisles. In 1909 the west end of the church, including the tower, was completed by J. J. Smith of Bideford. One of the features of the church is the wealth of fine Victorian stained glass, and the south aisle east window by J. Paterson, former head of Bideford School of Art.

496 Ashreigney, St James
Grade II*

Built in the 15th century but heavily restored in 1889-1890, it comprises a nave, chancel, south aisle and porch, and a tower to the north of the nave; a feature of some north Devon churches. The font is probably Norman and three of the Perpendicular windows have exceptional tracery. The royal arms of Queen Anne are displayed above the south doorway. Ashreigney parish church celebrates the Eucharist Sunday by Sunday with a faithful group of worshippers, while also active within the local community. There are numerous links between the local church and village organisations, putting a Christian presence, like the building, in the centre of the community.

497 Ashwater, St Peter ad Vincula
Grade I

Parts may be earlier, but dates predominantly from the 15th century and was restored in the 1880s. Consists of nave, chancel, north transept, south aisle, porch and west tower. There is a 12th-century font and high-quality 19th-century fittings including a reredos of carved timber, choir stalls, and carved rectangular bench ends which incorporate medieval work. The east window contains some medieval stained glass. On the south wall there are royal arms of 1638. All age groups in the village are thoroughly represented in the church family, which is outward-looking and has active links with needy people/communities across the world. Worship ranges from traditional to contemporary.

498 Beaford All Saints
Grade I

Part of the church, including the font, date from the Norman period. Having been rebuilt and repaired over the years, much of the current structure dates from the 14th and 15th centuries. The tower, which was rebuilt in 1802, and again in 1908, houses six working bells (re-hung in 1910), two of which are amongst the oldest in Devon – one being dated 1432. The beautiful eagle lectern of carved oak was worked by craftsmen of the firm of William Morris, and was added in 1940. Today, the church's welcoming congregation appreciate traditional Anglican worship and are very involved in the community life of the village.

499 Bideford, St Mary
Grade II*

In 2009, St Mary's celebrates the 750th anniversary of the building of its Norman tower! St Mary's was built in stone to replace the original Saxon church so is a great historical landmark in Bideford town centre. Now the church is the centre of many special occasions, whether a baptism, wedding or funeral. It is also at the forefront of other activities, with a Music Makers group for pre-school aged children, a Diner on a Friday for those in need of a meal, a church plant once a month with an informal feel and a variety of other groups such as Alpha, the Marriage Course and social afternoons.

TORRIDGE

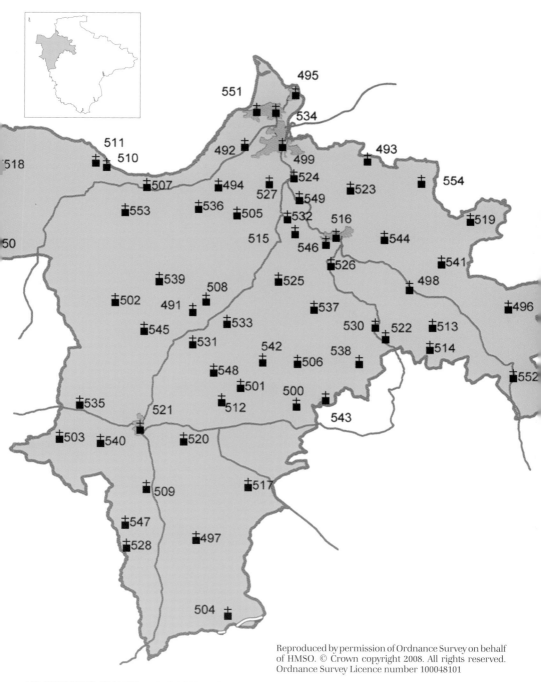

495

551

534

511
510
518

492
499

493
554

507
494
527
524
523

553
536
505
532
549
516
544
519

515
546
526
541

539
508
525
537
498
496

502
491
533
530
522
513
545
531
542
538
514
548
506
552

501
500

535
521
543

503
540
520

509
517

547
528
497

504

500 Black Torrington, St Mary
Grade II*

There was a Norman church here in the 12th century. The present building dates mostly from the 15th and 16th centuries, consisting of nave, chancel, north transept, south aisle with wagon roof and tower with six bells. A new chancel was built in 1900. The John Avery organ, built in 1791, was restored in 1987. Worship ranges from traditional to more contemporary and all are warmly welcomed to join us. We work closely together with the Methodist chapel to be a united Christian presence in our village. We enjoy strong links with the local primary school and are seeking ways of developing our links other local organisations.

501 Bradford, All Saints
Grade II*

This ancient church still retains its 12th-century font and south doorway. The north aisle dates from the 14th century, though the north windows and central arcade are 15th-century. The tower was rebuilt about 1550 and contains six bells. There are floor memorials to the Henscott and Arscott families and wall memorials to Bickford and Maynard. A small, friendly congregation worship here each Sunday. Services include Holy Communion, Morning Prayer and Evensong. Visitors can expect to be warmly welcomed. Set a little way out of the village, the peaceful atmosphere of the church encourages people to take the opportunity for quiet prayer and meditation.

502 Bradworthy, St John the Baptist
Grade II*

The Norman font is all that remains of the earlier church. The present church was consecrated in 1400. The leaning timbers of the roof have been described as, "forty arches all askew". The well-proportioned tower added in 1500 now has six bells. The nativity window is in memory of Dr Betts, the first of three generations from the same family who have now served the people of Bradworthy for 100 years. Inscriptions on the headstones in the churchyard make fascinating reading. Bradworthy village, with perhaps the largest square in the West Country, dates back to Saxon times. With many shops and facilities, Bradworthy is well worth a visit.

503 Bridgerule, St Bridget
Grade I

Perhaps dating from as early as 1041 the church was rebuilt in 1448 and re-dedicated to St Michael & All Angels. The 15th-century roofs still remain and the font is of great antiquity. The floor is of chequerboard slates laid on edge. Fr Kingdon, 70 years as incumbent, was responsible for most of the Tractarian furnishings, including the reredos, tabernacle for the reserved sacrament, the screens and statue of St Bridget. Thanks to the dedication of the congregation and the generosity of the village the fine peel of eight bells was hung on a new frame in 2006. There are important links with the church school and the Methodist chapel.

504 Broadwoodwidger, St Nicholas
Grade II

The first rector is recorded in 1288. At that time the church comprised a nave, chancel and transepts. There is a well-preserved Norman font. The church was restored in the 16th century with the addition of the porch, south aisle, a rood screen and carved bench ends. In 1900 a musicians' gallery was removed and an organ loft built in the north transept. The tower has six bells, dating from 1777. The medieval dedication has not been discovered; St Nicholas since 1883. The royal arms dated 1835 are on the north wall. There are a number of "listed" headstones in the churchyard. We offer regular worship to a large rural parish in a traditional style.

505 Buckland Brewer, St Mary & St Benedict
Grade II*

Built of sandstone and dating from about 1100, the church's main doorway is an excellent specimen of Norman work. The holy water stoup in the porch is 14th-century. Being 530ft above sea level, the church has been struck by lightning, destroyed by fire and was restored in 1880 having been struck by storms. The 76ft tower houses six bells. The doorway to the vestry is late Gothic. Beyond is the former schoolroom, believed to have been a chapel dedicated to St Stephen and now used for social and educational events, keeping Christianity at the heart of the village.

506 Buckland Filleigh, St Mary & Holy Trinity
Grade II*

Hidden among the woodlands, the churchyard looks past ancient yews and grassland to a lake in the valley beyond. The peace and tranquillity of the churchyard is also found in the church, which dates from the 13th century. The Fortescue and Browne families of Buckland House cared for it until 1952 and it is now the parishioners of this small rural community who continue the loving care. Services are mainly traditional with one family-orientated. The porch, bell tower, font and arcade with massive West Country granite pillars are probably 13th-century and the pulpit is made from Renaissance bench ends. The beautiful memorial stained-glass windows are mainly Victorian.

507 Bucks Mills, St Anne
Grade II

This church was built in 1861 by the Elwes family, the former landowners, for the estate workers. The entries in our visitors' book bear good testament to our policy of leaving it open at all times. The church, which nestles in the valley leading down from the A39 to the sea, is constructed from local stone and the remains of the quarry is now our car park. We have strong ties with the Braund Society, based on the descendants of the original inhabitants of Bucks Mills who have now spread worldwide. Our small but dedicated congregation are keen to make the church accessible to all.

508 Bulkworthy, St Michael
Grade II*

Said to be built by Sir William Hankford, Chief Justice of the King's Bench from 1414 to 1422, the church has a bell turret with two bells. The font has cable moulding. The pulpit is inscribed in memory of William Newcombe of Hankford, who died in 1854. Search for the panel nearly out of sight, which depicts the verse in St Matthew's Gospel, "And Jesus said to him, 'Foxes have holes and birds of the air have their nests; but the Son of man has nowhere to lay his head'" Matthew 8:20. An outside staircase leads to a parvise room over the south porch. The acoustics are excellent.

509 Clawton, St Leonard
Grade I

St Leonard's dates from the 14th century, built upon the site of an earlier church. There is an interesting Norman window in the chancel. Also of note are the barrel roofs in the side aisles, and in the sanctuary, the ancient piscina and unusual Victorian wall decorations. The font came from the earlier church, and local children have been baptised here for 1000 years. The tower has a peal of six bells and on its wall a royal coat of arms from 1662. We are a small active worshipping community, also involved with a local ecumenical "Fresh Expressions" group. Visitors are assured of a warm welcome.

510 Clovelly, All Saints
Grade I

Built on the site of an early timber cruciform church, the current building dates from the 12th century with the north aisle and rebuilding in the 13th. The arcade to the north aisle is of monolithic granite columns from Lundy. The front porch and font are Norman. The tower is only 54ft high but houses a peal of six bells with a 10cwt tenor. There is a fine wagon roof. The stained-glass windows date from the 1880s, one by Charles Kempe. There is a service most Sundays for the small welcoming congregation, two from the Book of Common Prayer and two from Common Worship per month.

511 Clovelly, St Peter

The building is about 250 years old, built of stone and cob on the right behind and below the New Inn part way down the street. It is owned by the Clovelly Estate Company, and All Saints is responsible for the upkeep. It was licensed for services in November 1947. It is quite plain inside apart from the murals – painted by local artist Fiona Creighton-Balfour in 1998 – which depict the angels Raphael and Gabriel and the Lamb on the Throne. There are no regular services held in the chapel.

512 Cookbury, St John the Baptist & the Seven Maccabees
Grade II*

Built in the Norman style, most of the present church dates from the late 13th century. The central arcade is Perpendicular (c.1500). Parts of the medieval screen have been used to panel the altar and for the base of the Victorian lectern. The present screen dates from the restoration of 1870 when a Jacobean pulpit from Launceston was installed. The church is lovingly cared for by the recently established Friends of Cookbury Church. Services are held in the summer months. Many visitors attend services on special occasions, such as our Advent Carol Service. The Russian Orthodox congregation come to worship here annually around the time of the feast of St John the Baptist.

513 Dolton, St Edmund
Grade II*

This church is built of local stone with fine narrow joints, Bath stone quoins and window surrounds, and natural slate roof. Square two-stage tower, upper part rendered and battlemounted. Simple porch with lancet archway. Three aisles with barrel roof ceilings and bosses. Nave flagstones cover burial vaults. Partly rebuilt in 1848. Six bells rehung in 1996. Unique Anglo-Saxon font formed from two blocks, one square, one tapered, with well-preserved interlace on all sides. Fine 1760 royal coat of arms. Recently a kitchen and toilet with disabled access have been provided inside the church. Average Sunday attendance around 40. There is a growing partnership with the Baptists.

514 Dowland, St Peter
Grade I

Founded by Walter de Clavil in 1132, it has very fine diagonally buttressed west tower with obelisk pinnacles. In 1970 the tower was completely repointed and a fallen pinnacle replaced. The five bells originally hung in 1886 were re-hung and dedicated in 1997. There are three bays with timber arcades which were restored in the 1960s. One of the church's finest features are the carved bench ends showing a series of symbols, badges and armorial charges two of which are Malchus's ear and the keys of St Peter. When entering the church one is impressed by the light and peaceful atmosphere. Services of Holy Communion and Morning Prayer are held on the first and third Sundays.

515 Frithelstock, St Mary & St Gregory
Grade I

This church dates from the 13th century with the only monastic remains in north Devon adjoining it. Notable features include the Norman font and medieval Barnstaple tiles. The royal coat of arms is the work of local and famous plasterer John Abbott. 15th-century carved pew ends and a small flight of stairs leads to an opening above the Jacobean pulpit, which was the entrance to the rood screen. There is a Green Man by the tower opening facing the altar. The six bells, two of which are medieval, are now being rung after many years of being silent. There is traditional worship by an ageing congregation.

516 Great Torrington, St Michael
Grade II

Like many churches dedicated to St Michael, this is on a hilltop. When the town fell to Parliament in 1646, prisoners were put in the church. During the night the gunpowder stored in the tower exploded, killing prisoners and guards and ruining the building. During the Commonwealth, Hugh Peters, chaplain to the army, preached the parliamentary cause in Torrington marketplace. Fourteen years later, at the Restoration, he was executed for treason. The Willis organ is a near twin of the organ in Truro Cathedral, and came here from Shirwell, Plymouth. The rood came from St Oswald's, Small Heath. The cobbled mound outside is a mass grave for victims of the explosion. The church is open during daylight. The Blessed Sacrament is reserved.

517 Halwill, St Peter & St James
Grade II*

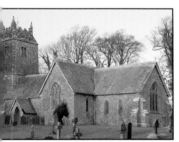

With the exception of the tower, dating from the 14th century, the whole church was practically rebuilt through the munificence of Squire Harris in 1879. It consists of west tower, nave, choir, sanctuary and superbly carved pulpit. The tower, surmounted by small battlements and corner pinnacles, contains a ring of six bells. Outside, in the angle of diverging churchyard paths, behind the lychgate, stands a massive stepped base of a very old granite cross. The worshipping community organises regular social activities in nearby Halwill Junction, working closely with the Baptist and Methodist congregations. Well-attended ecumenical services are held in the parish hall four times each year.

518 Hartland, St Nectan
Grade I

A collegiate church was founded here in c.1050 and dedicated to St Nectan, but the main surviving fabric dates from the 14th and 15th centuries. The church was restored c.1850 and in 1910-1911, but retains much early fabric and features. It comprises nave, chancel, north and south aisles, transept chapels and porches, and 128ft high west tower. Features of the interior include a 14th-century trefoiled piscina in the chancel; restored medieval wagon roofs; a fine 15th-century rood screen, with evidence of ancient colouring throughout; a restored medieval pulpit; and a late Norman font. The bells were cast in 1826. Throughout the church are 60 mural monuments on the walls and floors.

519 High Bickington, St Mary
Grade I

Comprises 12th-century nave, 14th-century chancel, truncated 12th-century south tower, and 15th-century south porch, north aisle and chapel, and west tower. The church was restored in 1876-1891. Internally, the evidence of the 12th-century church includes the right-hand jamb of the former chancel arch, south doorway, and the font. Other features include a 14th-century triple sedilia and piscina; a late-19th-century carved wooden reredos incorporating old carved panels; late-19th-century choir stalls incorporating late medieval and 16th-century bench ends; and a fine series (about 70) of mainly 15th and 16th-century benches. Four of the bells were cast in 1753, one recast in 1827 and three in 1911.

520 Hollacombe, St Petroc
Grade II

With striking views of Dartmoor, the Grade II church is in the small hamlet of Hollacombe. An aisleless nave probably of 13th-century origin has a small west tower dating from the 14th century. There is an old font with an octagonal bowl with circular basin. The east window is filled with stained glass representing the Nativity and Adoration of the Magi. The church underwent substantial restoration in the late 19th century and again at the beginning of the 21st, when the floors and pews were replaced. Worship is the traditional Book of Common Prayer 1662. Services are the first and third Sundays of the month.

521 Holsworthy, St Peter & St Paul
Grade II*

For nearly 1000 years, this church has stood on this site just off the Saxon square, now serving over 3000 people. Following the Reformation, the church has maintained an ecumenical relationship with the Roman Catholic Church, including a Saturday evening mass each week. On Sundays, there is Holy Communion (Common Worship), which is shared with another parish as we form a Mission Community with them. The parish Eucharist is a sung mass with choir and bells. We give thanks to God for this long and faithful tradition of worship and are committed to serving the people of Holsworthy into the future.

522 Huish, St James the Less
Grade II*

The church was largely rebuilt by G. E. Street in 1873-1874. Of the earlier church, only the tower, with foundations dating from1100, remains. Main features of this lovely small country church are the arcade of arches separating nave from south aisle, the soft colour of the Tisbury stone-clad interior, the massive hammer-beam roof of the nave, soft Devon marble sanctuary and chancel steps, and richly carved font and pulpit both in Caen stone. The tower contains three pre-Reformation bells. There is a listed churchyard cross dating to the 14th-15th century. The church, with monthly Eucharist and special services, continues to play an active part in the life of the wider community.

523 Huntshaw, St Mary Magdalene
Grade II*

This fine stone-built church was probably built in the 15th century. The tower with its newel staircase and wagon roof is typical of churches found only in Devon and Cornwall. The church boosts fine stained glass of the Victorian era and also some dating from the 13th century. The north arcade carvings and niches are exceptional for a small village church. Three bells in the tower, cast in the 17th century are no longer rung as their support cradle is now in very poor condition. The church attracts a loyal and diverse congregation drawn from within the Two Rivers ministry and enjoys two services monthly.

524 Landcross, Holy Trinity
Grade II*

Here, small is beautiful. On a hillside in one of Devon's smallest parishes, Holy Trinity's spiritual space is as special for solitary contemplation as full Songs of Praise. Formerly a Celtic "monastery in the marsh" and Catholic church of "Our Lady of Lancas", the present church of 1435 retains the Norman font in which the statesman George Monck was baptised in 1608. Its 15th-century wagon roof, 16th-century carved bench ends and 19th-century windows embrace worship of different ages and styles: BCP-based Communion, Taizé and Celtic services are part of Landcross' 21st-century mission to be a "Centre of Christian Spirituality" welcoming seekers of all traditions and none.

525 Langtree, All Saints
Grade II*

Dating from the 15th century, the church was one of only a few with no dedication – until 1994, when it was found to be All Saints. Its imposing sense of space is added to by a rare George II coat of arms (possibly originally Charles II), and finely carved 16th-century Flemish reliefs on the altar and sanctuary chairs. The font is possibly Norman. Outside are a 1641 sundial, and an unusual war memorial being the church clock. The peal of six bells is regarded as particularly good. Almost closed in 1990, a faithful congregation maintains regular worship to God, along with our Methodist friends.

526 Little Torrington, St Giles
Grade II*

The existing church probably stands on the site of an early-11th-century building. The dedication to St Giles, the patron saint of cripples, may be due to the presence of a leper hospital in the parish at Taddiport, which had probably been founded in the late 13th century. The door and font are very ancient, and there are some good wall monuments. The church is open daily. There is a service here every Sunday morning. The Blessed Sacrament is reserved.

527 Littleham, St Swithun
Grade I

This beautiful church shows the result of a very careful restoration by the Revd G. Morse in 1892 of a much earlier building. The north wall of the nave, north transept and chancel are 14th-century, the tower and south aisle are early-15th-century. Notable features include: a wall fresco in the Lady chapel, believed to be St Swithun; boldly carved pew ends in Renaissance style; 18th-century Flemish brass chandeliers; an ancient muniment chest; windows by C. E. Kempe; a magnificent oak rood screen; a large marble memorial to Lieut. General H. H. Crealock. We are a welcoming church, an active partner in a local team with services every Sunday.

THE CHURCHES
CONSERVATION TRUST

528 Luffincott, St James
Grade I

Set on a hill crest above the lovely wooded Tamar valley, at the end of a long lane with only a farm nearby, this little church is unassuming, but most appealing. It is mostly medieval, but the low tower was rebuilt in 1791 and there are delightful domestic Georgian sash windows on the north side. It has a barrel roof, continuous over nave and chancel, a simple 14th-century granite font and a fine group of slate headstones in the churchyard.

529 Lundy Island, St Helen
Grade II

This church was built in 1896 by J. Norton for H. G. Heaven, the then owner of Lundy Island. It comprises nave, chancel, transept, and porch under tower. It is built of granite in Gothic Early English style. The interior is of polychromed brick; red brick with black and white bands. The furnishings are mainly by Hems of Exeter. The reredos is on Purbeck marble colonnettes and with an alabaster carving, depicting the Last Supper. Other furnishings include the piscina and sedilia, and carved stone pulpit and square font. The stained-glass east window dates from the late 19th century. Five bells from the tower, now in the porch, are dated 1897.

530 Merton, All Saints
Grade II*

All Saints comprises nave, chancel, north aisle, south transept, western tower and south porch. It dates back to 1261 although nothing remains of the original except the Norman doorway and font, and the remains of a sepulchral arch in the transept. The church was rebuilt in the 1400s and restored by Medley Fulford in 1875. There are six bells in the tower, the oldest dating from 1420. A blue pig is depicted in the east window, unheard of anywhere else in England. There is a weekly service, an active Prayer Group and special events are held in the church on a regular basis.

531 Milton Damerel, Holy Trinity
Grade II*

This is a beautiful 12th and 14th-century church with a 1662 Restoration coat of arms of Good King Charles above the north door. There is a 14th-century sanctuary door in the south porch. As it enters the 21st century it has the same problem about numbers as it had in the 14th and 15th centuries. Being a plague village, much of the population died. We are still awaiting development next to the church, and hopefully those who now worship, having removed to other parishes to live, will be supported by some native worshippers. We invite others to come and join the monthly mass that takes place in this exquisite little church.

532 Monkleigh, St George
Grade I

Although dating from earlier times, the church is mainly 15th-century in the Perpendicular style with restoration in 1862. In a commanding position the church has a 70ft tower with six bells, chancel, nave, south or Annery aisle and porch. The Annery Aisle, approached through a fine early-16th-century parclose screen, contains the important canopied tomb of Sir William Hankford, Chief Justice of England 1414-1422, brasses to the St Leger family and 16th-century carved bench ends. The font is of Norman origin. We have a loyal village congregation and strong links with the local primary school. Other activities and support are provided through our five parishes network.

533 Newton St Petrock, St Petrock
Grade II*

With foundations dating to the 12th century, the oldest part of the existing building is the west tower, c.1350. The church was restored and enlarged in 1887 at which time Renaissance pew ends were discovered hidden under the flooring. These are now incorporated into the current pews and some, with carvings of the shields of noted Devon families, were used to construct the pulpit. The font is Norman and the altar table is Elizabethan. Services are held each week; we have a small but loyal congregation. At least once each month we worship together with our Baptist friends in the village and church and chapel together are the heart of our small community.

534 Northam, St Margaret
Grade I

Dating from Norman times, the north aisle was added in 1593, the date being recorded on the pillar nearest the chancel steps. Between 1846-1860 Parson Gossett paid for much of the restoration of the church. The tower is 170ft high and houses eight bells. The font was found buried under the tower in two pieces, restored in 1848 and put in its present position in 1865. The pulpit was given by F. T. Thorold Esq in memory of his mother, made of stone and south Devon marble. The organ is one of the finest instruments in the county, built by J W. Walker in 1866. Worship ranges from contemporary to traditional services for all ages.

535 Pancrasweek, St Pancras
Grade II*

The wagon roof gives outstanding acoustics to this church with origins in the 13th century and restored in the early 20th century with striking stencil work in the chancel. There is an interesting squint from the north transept (used as a vestry) to the altar. The peal of five bells, one said to be medieval, have a rich tone. The Wickett family created a memorial east window using 15th-century glass from Muchelney Abbey and presented a fine 16th-century Spanish processional cross. No longer a parish church, St Pancras is now a chapel of ease in the parish of Pyworthy. Without any village, the small congregation continues to maintain worship in this scattered community.

536 Parkham, St James
Grade II*

St James comprises a nave, chancel, north and south aisles, and its 84ft high tower, visible for miles, houses six 18th-century bells. Although originally built in Norman times, little remains of the church from this period except the font, set amid medieval Barum tiles, and the entry. The main body dates from 1450 but 16th-century extensions were added, the arches for which rest on granite piers from Lundy. Major restoration led to a rededication in 1875 by Frederick Temple, Bishop of Exeter and later Archbishop of Canterbury. The church, which is part of Hartland Coast Team, holds weekly Sunday services and is active in the village community.

537 Petersmarland, St Peter
Grade II

Very little is known of the church in medieval times. By the 19th century, it was largely dilapidated. It was later completely rebuilt in 1863-1865 by local squire, John Curzon Moore-Stevens, in high Victorian Gothic Revival style, except for the old tower. The tower was restored with buttresses added to the west. It still holds a peal of six. One is the oldest bell in Devon still being rung, dating from 1345. Its inscription reads *"Protege Virgo Pia quos invoco Sancta Maria"* (Holy Virgin, Saint Mary, protect those whom I call). Today the church still serves the scattered hamlets and farms of the parish.

538 Petrockstowe, St Petroc
Grade II*

The church stands in the heart of our busy village. The building dates from the 13th century but extensive rebuilding and enlargement took place in the 19th. You can still see the Norman piscina and font. An oak octagonal pulpit supported by local Hatherleigh stone bears the date 1631. There are some good stained-glass windows and a Father Willis organ built in 1872 at a cost of £120. A service is held every Sunday, including a united service with the Methodist chapel. There is a children's group called Kingdom Kids, a choir and a team of young bell-ringers. All are welcome to visit.

539 Putford, St Stephen
Grade I

Serving the scattered houses and farmsteads of West and East Putford, the church nestles in peaceful isolation out of sight to all except visitors and worshippers. Items of interest include an oddly shaped Norman font, a south door inscribed 1620 with stoup set into the wall, 14th-century timbers in the north transept, chancel floor tiles made in Barnstaple and a royal coat of arms for Queen Anne (AR 1714) on the north wall. The 15th-century tower contains six bells. In 2006 the church underwent a major restoration. Funded chiefly by English Heritage, the innovative fundraising ideas arranged proved that, in terms of community spirit, Putford is far from sleepy.

540 Pyworthy, St Swithun
Grade II*

Dedicated in 1334, the church was a pre-Conquest foundation. The atmosphere is enhanced by the light from the clear glass in the east window. The wood of the wagon roof is complemented by recent carved features by a former churchwarden. The church is noted for concerts and recitals to support the fabric and charitable causes. Situated at the heart of the village across the road from the church school and open in the day it is well visited (sometimes also by barn owls). The generosity of the community has recently enabled the sound system to be enhanced, and an induction loop added.

541 Roborough, St Peter
Grade II*

Standing prominently in the hilltop village of Roborough, St Peter's serves a rural parish with Communion, Morning Prayer and family services. The present church probably dates from the late 15th century, but was heavily restored in 1868: externally Victorian fittings predominate, giving the church its 19th-century ambience. The squat and square west tower is a survival of the medieval church and carries a peal of six bells last re-hung in 1995, an act of confidence by the small but effective congregation that St Peter's will continue to serve its community of scattered farmsteads, with a welcome to visitors into the new millennium.

542 Shebbear, St Michael
Grade II*

The church of St Michael is of Saxon origin. However, the annual ritual of "the stone" suggests a site of pre-Christian activity. The first church consisted simply of a nave, with the south aisle and Norman doorway added later. Three key features are the oak pulpit, the recumbent life-size effigy of Lady Prendergast and the depiction of a First World War aeroplane in a window. There are six bells. Four were cast in 1792 and two in 1863. In 1815 some left the church to form the Bible Christian movement; however, today all Christians in the village work together to ensure a variety of opportunities for worship and fellowship.

543 Sheepwash, St Lawrence
Grade II*

Believed to be the third church since the 14th century, Lord Clinton rebuilt it in 1880 for £1600. It consists of a vestry, organ chamber, nave, chancel, tower and porch. William Morris Pepper designed the beautifully stained east window in 1881 and glazed the other windows, all images of English saints. The chancel has a hammer-beam roof decorated with trumpet-holding angels. The font is Norman. The oak lectern is in the form of an eagle and the pulpit is carved with Moses and Christ. A previous chapel at Upcott has links to Torre Abbey. Today a small but faithful congregation works well with Methodists and Baptists in the village.

544 St Giles in the Wood, St Giles
Grade II

Records indicate the founding of a church on this site in 1309. It was completely rebuilt in the 16th century and extensively restored in 1862-1863 by the Hon. Mark Rolle of Stevenstone. Victorian features include a handsome alabaster and marble pulpit. In 1967 part of the south nave was enclosed to create the Mary Withecombe chapel, a great asset for our smaller congregations. Sunday services include both Common Worship and Prayer Book with a bimonthly family service. "Seekers", for our children, is held fortnightly. The six bells are rung for many services. The church, opened daily, is also used for concerts and other functions with great support from the community.

545 Sutcombe, St Andrew
Grade II*

Close by the porch lies buried Emma Harrison, wife of a former rector and sister of Isambard Kingdom Brunel. A carved Green Man in the porch welcomes the visitor. Founded in Norman times, the church was rebuilt and extended in the 15th century with the addition of the south Thuborough aisle. The carvings on the pew ends and 16th-century pulpit are a real joy. The screen dates from the early part of the 20th century but careful inspection will reveal some of the ancient original. The tower has six bells. To the north of the church are three old almshouses, restored in recent years and now used for their original purposes.

546 Taddiport (Little Torrington), St Mary Magdalene
Grade II*

The inconspicuous little medieval chapel of St Mary Magdalene on the bank of the Torridge is a hidden gem. It was built to serve the leper hospital outside the town of Great Torrington. The rector of Little Torrington is usually the chaplain, but the building belongs to trustees. There are old texts painted on the walls inside evidently referring to misappropriation of some of the Magdalene lands in the past. The church is open daily. There is a service every Sunday. The Blessed Sacrament is reserved.

547 Tetcott, Holy Cross
Grade I

Situated on the Arscott estate, Holy Cross is a mostly 13th-century building, with a 15th-century tower and 19th-century vestry, and was restored in 1890. It comprises nave, chancel, west tower, south transept, vestry, and south west porch. Internally, the chancel fittings are early-20th-century with a timber reredos, altar, and poppy-head choir stalls. The timber drum pulpit is probably also early-20th-century. The font is 12th-century. There are some unusual rustic early-16th-century benches, carved with leaves and architectural detail. The south transept is the Arscott family pew and contains some 17th-18th-century woodwork which has been incorporated into the seating. There are several good wall monuments. Some stained glass by Hardman.

548 Thornbury, St Peter
Grade II*

Here is a place where God has been worshipped by his people for 800 years. The Perpendicular-style church today comprises: nave with significant remains of the Norman church, including entrance doorway and font; 14th-century south transept and chancel with piscina; 15th-century north aisle and 14th-century tower containing a well used peal of five bells dating from 1876. Substantial restoration occurred in the 1870s. An important alabaster tomb with effigies is that of Humphrey Speccot, d.1590. There are several stained-glass windows. We are active with a Christian presence in our scattered community. Our small but outward-looking congregation celebrates two Eucharists, a traditional Evensong and a well-supported family service each month.

549 Weare Giffard, Holy Trinity
Grade I

The nave and chancel are 14th-century, though the Norman font, effigies of crusader Sir Walter Giffard and his wife Alice (1243) and tile shards (1280) suggest an earlier church on the site. The roof is probably the work of craftsmen who built the magnificent hammer-beam roof in Weare Giffard manor. The Lady chapel, south aisle, porch and (six bell) tower are 15th-century. Carved bench ends (from 1510) are fine examples of heraldic design. Some windows contain medieval glass, with a millennium window celebrating 2000 years of Christianity. A medieval wall-painting depicts the martyrdom of St Sebastian. The church is open daily and the congregation is very warm and welcoming.

550 Welcombe, St Nectan
Grade II*

Initially a chapel of Hartland church, and later gifted to the Abbey, St Nectan's Welcombe was founded in the 11th century, and the font dates from that period. The 14th-century screen is one of the most primitive examples of a great Devonian art, and the wall plates, alone in Devon apart from Exeter Cathedral, retain their original colouring. Hawker of Morwenstowe insisted on opening the ancient vestry door during baptisms to let the devils depart; today the vestry is used by an active and growing Sunday School. Worship ranges from traditional to modern, alongside weekly Bible studies and a growing band of bell-ringers, who call everyone from this small friendly community to worship Christ.

551 Westward Ho! (Northam), Holy Trinity

The Revd Isaac Gossett saw a need for a church at Westward Ho! So he commissioned W. Oliver of Barnstaple to draw up plans. Work began in 1868. The church was opened in 1870 at a cost of £1,800. The service was conducted by Frederick Temple, later Archbishop of Canterbury. The church is very light with plain glass with a wonderful view. The basic structure of the building has hardly changed since its completion. The dressings around the doors and windows are of Lundy granite. The side chapel, a gift to mark the Coronation of King George VI and Queen Elizabeth in 1937, is used for quiet prayer. Services are held regularly.

552 Winkleigh, All Saints
Grade I

In the centre of the village, this impressive Grade I church dates from around the end of the 12th century, though it was extensively repaired in the 14th (some of the stained glass remains) and restored in the 19th and 20th centuries. It has many interesting features including richly carved and beautifully decorated cradle roofs, with numerous angels, wall (sgraffito decoration) and screen. The tower contains a fine peal of eight bells, regularly rung. Close by is a small room used by the active Sunday School. Worship is traditional and centred on the Eucharist and includes people of all ages working to be a church for the whole parish.

553 Woolfardisworthy West, All Hallows
Grade I

The church was originally a chapelry dependent on the parish church of Hartland and became separate during the Reformation. The porch and font are Norman and the tower is the only example from the 13th century in north Devon, with a south-facing external stairway. There is a ring of six bells which were added in 1826. The north aisle and nave have a collection of interesting bench ends thought to have been carved in the 15th century. All Hallows has a ten-year-old covenant with the Methodists. Once a month there is an open worship service, to encourage people who are not familiar with church to join us.

554 Yarnscombe, St Andrew
Grade II*

The first recorded incumbent was appointed in 1269 shortly after the building of the nave and chancel, along with the tower which may have an earlier Norman origin. The south aisle and porch were added 200 years later, with some major alterations in the 19th century. There is some medieval stained glass in the south aisle and the font dates probably from Tudor times. The six bells, the earliest dated 1440, are rung regularly. Lying close to the heart of the village, the church holds a service every Sunday. It is open during daylight hours for those who wish to pray in a quiet, holy place.

WEST DEVON

This area includes most of Dartmoor National Park, the market towns of Okehampton and Tavistock, and myriad small and often remote villages. The area prospered from the wool trade and is the home of tin-mining in Devon with its stannery towns. Mostly deeply rural, agriculture has always been important here. At the heart of the Moor stands Princetown, with its famous prison, and three of the area's 64 Anglican churches.

555 Beaworthy, St Alban
Grade II

Beaworthy Church was largely rebuilt in 1871 by Samuel Hooper of Hatherleigh, but parts of the building showing a much earlier church still exist. There are two carved Norman stones in the porch, and the base of the tower is thought to be medieval, perhaps 14th-century. There is only one stained-glass window, situated in the west wall and believed to date from 1813. The church consists of a nave, chancel and tower; it is small and simply furnished and a focal point of the village. The congregation although small is very friendly and welcoming. There are both traditional and contemporary services.

556 Belstone, St Mary
Grade II*

The church has a 15th-century tower, 16th-century south aisle, and nave, chancel and north porch which were rebuilt during a major restoration of 1881. It is constructed of granite. It comprises nave and chancel under a continuous roof, south aisle, west tower, vestry and north porch. The fittings and furnishings include an altar piece of 1912 comprising oak panels either side of a painting of the Madonna and Child, and the rood beam with a bronze figure of Christ, which is a First World War memorial. The pulpit, lectern and prayer desk are late-19th and 20th-century, all made of oak with some good carving. The octagonal granite font dates from the 15th century.

557 Bere Alston, Holy Trinity

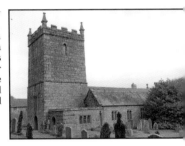

The present church was built in 1848 as a chapel of ease for the large mining population in Bere Alston, which is part of the parish of Bere Ferrers. It was dedicated on 16 July that year but not consecrated for another 23 years. The building is cruciform with an open and airy feel, and an illuminated cross on its roof can be seen from all parts of the village. Mission, community and tradition are central to Holy Trinity's identity, with strong links with all of village life and BCP and Common Worship services in traditional language assisted by a robed choir. It is always warm and welcoming.

558 Bere Ferrers, St Andrew
Grade I

The church was built during the 13th century, helped by the revenues from the Bere silver mines. The east window, known as the "pilgrim window", contains some of the oldest glass in England, installed by Sir William de Ferrers II, himself a pilgrim, in the early 14th century. At the west end is an early Norman baptismal font, made of local stone and lined with lead. The oak pews date back to the early 16th century. A fireplace in the north transept kept the lord of the manor warm and the squint gave a view of the altar. The church is part of the life of the community and welcomes visitors.

559 Bondleigh, St James
Grade I

Bondleigh is a small parish in the Taw Valley near North Tawton. The church is mainly 15th-century with 16th-century additions. The layout of the chancel and nave is similar to that of the original Norman church but the north aisle is late-16th-century. The church was restored in 1890 when several windows were renewed. The font is Norman and other Norman features are the south door and two capitals on the east wall of the aisle. There are fragments of medieval glass in some windows. Several 16th-century bench ends remain and the design of one of them is reflected in the Millennium window of 2000.

560 Bradstone, St Nonna
Grade I

THE CHURCHES CONSERVATION TRUST

This small church is set high above the Tamar on the approach to the ancient crossing into Cornwall at Greystone. The dedication to a Celtic saint in a Saxon settlement is unusual, and there is some evidence that the original dedication was to St Christopher. A simple interior and clear glass provide a peaceful atmosphere and the sense of centuries of prayer. There is a peal of six bells which is popular with ringers. Now in the care of the Churches Conservation Trust, the church still hosts a well-attended Benefice Service each year. Adjacent is Bradstone Manor, and the ancient "Broadstone" stands in a hedge nearby.

561 Bratton Clovelly, St Mary the Virgin
Grade I

The church site has been used from before Saxon times; the door step is a carved stone from the Dark Ages. The existing building is 14th-century, the structure suggests that a much larger cruciform church was intended. The floor unusually slopes down to the altar. The striking wall paintings uncovered in the 1980s are 17th-century, depicting the prophets on the north wall, the disciples on the south, plus various texts. Much of the interior fabric and the stained glass were replaced in the 19th century, also the alabaster reredos; the bells were cast by Pennington in 1767. The church serves the community and school spiritually and practically.

562 Brentor, Christ Church
Grade II

This church is situated within the village of Brentor, but built as a chapel of ease to the more famous church of St Michael, Brentor. It was built in 1856 by Richard Gosling of Torquay, and financed largely by Mrs Isabella Holwell, Admiral Octavius Vernon and Mrs Danby. It cost £1,003 to build. It comprises nave, chancel, west tower, north west porch and south east vestry. Internally, there is a set of contemporary glass by Alfred Beer of Exeter: pictorial in the east window, and the window opposite the north door commemorating Isabella Holwell. The granite font is probably of 1856, although the font cover and other fittings date from the 1930s.

563 Brentor, St Michael
Grade I

This small church is located on the summit of a tor on Dartmoor; a well-known landmark for miles around. The earliest record of the church is before 1150, although the church as it stands today is probably largely 13th-century with 15th-century alterations and a 15th-century tower. It was restored in 1889-1890. There is one lancet window only to the north and south sides, and an east window. Internally, there is a 15th-century octagonal font, a pulpit of 1884-1890, and contemporary benches and altar rail. The east window is by James Paterson, 1971. The church is lit by gas lights, and holds services in the summer months only, but is open for visitors daily.

WEST DEVON

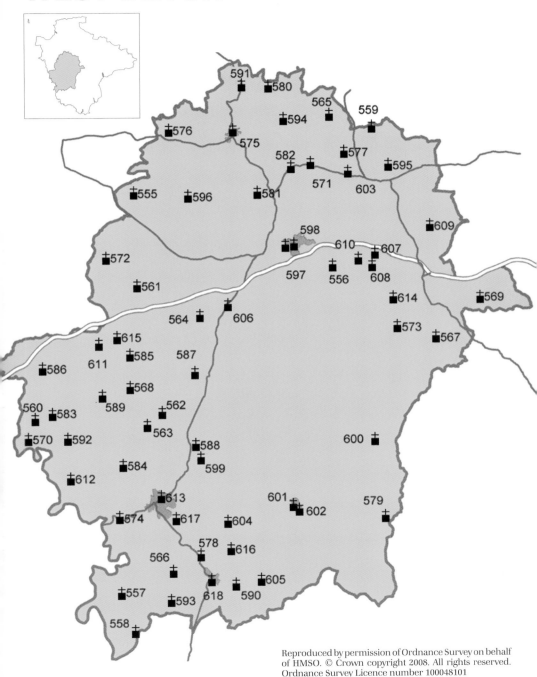

591
580
565
559
594
576
575
582
577
595
581
571
603
555
596
609
598
572
610 607
561
597 556 608
614
564 606 573 569
567
615
585 587
586 611
568
560 562
583 589 563
570 592
600
588
584 599
612
601 602 579
613
574 617 604
578
566 616
605
557 618 590
593
558

564 Bridestowe, St Bridget
Grade II*

Completed c.1450, the present church is the third to have been erected on the site. It is set in a large churchyard, whose main entrance is framed by a Norman arch, dating from a previous church which was eventually converted into a Poor House, itself demolished in the early part of the 19th century. The royal coat of arms is one of a very limited number, displaying the pattern of Queen Anne. Of the stained glass, the oldest is the west lancet window depicting St Bridget carrying lilies and shamrock. The painting of St Francis of Assisi on Dartmoor now hangs in the chancel and was completed in 1976.

565 Broadwoodkelly, All Hallows
Grade I

The parish church of All Hallows is mainly of Perpendicular period c.1350-1539 considerably rebuilt in the late 15th and 16th centuries and then restored in 1867-1868. The ancient porch is inscribed by Robert Wollan 1694. In the north window of the chancel is preserved old glass dated 1523 which shows the Madonna, two women kneeling and a saint holding a head and carrying a monk's scythe. The east window depicts the Good Shepherd and Sts Peter and Paul. The organ was removed from the cloisters of Westminster Abbey in May 1873. The holy water stoup in the porch and the piscina in the lady chapel are some 700 years old.

566 Buckland Monachorum, St Andrew
Grade I

A small wooden church was built in 900. This was replaced in 1350 by a more substantial cruciform stone structure. In 1490 the present building was erected with much of the stone salvaged from its predecessor. In 1581 Sir Francis Drake bought Buckland Abbey and worshipped at the church. Aspirations for church life at Buckland are that we are passionate about our faith, seeing the Bible as God's heartbeat, and looking to be enlivened by the Holy Spirit. Prayer underpins church life. We are always pleased to offer a warm welcome to visitors.

567 Chagford, St Michael the Archangel
Grade I

Walkers and shoppers flock to this attractive stannary town where the square tower of the church, dedicated in 1261, with its eight bells dominates the square. The interior has octagonal monolithic granite columns and medieval parclose screens. Herbert Read of Exeter made the beautiful rood screen, carved oak pews and pulpit. Modern re-ordering has provided facilities for the choir and ringers (1961) and kitchen, toilet and a graceful balcony (2007). Visitors hear tragic stories of Sydney Godolphin and Mary Whiddon and view the intriguing "Tinners' Hares" motif. Chagford, principal village in the Whiddon Parishes of Dartmoor, has a church school, lively eucharistic worship, and an ecumenically funded youth worker.

568 Coryton, St Andrew
Grade II*

This church has a 13th-century chancel, 15th-century nave, 16th-century tower, 19th-century porch and north aisle. It was substantially restored in 1885. It comprises nave and chancel, west tower, south porch, north aisle and transept. The bowl of the square font is probably 15th-century, the rest of the interior is largely of 1885, including the arcades, chancel arch, chancel roof with carved bosses, pews, and rectangular pulpit. Fixed to the east end of the north aisle are 1840s commandment boards and creed above a stone painted with fleur de lys. Four of the stained-glass windows are by Kempe & Co. The Newman family who financed the 19th-century north aisle purchased the Coryton estate in 1809.

569 Drewsteignton, Holy Trinity
Grade I

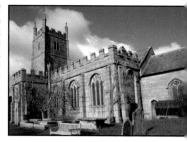

This spacious church, dominating the village square, was built of granite during the 14th and 15th centuries. However, the base of a Norman font suggests that there was an earlier building here. The north aisle, being more decorative, appears to be later than the south aisle where the porch has a parvise over. The chancel was rebuilt in 1861. The centre block of pews (1931) commemorates Julius Drewe of Castle Drogo. Nearby is the church house (1546), now the village hall. Each month there are services of all types with an active Sunday Club, support for the Youth Club and connection with an African farming charity.

570 Dunterton (Milton Abbot), All Saints
Grade I

Close to the border with Cornwall, All Saints stands alone, without an associated village. It was built probably early to mid-14th century. The nave has largely been rebuilt, with the north aisle and the west tower added in the 1460s. The south porch is late-15th-century. Internal features include the original wagon roof to the nave and chancel with moulded ribs and carved bosses. The majority of the furnishings and fittings are 19th-century, apart from the 18th-century hexagonal timber pulpit on a granite base, and the piscina in the chancel, which is 14th-century. There are a number of monuments, dating from the 17th century onwards.

571 Exbourne, St Mary Blessed Virgin
Grade II*

The church contains some 14th, 15th and 16th-century fabric, and was restored and added to in 1884 by R. M. Fulford. It comprises nave, chancel, south aisle, south porch, and west tower. The chancel shows evidence of the earliest work with an early-14th-century east window; the nave probably dates to the early 15th century and the tower may be of the same date. Internal features include the restored 15th-century rood screen, the panelled pulpit inscribed "S.W.1665", the font which is a probably made of parts from several different fonts, and other woodwork by Herbert Read of Exeter, including Arts and Crafts pews. There are two listed chest tombs in the churchyard.

572 Germansweek, St German
Grade II*

This church dates mainly from the 12th and 13th centuries, with 14th and 15th-century additions. The first surviving written reference to St Germanus' Church occurs in the latter part of the 13th century. On 5 July 1270, John de Weston, then Lord of the Manor of Germansweek, gave the patronage of the church to Frithelstock Priory. Re-roofed and extensively restored in 1875, the period of the present furniture. The five bells were recast and re-hung in 1872 and re-hung again in 2007. Set on the edge of the village, among trees, views westward over the reservoir and setting sun, deeply spiritual and healing atmosphere. Services first and third Sunday.

573 Gidleigh, Holy Trinity
Grade I

Set in a green bowl, high in the heart of Dartmoor, Holy Trinity stands beside the ruins of a fortified castle, and has a stream flowing through the beautiful churchyard. We know of the existence of a Saxon chapel here since 1066 and it is believed that for many years before there was a wooden or stone place of worship on or near the site of today's church. This much-loved granite church with a wonderful rood screen dating from 1530, imparts a feeling of peace and tranquillity. Its tree-like arches open up the body of the church with light and a sense of space, inviting visitors to explore their spirituality.

574 Gulworthy, St Paul
Grade II

"The miners' church" set centrally in the parish, which is bounded by the Tamar Valley border of Cornwall and part of the World Heritage Miners' Site, was given to the people by Francis, Duke of Bedford in 1856. The Duke encouraged prayer and learning for his employees. In the churchyard can be found the graves of many miners. Stone-built with nave, chancel, north and south transepts and south porch, features include the Commandments set in stone tablets behind the altar where below the window is a rich setting of period tiles. Weekly Communion and occasional Evensong is held. There is close contact with the primary school next door.

575 Hatherleigh, St John the Baptist
Grade I

Most of the present church is 15th-century on pre-Norman foundations. In 1990, the spire was blown down, devastating the interior. The story of the repair can be seen on the wall near the door. Angels look down from the barrel roof and slender granite piers divide the aisles, making the church seem very spacious. The font is 12th-century. Some of the carved pew ends are 16th-century. The reading desk and the Jacobean pulpit had parts of the rood screen incorporated into them in the 19th century. Traditional services are held every Sunday, with a more informal family service once a month.

576 Highampton, Holy Cross
Grade II*

This small medieval church still has a Norman south doorway and Norman font. The north aisle was added in 1834 and the interior was restored in 1869. The stained-glass east window was made in 1871 by Clayton and Bell. Two of the three bells in the tower are mid-15th-century; the tenor bell dates from 1555. Services of worship take place twice a month in this lovingly looked after church. A warm welcome is always extended to visitors. The church is an integral part of our small rural community and we are exploring new ways of serving this community. We value our links with the local primary school.

577 Honeychurch, St Mary
Grade I

This is one of the smallest and most unspoilt churches in England. "Huna's Church" was founded by a landowner in the 10th century. It dates from the 12th century. It is a little Norman church of nave and chancel to which a small western tower and south porch were added. There are two 12th-century corbels either side of the door. The medieval benches on the north side of the nave date from the 15th century. A part of an Elizabethan mural still remains on the north wall. Services are held every first Sunday in the month. The church is always open so visitors may come at any time and share our history.

578 Horrabridge, St John the Baptist
Grade II*

This church was built in 1893 as the parish church of the newly formed ecclesiastical and secular parishes of Horrabridge. It is built close to the site of a medieval chapel belonging to the monks of Buckland Abbey and the large corbel stone of this building is displayed outside the church. A porch was added at a later date and one of its distinguishing features is the red mortar used between the bricks to represent the Holy Spirit. St John's remains the focal point of the village and its worship has been enhanced recently by going into a covenant arrangement with Horrabridge Methodist Church.

579 Huccaby Chapel (Princetown), St Raphael
Grade II

St Raphael is the only Anglican church with this dedication in the country. It was built in 1868 by the Revd Morris Fuller as a chapel and school. The vestry was added in the 20th century. It comprises simple nave with south porch and vestry at the west end with a single pitched roof. There is a granite bell flitch to the west end of the roof. Built of granite, and partly rendered. The interior is simple, with fittings including benches, plus some 19th-century school desks, the altar, and an oak lectern. The east window is a representation of the Good Shepherd, and is a memorial to Edward Arthur Adams who died in 1888, aged 11.

580 Iddesleigh, St James
Grade I

The church stands well with magnificent views south to Dartmoor. The building is predominantly 15th-century, with some 19th-century restoration. There are excellent wagon roofs in both aisles. Roof boss designs include The Three Hares, Fox and Geese and a face. The font is Tudor, the cover Jacobean. Half of the 15th-century screen remains. In the north chancel is an effigy of a recumbent knight c.1250, probably a Sully. The Revd Jack Russell was curate here when his father was rector in the 1840s. Current congregations are encouraging: over 10 per cent of the parish adult population on average. The church is an important part of village life.

581 Inwardleigh, St Petroc
Grade II*

This little church has a fine Norman font and fragments of 14th-century glass in the east window of the north aisle, a wagon roof and a 16th-century arcade. There are some Barum tiles by the chancel steps, the arms of George III, and some 17th-century memorial slabs on the floor. A modern millennium window is a colourful celebration of the countryside and the life of St Petroc. We are a welcoming church and we like to make all visitors comfortable. The pattern of the seasons is marked particularly in our worship on Plough Sunday, Rogationtide and Lammas.

582 Jacobstowe, St James
Grade II*

Stowe is the Anglo-Saxon for a meeting place. It is therefore possible that the promontory on which St James stands has been a general meeting place since the 7th century. Today it is used by the 120 souls widely distributed in this large rural parish, a number unchanged since Domesday, for general socialising and the worship of God. It is a simple church with few embellishments but it has a feeling of timelessness and peace that is frequently commented upon by visitors. Over 2000 are buried in the churchyard, 1500 of whom have been recorded since 1580.

583 Kelly, St Mary the Virgin
Grade I

Consecrated in 1259, only a 14th-century capital remains from the earliest period. The present building is largely Perpendicular, with an interior remodelled in 1865. The chancel was rebuilt in 1710, and the tower, which had become ivy encrusted and dangerous, was rebuilt in 1885. It has six bells and holds a special place in the history of Devon ringing. There is 15th-century glass in one window, the remainder being the work of the 19th-century Lavers and Barraud studio. Although we are a small parish, we gain strength today from being a part of the Lifton Benefice, and seek to encourage the next generation.

584 Lamerton, St Peter
Grade II*

This church has origins in the late 14th century, was restored in the 19th century, but in 1877 was destroyed by fire (apart from the tower), and was subsequently rebuilt. It comprises west tower, nave, chancel, north and south aisles, and south porch. The bell-frame is by the Whitechapel foundry, and the bells by John Warner and Son, London. Internally, fittings include two sedilia and piscina; 19th-century pews and pulpit; carved wooden painted royal arms of George III; organ by J. W. Walker and Sons, London, 1880; and a 19th-century granite font. There are a number of monuments, mainly dating from the 19th century, but including the Tremayne family monument, dated 1588 and rebuilt by Arthur Tremayne, 1707.

585 Lewtrenchard, St Peter
Grade I

The original church on this site was entirely rebuilt in 1261 and re-dedicated to St Peter. The present church was built in 1520 and in 1523-1524 the interior was enriched with carved pew ends and a carved wood screen. In 1832 Charles Baring-Gould was instituted to the family living at Lewtrenchard. Sabine Baring-Gould (author of 'Onward Christian Soldiers' etc) became heir to the estate. In 1881 he became squire and parson of Lewtrenchard where he remained living until 1924. The church is open every day of the year for visitors and services are held three Sundays a month.

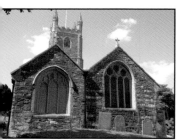

586 Lifton, St Mary
Grade I

Parts of the chancel date from the 14th century, the remainder is 15th-16th-century. It comprises nave, chancel, south aisle, south chancel chapel, west tower, north porch and vestry. It was restored in 1871. Interior features include a timber reredos of 1910; a 14th-century piscina; a 12th-century font with a square bowl; and a timber drum pulpit and eagle lectern, both also of 1910. The pews and choir stalls with poppy heads date from the 1871 restoration. There are a number of monuments including one of the 17th century to members of the Harris family, which dominates the north wall of the chancel. The stained-glass east window of c.1905 is probably by Drake of Exeter.

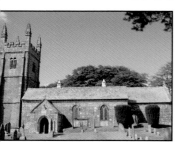

587 Lydford, St Petrock
Grade II*

Standing in the ancient Saxon burgh, with a pre-Norman font, this church formally served most of Dartmoor. The original building was probably destroyed by Vikings in 997. It was stone built in the 13th century and rededicated by Bishop Bronescombe in 1260. The tower was added in 1450 and has six bells which are rung regularly. In 1890 the church was restored and the north aisle added. The Pinwell screen and Herbert Read pew ends are 20th-century. The Watchmaker's Epitaph (now inside) is one of the listed headstones. A good congregation, supported by choir and organists, attend different services every Sunday. The church is always open for visitors.

588 Mary Tavy, St Mary
Grade I

The nave and chancel have origins in the 14th century, with the second phase of building dating from the early-15th century; the west end of the aisle was rebuilt and the porch added mid-15th century, restored in 1893. It comprises nave, chancel, south aisle, west tower, south porch and south transept. Internal features include the door to former rood stair in the north wall, the 19th-century wooden pulpit, the granite font, a 15th-century piscina, and the late-19th-century carved wooden rood screen. The bell-frame dates from the mid-19th century with two of the bells dated 1720 and 1809. The fine stained glass is by the Kempe Studios, and dates from 1893-1895.

589 Marystowe, St Mary the Virgin
Grade I

Parts of the south doorway date from the 12th century; the chancel is 14th-century, and the nave, north aisle, chancel chapel and tower are of the late-15th and 19th centuries. Heavily restored in 1866. Internal features include the 14th-century double sedilia; a fine 12th-century font with a square bowl, almost identical to that at Lifton Church; three bays of the late-15th-early-16th-century rood screen re-used as the tower screen; and a drum pulpit of 1903-1905. The north chancel chapel is dominated by a massive monument to Sir Thomas Wise of Sydenham, d.1629, with two effigies on a Caen stone base, and other members of the Wise family positioned on the plinth.

590 Meavy, St Peter
Grade I

Norman in origin, the nave, aisle, south transept and west tower were added in the 15th century with Victorian restorations, including oak carvings of local wildlife. Cut in stone between the two altars is a hagioscope. It is believed that monks from Plympton, Buckland and Buckfast celebrated mass here. The lectern was carved in Oberammergau. The local Drake family worshipped in the lady chapel. Named from the famous tree growing by the lychgate the church house became the Royal Oak Inn. The six bells sound out over the Dartmoor countryside. In this well-loved church there is a warm welcome to the traditional weekly services and the church-aided school maintains a close link.

591 Meeth, St Michael & All Angels
Grade II*

A cobble path laid by Napoleonic POWs in 1818 leads through an early Norman porch with carved roof bosses into this small church, open daily. Fine carved bosses adorn the 15th-century wagon roof. The font is Norman, its cover Tudor. Remarkable and beautiful, the plaster coat of arms of 1704 is probably the work of Abbot of Frithelstock. Restored in 1991, the two Stadler and two medieval bells are rung for worship. Though small, the church is active in its witness, at the heart of many events in this rural community as it has been for over 1000 years, and supportive of the needy further afield.

592 Milton Abbot, St Constantine
Grade I

St Constantine is an impressive building dating from the 14th century standing in the centre of the village of Milton Abbot. This church belonged to the monks of Tavistock Abbey and in 1155 changed from having a rector to a vicar. The basic Hurdwick stone is 15th-century and there are traces of 14th-century work in the tower and the main door. Restoration work was carried out in 2003-2004 to the beautiful 15th-century ceiling with its carved bosses. There are large stained-glass windows on three sides and a fine peal of bells. Over the main porch is a sundial dated 1726.

593 Milton Combe, Holy Spirit
Grade II

Prebendary Hayne, a visionary vicar between 1860 and 1925, conceived and planned the Church of the Holy Spirit, Milton Combe. Weekly services draw a faithful congregation, whose organist Minnie Grainger has played for over 65 years.

594 Monkokehampton, All Saints
Grade II

Nestling in the Okement Valley, All Saints consists of a chancel and single aisle nave. Following a fire in the mid-19th century all except the medieval tower was rebuilt in typical Victorian style with the colourful east window coming from the Great Exhibition of 1851. There are other interesting stained-glass commemorative windows. There is now need of much refurbishment. This small rural parish has seen very little development, thus a declining congregation. Attendance at the twice-monthly services features a wide age range. The former village school built in the churchyard is being transferred to a Village Hall Trust.

595 North Tawton, St Peter
Grade I

We have celebrated 750 years since the first listed rector at the church. The main building is 14th-century, the south porch dates from the 15th century, and aisles were added later. The 18th-century sanctuary was supplied by Robert Hole, the last of 200 years of incumbents of the Hole family. Little stained-glass windows at the middle of the north wall are all that remains of the medieval windows. The top of the spire, burnt in a fire in the 19th century, suffers from a "quick repair job". We have a Sunday Club, Youth Group and toddler group, and run Alpha courses.

596 Northlew, St Thomas of Canterbury
Grade I

This well-loved parish church originated in Norman times, replacing an earlier Saxon church. Restoration took place in the 15th century, with some Victorian alterations. The pew ends, some dating from 1537, are beautiful. There is a fine barrel roof over the north aisle and we are proud of our elderly Henry Willis organ which came from a London church in the late 1800s. The rood screen was damaged during the Reformation and was finally restored as a War Memorial in 1923. We have a vibrant congregation who are passing the Word of God on to future generations; enthusiastic choir and bell-ringers and strong links with school and village.

597 Okehampton, All Saints
Grade II*

A church has existed here since Saxon times, prior to the first recorded consecration in 1261. The current building, mostly dating from 1842, has recently undergone extensive refurbishment to enable more flexible use. Although the church is on the edge of the town, we seek to be at the heart of the community. We are a growing church, with a good range of ages and backgrounds. We have a strong musical tradition with two choirs and a dedicated team of bell-ringers. We try to offer a range of worship to suit all tastes from informal to formal and from modern to traditional. You will be most welcome to join us.

598 Okehampton, St James
Grade II*

St James is not strictly an Anglican church, being a "mayoral chapel" and cared for by trustees. The parish church is out of town and up the hill and the little chapel was consecrated to enable parishioners to worship when the weather made it difficult to get there. Its tower, standing almost in the middle of the street, is the most commonly photographed feature of Okehampton. Although no longer used for Sunday worship, it is always open in the daytime and provides a quiet sanctuary in a busy town. It contains many interesting features and a guide book and history is available. There is a service of Holy Communion every Thursday.

599 Peter Tavy, St Peter
Grade I

1185 is the earliest recorded date, but it has been rebuilt and enlarged three times in its life. The north aisle was the last addition in 1692. Most woodwork is either oak or pitch pine and fairly modern, though examples of the older work, a screen made of even earlier panels, and two painted panels depicting apostles from the old rood screen, may be seen in the church. A fine tower with 15ft 6in pinnacles, houses six bells which were hung between 1720 and 1790, replacing bells hung 1553. The church, now part of a larger benefice, also has a good rapport with our friends in the Methodist Church in Peter Tavy.

600 Postbridge, St Gabriel
Grade II

This church was originally built as a school-cum-chapel in 1869, the collection for its construction having been instigated by the Revd W. H. Thornton, incumbent of North Bovey. It became the village church in 1934. The work was commissioned by Mrs Pethybridge, in memory of her two brothers. The beautiful wood carvings of biblical scenes decorating the pews are the work of Miss Pinwell. The two icons were gifts from a former Postbridge resident, a Cypriot who commissioned the icon of St Gabriel from a monastery in Cyprus. The small graveyard is detached from the site, at the end of the lane, the earliest headstone bearing the date 1909.

601 Princetown, St Michael & All Angels
Grade II*

THE CHURCHES CONSERVATION TRUST

Is unique in the fact that it is the only English church built by prisoners of war. Built of plain granite it was started in 1812 by French prisoners, and completed by American prisoners in 1815. The main memorial is to Sir Thomas Tyrwhitt, 1762-1833. As secretary to the Prince of Wales it was he who founded both Princetown and the prison. The stained-glass east window was installed in 1910 as a memorial to the Americans who died in Dartmoor Prison. In 2001 the church came under the control of the Churches Conservation Trust and is used for occasional services. It is still a focus of Christianity for both locals and visitors alike.

602 Princetown, United Church (Tor)

A new build behind the former Wesleyan chapel, completed in 1983, it is centrally located in the moorland village. With a plain rendered exterior, it is a multi-use building, disabled-friendly throughout, with an intimate worship area. This hosts services for the Ecumenical Partnership supported by the Tavistock Methodist Circuit and the Ashburton and Moorland Team Ministry. Alternating services, held weekly, follow the traditions of both Anglican and Methodist alike. Apart from the church it provides a large hall, lounge, kitchen and other associated areas. Actively supporting the pre-school and other groups and clubs, the building forms a focus to draw the local community together.

603 Sampford Courtenay, St Andrew
Grade I

This 15th-century, embattled, granite church, with a most majestic tower housing six bells, has a wide, well-lit nave with open aisles of four bays. A number of fine bosses, including two noted Green Men, grace the wagon roofs. The font, with its Purbeck marble top, was constructed around 1100. During restoration in 1899, chairs temporarily replaced the pews, but have remained in situ. A permanent display depicts the Prayer Book Rebellion of 1549, which began outside the adjoining church house. Traditional weekly services and a monthly family service are held, with the successful choir performing additional concerts. A flourishing team of bell-ringers ring for every service.

604 Sampford Spiney, St Mary
Grade I

There is no record of the date of the foundation of this parish church, but it is mentioned in a taxation return of 1291. It is believed that the original church was built around 1250 and was the chapel to Sampford Manor, mentioned in the Domesday Book. In the reign of King Edward III the church was put under the control of Plympton Priory by the Bishop of Exeter in 1334. In the early-16th century, the tower and south aisle were added to the church and in 1547 the patronage of the church was granted to the Dean and Canons of Windsor.

605 Sheepstor, St Leonard
Grade I

Situated near Burrator reservoir, this granite church dates from the late-15th century and was restored in 1862. It comprises nave, chancel, south aisle, north transept, west tower and south porch. Internally, there is a rood screen of 1914 which is an exact replica of that removed in 1862; and a 15th-century granite octagonal font. Also of interest are the memorials to the Elford family who were gentry of the parish, including that of 1641 to Elizabeth Elford. The churchyard contains a large red granite sarcophagus to James Brooke, first rajah of Sarawak, who bought the Burrator estate in 1858, and an unusual cyclopic granite boulder to the second rajah, Charles Brooke.

606 Sourton, St Thomas a Becket
Grade II*

This little church on the edge of Dartmoor is mainly 15th-century with some earlier features. The medieval wagon roofs still retain traces of colour. The original wall plate in the north aisle has carvings of angels holding shields, the work of local craftsmen. Herbert Read restored the coat of arms of Charles II in 1916, conserved in 1996. The Granite Way, just above the churchyard, brings in many cyclists and walkers who comment on the tranquillity and peaceful atmosphere in the church. There is a small but welcoming regular congregation for Communion or family service each Sunday.

607 South Tawton, St Andrew
Grade I

Built in granite, most of the present church dates from the 15th century, but its origins lie in the 11th. It consists of nave, two side aisles with chapels, porch and a 75ft high tower. The wagon roof has over 170 late medieval carved bosses. The church was extensively restored in 1881. The chancel screen dates from 1902. Memorials include an effigy of John "Warrior" Weekes of North Wyke, dated 1572 and the Burgoyne Memorial dated 1651. The old thatched church house was built soon after 1490 and is of great historic interest. It is used for church meetings and events and is open to the public during the summer.

608 South Zeal, St Mary
Grade II*

This much-loved granite chapel lies in the centre of the village in the old market place. It is a simple rectangle of large granite blocks on granite boulder footings with a bell gable at the west end, and was probably built in 1713 on the foundation of an earlier building, possibly a Weavers' Guild chapel. It was used as a school from 1773 until restoration by William Lethbridge in 1877, when it became a chapel of ease to South Tawton. The interior was refurbished in 2002 for more informal services and meetings and is in regular use. The 18ft market cross at the end of the churchyard is probably 14th-century.

609 Spreyton, St Michael
Grade II

This church dates from 1451. It is a simple peaceful building with stained-glass windows at each end; one depicts our Lord, the Blessed Virgin and St John, the other St Michael. Granite pillars and arches support the chancel roof with bosses including tinners' rabbits and a Green Man. The altar stone is one piece of granite. There is a Norman piscina, two ancient fonts, a priest's door and rood stairs. The six-bell tower summons us to weekly services. Set in a green and tranquil churchyard, which includes the grave of Tom Cobley, there are magnificent views of north Dartmoor approached down an avenue of limes.

610 Sticklepath (Belstone), St Mary's Chapel

Built in 1871, it consists of nave with apsidal chancel, north porch, and vestry, and was constructed of local stone (mainly granite).

611 Stowford, St John the Baptist
Grade I

The church dates back to the 14th century, with later 15th and 16th-century additions. The font is 12th-century. In 1874 Sir Gilbert Scott was asked to restore the interior of the building. There are many fine monuments belonging to the Harris family of Hayne. By the gate is a strangely shaped stone, called a gunglei, dating from the 7th century, believed to be the gravestone of St Curig's father. In 2006 the tower was restored. The village congregation is small, but boosted by members of the benefice. The Eucharist is celebrated twice a month on a regular basis, and there are special services at the appropriate times of year.

612 Sydenham Damerel (Lamerton), St Mary
Grade II*

The tower and porch date from the 15th century, but the rest of the church was rebuilt in the late 1950s after being destroyed by fire. It was built on a slightly smaller scale, without an aisle. It comprises nave, chancel, west tower and south porch. Some medieval stonework from the windows was incorporated in the rebuilding. Built of granite, the nave and chancel are narrow, and under a single roof. The interior dates from the 1950s, but includes a 15th-century octagonal font. There is a peal of six bells, five dating from 1770, one from 1912. There are a number of good 17th and 18th-century slate headstones in the churchyard.

613 Tavistock, St Eustachius
Grade II

The parish church of St Eustachius stands at the very heart of the town of Tavistock, and was built 1285-1324, and dedicated in 1318. Immediately to its south lie the ruins of Tavistock Abbey, founded by Ordulf in 981, and destroyed at the Dissolution of the Monasteries in 1539. Many fragments of the abbey stonework are to be found around the town. From this site of ancient prayer, the current congregation worships daily together, extends a warm welcome to many visitors, is passionate about pastoral care for those in need, deepens faith through study, and rejoices in work with other denominations in the town, and in its links with the church in Melanesia.

614 Throwleigh, St Mary the Virgin
Grade I

The earliest indication of a church on this site is found in documents dating from 1248, but the present building is predominately 15th-century. Internally it was heavily restored by the Victorians, although it now has a simpler aspect. There is a fine peal of six medieval bells, which are rung regularly, and some interesting roof bosses including the three hares and the Green Man in the north aisle. There are some original windows incorporating stained glass by Sir Ninian Comper. This well-loved church is now part of the United Benefice of Whiddon Parishes but still has regular services of early-morning Communion and mid-morning Matins.

615 Thrushelton, St George
Grade I

St George's has traditionally been known as the farmers' church. It is surrounded by farmland, so many visitors will enjoy the peaceful environment. The first mention of a church at Thrushelton is in 1334. The present church was built in the 14th century, and enlarged in the 15th. The church consists of a south aisle and chapel, chancel, nave and arcade .The west tower is also 15th-century and has six bells. The building by the gates was built as a Sunday School and a vestry in 1833 for £45. An avenue of 20 lime trees leads from the gates to the church. There is traditional style worship most Sundays.

616 Walkhampton, St Mary the Virgin
Grade I

With its 85ft tower, sited on a hilltop on the south west edge of Dartmoor, half a mile from the village, the church is a prominent local landmark. The present Perpendicular Gothic style building dates from 1450, featuring a plain, largely unadorned, interior. A substantial refurbishment was undertaken in the 1850s, financed by subscription and the Lopes family. Serving the village and surrounding hamlets, the church congregation actively participates in community life. A project to add a kitchen, toilet, and a gallery for bell ringing will see the building continue to serve God and the community well into the 21st century.

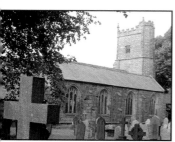

617 Whitchurch, St Andrew
Grade I

St Andrew's is a living church with a rich architectural and spiritual history. Christians have been worshipping here for over 700 years with the earliest records starting in 1288. The chancel dates from the 14th century and the slate panels from c.1530. The outer doorway, stone benches and holy water stoup in the porch are among the oldest parts whilst the Margaret Chapel, bells, bell tower and stained-glass windows are Victorian. Today St Andrew's is a thriving church embracing a broad range of traditions and crossing cultural and generational boundaries. At the heart of this Christian community is its mission statement – to reach out with the love of Christ.

618 Yelverton, St Paul
Grade II

The decision to substitute Ham Hill stone for the interior rather than granite when this church was built in 1910-1912 was a happy one, giving it a warmth that comes alive on a late sunny afternoon. A fine example of Nicholson and Corlette's work, its spacious unity is its charm. Sadly the gift of Yennadon ironstone outside has not been so successful, Dartmoor weather finding it out. Recent generosity by church and village has provided an answer we trust will not fail. Worship is responsive to the needs of a diverse population having deep roots in ordered Anglicanism yet needing fresh expressions of lively faith for our day. Open daily.

INDEX OF CHURCHES

Churches are listed by place name first. The numbers in brackets are OS grid references.

GLOSSARY

(refers to *Foreword*, *Introduction* and the articles *St Peter's Cathedral: It's Life and History*, *A Church of Two Thousand Years* and *Understanding Devon's Churches*)